D0566838

Australia's Changing Population

Australia's Changing Population

Graeme Hugo

TRENDS AND IMPLICATIONS

Melbourne
Oxford University Press
Oxford Wellington New York

The support of the Department of Immigration and Ethnic Affairs in the production of this book is gratefully acknowledged.

OXFORD UNIVERSITY PRESS

Oxford New York Toronto
Delhi Bombay Calcutta Madras Karachi
Singapore Hong Kong Tokyo
Nairobi Dar es Salaam Cape Town
Melbourne Auckland
and associates in
Beirut Berlin Ibadan Nicosia

First published 1986

National Library of Australia
Cataloguing-in-Publication data:
Hugo, Graeme J., 1946– .
Australia's changing population.

Bibliography.
Includes index.
ISBN 0 19 554680 6.

1. Australia—Population. 2. Australia—Population policy. I. Title.

304.6′0994

Edited by Sarah Brenan
Designed by Peter Shaw
Cover design by Guy Mirabella
Typeset by Asco Trade Typesetting Ltd, Hong Kong
Printed by Impact Printing, Melbourne
Published by Oxford University Press,
7 Bowen Crescent, Melbourne
OXFORD is a trademark of
Oxford University Press

Contents

Foreword

Population trends affect us all in many ways. Education, the labour market, social welfare and security, health, economic development and marketing are just some activities influenced in some way by changes in the size or characteristics of the population. It is, therefore, important that planners at all levels of government, private enterprise and the community be aware of population developments and how they impact upon areas of concern to them.

Regular monitoring of population trends is essential if planning is to proceed on a sound footing. The Census of Population and Housing enables detailed analysis of the complex interrelationships between population trends and the broad range of policy areas affected by them.

As part of my Department's population monitoring role, the National Institute of Labour Studies was commissioned in 1982 to undertake the first comprehensive policy-related research of census results. *Australia's Changing Population: Trends and Implications* is the final report of this study.

The findings of the report reflect the important and wide-ranging implications of Australia's demographic trends. Rather than being the final word, however, they should be seen as the starting point for more detailed research in specific policy areas. I urge planners in both the public and private sectors to reflect upon those issues of relevance to them and to take up where this study ends.

CHRIS HURFORD
Minister for Immigration and Ethnic Affairs

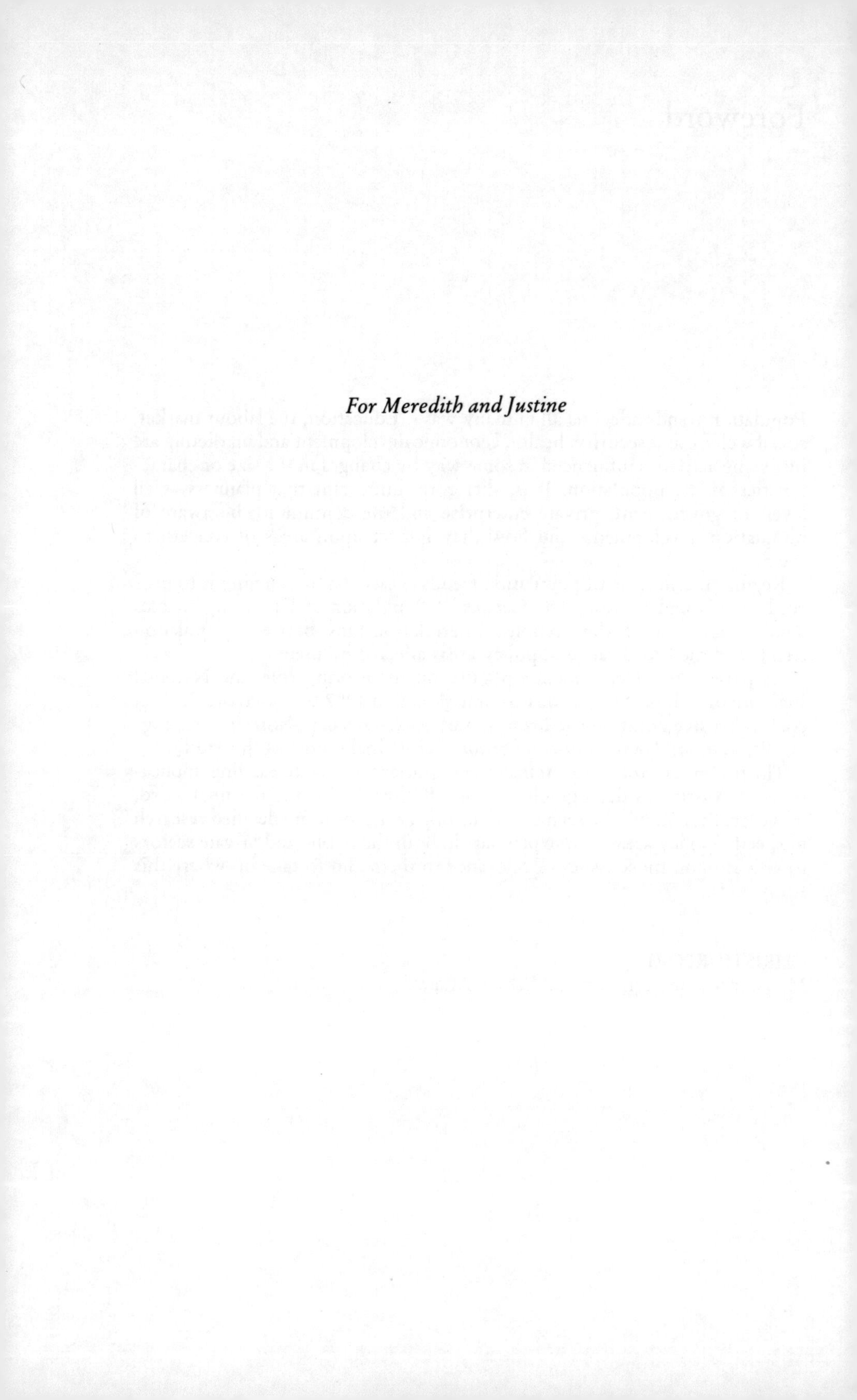

For Meredith and Justine

Preface

This book is one of the outputs from a major research project based primarily on the results of the 1981 Australian Census of Population and Housing. The study was funded by the Commonwealth Department of Immigration and Ethnic Affairs, and was undertaken at the National Institute of Labour Studies in the School of Social Sciences at the Flinders University of South Australia. The aim of the study was to elucidate the major demographic trends in Australia, especially as revealed by the results of the 1981 census, and to draw out their meaning for policy and their implications for the future. In the course of the two and a half years of the project (June 1982 to December 1984) many organizations and individuals have greatly assisted me.

First I am indebted to the Australian Bureau of Statistics, both in Canberra and Adelaide, for making available the bulk of the data upon which the study is based. The unfailing helpfulness and co-operation with which my requests were met, as well as the Bureau's professional advice, was a major factor in the success of the project. In particular the support of Mr John Cornish is gratefully acknowledged. The Population and Research Branch of the Department of Immigration and Ethnic Affairs has contributed much more than funding to this study. They have been a constant source of helpful comments and encouragement, and in particular the support and help of Mr Bob Goddard and Ms Lois Sparkes have been greatly appreciated by the author. The steering committee of the project comprised members of the Department of Immigration and Ethnic Affairs, Australian Bureau of Statistics, Bureau of Labour Market Research and the Industries Assistance Commission and their advice and encouragement was always supportive and helpful. It is not possible here to name separately all the many individuals, institutions and departments who provided data or comments on the working papers but I would like to express my gratitude to the many who helped so materially in the successful completion of the project. Of course, the views expressed in this study are not necessarily those of any of the organizations mentioned here and I take sole responsibility for them.

The census study was conducted within the National Institute of Labour Studies and its support is gratefully acknowledged; in particular I wish to express my appreciation of the support and help of Professor Richard Blandy, the Director, and Mrs Helen Lindner. The Flinders University of South Australia made many contributions to the study through provision of access to computing and other university facilities and its support was critical to the success of the project. I would also like to thank sincerely my colleagues in the discipline of geography who allowed me to be seconded on a half-time basis to do the study and who were a source of support and stimulation not only throughout the project but the entire time I have been at Flinders University.

My special thanks go to my research colleagues at Flinders University who shared the experience of working on the project and who not only demonstrated the highest degree of skill and dedication but also managed to remain unfailingly helpful, happy and unfazed throughout the rather heavy work programme of the project. The research was completed by a small team comprising Ms Frances Robertson (programmer), Ms Deborah Wood and Ms Janet Mattà (research assistants) in addition to the writer. Under the Commonwealth government's work experience programme we were fortunate to gain the services for short periods of Ms Joanne Bromilow, Ms Yvonne Logan and Ms Gillian Humphries, all of whom proved very capable and made a significant contribution to the work of the project. There was a heavy typing load associated with the project and I would like to express my deep appreciation to the following, who all assisted in this at some stage—Ms Lindy Dodd, Mrs Jean Lange, Ms Angela Fletcher, Ms Margaret Bennett, Mrs Joan Marshall, Mrs Ann Gabb, Mrs Barbara Leonard, Ms Leonie Koop and Ms Chris Godfrey.

Finally I'd like to thank my family, Meredith and Justine, for their patience and understanding and putting up with my preoccupation with this work over the last two and a half years.

GRAEME HUGO
1986

1 Introduction

Australia's population is undergoing gradual but profound change. Fertility rates are near record low levels, older Australians are living longer, the number and proportion of older people are increasing at unprecedented rates, Australians are earning their living and grouping themselves into households and families in new and different ways, there have been significant shifts in the ethnic composition of the population and there have been radical changes in the patterns of population movement within Australia. These and other demographic shifts present Australia's policy makers and planners in both the public and private sectors with a major challenge. There is almost no major planning or policy issue facing contemporary Australia which does not have a demographic dimension. Yet, paradoxically, this dimension has received very little explicit attention among policy makers and planners, and public awareness of population issues has remained very limited. This is partly because the gradual nature of these changes tends to mask the profound ways in which they are reshaping society.

The aim of this book is to describe and analyse this evolving demographic context in Australia—to identify the major significant shifts which are occurring, to explain them insofar as this is possible and spell out several key problems that policy makers can expect to face. In particular, the results of the 1981 Australian Census of Population and Housing are the basis of an integrated demographic analysis of a range of population trends in the late 1970s and early 1980s. In the past deficiencies in planning the allocation of scarce resources in Australia, within all three tiers of government as well as in the private sector, can be directly traced to a lack of availability of (or failure to consider) up-to-date information on demographic trends and their linkages with social and economic factors. I hope that the publication of this book will make it possible to avoid some of the mistakes of the past.

I have tried in this study to discuss the issues in such a way that they can be understood by, and of use and interest to, a wide audience. Accordingly, much of the detailed demographic analyses and data on which the discussions are based is not presented within the book. They can be found in a series of detailed working papers which preceded this study. My aim here is to elucidate the major demographic trends in contemporary Australia and their implications for the future, without resorting to a large amount of technical detail.

While a major concern is to address an audience of policy makers and planners in the public and private sectors I feel that an understanding of such population issues is of even more fundamental significance to the general community. Any citizen's understanding of the contemporary dynamics and future of their local community, their state, the nation and the world is greatly enhanced by a knowledge of present, past and likely future population growth and composition at those various levels. There is a population dimension to most of the major social and economic changes occurring within contemporary Australia and a thorough knowledge of that dimension not only assists in the understanding of wider societal forces and processes but is also of substantial intrinsic interest. The growing recognition of the fundamental role of demographic processes in societal change is evidenced in many ways. There is, for example, increasing pressure to give students at secondary and tertiary level an understanding of the basic processes shaping the size, growth, composition and distribution of populations. Moreover, it is a rare week that goes by without some population-related issue gaining prominence in the popular media. Issues such as the 'greying' of Australia, the scale and composition of immigration, the declining numbers of children entering schools, changing patterns of family formation and dissolution and the decline or growth of particular towns, suburbs or regions are continually being discussed and debated. Unfortunately, much of the information which finds its way into such discussions in the media is only partly accurate or representative, or is significantly misinterpreted. Hence, another objective here is to promote a greater knowledge in the community generally regarding population trends and their implications.

Demographic changes—such as fluctuations in birth and death rates, internal and international migration, the timing of child-bearing, or the way the population groups itself into households—can influence the pattern of demand for services and consumption of resources in at least four ways. First, and most obviously, variations in the overall rate of growth of the population will be reflected in fluctuating levels of demand and need for goods and services. Second, since many such demands and needs are strongly concentrated in particular age groups, changes in the age structure of a population will cause variations in both the level and type of demand for particular resources and services. Similarly, changes in other characteristics of the population (e.g. in ethnic composition) are influential in shaping the pattern of demand. Third, many services are consumed by families or households rather than individuals, so that changes in the way and extent to which the population forms new households will influence the level of demand. Finally, the migration patterns of the population within Australia will alter the spatial distribution of demand for services. Accordingly, this study considers contemporary and likely future trends in each of those demographic processes in Australia and discusses their implications. To begin with, however, I will summarize the major changes which have occurred in the growth of the Australian population over the post-World War II period, since the impact of these changes will continue to be felt throughout the 1980s.

Figure 1.1 Population growth in Australia, 1851–1983, and projected growth, 1981–2001

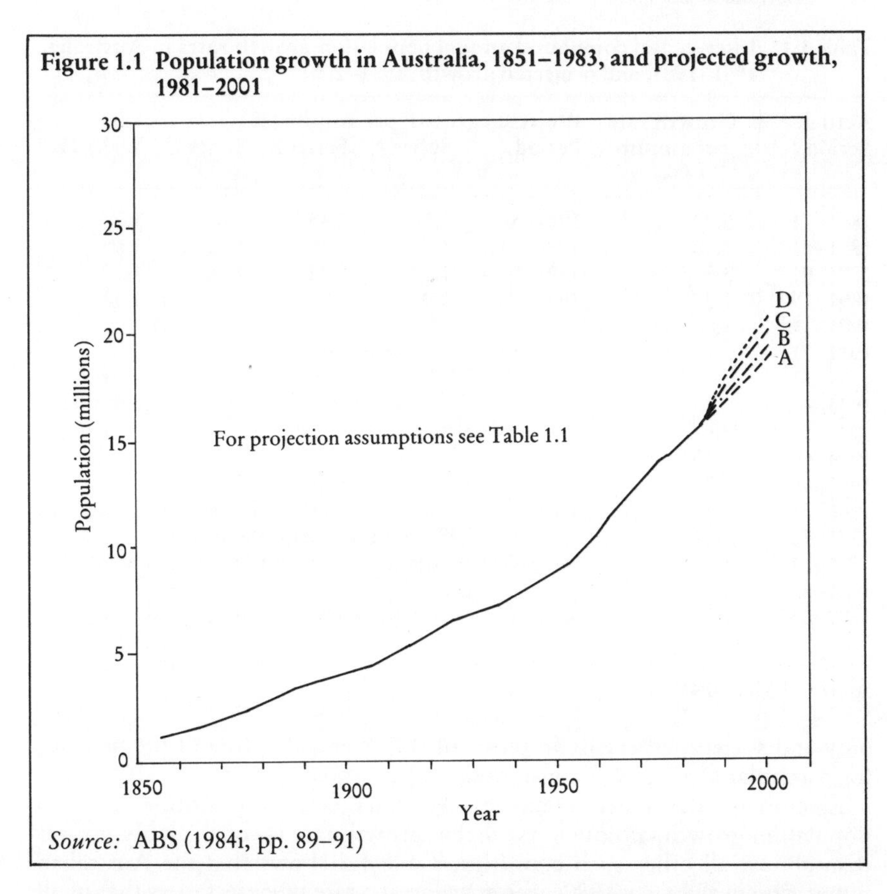

Source: ABS (1984i, pp. 89–91)

AUSTRALIAN POPULATION GROWTH SINCE WORLD WAR II

The total population of Australia on the eve of European settlement has been estimated at around 300 000. It took more than half a century for the European population to attain this figure and it was in the late 1850s that the population passed one million. Figure 1.1 shows the subsequent trajectory of growth, and we are especially interested here in the post-World War II period. It is clear from the graph and from Table 1.1 that Australian population growth rates in the late 1940s, 1950s and 1960s were at their highest level since the early colonial days of mining booms and rapid expansion of the agricultural frontier. In the mid-1970s however, the tempo of growth slackened and fell below one per cent per annum for the only time during the post-war period in 1975. Although there has subsequently been an increase in the rate of growth, the population in the early 1980s was increasing only slightly more than half as fast as in the 1950s and 1960s. Like the United States and most sections of the so-called 'developed world', Australia has undergone a transition from rapid to slow population growth. This slowing of population growth has major implications for the nation's future econ-

Table 1.1 Inter-censal compound annual population growth rates in Australia, 1861–1983, and projected growth, 1981–2001

Actual Period	Growth rate per annum (%)	Projected growth per annum (%) Period	Series A	Series B	Series C	Series D
1861–71	3.70	1981–86	1.36	1.45	1.67	1.77
1871–81	3.08	1986–91	1.20	1.35	1.50	1.65
1881–91	3.51	1991–96	1.08	1.22	1.36	1.50
1891–1901	1.80	1996–2001	0.95	1.08	1.22	1.34
1901–11	1.63					
1911–21	2.03					
1921–33	1.85					
1933–47	0.85					
1947–54	2.47					
1954–61	2.25					
1961–66	1.98					
1966–71	2.21					
1971–76	1.44					
1976–81	1.24					
1981–82	1.71					
1982–83	1.32					

Projection assumptions

Series A: TFR (total fertility rate—see Chapter 3) declines to 1.9 in 1987 and is constant thereafter
Mortality declines
Net immigration = 75 000 p.a.

Series B: As for A, except TFR recovers to 2.11 in 1987 and is constant thereafter

Series C: As for A, except net immigration = 125 000 p.a.

Series D: As for B, except net immigration = 125 000 p.a.

Source: ABS (1984)

omy and society, especially in terms of the level and nature of the demand for particular services and consumption of resources.

Like many developed countries Australia faces a transition to zero population growth, although its current growth rate is considerably greater than almost all other such countries. Table 1.2 shows that the Australian population in the early 1980s was growing at a rate twice as fast as that of all developed countries taken together, three times as fast as Europe and half as fast again as North America. While these differentials are obviously a function of the fact that Australia (and the United States and Canada) have continued to take in significant numbers of immigrants, this is only part of the story. It can be seen from Table 1.2 that the rate of natural increase of the population was higher than that of developed countries generally and more than twice that of Europe. This is due not so much to Australia having intrinsically higher fertility or lower mortality than Europe, but more to the young age structure forged by the post-war baby and immigration booms which results in a greater proportion of the adult population being at child-bearing age. In some European countries, on the other hand (e.g. Denmark, Federal Republic of Germany, German Democratic Republic, Hungary) the age structure of the populations is such that there are such high proportions of the total population in the older age groups that total births were outnumbered by total deaths during the early 1980s. Thus, although Australia does appear to be moving toward zero population growth—and in fact has fertility levels below those necessary to maintain zero growth in a stationary

Table 1.2 Population growth and natural increase rates in the early 1980s: Australia and other countries compared

	Annual growth rate 1980–83	Annual natural increase rate 1981–82
More developed countries	0.6	0.6
North America	1.0	0.7
Europe	0.5	0.3
Australia	1.5	0.8
Less developed countries	2.1	2.1

Sources: US Bureau of Census (1983b); Population Reference Bureau (1984)

population—Australia's population is still growing. It is very important to realize this. In fact, Table 1.2. indicates that in the early 1980s Australia's population was growing at almost three-quarters the level of the less developed nations of the world taken as a group.

Not only is Australia's population still growing in the mid-1980s but this growth is almost certain to continue for several decades, even if fertility remains below replacement levels. Figure 1.1 and Table 1.1 present recent population projections made by the Australian Bureau of Statistics (ABS) and indicate that each of the four scenarios for the future envisages a continuation of growth until the end of the century. Of the various scenarios it is the lower immigration levels of Series A and B which at present seem most likely to prevail. Even under the low-fertility assumption of Series A (Table 1.1) there is a gradual decline in the rate of growth but the rate will only fall below one per cent per annum during the last five years of the century. Nevertheless, if low fertility persists and if there were zero immigration, natural increase would virtually cease in the early part of next century. With immigration assumptions at the Series A level, natural increase would not cease until the second half of the next century.

The transition to zero population growth has very important implications for policy makers and planners in Australia. Most of the contemporary senior managers and policy makers in the Australian private and public sectors have gained their formative experience during the unprecedented rapid growth years of the 1950s and 1960s. The demographic context in which they will work over the next two decades will be quite different. Not only will it be one of low (and almost certainly decreasing) rates of overall population growth, but it will be one of a changing distribution of this growth between regions and between particular groups in Australian society. Moreover, other unprecedented changes, some associated and interrelated with the transition to zero growth, will also occur. These include the ageing of the population, shifts in the composition of families and households, changing roles of women and changes in the size and composition of immigration to Australia.

I will examine separately each of the demographic processes influencing contemporary population change in Australia, but first it is important to give an outline of how demography developed in this country.

THE STUDY OF AUSTRALIA'S POPULATION

Although the formal study of Australia's demography within the nation's universities is a relatively recent (post-war) phenomenon, sound demographic analysis of the Australian population can be traced back almost a century. In particular, attention should be drawn to the work of T.A. Coghlan, the Government Statistician of the colony of New South Wales in the latter part of the nineteenth century; G.H. Knibbs, the Commonwealth Statistician from 1905 to 1921, and writers like Borthwick (1891). However, the key figure in the development of Australian demography has been Professor W.D. Borrie, whose work in the early post-war years and his establishment in 1952 of the world's first Department of Demography in the Australian National University (ANU) initiated a new era of research into Australia's demography. Under Professor Borrie and the current head, Professor J.C. Caldwell, the department awarded 116 higher degrees in demography up to 1984, a significant proportion of which were for theses on Australian topics. It has become a major force in world demography. Two major initiatives of the department in the 1970s saw a quantum leap in our knowledge and understanding of demographic change in Australia. These were the National Population Inquiry (NPI) headed by Professor Borrie between 1971 and 1975; and the Australian Family Formation Project headed by Professor Caldwell, which included a major field survey of Melbourne in 1971.

While the work of the ANU department expanded, there were a number of other developments which also added to the amount of research on Australian population and the depth of knowledge concerning it. Research into Australian mortality change had developed under H.O. Lancaster at the University of Sydney in the early post-war years and then was expanded by Pollard and his colleagues at Macquarie University. It was at the latter that the first of a series of undergraduate courses in demography was established in 1968. Other universities have included demography courses in mathematics, geography, social science, economic history, economics and medicine programmes (see, for example, Caldwell and Cameron 1972).

Outside the university sector the Australian Bureau of Statistics in the later 1970s greatly expanded its research staff and periodically published analytical studies as well as continuing its long-established function of collecting and processing population data. The 1970s also saw the somewhat belated emergence of a wider recognition that a thorough and informed knowledge of changes in the population is an essential foundation for the development of policies and planning at the various levels of government. In particular, the Department of Immigration and Ethnic Affairs (DIEA) formed a Population Branch which has played a leading role in promoting applied research into Australian population trends and in generally raising awareness in the public sector of population trends and their implications. Most State governments have created small population units over the last decade to advise them on prevailing demographic trends and their implications, and to prepare population projections. The increasing momentum is seen in the annual Commonwealth/State population workshops which have been held since

1978. In 1980 an Australian Population Association was formed to foster the awareness of population issues and encourage a broad discussion of population issues within the Australian community. By 1984 the Association had over 300 members and had begun publication of a journal devoted primarily to the dissemination of information, analyses and views on Australia's population and related issues.

In the 1970s there were several developments in the study of Australia's population which in some ways form a departure point for this study. In particular, the publication of the report of Professor Borrie's National Population Inquiry (1975), its supplementary report (1978) and a number of associated monographs and papers marked a watershed in the analysis of Australian demographic trends and more particularly the making available of the results of such analyses to policy makers and planners. However, most of the NPI analysis refers to 1973 or even earlier (especially 1971 census results) and the past decade has seen significant changes within Australia. The present study partially seeks to update the NPI's findings using more recent data, especially the results of the 1981 census. However, the present study differs significantly from the NPI in that it does not seek to provide the detailed historical analysis which is so excellently done in the NPI; nor does it seek to produce a set of detailed projections of Australia's future population, which was a major task of the NPI. In addition, this study has a less purely demographic focus in that the emphasis is upon elucidating trends and their policy implications.

Late in the 1970s a major project was initiated to produce a monograph on Australia's population as part of the United Nations Economic and Social Commission for Asia and the Pacific (ESCAP) country monograph series. Based primarily on results of the 1976 Australian census, its 580 pages (ESCAP 1982) present a comprehensive statistical picture of Australia's population in the mid-1970s. It was prepared by some twenty academic demographers and Commonwealth government departments. The present volume does not seek to duplicate the work of this study, especially in the presentation of detailed statistical material. Again I seek more to elucidate trends, as well as to bring the picture up to date.

A third major initiative of the 1970s which should be mentioned here is the ANU Department of Demography's Australian Family Formation Project. Many of the publications arising from that project are referred to in this study. Although we are not seeking to present a comprehensive review of the literature on Australia's contemporary demography here, some other works should be mentioned. Price's series of monographs, bibliographies and digests on immigration to, and settlement in, Australia are the basic works in this important area. The Australian Academy of Science has produced a series of monographs on immigrants in Australia and a substantial volume on the implications of Australian population trends (Borrie and Mansfield 1982). The Australian Bureau of Statistics has also in the 1970s extended its publishing beyond purely statistical material. Especially notable here are the census monographs using internal migration data from the 1971 (Rowland 1979) and 1976 censuses (Maher 1984). There have also been series of occasional, technical and demography research papers produced by ABS since the late 1970s. More recently the Bureau has produced a series of focused compilations of social statistics including brief commentaries on those statistics. In particular a regular series of social indicators has been initiated and especially useful special volumes on Australia's aged population in 1982 and Australian families in 1982 have been prepared. In association with the Division of National Mapping and with the co-operation of the Institute of Australian Geographers, social atlases based on the results of the 1981 census have been produced for Australia's seven major cities. These volumes provide a useful spatial perspective on many of the trends revealed by the 1981 census and are valuable companion works to this study. Finally, the Division of National Mapping's map of Australia's population distribution at the 1981 census is an excellent and highly skilful presentation which also is a useful adjunct to the present study.

Several government departments have useful serial publications. The Department of Immigration and Ethnic Affairs (DIEA) produces the annual *Australia's Population Trends and Prospects* (formerly *Review of Australia's Demographic Trends*) and the Australian Council on Population and Ethnic Affairs' *Population Report* series are most notable here. In addition most State governments produce an annual review of demographic trends within the State, as well as occasional publications on projections. Compilations of the papers presented at two recent conferences also should be included in any review of the available literature on Australia's population. These include the papers presented at the first Australian Population Association conference (1982) and those in the seven volumes of proceeding of the Australian family research conference (1983) organized by the Institute of Family Studies.

The above is by no means a comprehensive listing of recent demographic research into Australia's population, but it is indicative of the growing interest and activity in this area. However, it would be difficult to argue that enough is being done, especially in the area of interpretation of demographic trends in such a way that they can be used by planners and debated by the community. Much of the planning that is undertaken in our community remains uninformed, partially informed or ill informed about current and impending demographic change. In the mid-1970s the NPI report's findings of a slowdown in population growth and its likely continuation came as a huge shock to many Australian planners who had predicated their plans on a continuation of 1960s growth patterns and had not sought informed analysis of recent and impending population change. For example, Birrell (1975, pp. 87–8) pointed out with respect to metropolitan urban planning that

> the politicians and planners responsible for such planning have been reluctant to acknowledge that recent demographic trends may be maintained over the long term. They are continuing to make decisions which reflect 1960s trends.... This may well be leading to premature commitments of scarce capital such as to unnecessary water supply projects, unnecessary satellite towns and superfluous zonings of land for urban purposes.

Such statements could apply to many areas of social planning at that time. Although today there is a greater appreciation of contemporary population trends, planners often fail to make full use of the work of trained demographers. We are still too frequently surprised by changes which could have been anticipated by even relatively unsophisticated demographic analysis. It is one of the objectives of this study to assist planners and policy makers in avoiding such unwelcome surprises.

POPULATION POLICY IN AUSTRALIA

One can identify two major areas in which there is an interface between population trends on the one hand and policy making and social and economic planning on the other. The first is in using knowledge of recent and impending demographic change to guide policy makers in their allocations of resources between groups, regions and sectors and in planning the provision of services, housing etc. However, Australian governments have also initiated policies which have influenced the nation's demography. Some are policies which have explicit population objectives while other government actions initiated without such objectives often have hidden implications for population growth, structure or distribution. Indeed, in some cases such indirect policies are more influential in shaping demographic trends than more explicit policies.

In the long history of public debate, government policy formulation and attempted intervention concerning Australia's population there have been three predominant themes:

1 the size and overall growth (or more often the lack of growth) of the national population;
2 the ethnic/racial composition of the population;
3 the spatial distribution of the nation's population.

Extended consideration of these themes is taken up at appropriate points in this study and I will make only a few introductory and summary remarks here.

Since the early years of white settlement the catch-cry of 'populate or perish' has had no shortage of supporters in Australia. The period following Federation especially saw descriptions of Australia's inestimable resource endowments and a push for massive population growth. Such optimism did not go unchallenged by those whose knowledge of Australia's potential for further closer rural settlement was based on scientific appraisal of land capability. Powell, for example, has written entertainingly and authoritatively of the debate during the inter-war years between the boosters of 'Australia Unlimited' and the geographer T. Griffith Taylor (in Birrell et al. 1984). While the debate in the 1980s hasn't generated as much heat and public interest as that of the inter-war years it is, nevertheless, alive and well. This can be seen in the publication in 1984 of a major study arguing that Australia should seek to attain a zero growth situation as rapidly as possible, both because of the vulnerability of the natural environment and limitations of

Australia's resource base to meet the demands of a larger population, and also because of the 'social consequences' of population growth at a time of economic recession, high unemployment and structural change (Birrell et al. 1984).

Much of the debate hinges upon Australia's capacity to absorb further population growth—a subject which was devoted substantial attention in the NPI Report (1975, Chapter XVIII). The bio-physical restraints on growth are difficult to estimate, since they can be affected by technological change and willingness or otherwise of the population to forgo current or higher standards of living and consumption of resources. However, an authoritative Commonwealth Scientific and Industrial Research Organisation (CSIRO) assessment (Gifford et al. 1975), summarized in Table 1.3, estimated that at present levels of technology and taking purely food and water criteria as limits to growth, some sixty million people could be supported on present Australian diets on food produced in Australia without real danger to the system. However, currently Australia exports 65 per cent of its food production and if this was directed to internal consumption it would have a highly detrimental impact on countries currently reliant upon food imports from Australia and on Australia's export income. At that export level, Gifford et al. have estimated that Australia could support only 22 million people if it were to expand its food production to the maximum attainable, given present technological levels. The upper limits imposed by water are somewhat higher, but it must be remembered that the majority of Australia's water resources are north of the Tropic of Capricorn, which is home to only

Table 1.3 Estimated bio-physical constraints on the total population which could be supported in Australia

Bio-physical constraints	Stable population supportable (millions)
Water	
(a) no expansion of irrigation; present per capita use of domestic, municipal and industrial water	320
(b) irrigation expands to maximum irrigable area; present per capita use of urban water	140
(c) as (b), but with per capita urban water use at present USA level	60
Food	
(d) estimated potential arable land area put into crops and sown pasture and irrigated culture in same proportions as now; present per capita food consumption; no food export	82
(e) as (d), but with present per capita food consumption	60
(f) as for (e), except that 50 per cent of food produced is exported	30

Source: Gifford et al. (1975, p. 221)

a small minority of Australia's current population. Such figures taken alone are unrealistic, as food and water are not the only resources which are exploited by population growth (see Nevill, Lowe and French, all in Birrell et al. 1984). Moreover, they beg the question of how increases in population are to be absorbed into an economy in which capital and technology investment is displacing labour. However, the figures are nevertheless instructive—it will no doubt come as a shock to many that the upper limit set by food and water, given more or less stable technological conditions and standards of living, is estimated to be only 22 million. This is a salutory warning that while the statement by the National Population Inquiry (1978, p. 724) that 'By any international comparison Australia is rich in resources, and on a *percapita* basis fantastically rich' has validity, there are very real biophysical limits on population growth and while these are not likely to 'bite' in the near future they must be carefully weighed up in any attempt to formulate a national population growth policy.

In the relevant chapters of this study, attention is focused upon policy options influencing mortality, fertility and immigration, and therefore population growth. In any time period total population change is the combined result of all three processes and if intervention is contemplated it must be via one or more of those processes. With respect to mortality, a universal policy goal must be to assist all of the countries' citizens to live as long as possible: this is discussed in Chapter 2.

With respect to fertility, the official policy is evident in a statement to the International Conference on Population in Mexico City in 1984 (Department of Immigration and Ethnic Affairs 1984a, p. 41):

> The Australian Government adheres to the principle that people should be free to choose the number and spacing of their children and their place of living within their own country. Each person should also have equal opportunity for social and economic wellbeing including equal access to education, health care and welfare of a high standard.

However, as is pointed out in Chapter 3, there are many implications for policy makers from contemporary fertility trends. Pressure groups within and outside government have argued for programmes with pro- or antinatalist intentions. However, it is unlikely that explicit interventionist policies with respect to fertility will be pursued by Australian governments in the near future, although policies in other areas may affect fertility indirectly. These would include policies and programmes which impinge upon child care, taxation of family units rather than individuals, sex education, contraceptive availability and cost, and so on.

There can be no question that the most flexible measure available to Australian governments to control the rate of population growth is immigration. This is taken up in more detail in Chapter 4, but it should be stressed that significant changes in immigration policy since 1970 have greatly restricted the degree of flexibility available to governments in turning the immigration tap on or off. Moreover, for the first time in the post-war period the early 1980s saw a departure, albeit a brief one, from the bipartisan

Table 1.4 Numbers of permanent settlers in Australia whose previous place of residence was an Asian country, 1970–84

Year	Total settlers	Total from Asia	Percentage from Asia
1970	185 325	9 634	5.2
1971	155 525	11 264	7.2
1972	112 468	9 302	8.3
1977	75 640	14 949	19.8
1978	68 419	19 355	28.3
1979	72 236	22 984	31.8
1980	94 502	25 173	26.6
1981	118 735	27 012	22.7
1982	107 171	23 790	22.2
1982–83	93 009	25 771	27.7
1983–84	68 824	26 448	38.4

Note: Asia is taken to include the following countries—China, Taiwan, Japan, Hong Kong, North and South Korea, Macau, Mongolia, Brunei, Burma, Indonesia, Kampuchea, Laos, Malaysia, the Philippines, Singapore, Thailand, Vietnam, Afghanistan, Bangladesh, Bhutan, India, Iran, Maldives, Nepal, Pakistan, and Sri Lanka.
Source: ABS overseas arrivals and departure bulletins

approach to immigration policy adopted by the two major Australian political parties. Clearly it is in the area of immigration that most public debate and the greatest concern of policy makers with population growth will be focused. There are powerful lobbies within Australian society, many of which cut across conventional political allegiances, for both increasing and reducing immigration levels. Thus some employer groups, ethnic communities, industrialists, the housing industry, humanitarians and liberals have supported the increased immigration lobby; while those speaking out against immigration have included intellectuals, conservation groups, racist lobbies and unions.

The size of the immigration intake is only one dimension of the public debate on immigration. The ethnic, and especially the racial, composition of the immigration intake has long been a matter of considerable public concern. It was not until the early 1970s that the last vestiges of the 'White Australia Policy' were removed from Australia's immigration policy. Prior to World War II, this had involved an almost total rejection of non-Europeans wishing to settle in Australia. However, as has been well described by Price (1975), the policy was dismantled and through the 1970s the non-European intake began to rise. By 1983–84, 38.4 per cent of permanent settlers arriving in Australia were of East, South-east and South-central Asian origin. However, as Table 1.4 shows, there was little change in the *numbers* of immigrants of this origin in the early 1980s; the reduced intake of other groups resulted in the proportion of Asian origin increasing substantially. This is also evident in Figure 1.2, which shows trends in the arrivals of both permanent settlers and long-term visitors over the last quarter-century, and the numbers arriving from Asian countries. This shows that

Figure 1.2 Permanent and long-term arrivals in Australia from Asian countries,[1] 1958–84

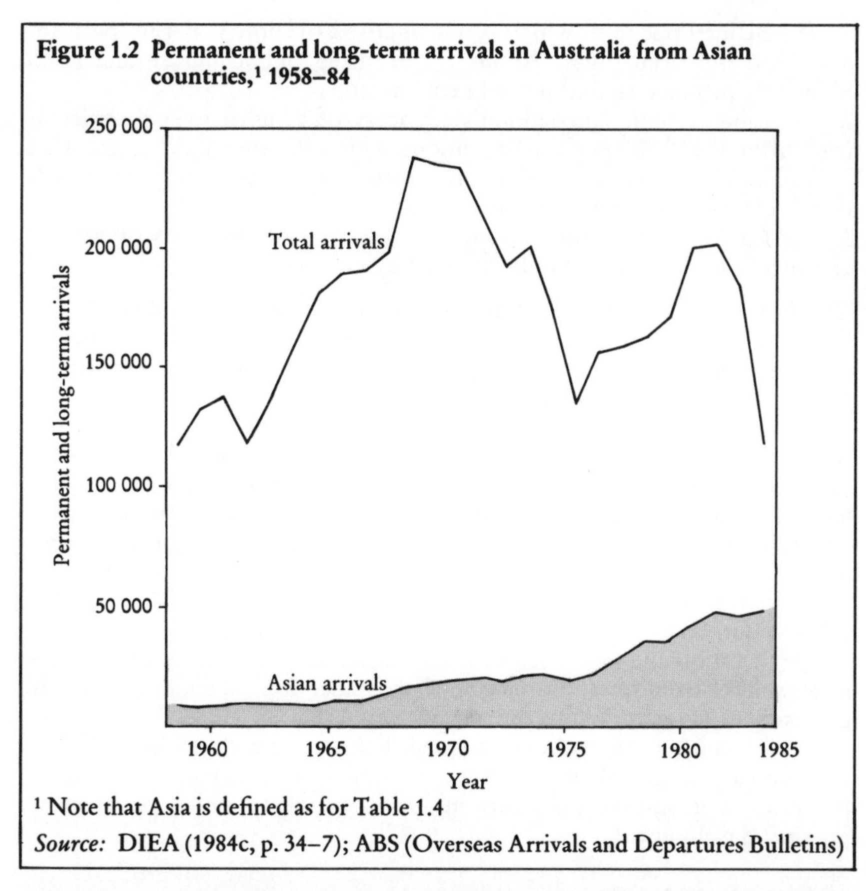

[1] Note that Asia is defined as for Table 1.4

Source: DIEA (1984c, p. 34–7); ABS (Overseas Arrivals and Departures Bulletins)

there were two significant upturns in Asian immigration over the period since the removal of the White Australia Policy in the early 1970s. These were in the late 1970s, when Australia began to take substantial numbers of Indo-Chinese refugees; and in the 1980s, with the increased numbers of persons of Asian origin coming to Australia under the family reunion scheme.

Despite the small size of the Asian intake and the relative stability of numbers during the 1980s, there has been growing criticism from within the community. This was especially so in early 1984 when Professor Geoffrey Blainey publicly stated that he considered the Asian component of immigration to be too large and that it threatened to strain community tolerance, especially among the poor and disadvantaged. This sparked off a resurgence of public discussion about the racial composition of immigration and it is certain that this debate will continue. Unfortunately, much of that debate is being conducted in a heated, confrontationist, totally dogmatic and bigoted way. Price (1984, p. 14) recognizes three main positions in contemporary Australia on this issue, leaving aside 'extremists on both sides, some apparently unable to conduct a rational discussion'. These are:

1 the Blainey position, which is not opposed to some non-European immigration but argues that Asians are arousing public unease and could ultimately produce an outburst of racial hostility;
2 the Liberal/National coalition's advocacy of a higher overall settler intake (around 100 000 per annum) among which the annual Asian intake of around 20 000 to 30 000 would not be so prominent, thus restoring the traditional 'balance' in Australia's immigration;
3 the Labor government's standpoint, i.e., a rejection of its opponents' arguments as racist and completely unacceptable.

The fact remains that at present, employing a reasonable definition of 'Asian', some 2 per cent of the Australian population belongs in that category and if present trends continue unchanged until the end of the century the proportion would be no more than 4 per cent.

The third major area of population policy debate in Australia relates to the spatial distribution of the population. Although considerable debate has surrounded attempts to redirect population growth within major cities (Burnley 1980, Chapter 12) and to populate and develop the northern third of Australia (Davidson, 1965), most attention has been focused on a perceived need to decentralize population growth away from the capital cities, especially in the twenty-five years since the war. As Stilwell (1974, p. 153) pointed out, 'State governments have long accepted the general rationale for decentralization and have used various policies to achieve these ends'. These policies have from time to time gained assistance from the Commonwealth government (Logan, Whitelaw and McKay 1981, pp. 108–13). However, their success has been extremely limited. During the early 1970s a Ministry of Urban and Regional Development was established, only to be abolished a few years later, and Australia currently lacks a coherent policy of urban and regional development.

SOURCES OF DATA

The major source of information used in this study is the Australian Census of Population and Housing conducted on 30 June 1981. The census attempts a complete enumeration of all Australians, and collects a range of social, economic and demographic information from them. This was the eleventh census this century and they have been conducted quinquennially since 1961. It was a *de facto* count, assigning people to their location on the night of the census, although information was obtained to allow population totals to be estimated on a place of 'usual residence' basis. The Australian census has a very low under-enumeration rate by any international standard, especially considering the vast geographical area to be covered. The 1981 census post-enumeration survey indicated that 1.9 per cent of Australians were missed by the census, a significant improvement over the 2.7 per cent at the 1976 census (Doyle 1982). The under-enumeration rate, however, was not evenly spread across the total population but was higher, for example, among males (2 per cent) than females, among the young (over 3 per cent among those aged 15–24), in Queensland (3.1 per cent) and the Northern Territory

(5 per cent). In Chapter 8 the apparently substantial under-enumeration of the Aboriginal population is discussed. Nevertheless, despite the (generally small) biases introduced by under-enumeration and non-response to some questions (Doyle 1982), the census remains the single most important source of demographic, social and economic statistics available for planning at all levels in the Australian community. It is unique in providing reliable knowledge of the numbers and characteristics of the population living in areas ranging from the nation down through a hierarchy of regions to collection districts generally containing between 200 and 800 persons. The data provided are comparable across the country, and to some extent with previous censuses, allowing change to be measured and studied, and they provide the benchmark for projections and estimates and for testing the quality of statistics available from other sources.

Topics covered by the census are restricted to a limited number of factual questions. The Census and Statistics Act under which the 1981 census was conducted makes several topics mandatory—age, sex, duration of marriage, marital status, relationship to head of household, religion, birthplace, period of residence in Australia, citizenship, occupation and material of outer walls and number of rooms in dwelling. These topics are consistent through most recent censuses, and have been supplemented by additional questions which have varied from year to year. The 1976 census questionnaire was by far the largest ever used in Australia and collected a large array of information on leisure and recreation, health and welfare, labour force and housing. Budget constraints and changing government priorities resulted in a considerable contraction of the topics covered in the 1981 census, which are listed in the Appendix.

Census data are available in a wide variety of forms, most of which have been employed in some way in this study. These are well documented in Australian Bureau of Statistics publications (listed in the ABS publication catalogue) and only a few points are made here. The results of each census question are presented in one-way tabulation or cross-tabulation form. Hence, for most analyses of census data aggregate data must be employed. Scrupulous care is taken to preserve individual confidentiality. In the past, the restriction of availabe census data to such aggregate forms has limited the types of analysis that could be completed, although the ABS produced certain matrix tapes of detailed cross-tabulations on demand from researchers and planners. A very welcome innovation in the output from the 1981 census was the production for public use of one per cent sample tapes for unidentifiable individuals and households. This has opened up a wide range of research possibilities in allowing us to explore the inter-relatedness of particular characteristics of the population as well as their housing and living arrangements at a level of detail not previously possible. Such data allow researchers and planners to evaluate the requirements of particular groups of people, at least broadly, in a number of significant areas. Of course the samples represent only a small part of the Australian population, and in some detailed cross-tabulations the probability of sampling error is significant. Nevertheless, the sample of the census is larger than any available sample surveys and contains nearly all the data on individuals and households gathered at the census. As Siegel and Taeuber (1982, p. 148) point out these unit sample tapes 'permit do-it-yourself statistical analysis to answer questions that a particular service provider or academic researcher needs answered'. This is the first time Australian census data have been made available in this form, and extensive use has been made of the tapes in the present volume.

Although this study is based primarily on the 1981 census, a range of other sources has been employed. Most of these are derived from the Australian Bureau of Statistics. In particular, the ABS collates birth, death, marriage and divorce statistics, and these are used extensively in Chapters 2 and 3. Australia's vital statistics are of excellent quality, as are the overseas migration statistics which are also collated by ABS and used in Chapter 4. In the other chapters, use has been made of the results of household sample surveys regularly conducted by the ABS on topics of a demographic, social and economic nature. In particular, surveys of the labour force, internal migration, health, birth expectations, income and housing, families and handicapped persons are used here. The surveys are based on a carefully drawn-up and maintained sample frame and usually cover two-thirds of one per cent of the national population. In sum, Australia is fortunate to have such comprehensive and accurate demographic data, and it is unfortunate that these data have not been anywhere near fully exploited by planners and policy makers. I hope that this study demonstrates the potential utility of these data and that it will encourage more intensive use of these sources in the future.

CONCLUSION

The decade since the publication of the Report of the National Population Inquiry has seen rapid and significant demographic, not to mention social and economic, changes within Australia. Indeed, the demographic shifts experienced by Australia during the 1970s were surprising to many, and the question must be asked as to whether the changes in the 1980s will be as startling. Analysis of data from the 1981 census provides some clues to demographic trends in the 1980s. Moreover, many demographic changes can be readily anticipated—the probable numbers of people aged 65 years and over, the number of school entrants, etc. On the other hand, uncertainty surrounds such questions as: How many children will be born? How many people will migrate to Australia? Where will Australians live? Demographers have no special window to the future which is denied to other social scientists; however as Morrison (1978, p. 1) points out, analysis of major demographic changes 'can draw attention to emerging and approaching issues associated with these shifts and set the stage for public debate on timely actions for dealing with those issues'.

The population projections and forecasts referred to earlier suggest that the immediate outlook for the rest of this century is for a continued low rate of population growth. How is such a pattern occurring, and why? The social, economic and political explanations for the slowdown are complex, but some light can be shed on them and on the future outlook by examining separately each of the demographic processes which affect regional population growth. The demographic processes which together determine the degree of population change in a region are mortality, fertility and in and out migration. Each of these processes will now be taken in turn, their recent trends examined and future outlook discussed. We will then proceed to an examination of aspects of the changing spatial distribution and composition of the population.

2 The Changing Way of Death in Australia

In recent years there has been mounting concern about the capacity of the Australian economic, social welfare and health systems to cope with the rapid ageing of the population. One of the major factors underlying this concern is the recent increases in life expectancy which have occurred among older Australians. In this chapter I examine the nature, scale and significance of recent changes in mortality in Australia. It is arguable that Australia has entered a completely new phase of changes in mortality levels, causes and differentials. This is extremely important to planning, in both the private and public sectors, so the final part of the chapter assesses the implications of these changes for the near future, especially in demand for health and other services. In passing it should be mentioned that while there is no more important national policy goal than to have citizens live as long as possible and for there to be equality among them in the face of death, there are some other considerations to be confronted. As medical technology allows increasing numbers of Australians to survive to older ages, despite their having seriously debilitating conditions, there will be need for society to consider the complex bio-ethical issues relating to life with dignity, euthanasia and the right to die and for the public discussion of these issues in relation to basic human rights.

There have been few greater achievements in Australia during the last century than the reduction in mortality, which has extended the expectation of life at birth of females by some 29 years and males by 25 years. Only a handful of European countries and Japan have lower mortality levels than Australia. By the early 1970s it was considered that these improvements in mortality had levelled off. The National Population Inquiry (NPI) Report published in 1975 conducted a thorough analysis of mortality trends in the previous century, and especially in the post-war period, and found that 'barring any major disasters, future changes in mortality are unlikely to have any significant effect upon demographic aspects of growth' (p. 39). Further, it was stated that there was 'little evidence which suggests that a major improvement in mortality rates is imminent. If population changes were only a function of mortality, future population could be projected with great certainty'. Similar statements were made by demographers in other advanced-economy countries. However, the population projections based on these assumptions were found by the early 1980s to heavily under-predict the numbers of older persons, largely because there was an almost universal failure to anticipate large decreases in the mortality of older people.

THE EPIDEMIOLOGIC TRANSITION IN AUSTRALIA

Mortality levels at present are the lowest ever recorded in Australia. In 1982 the Crude Death Rate (CDR) was 7.6 per thousand (ABS 1983a, p. 2) compared to 17.9 in 1860. The CDR, however, is a poor measure of mortality, for it does not account for the age structure of a population. A more accurate measure of mortality which takes account of the age structure is the 'expectation of life'. This measure refers to the average number of years a person of a given age can expect to live if the present mortality rates at all ages for a given period are maintained over their lifetime. There has been a fairly steady increase in the expectation of life at birth. For example in 1870 an Australian-born male child could expect to live 46.5 years, while a female child could expect to live 49.6 years (Young and Ruzicka in ESCAP, 1982, p. 167). By 1946–48, life expectation at birth had reached 66.1 years for males and 70.6 years for females, and by 1983 this had increased to 72.1 and 78.7 for males and females respectively.

The patterns of mortality change over the last two centuries in developed countries have been so similar that Omran (1971) put forward a model to describe those changes. His 'epidemiologic transition' model comprises three stages (each of which is characterized by particular patterns and causes of death), through which societies progress as they experience economic development and social change. These stages are:

stage 1, in which mortality is very high and fluctuating and the main cause of death is infectious disease and epidemics—famine and pestilence are very influential;
stage 2, characterized by a progressive decline in mortality in which epidemics become less frequent and less catastrophic—however, infectious diseases like diarrhoea, tuberculosis and cholera remain very important causes of death;
stage 3, in which mortality stabilizes at a low level, and degenerative and man-influenced diseases such as heart disease and cancer become predominant.

I will show later that the Aboriginal population remained in the first stage of this transition until relatively recently. However, the white population was into the second stage of the transition by the time of their initial settlement in Australia. Figure 2.1 shows the steady improvement over the next century and Young and Ruzicka (1982) in their examination of the changing patterns of cause of death in Australia identify two distinct periods which broadly conform to the second and third stages of Omran's transition. They show that the transition from the second to the third stage occurred in the early years of this century, with infectious diseases gradually being reduced in significance and accidents and degenerative diseases assuming greater

Figure 2.1 Expectation of life at birth in Australia, 1870–1982

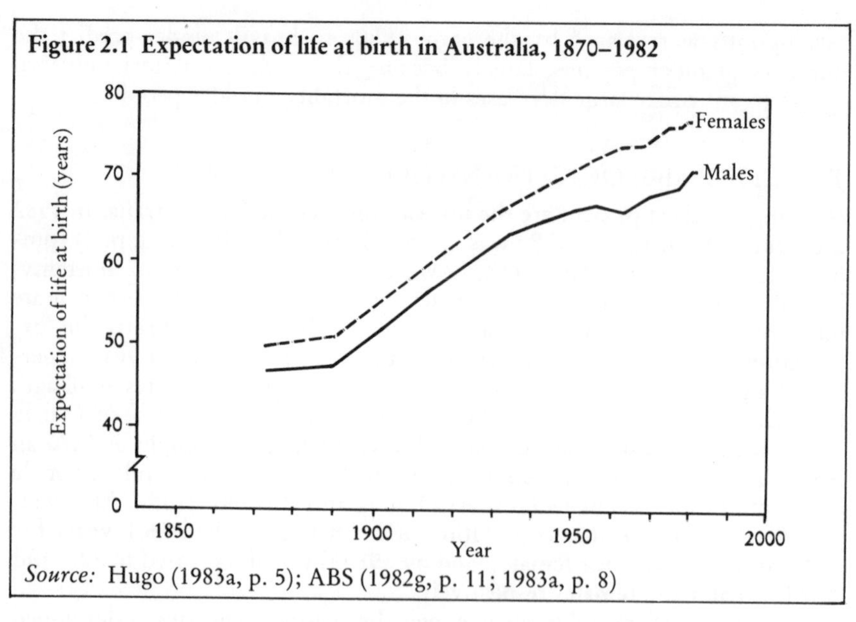

Source: Hugo (1983a, p. 5); ABS (1982g, p. 11; 1983a, p. 8)

importance. Although changing classifications render any attempt at comparisons over time difficult, Young (1976) has shown the dramatic decline in deaths of infant and young children from diarrhoea and deaths from such infectious diseases as tuberculosis, typhus, typhoid, scarlet fever, cholera, dysentery and smallpox: these accounted for 40 per cent of deaths around the turn of the century but now are the cause of less than 1 per cent of all Australian deaths. The most important reasons for the changes were improved nutrition levels, rising standards of living, introduction and development of sanitary engineering measures such as water control, sewerage, etc., and isolation of infected agents in hospitals. Young shows that these were more important than developments in therapy.

Over the century preceeding 1971, the largest improvements in mortality were among infants, dependent children and women of child-bearing age as Table 2.1 demonstrates. Declines in infant mortality have been huge over the last century. In South Australia, for example, whereas in 1876 149 out of every 1000 children born died before they reached their first birthday, this had been reduced to 8 per 1000 by 1981. The massive improvements prior to World War II were largely due to control of infectious diseases. Even during the post-World War II period the Australian infant mortality rate has dropped precipitously, from 27 (per 1000) in the late 1940s to 16.2 in the early 1970s and 10.3 in 1982 (ABS 1983a; Wood and Hugo 1983, p. 12). Young and Ruzicka show that these post-war improvements have been due principally to large reductions in the number of high-risk births on the one hand, and developments in medical technology and maternal and child nutrition enhancing the survival rate of children on the other. By the 1980s fewer than ten other countries had lower infant mortality rates than Austra-

Table 2.1 Improvements in expectation of life in Australia at selected ages, 1870–1970 and 1970–81

Age in years	Males 1870–81 to 1970–72	Males 1970–72 to 1981	Females 1870–81 to 1970–72	Females 1970–72 to 1981
0	21.9	3.5	25.0	3.8
10	10.5	2.8	14.4	3.3
20	9.4	2.7	13.1	3.2
30	7.6	2.7	10.9	3.1
40	5.4	2.5	8.2	3.0
50	3.1	2.3	5.8	2.7
60	1.6	2.0	4.2	2.4
70	0.6	1.4	2.7	1.9
80	0.1	0.8	1.2	1.2

Sources: Young and Ruzicka (in ESCAP, 1982, p. 167); ABS (1982a, p.11)

lia. Table 2.1 also shows that over the 1870–1970 period there was a major improvement in the survival of young adult women. This was due to the virtual elimination of maternal death because of greatly improved birth practices, nutrition, etc.

It can be readily seen in Table 2.1 that the 1970s saw a significant improvement in the survival of all age groups in the Australian population. As was the case for the preceding century, there were major increases in the life expectancy of infants and young children. However the 1970s saw unprecedented major improvements in the life expectancy of older adults. Over the 1971–81 period, the life expectancy of 50- to 60-year-old Australians increased by more than two years and that of those older by more than one year. In the case of males, these improvements were as large as, or larger than, improvements over the entire previous century.

The improved expectation of life at older ages has been primarily due to greatly reduced death from ischaemic heart disease during the 1970s. In 1968 there were 337 deaths from ischaemic heart disease per 100 000 Australian men, whereas the rate in 1982 was down to 250 (the equivalent figures for females were 219 and 177). The major reasons for the sharp decrease in death rates from these diseases have not been fully explored, but they can be divided into two categories. First there is a set of lifestyle factors: fewer men were smoking (this was especially true of middle-aged men), and people generally were consuming smaller amounts of animal fats and exercising more. Second, there have been medical advances, such as improved techniques of diagnosing coronary artery disease, better information and screening programmes, more intensive care and coronary care units, improved drug and surgical treatment (especially the development of coronary bypass surgery); and increased use of medical services has enhanced the chances of early detection of the disease.

The unprecedented nature of the mortality improvements since 1970 should be stressed. This is the first time in our history that improvements at older ages have played a major role in overall reduction in mortality. This has also been observed in other developed countries, particularly the United States (Crimmins 1981). This would suggest that we may have entered a completely new phase of changes in mortality levels, causes and differentials which would perhaps warrant the addition of a fourth phase to Omran's epidemiologic transition. This phase would comprise the following elements:

- significant mortality decline in middle- and older-age groups as well as among infants;
- significant declines in death rates from some of the major degenerative diseases—especially ischaemic heart disease and cerebro-vascular disease;
- a reversal of the trend toward widening of sex differentials in mortality;
- increased levels of chronic disease among middle-aged and older groups; and
- a recognition that changes in diet, smoking, alcohol consumption, exercise and exposure to stress are necessary to reduce mortality from degenerative disease, as well as diagnostic, surgical, and other medical advances.

Accordingly we can posit a considerably expanded version of the epidemiologic transition model such as that presented in Table 2.2.

MORTALITY DIFFERENTIALS

The overall mortality experience for the whole of Australia hides differences that exist between, for example, the sexes, different population groups including Aborigines, different regions, different occupational groups and so on. The study of these mortality differentials can be important in identifying disadvantaged groups in society, thereby enabling the planning of the most equitable provision of health services and other facilities.

Sex differences in mortality

One of the most distinctive features of current mortality levels in developed countries is the marked difference between the sexes in the expectation of life. It has been estimated that if everything else was held constant and only genetic factors were allowed to have an impact, females would on average live two years longer than males (Pressat 1970). Yet in contemporary Australia, as well as the US, Canada and many European countries, the expectation of life at birth of females is six to eight years greater than for men. A number of social and environmental factors are assumed to intervene to extend this difference. Moreover the decline in overall mortality over the last century has also seen an ever-increasing divergence in the mortality experience of the sexes (Figure 2.1). In 1870 the gap between male and female life expectancy at birth was 3.2 years; by 1965–67 this had increased to 6.5 years, and in 1981 it had reached a peak of 7.1 years. However Lopez and Ruzicka (1977, p. 87) have pointed out that

> the magnitude of this differential has been progressively diminishing in recent years and unless there are significant changes in the current mortality pattern for Australia, it appears likely that the gap in life expectancy at birth for the sexes will stabilize somewhere between 6.5 and 7 years.

Table 2.2 The epidemiologic transition: an expanded model

Stage		Indicative mortality levels			Mortality differentials		Main causes of death	Major initiatives to reduce mortality
		IMR	E_0^0	E_{50}^0	Sex	Socio-economic		
I	High and fluctuating mortality	200	40	10	Low	High	Infectious disease associated with epidemics, famine and pestilence	Famine relief, improved diet, sanitation, water control
II	Progressive declines in mortality, predominantly in younger ages	100	50	24	Increasing	High	Infectious disease, but epidemics less frequent and catastrophic	Public health and sanitation, improved nutrition, hospital development
III	Stable mortality at a low level	12	70	25	High	Decreasing	Degenerative disease such as cancer, heart disease and accidents dominate	Therapy developments, medical breakthroughs
IV	Further declines in mortality, especially at older ages	9	75	30	Decreasing	Decreasing	Degenerative disease and accidents	Lifestyle changes (diet, exercise, etc.), medical breakthroughs

Note: IMR = infant mortality rate (infant deaths per 1000 births)
E_0^0 = life expectancy at birth
E_{50}^0 = life expectancy at age 50
Source: adapted from Omran, 1971

In fact there was only a small decline in the differences in life expectancy at age 0, from 7 years in 1975–77 to 6.95 years in 1978 and thereafter an increase to 7.08 years in 1980. Since then the decline has resumed, with the difference being 6.63 years in 1983. It is probably too early to suggest that this is the beginning of a long-term trend however.

There are two groups of theories which explain the mortality differential between the sexes (Lopez and Ruzicka 1977, p. 87). The first relate to the apparently greater biological and constitutional resistance to degenerative diseases among women (Madigan 1957). The alternative theories are based on the fact that many of the behavioural patterns of men are less conducive to longevity. The higher incidence of premature male mortality from degenerative diseases such as heart disease, cerebro-vascular disease and cancer among those 50 years and over is undoubtedly associated with higher incidence of occupational stress, and higher levels of alcohol consumption and tobacco smoking among men. Retherford (1972) has demonstrated that higher incidence of cigarette smoking among males accounted for 47 per cent of the sex differential in mortality between ages 37 and 87 in the United States. The higher incidence of motor vehicle accidents among males in their late teens and early 20s is also an important contributing factor in the difference in mortality between the sexes.

The reasons for the narrowing of sex differentials in mortality in recent years are less clear. They are partly due to significant reductions in the male mortality rate at ages 15–24 from motor vehicle accidents (associated with seat belts and perhaps random breath testing); but the greatest reductions in the male mortality rates have been from cardio-vascular disease for those aged between 40 and 60 years, and this alone will have reduced sex differentials in mortality. However, the main explanation of the convergence in sex mortality differentials may lie in the pervasive changes in women's lives in recent years. The increasing involvement of women in the workforce outside the home and in public activities is altering their relative risks. As women are exposed to greater stress and as their behaviour patterns, including increased alcohol consumption and increases in cigarette smoking become similar to those traditionally associated with men, then the differential in mortality between the sexes can be expected to decline even further until perhaps the difference is accounted for only by biological-genetic factors. In this context, it should be noted that in recent years there has not been as great an improvement in death from cardio-vascular disease among women as among men.

The difference between male and female mortality levels has some significant implications for the planning of services for the aged population, since the number of women living to older ages is much greater than for men. Table 2.3 shows the decrease in the sex ratio with increasing age. Six out of ten Australians aged over 65, and nearly three-quarters of those aged 85 or more, are women. Care of the aged thus becomes largely the care of aged

Table 2.3 Sex ratio among Australians at selected ages, 1976, 1981 and 1983

Age	Sex ratio (males/1000 females)		
	1976	1981	1983
60–64	923	908	924
65–69	880	874	863
70–74	792	781	782
75–79	627	688	683
80+	462	451	462
Total population	1004	996	996

Source: ABS (1982b, pp. 18–19, 33–4; 1984a, pp. 4–5)

widows and spinsters. This is especially so when it is considered that because most men are outlived by their wives, they tend to be nursed through illness and disability associated with old age by their wives and hence the probability that they will need institutional assistance is low.

Aboriginal mortality

The largest differentials in Australian mortality patterns are those which exist between the Aboriginal and non-Aboriginal populations. Information on Aboriginal mortality is limited, but the scale of inequality is evident in the estimates of recent infant mortality rates (IMRs) in Table 2.4. Despite a dramatic decline in the IMR from around 138 deaths per thousand in the mid-1960s, in 1980 the rate was still three times that of the non-Aboriginal population at 32.7. The major causes of the excessive Aboriginal deaths at the young ages are gastro-intestinal and respiratory infections and accidents. In principle almost all such deaths are preventable.

Data for adult mortality among the Aboriginal population are even more limited than that for infants. Thomson (1982, 1984a & b) quotes a 1978–79 study based on rural New South Wales data which reported a life expectancy at birth for Aborigines of both sexes of 52.7 years compared to 72.2 for the total population. The age-standardized death rate for adult male Aborigines was almost four times greater than that for the total adult population, while the female rate was three and a half times greater. The age-specific death rate for the Aborigines between the ages of 35 and 44 was ten times greater than for the non-Aboriginal population. The breakdown of causes of Aboriginal death studied by Thomson shows a high proportion of deaths from pneumonia, infectious and parasitic diseases, and alcohol-related disorders such as cirrhosis and pancreatitis. In 53 per cent of adult male deaths and 21 per cent of female adult deaths reported among Aborigines, alcohol was mentioned as a significant medical problem.

A parliamentary report by the House of Representatives Standing Committee on Aboriginal Affairs (1979) concluded that 'the standard of health of Aboriginals is far lower than that of the majority of Australians and it would not be tolerated if it existed in the Australian community as a whole'. There can be no doubt that the mortality and health levels among the Aborigines are the worst of any group in Australian society. There can be equally no

Table 2.4 Aboriginal and non-Aboriginal infant mortality rates, 1976–80

Year	Infant mortality rate	
	Aboriginal	Non-Aboriginal
1976	51.6	12.8
1977	50.6	11.5
1978	38.8	11.5
1979	31.7	10.9
1980	32.7	10.2

Source: Thomson (1982, p. 3)

question regarding the causes of these inequalities. Thomson (1984a, p. 946), in demonstrating the failure of more than a decade of special Aboriginal health programmes to attain the goal of equal health status, succinctly and accurately identifies these inequalities as stemming from

> the extreme social inequality experienced by Aborigines. This social inequality is characterised by poverty and powerlessness, and is directly related to the dispossession and discrimination to which Aborigines have been, and are still being, subjected.

Mortality differences between birthplace groups

In Australia at the 1981 census some 20.7 per cent of the total population was born overseas. Hence any differences in the mortality and morbidity experience between the major birthplace groups and the Australian-born are likely to have some impact not only upon overall mortality levels, but on demand for health services of various kinds. In general, immigrants tend to have lower levels of mortality than the Australian-born. This is apparent in Table 2.5 (drawn from the work of Dunt 1982), which shows that for both

Table 2.5 Standardized mortality rates of persons aged 25–64 years, for major birthplace groups, 1970–72

Cause of death	Sex	Place of birth			
		Australasia	Britain & Ireland	Southern Europe	Other European
Ischaemic heart disease	M	111	88	44	89
	F	107	83	38	64
Malignant neoplasm	M	99	111	75	98
	F	101	108	81	104
Cerebro-vascular disease	M	110	73	47	73
	F	111	64	55	51
'All other causes'	M	107	70	51	80
	F	108	53	47	63
Motor vehicle accidents	M	100	83	98	117
	F	100	100	100	115
Bronchitis, emphysema and asthma	M	111	100	26	41
	F	111	89	22	33
Suicide, self-inflicted injuries	M	100	92	65	138
	F	100	100	43	143
Hypertensive disease	M	112	50	50	75
	F	120	80	40	80
Other heart disease	M	107	61	46	69
	F	100	75	50	63
All causes	M	105	89	59	91
	F	105	84	60	80

Note: rate for total population = 100
Source: Dunt (1982, p. 219)

sexes and most causes of death Southern Europeans had significantly lower mortality than not only the Australian-born but also the British/Irish and other Continental European-born population.

Several explanations have been advanced to account for immigrants' lower death rates (Wood and Hugo 1983, pp. 21–8) and these are summarized below.

1 Immigration to Australia is a selective process and in fact involves a formal selection programme whereby healthier people are much more likely to be chosen to migrate;
2 It is possible that migrants' behaviour patterns and environment prior to migration are conducive to longevity;
3 A third explanation, considered by Powles and Birrell (1977), is that migrants came from populations with more favourable genetic constitutions;
4 A fourth hypothesis is that it may be something specific in the diet, behaviour and lifestyle of particular immigrant groups which explains their lower mortality rates in comparison to the Australian-born. McMichael (1982), for example, has recently summarized evidence on dietary differences between Australia and the countries of origin of Southern European immigrants and concludes that there are differences in sources of both fat and protein intake (i.e., whether animal or vegetable). Clearly this may be a factor in differential mortality. However, immigrants' food habits do change and move towards those of the Australian-born majority, and this also may be a factor in the convergence of mortality rates with period of residence.

Mortality differences between occupational groups

The linkages between ill health and occupation are both indirect and direct. First, occupation tends to be strongly associated with income, lifestyle, socio-economic status, behaviour patterns and place of living, which in turn have major implications for health and relative exposure to risk of contracting (and dying from) particular diseases. Second, certain occupations involve higher relative health risks. Recent studies have confirmed the existence of strong occupational differentials in mortality in Australia (e.g., Dasvarma 1977, 1980; McMichael and Hartshorne 1980, 1982).

Differences in Standardized Mortality Ratios (SMRs) for males aged 15 to 64 years in different occupational groups for the 1968 to 1978 period are shown in Figure 2.2. The SMRs show wide differences between the so-called white- and blue-collar occupational groups. Of the nine occupational groups, the professional, technical, administrative, executive and managerial groups had the lowest SMRs—some 11 per cent below the national level so the difference was statistically significant. On the other hand, miners and quarrymen had SMRs some 90 per cent greater than average, those employed in transport and communication had SMRs one-quarter higher and craftsmen, labourers, members of the armed forces and men employed in service, sport and recreation all had SMRs significantly higher than the national average.

Figure 2.2 Standardized mortality ratios by occupational groups for all causes of death in Australian males, 1968–78

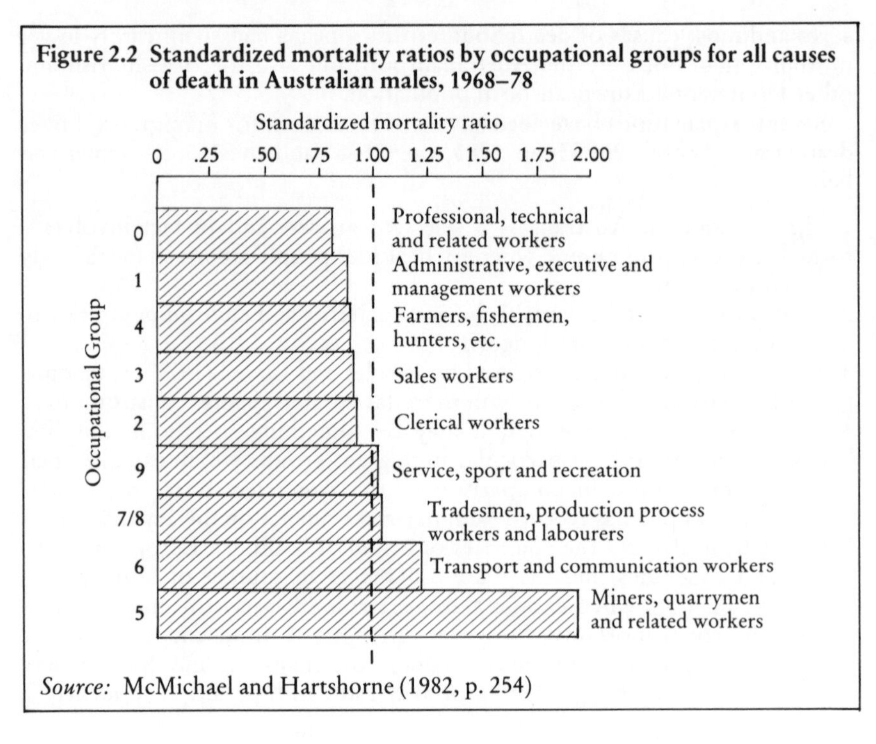

Source: McMichael and Hartshorne (1982, p. 254)

Spatial differences in mortality

To a large extent, differentials between different areas are a spatial expression of the socio-economic and demographic differentials briefly discussed above. That is, they reflect the relative distributions of the various socio-economic, birthplace and occupational groups which in turn are associated with differences between groups in their lifestyle, diet, behaviour, work patterns and inequalities with respect to access to health services, housing, education etc. In some cases, however, the environmental factors (such as types of pollution) or particular patterns of behaviour which are spatially concentrated may have an independent association with specific mortality patterns.

Differences in mortality between the Australian States were substantial in the nineteenth century (Young and Ruzicka in ESCAP, 1982), but as overall mortality has declined so these differences have diminished. The most striking pattern is the substantially higher mortality in the Northern Territory (1983 life expectancies at birth were 64 for males and 69 for females, compared with 71 or more and 78 or more in all other States), a pattern associated with its substantial Aboriginal population and 'frontier' character. On the other hand, South Australia and Western Australia have a constant pattern of below-average mortality.

Studies of regional variations in mortality are constrained by the small population size of local government areas in Australia. Burnley (1977) found a general negative correlation between the socio-economic status of suburbs in metropolitan Sydney and their SMR. A similar pattern was found to prevail in Adelaide (Hugo, 1983a, pp. 10–11). Spatial patterns of infant mortality are especially interesting since the IMR is very sensitive to socio-economic conditions. Studies of infant mortality have been made for most of Australia's major metropolitan areas (e.g. Burnley 1977; Wilson 1972, 1979; South Australian Health Commission 1980; and Dyer 1979). Dyer, for example, concluded from his study of data on Adelaide 1966–75 that babies born and living in the city of Adelaide and surrounding inner suburbs had a risk of infant death some two to three times higher than children living in the outer suburbs. However, all these studies were based upon aggregate infant death data provided by the Australian Bureau of Statistics. These data (especially in earlier years) suffer from several limitations, such as late registration and the occasional misreporting of place of residence whereby the infant death is allocated to the local government area in which the infant death occurred (often at a hospital) rather than the infant's parent's place of usual residence. These limitations can lead to spatial errors and the exaggeration of patterns of infant mortality. This is shown by Wood (1982) who used data directly obtained from the matching of birth and death certificates to examine the changing spatial distribution of infant mortality in metropolitan Adelaide between 1970 and 1981. She found that the IMR was significantly higher than average in the areas of lower socio-economic status to the north, west and south-west of the city centre, although the differences were not nearly so marked as those measured by Dyer using uncorrected data. Her study showed that between 1970 and 1981 the eastern, higher-status local government areas continued over the years to be areas of lower IMRs, while the industrial, lower-status areas of Marion, Port Adelaide, Thebarton, Hindmarsh, Enfield, Salisbury, Elizabeth and Munno Para persisted as areas of higher IMRs. Moreover the differential between the lesser and more affluent suburbs had increased over time.

CHANGING PATTERNS OF CAUSE OF DEATH

It was shown earlier (Table 2.2) that over the last century Australia passed through an epidemiologic transition, from a pattern where infectious diseases were the dominant cause of death to one where death from such diseases was negligible. By the 1940s many infectious and parasitic diseases had been brought under control and degenerative diseases had become the major causes of death. In 1982 ischaemic heart disease accounted for more deaths than any other cause, accounting for 29.9 per cent of all male deaths and 26.1 per cent of all female deaths. Malignant neoplasms (cancer) were the second most common cause, accounting for 22.4 per cent of male and 20.8 per cent of female deaths. Cerebro-vascular disease accounted for another 8.9 per cent of male deaths and 16.2 per cent of female deaths. These three major causes of death accounted for 61.2 per cent of all male deaths and 63.1 per cent of all female deaths in 1982 (ABS, 1983a).

The incidence of death from heart disease began to increase noticeably in the late 1950s and early 1960s, reaching a peak in 1966 and 1968 of 374 deaths per 100 000 males and 266 for females in 1968. Since the late 1960s, however, the number of deaths from heart disease has continued to decline, reaching 250 for males in 1982 and 177 for females.

The decline has occurred almost uniformly throughout the population, as it has occurred in most age groups and for both sexes simultaneously (Dobson et al. 1981, p. 411). Moreover, a similar pattern of progressive increase and then sharp decrease occurred simultaneously in the United States. Mortality due to cardio-vascular diseases in the United States decreased by more than 30 per cent in the last thirty years, 20 per cent between 1970 and 1980 (Levy and Moskowitz 1982, p. 121).

It is clear that the decline in death from cardio-vascular disease is the major reason for the unexpected and unprecedented improvement in the expectation of life among older Australians. As Crimmins (1981, p. 241) points out in the American context, it is difficult to isolate one factor or group of factors which can explain the decline but as mentioned earlier they can be broadly grouped into those related to medical and therapeutic developments and those involving lifestyle changes. However there would appear to still be considerable scope for improvement in mortality from cardio-vascular diseases. It remains the largest killer in Australia. Each day some eighty-five Australians die of ischaemic heart disease—and it is not simply the very old who succumb to heart attack. Powles (1982, pp. 75–89), in his study of 'premature death' (i.e., deaths to persons aged 15 to 64 years), has estimated that some 16 per cent of lost life years between the ages of 15 and 64 in 1978 were attributable to death from heart attack. Moreover, the recent improvements notwithstanding, Australia remains high among the developed countries in the level of death from heart disease (Wood and Hugo 1983, p. 51).

Unlike death rates from heart disease, those from malignant neoplasms have steadily increased over the period 1950 to 1982. In 1950 the death rate from this cause for males was 130 and this had increased to 187 in 1982; while for females the death rate continued to increase from 125 in 1950 to 141 in 1982. The increase has thus been much greater for males than females. Elsewhere (Wood and Hugo 1983, pp. 54–68) it is shown that trends in death from cancer vary with the type of cancer. This is because cancer is not a single disease that takes a single form—it has many forms and occurs in many sites in the body and the techniques of diagnosis and treatment differ by site. Because of space limitations we will deal here with only two of the major forms of cancer. Note that in any analysis of changing causes of death, problems arise from changes in the diagnosis. In the case of diseases such as cancers, the greater awareness of those diseases may have resulted in seeking of treatment earlier and causes of death being listed differently.

Lung cancer is the most significant cause of cancer death and its incidence is increasing at a faster rate than all other forms of cancer combined. The male death rate from lung cancer increased from 42 deaths per 100 000 in 1968 to 56 in 1982. The ratio of male to female deaths from lung cancer was 7.9 in the mid-1960s but had reduced to 4.0 in the early 1980s, due mainly to the increased incidence of cigarette smoking among women.

With lung cancer mortality increasing faster than any other form of cancer mortality, the prevention and/or treatment of this disease is of particular significance. The need for primary prevention (that is, reduced cigarette smoking) is fundamental in trying to combat this disease, for by the time the symptoms appear, the prospects for survival are generally poor. Data from the South Australian cancer registry unit (South Australian Health Commission 1983) for the period 1977–81 indicate that the survival rate one year after cancer diagnosis is only 32 per cent and four years after, approximately 14 per cent; and these figures do not speak of the suffering that may be associated with 'survival'.

The full impact of the detrimental effect of smoking on the health of Australians has been graphically demonstrated in a number of recent papers. The Surgeon-General has estimated that some 10 per cent of all deaths occurring in Australia are attributable in some way to use of tobacco (via lung cancer, coronary heart disease, bronchitis and emphysema and still-births to tobacco-using expectant mothers). Armstrong and de Klerk (1981) have estimated that in 1978 cigarette smoking caused 10 434 premature deaths and this represented a total loss of about 156 730 person-years of life of which 70 005 were lost before the age of 70 years. An official estimate in the United States indicates that 80 per cent of all lung cancer would be prevented if people stopped smoking (Crimmins 1981, p. 247).

Cancer of the breast is the major cause of death among Australian women, occurring at a rate of around 24–25 deaths per 100 000 over the last fifteen years. There have been reductions in death rates from breast cancer for some age groups. It has been found (South Australian Health Commission 1983) that the survival rate one year after detection is about 92 per cent and four years after nearly 70 per cent. With such high survival rates, early detection is important and self-examination has a fundamental role. It is clear that better methods of diagnosis, earlier detection and greater public awareness fostered by information campaigns have played a role in the improvement in mortality rates from breast cancer. Improvements in radiation therapy, chemo-therapy and surgical techniques may also have contributed.

For both heart disease and cancer, male death rates have long been significantly higher than for females. For the third major cause of death, cerebro-vascular disease, however, the female death rate is higher. In 1982 cerebro-vascular disease accounted for 9.9 per cent of male deaths and 16.2 per cent of female deaths. Until the late 1960s male death rates from cerebro-vascular disease remained steady at around 100 deaths per 100 000, and female rates fluctuated between 125 and 142. Since the early 1970s, however, the rates have declined to the 1982 levels of 110 for females and 74 for males. The reasons for the decline are believed to be associated with improvements in the management of hypertension (Roder 1980). Increasing community awareness of the consequences of alcohol consumption, smoking, diet and degree of fitness may also have had a positive effect.

The next most important cause of death is accidents, especially motor vehicle accidents. Accident death rates peaked in 1970 at 46 per 100 000 for males and 17 for females. Since 1970, the figures have generally declined to reach a low of 33 deaths per 100 000 for males and 11 deaths for females. This decrease could partly be explained by the introduction of compulsory wearing of seat belts and more recently the introduction of random breath testing. Nevertheless, the concentration of this cause of death in younger age groups makes it a major area of community concern. Moreover, as Hetzel (1982, p. 68) explains, there is a strong association between alcohol consumption and road crashes, with at least one-third of drivers killed on the road having excessive blood alcohol levels.

Suicide accounted for only 1.5 per cent of Australia's total deaths in 1982. Nevertheless, it has particular significance as a cause of death for people aged between 15 and 44. Suicide accounted for 23 deaths per 100 000 in 1982 among persons aged 25 to 44. Moreover, the number of suicides is probably understated, as it is possible to take one's life in such a manner that suggests to others that the action was not deliberate. A study by Clifford and Marjoram (1979) of suicide in South Australia found the suicide rate among the unemployed (particularly unemployed males) was much higher than the rates for those who were either employed or not members of the labour force. Suicide for both sexes was also found to be higher for widowed and divorced persons than for those who were married. Also, in 1981, rates for people never married were higher than for the married, except for women aged 15–24 and 65 years and over.

MORTALITY AND MORBIDITY

It is somewhat paradoxical that while Australia has excellent data on mortality there is a lack of comprehensive, representative and accurate data on morbidity, well-being and disability in the population. Unlike the United States we have no national health survey to assist health planners, and they are forced to rely on case studies or the Australian Health Survey of 1977–78 and the Survey of Handicapped Persons of 1981. The latter two national sample surveys were both conducted by ABS but are of limited utility since they rely upon self-attributed degrees of health and are thus subject to considerable response error. Nevertheless they do give some broad indications of the incidence of morbidity and disability in the Australian population. Table 2.6, for example, shows the incidence of handicap among specific age groups.

Among the several patterns in evidence, the following appear especially significant:

1 There is a rapid increase in the rate of disability with older age, with 44 per cent of those aged 75 years and over having some disability. (A handicapped person is one who is limited to some degree in his/her ability to perform activities or tasks in self-care, mobility, communication, schooling or employment.)

2 Older people have a much higher incidence of severe handicap, which was defined for the purposes of the ABS survey as one where personal help or supervision is required or the person is unable to perform one or more of a series of activities related to self-care, mobility and communication.

Table 2.6 Incidence of mild, moderate and severe handicap among Australians, by age, 1981

Age group	Mild handicap Rate per 1000	Moderate handicap Rate per 1000	Severe handicap Rate per 1000	Total Number ('000s)	Rate per 1000
5–14	0.37	0.45	1.60	97.0	3.75
15–44	0.73	0.80	1.41	158.6	2.30
45–54	2.43	2.71	3.61	157.8	11.65
55–64	5.43	4.69	5.75	260.7	19.25
65–74	8.46	5.45	9.61	220.5	23.53
75+	8.95	6.02	29.49	230.4	44.46
Total	1.98	1.70	3.44	1264.6	8.47

Source: Calculated from ABS 1981a, 1982b

The incidence of illness in the Australian population as measured at the 1977–78 Health Survey is shown in Figure 2.3. The concentration of incidence of chronic disease in older age-groups is readily apparent, as is higher incidence of illness and consultation with doctors.

Older people also have above-average rates for hospital admissions in the year preceding the survey. (There were equally high hospital admission rates for young adults, but this was mostly for childbirth or acute—especially accident-related—ailments.) Clearly with the longer survival of older people there are major implications for the future level of demand for health services. Moreover, demand will shift from the acute ailments of the young, to the chronic sicknesses of the old. Much of our medical system was established in the 1950s and 1960s when the population was extremely young and growing rapidly and hence was set up to provide the relatively short-term, very intensive specialized care demanded by acute illness, and not the less intensive, longer-term and less technologically sophisticated care more appropriate to chronic illness.

The changing relationship between age-specific levels of disability and morbidity in the population on the one hand, and levels of mortality in that population on the other, is obviously complex. The lack of a set of time series morbidity and disability data effectively precludes examination of these relationships in the Australian context. However, a study by Verbrugge (1984) of the United States annual health surveys between 1957 and 1981 shows that the *decrease in mortality* in older ages has been accompanied by *rising morbidity* among middle-aged and older people. There has been a slight decline in the incidence of acute conditions, but there has been an increase in both the incidence and the degree of limitation imposed by chronic conditions. The percentage of people limited in both major (job or housework) and secondary activities has increased steadily for middle-aged and older people. Verbrugge suggests (pp. 508–10) that the most plausible reasons for this increased morbidity are people's greater awareness of their diseases due to earlier diagnosis, earlier accommodation to the limita-

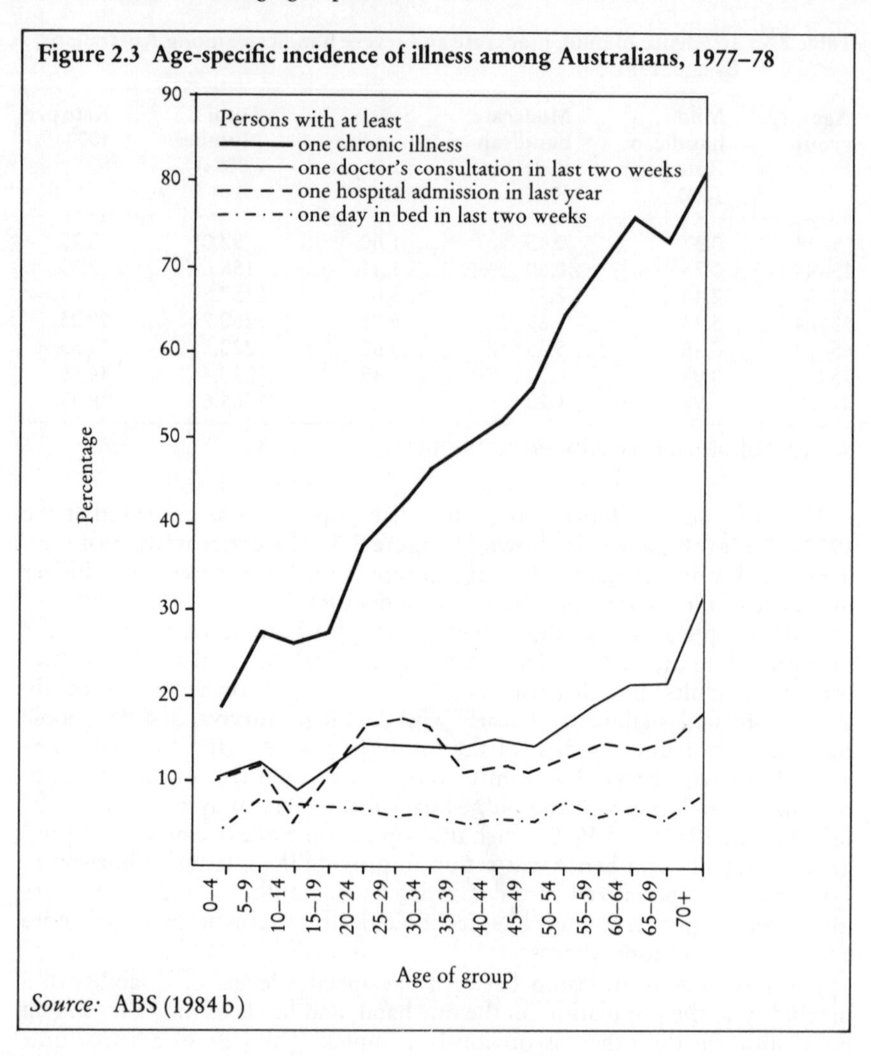

Figure 2.3 Age-specific incidence of illness among Australians, 1977–78

Source: ABS (1984 b)

tions of those diseases and lower mortality. She explains the latter in the following manner (p. 507):

As mortality rates drop, some people are "rescued" from death and remain among the living. Most of those "new survivors" are ill with chronic diseases (but not so ill as those who die). By staying alive for a while, they have more years for their illnesses to advance into severity and more time to develop other chronic conditions, both killers and non-killers. The survivors may actually be more susceptible to new illnesses than their healthier age peers are, this is an intriguing question.

It is not unreasonable to suggest that such patterns as those documented by Verbrugge apply in Australia, given the similarity of patterns of mortality and morbidity in the two populations. If people who are 'rescued from death' swell the numbers of those with chronic conditions in Australia, then planners will need to adjust services accordingly: any future improvements in mortality will mean more older people seeking services, and they will be on average more severely incapacitated.

FUTURE MORTALITY PATTERNS

It was indicated earlier that the constant mortality assumptions used in the population projections made by the National Population Inquiry of 1975 unexpectedly proved a source of error. This provides a salutary lesson against making definitive pronouncements about the future course of mortality in Australia. Too little is known about the determinants of the distinctive mortality decline of the 1970s for us to have complete confidence in predicting either its continuation or termination. Some commentators have suggested that 'There is little basis for anticipating major increases in life expectation (in the next several decades) and it is visionary to anticipate extension of human life span' (Siegel 1979, p. 15). However Crimmins (1981, p. 248) reports that other experts in the United States suggest that 'we are witnessing the beginning of a new phase of mortality decline in which advances in regard to the treatment of cardiovascular diseases take up the role played from 1940 to 1954 by antibiotics reducing mortality due to infectious diseases'. Indeed, a recent analysis by Manton (1982, p. 195) reaches a conclusion the reverse of Siegel's—'it seems quite possible that real increases in life span are being manifest and the terminal age of the survival distribution is increasing'.

Before discussing some projections of future Australian mortality rates, let us briefly examine some of the assumptions made in recent projections for overseas societies experiencing mortality decline similar to Australia's. For example, official projections produced by the United States social security actuaries are based on three sets of future mortality scenarios based on observed trends and 'judgements' regarding future trends. All three assume some increase in life expectancy, with the first (I) representing a slowing down in the rate of improvement of recent years, the second (II) a continuation, and the third (III) an acceleration of current rates of decline in mortality. The alternative scenarios are presented in Table 2.7 and they produce projections of the United States population aged over 65 years which range from 34.6 to 39.4 million.

The Australian Bureau of Statistics has made a close study of age-, sex- and cause-specific mortality rates for Australia over the last two decades. This has been used as the basis for the most recent official population projections (ABS, 1982c) which include four series of projections, all of which have the same set of mortality assumptions. The most basic assumption is that mortality declines will continue. It is assumed in the projections that the rapid rate of decline of the 1970s will continue up to 1986. Accordingly rates for the period 1976–80 for each cause of death have been projected from 1981 to 1986 using the rate of decline for the 1971–80 period. Thereafter

Table 2.7 Life-expectancy change in new social security forecasts for the United States

	Projected life expectancy (years) Expectation of life at birth			Expectation of life at age 65		
	I	II	III	I	II	III
Men						
1980	69.8	69.8	69.8	14.3	14.3	14.3
2000	71.4	72.9	75.9	15.0	15.8	17.4
2020	71.8	73.8	77.7	15.3	16.4	18.8
Women						
1980	77.7	77.7	77.7	18.7	18.7	18.7
2000	79.4	81.1	84.9	19.8	21.1	24.2
2020	79.9	82.1	87.2	20.2	22.0	26.1

Source: Manton (1982, p. 231)

there is an assumption that the rate of decline will decrease somewhat, at the overall rate of decline for the 1961–80 period. The projected annual changes in mortality rates are shown in Table 2.8. They reflect an increase in expectation of life at birth of 2 years for males and 2.3 years for females up to the year 1995. The increase in the expectation of life at age 50 is from 25.1 to 26.5 years for males and 30.3 to 31.9 for females (Gogulapati et al. 1984). These assumptions are broadly in line with those of the United States social actuaries considered earlier. There certainly would appear to be some good reasons to anticipate further declines of mortality in Australia. They are:

1 Australia, as was shown earlier, still has quite high levels of death from cardio-vascular diseases in comparison to other developed countries. Presumably this leaves considerable scope for improvement—especially with respect to lifestyle and dietary adjustments. Also there is little reason to anticipate that the medical advances of recent years will not be continued to some extent. Levy and Moskowitz (1982, p. 128), for example, point to many promising developments in diagnostic screening and monitoring, surgery, repair of blood vessels, coronary care, chemo-therapy, etc., and conclude that it is possible that there is no cardio-vascular disorder so complicated that it does not have the potential to be fully understood and controlled. However it is clear that much of the future improvement will depend upon more effective public education and information about risk factors and the need to change certain behaviour patterns.

2 Many of the arguments outlined above apply also to death from cerebrovascular disease.

3 The future pattern of death from cancer is much more problematical. At present, while there are steady improvements in diagnosis and treatment for some cancers, the greatest decreases in mortality would be achieved by elimination of smoking, dietary changes, more active leisure pursuits and so on. Whether current trends in this direction will have some impact will of course show up as the age groups who have changed their lifestyle at a comparatively young age move into the high-risk older age groups.

Table 2.8 Projected short-term and long-term percentage annual changes in mortality rates in Australia, 1981–95

Age (years)	Short-term (1981–87)		Long-term (1987–95)	
	Males	Females	Males	Females
0	−5.9	−5.3	−2.5	−2.5
10	−2.8	−3.5	−2.1	−2.4
20	−1.0	−1.6	−1.0	−1.3
30	−1.4	−2.8	−0.9	−1.8
40	−1.9	−3.4	−0.9	−1.5
50	−2.6	−3.3	−0.9	−1.2
60	−2.5	−3.1	−0.6	−1.1
70	−2.4	−3.0	−0.4	−1.1
80	−2.2	−3.0	−0.3	−1.1
90	−2.2	−3.0	−0.3	−1.1

Source: Gogulapati et al. (1984, p. 45)

4 No improvement in the rates of mortality from accidents, especially motor vehicle accidents and suicide, could be confidently predicted at present.

In summary, the assumed future mortality rates used by the ABS appear realistic, and if anything may be a little pessimistic, at least in the short term. In the long term they may be too optimistic; indeed, in the next set of ABS projections there will be an assumption that the mortality improvements will cease in 1995.

SOME POLICY AND PLANNING IMPLICATIONS

At several points in this chapter it has been pointed out that changing levels and patterns of mortality in Australia have important implications for policy makers and planners. This applies not only in health services, but also in a wide range of other areas within both the public and private sectors. As was correctly indicated by the National Population Inquiry (1975), changes in future mortality patterns will make little difference to the projected number of persons *under* retirement age, since most women survive to the end of their child-bearing years. However, the same cannot be said for their impact upon projections of the number of persons *over* retirement age. This has been demonstrated elsewhere (Hugo, 1984a) where projections of the population aged 55 years and over for 1981, made less than a decade earlier, are compared to the relevant 1981 census data. NPI projections published in 1975 under-projected the 65+ population by 160 787, a discrepancy of 11 per cent. The 1976 ABS projections produced a 9.2 per cent underestimate and those of 1978 a 2.9 per cent underestimate. More than 90 per cent of this discrepancy is accounted for by over-prediction of mortality among older Australians. This in fact was the experience for most of the developed world (see Manton 1982, p. 229, for instance, on the US). Hitherto, changes in mortality have been deemed to *not* be a major determining factor of the overall growth and structure of the Australian population and of the numbers and proportion of the elderly in the population. It has been assumed that the variations in growth of the aged over time is purely a function of the size of cohorts entering the older age years and hence determined largely by past patterns of fertility and immigration. However, the findings of this chapter would suggest that changes in mortality are becoming increasingly significant in determining the growth of the aged population, and that great care must be taken in establishing the mortality assumptions in projections. Planning for provision of pensions, health services, accommodation for the aged, etc., relies upon such projections and it is important to obtain figures which are reasonably robust at least over a five- to ten-year planning period.

The crucial point is that recent and impending mortality improvements are having and will continue to have a significant impact on the growth of the Australian aged population. Improvement in longevity during the 1970s alone has added over two million person-years more than would have been the case had mortality levels remained stable. These implications are taken up in some detail in Chapter 6, but it should be mentioned here that the greatest errors in the 1975 projections of the aged population occurred in the oldest age groups. These errors are of particular significance, since it has been shown that among the very old population there is an extremely high risk of chronic disease, morbidity and disability, and thus higher use of medical services. For example, an ABS survey of 1977–78 found that 70.2 per cent of persons aged 65 years and over had visited a doctor in the previous three months (75.2 per cent of those aged 75+) compared to 45.3 per cent of the population aged under 65 (ABS 1982d, p. 21). Similar patterns apply to use of hospital facilities (ABS 1982d, p. 22). Hence the total overall demand for health care will increase rapidly. Moreover, the nature of care required by the elderly differs from that of the younger population, with less emphasis on treatment and care of acute conditions and more on long-term chronic disease. Table 2.9 shows that public expenditure on health services

Table 2.9 Estimated average hospital and community health expenditure per head of population in Australia by age group, 1981–82

Age	Expenditure per capita ($)	Percentage of average for total population
0–15	95	36
16–24	134	50
25–39	173	65
40–49	181	68
50–54	271	102
55–59	392	147
60–64	498	187
65–69	623	234
70–74	726	273
75+	1825	686
Total population	266	100

Source: Social Welfare Policy Secretariat (1984, p. 43)

for the 75+ population is more than six times that of the average for the total population. Clearly the increase in longevity demonstrated here will place disproportionately great pressure on funding of health services.

Earlier it was suggested that improvements in mortality rates are probably accompanied by a higher rate of morbidity among older Australians. The task facing Australia's health delivery system is daunting enough without any increase in the incidence of illness in older age groups. If we assume that 1977–78 levels of chronic conditions will apply over the next three decades, the pattern of increase in numbers of people suffering chronic conditions will be something like that in Table 2.10. The table shows that there were over a million older Australians with chronic conditions in 1981—207 400 with conditions which confine them to bed or to the home. The projections suggest that there will be an increase of 84 per cent over the next three decades in the number of older persons with chronic conditions, and 105 per cent in those with limiting chronic conditions, while the increase in the total population will be less than half this (37.7 per cent). Similarly, if we extrapolate from rates of incidence of handicap from the ABS survey of handi-

Table 2.10 Projected increases in the number of aged persons with chronic conditions, limiting chronic conditions and handicaps, 1981–2011

	Age group (years)			
	65–69	**70–74** '000s	**75+**	**Total 65+**
Chronic conditions				
1981	391.1	316.9	424.9	1132.9
1991	477.8	397.3	640.4	1515.5
2001	459.8	466.6	848.5	1774.9
2011	622.7	502.3	960.0	2085.0
Percentage change 1981–2011				+84.0
Limiting chronic conditions				
1981	32.1	33.3	142.0	207.4
1991	39.3	41.7	214.0	295.0
2001	37.8	49.0	283.5	370.3
2011	51.2	52.8	320.8	424.8
Percentage change 1981–2011				+104.8
Handicapped				
1981	114.2	106.3	230.4	450.9
1991	142.0	136.3	367.1	645.4
2001	136.7	160.1	486.3	783.1
2011	185.1	172.4	550.2	907.7
Percentage change 1981–2011				+101.3
Percentage change in total population 1981–2001				+37.7

Note: These projections are based on net migration of 75 000 persons per annum (ABS, 1982c); while the incidence of chronic conditions and handicap is based on 1977–78 and 1981 surveys conducted by ABS and assumed to remain constant throughout the projection period.
Source: based on ABS 1981a, 1984b

capped persons in 1981 the number of older persons with handicaps will *double*, to nearly one million persons within thirty years.

Clearly the changing mortality patterns among Australia's aged population have major implications for policy and planning in the area of public health. They also have important impacts upon planning for provision of pensions, specialized accommodation and other services for older people. These issues will be taken up in Chapter 6. We shall now turn briefly to some other policy implications arising from the analysis of mortality patterns in this chapter.

Wide mortality differentials have been identified for groups such as the Aborigines, particular occupation groups and particular regions. In Australia, however, there is a lack of studies of the extent to which these differentials are in fact the result of social class or status differences in risks of dying. One reason is the lack of suitable data. There is at present little socio-economic information recorded on death certificates, although in the case of infant mortality it is possible to match the birth and death certificates to gain greater insight (Wood 1982). The fact that some overseas-born groups who migrated to Australia in the immediate post-war period have very low mortality rates from particular degenerative diseases presents a unique opportunity to undertake epidemiological studies of these groups as they enter the higher-risk middle and older ages. Such studies may throw light on the correlates and perhaps even some causes of the major degenerative disease killers of Australians.

Special attention must be drawn to Aboriginal mortality levels. As Thomson (1984a, p. 946) points out, health programmes alone are unlikely to achieve the goal of Aboriginals being as healthy as other Australians. Such programmes must be integrated with 'Broad wide-ranging programs ...aimed at alleviating Aboriginal poverty and powerlessness, at redressing the persisting effect of dispossession, and at eliminating discrimination'.

What are the implications of our examination of changing mortality patterns for more general health policy? Several issues have been touched on in the discussion but we should draw particular attention to the following. First, it must be stressed that there is still substantial scope for reducing mortality in Australia even without any further major medical breakthroughs or major extension of the life span. Powles (1982, p. 76) estimated that (at 1977 death rates) 27 out of every 100 Australian males aged 15 could expect to die before reaching 65. Most Australians die of the 'diseases of affluence' (Hetzel, 1982) and the incidence of such diseases can be greatly reduced through adjustments in lifestyle. This would suggest that policies and programmes that place emphasis on preventative medicine, greater community awareness and carefully targeted legislation should have a more significant role than in the past. The full impact of such programmes may not be felt in the short term. Clearly people currently nearing old age who take up a more healthy lifestyle after forty years of heavy smoking, substantial alcohol consumption, poor diet and an inactive lifestyle can hardly anticipate a major reduction in their chances of contracting one of the diseases of affluence. Perhaps the major effects of the 'Life Be In It' and 'No Smoking' campaigns will not be felt in our health delivery system for several decades.

This is not to say that medical technology does not have a role in improving the survival chances of Australians. Manton (1982) lists an impressive array of new and impending innovations in the management of chronic circulatory disease, and to a lesser extent in early diagnosis and treatment of specific forms of cancer. Such innovations in medical science, however, can only be effective in reducing mortality when they are widely available.

CONCLUSION

The experience of the 1970s should warn us against making definitive pronouncements about the future course of mortality in Australia. Even now we know too little about the causes of the distinctive 1970s mortality decline to have much confidence in predicting its future course. However, it is clear from the discussion here that future mortality changes will have a major impact in many important policy areas, so that major research efforts to understand these changes should be accelerated. In particular, there is a real need in Australia for an annual national health survey along the lines of the United States model, not just for studies such as that proposed here but for early detection of trends in morbidity and appropriate targeting of preventative programmes. To a large extent, further improvements will be dependent upon changes in behaviour and such programmes are, therefore, essential.

3 Baby Booms and Baby Busts: Contemporary Fertility in Australia

Of all the demographic changes which have reshaped Australian society during the post-war period none have been so wide-reaching in their effects as the changes in patterns of fertility and family formation. Yet paradoxically, with the notable exception of the work of demographers associated with the National Population Inquiry and the Australian Family Formation Project at the Australian National University during the 1970s, and more recently the work of the Institute of Family Studies in Melbourne, there have been only limited attempts by Australian social scientists to investigate the causes and consequences of the dramatic post-war changes in fertility patterns. Much of the work has been restricted to charting the patterns of change and little to seeking an understanding of the fundamental forces shaping those patterns. Moreover, in our attempts to project future patterns of population growth in Australia there is no greater uncertainty than over how many children will be born over the next decade.

The present chapter concentrates upon contemporary patterns of fertility in Australia, especially since the publication of the report of the National Population Inquiry (1975, 1978). The NPI report was a milestone in Australian fertility studies, presenting a thorough demographic analysis of fertility and family formation up to the early 1970s, concentrating especially upon the post-war period. Similarly, the publication of Ruzicka and Caldwell's 1977 monograph entitled 'The End of the Demographic Transition in Australia' was of major significance, since it adopts an historical and longitudinal approach and considers Australian fertility change within a theoretical framework. A subsequent paper by Ruzicka and Caldwell (Chapter IX in ESCAP 1982, vol. 1) updated the findings of this study to around 1978, while Caldwell (1984) and McDonald (1984) have shed further light on recent fertility trends and their causes.

AUSTRALIA'S FERTILITY TRANSITION

The most familiar of population models is the so-called 'demographic transition model' which in its traditional descriptive form states that as economic development and social change proceed in a society there is a definite sequence of changes in fertility and mortality, as shown in Figure 3.1. The model describes a transition from a traditional society in which high fertility is cancelled out by high mortality to give slow population growth, to a modern

Figure 3.1 Traditional form of the demographic transition model

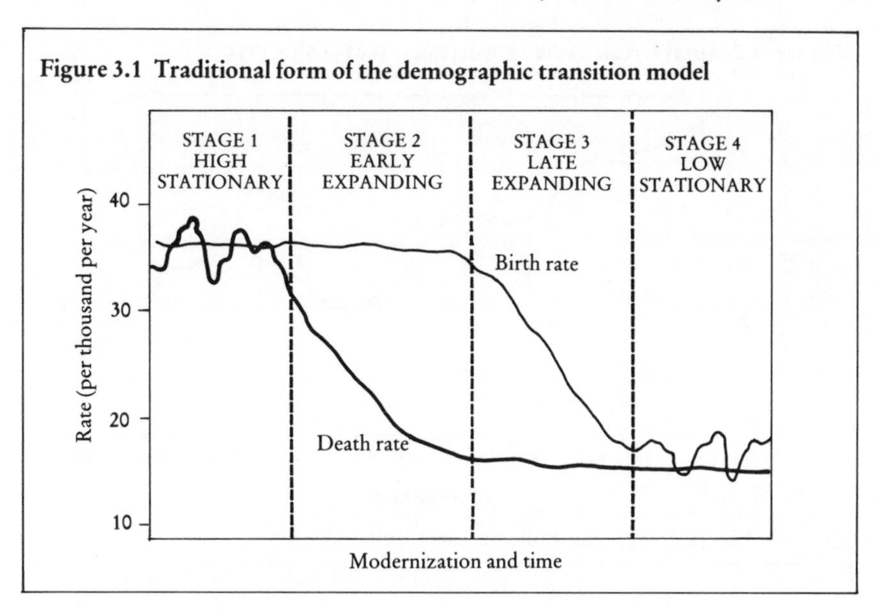

society where stability is brought about by low fertility and mortality levels. Conventional versions of the model suggest that the transition is initiated when the onset of 'modernization' leads to improved living conditions and control of disease and an associated decline in death rates. At first fertility rates remain high so that the early stages of the transition are ones of substantial population growth. There is a lagged reduction in the birth rate, so that in a third stage population growth rates level off as the birth and death rates begin to converge. The fall in fertility is traditionally ascribed to a perceived increase in the burden of rearing and educating children due to the forces associated with the growth of an urban industrial society (greater emphasis on individualism and less on the traditional family, etc.), and the greatly improved probability of survival of infants and children supported by improved methods and more widespread knowledge and practice of contraception. Recent work has shown that this model, together with the associated explanation of the transition from a pattern of high and stable to declining fertility, has by no means been universally applicable. Much current research effort, both in historical demography of developed countries and in contemporary Third World countries, has sought a more satisfactory theory to explain this transition to low and stable fertility.

A century ago Australian women were bearing on average more than six children, while today the average is less than two. This transition from high to low fertility can be seen in Figure 3.2, which traces changes in Australia's Total Fertility Rate (TFR) over the past 120 years. The TFR indicates the average number of children that would be born alive to a woman during her lifetime if she were to pass through all her child-bearing years conforming to the age-specific fertility rates of a given year. As in much of the Euro-American world, the transition toward smaller families was initiated

Figure 3.2 Total fertility rate in Australia, 1861–65 to 1984

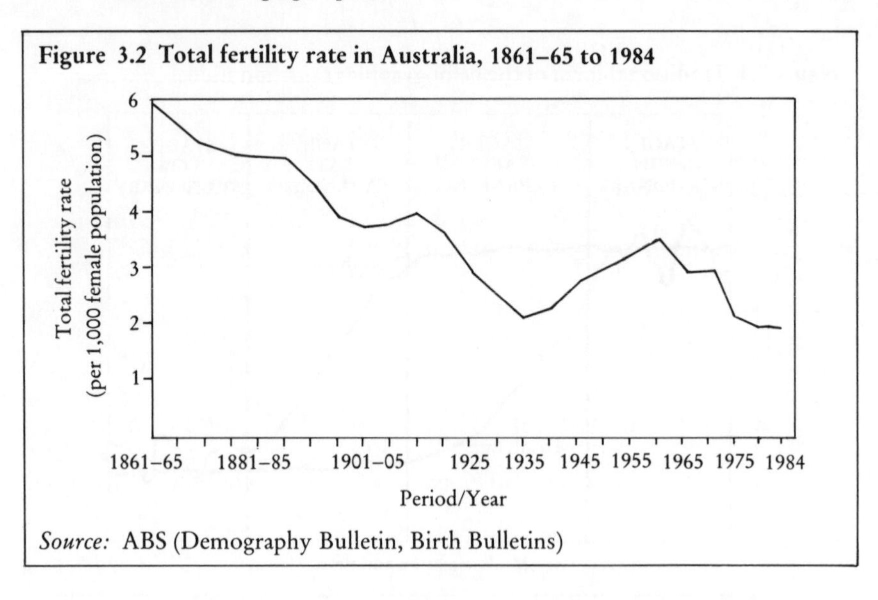

Source: ABS (Demography Bulletin, Birth Bulletins)

during the 1870s (Ruzicka and Caldwell 1977). The causes of this are not yet fully understood but Caldwell attributes it to a reversal in the net (lifetime) inter-generational transfers of wealth away from parents and toward children which in turn is brought about by a number of wider social changes, especially the introduction of mass compulsory schooling (Caldwell 1982a; Stevenson 1982). During the depression of the 1890s, the decline of fertility steepened, continuing into the early part of the new century. This prompted the appointment of a Royal Commission into 'The Decline of the Birth-Rate and on Mortality of Infants in New South Wales' (Hicks 1978). There was thereafter a stabilizing of fertility levels, but by the 1920s the fertility decline had resumed and this was greatly accelerated during the depression years of the 1930s, reaching a TFR below replacement level (2.115) for the first time.

There was a major upswing in fertility during the so-called 'post-war baby boom', the causes of which have been comprehensively dealt with in the report of the National Population Inquiry (1975). These included the following:

1 A 'marriage boom' encompassing a reduction in the average age at first marriage of women and an increase in the proportions of women marrying (McDonald 1974). Ruzicka and Caldwell (1977) attribute more than three-quarters of the 'baby boom' to the 'marriage boom'.
2 A 'catching up' of births postponed during the depression and war years.
3 The effects of the post-war acceleration in net immigration gains, which were highly selective of young adults.
4 An increase in ex-nuptial births.
5 Reduced involuntary childlessness due to increased knowledge of sub-fecundity and medical treatment of it.

By 1961 the Australian TFR stood at 3.55 but there was a sharp decline to 2.88 in 1966 and stabilization until the early 1970s when the decline resumed at an unprecedented rate with annual reductions of 0.2 in the TFR until it fell below replacement level in 1976. The fall continued until 1978 when a TFR of 1.94 was recorded. There has been some evidence of stabilization since then. The dramatic nature of the decline in fertility in the 1970s must be stressed. The TFR fell by more than one-third. Caldwell (1984) has pointed out that this decline was faster than in any European or North American country.

The overall decline in fertility and the fluctuating changes in the downward trend are reflected in changes in the Net Reproduction Rate (NRR) shown in Figure 3.3. The NRR is the average number of daughters that would be born to a woman if she passed through her lifetime from birth conforming to the age-specific fertility *and* mortality rates of a given year. An NRR of 1.00 is equal to *replacement level.* The latter is the level of fertility at which a cohort of women on average have only enough daughters to replace themselves. In 1947 the NRR was 1.42, but thereafter began to increase during the period of the 'baby boom' to 1.50 in 1954 and 1.67 in 1961. With the decline in fertility levels from the early 1960s the NRR fell to 1.36 in 1971. Figure 3.3 shows that from this point on, the NRR declined even more rapidly and has been below replacement level since the mid-1970s, reaching its lowest recorded level of 0.902 in 1980. In 1981 it recovered a little but still remains well below replacement level.

Ruzicka and Caldwell (ESCAP 1982) point out that this low NRR implies that if there is not a positive balance of net migration and if such low levels of fertility and the current levels of mortality are maintained over several

Figure 3.3 Net reproduction rate, 1971–83

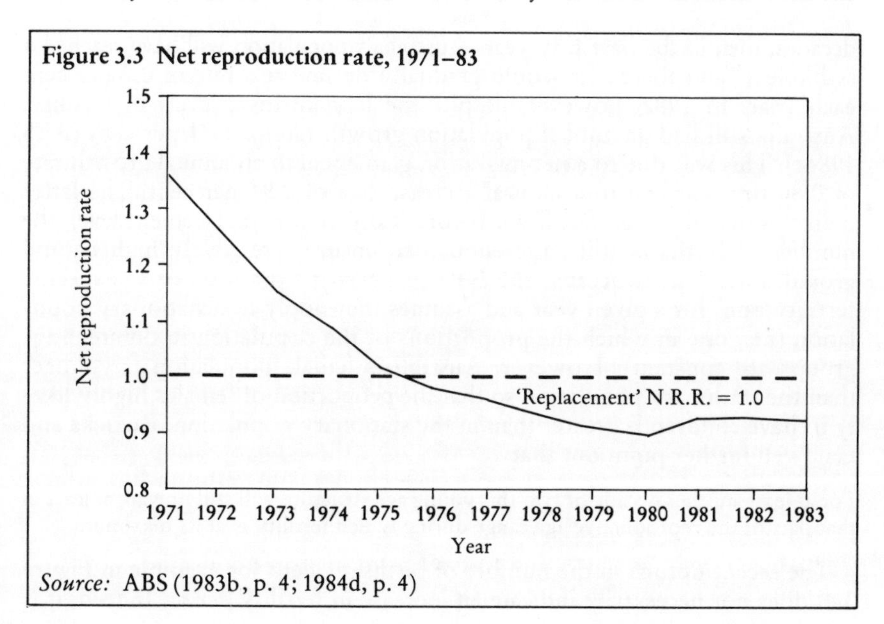

Source: ABS (1983b, p. 4; 1984d, p. 4)

Figure 3.4 Total number of births in Australia, 1950–84

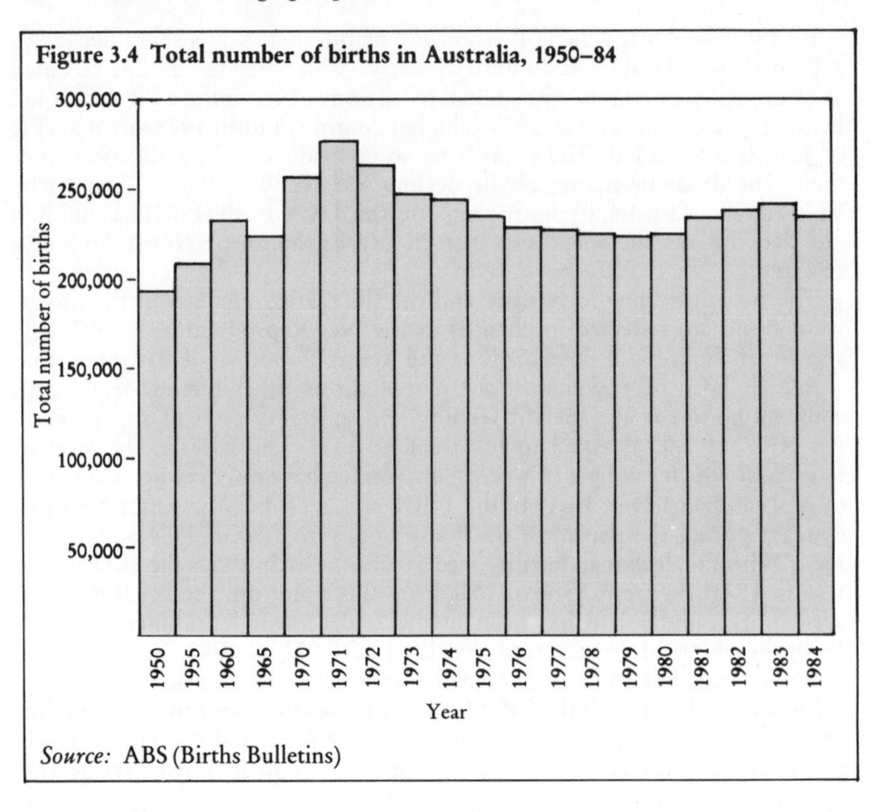

Source: ABS (Births Bulletins)

decades, then in the next fifty years Australia's population will have reached a stable level and thereafter would gradually decline at a rate of 0.2 per cent each year. In 1982, however, despite the low intrinsic levels of fertility, Australia still had an annual population growth rate of 1.71 per cent (ABS 1984c). This was due to a net migration gain equal to an annual growth rate of 0.86 per cent and to a natural increase rate of 0.84 per cent. The latter indicates that although fertility is theoretically below 'replacement level' the number of births is still large enough to ensure a relatively high natural growth rate. This is because the NRR is derived from a set of age-specific fertility rates for a given year and assumes they apply to a stationary population (i.e., one in which the proportions of the population in different age groups are constant). However, Australia's female population is younger than the stationary population so that the proportion of females highly likely to have children is greater than in the stationary population. Ruzicka and Caldwell further point out that

> For at least another decade or two this young age structure will still prevail, at least in that part of the reproductive age range during which fertility is at its maximum.

The recent upturn in the number of births, evident for example in Figure 3.4, does not necessarily indicate an increase in fertility *per se*. Indeed, it is

Figure 3.5 Age-specific fertility rates, 1961–84

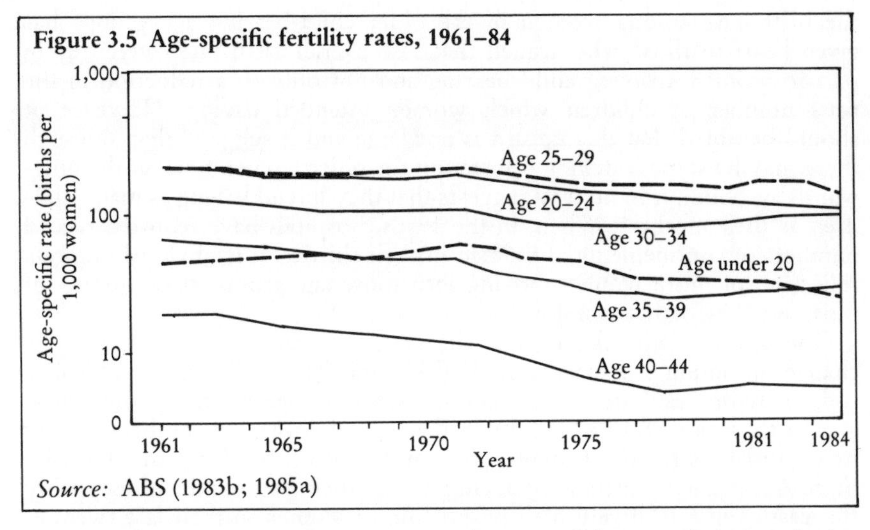

Source: ABS (1983b; 1985a)

more a reflection of the changing age structure of the population. It is the beginning of an 'echo' effect of the post-World War II baby boom as the large cohorts of children born in the 1950s and 1960s begin to marry and have children. This was anticipated by commentators in the 1970s (NPI 1978).

Trends in age-specific rates over the last two decades show declines in all ages and a general steepening of the decline during the 1970s (Figure 3.5). However the patterns and degree of decline have been different for each age group. For example, for women aged 15–19 birth rates increased after World War II to reach a high point of 54.21 in 1971 before declining sharply through the 1970s to a low of 27.6 in 1980. For the group aged 20–24 years, birth rates began to decline much earlier, in 1961, and did so continuously, reaching a low point of 106.9 in 1980. Similar patterns prevailed for the 25–29 and the 30–34 age groups, although in the latter case the lowest level was reached in 1976 and has subsequently increased slightly. Among women in the older child-bearing ages of 35 years and over, there was an initial catching up of births in the immediate post-war period followed by more than thirty years of decline before there was a slight increase in 1979. Although all these age groups participated in the decline the biggest decline over the period 1966 to 1980 was for those women aged 35 and over. Clearly, however, the *numbers* of births 'lost' involved in this change were small compared to those 'lost' through the decline in the peak child-bearing age groups. In the 1970s there was a decline of 25 per cent or more in fertility in all child-bearing age groups. The decline in the 20–24 age group is particularly significant, since it was the peak child-bearing age group in the late 1950s whereas the current rate is now less than half of what it was during that period.

In 1981, for the first time since 1972, age-specific birth rates rose marginally for every five-year age group from 15 to 44. The slight upturn in the birth rate among women in the older child-bearing age groups has given heart to those who argued that low overall birth rates were due in part to women *delaying* child-bearing and not only to a reduction in the total number of children which women intended having. However, it should be noted that this upturn is not large and it suggests that although there may be some 'catching up' among the older women born in the post-war baby-boom, it in no way suggests that they intend having as many children as their mothers. When, in the 1980s, hospitals have reported record numbers of confinements of women in their thirties, it is obviously more a reflection of more women moving into those age groups than women of those ages having more children.

One of the major elements in the recent overall decline in fertility is changes in timing and spacing of child-bearing. The decline in total fertility is partially the result of substantial increases in the age at which women first give birth. From 1971 to 1982 the median age of Australian mothers at their first nuptial confinement increased from 23.2 years to 25.5 years. Clearly, more Australian women are delaying having their first child and inevitably this results in a relatively high proportion of women in their late twenties and early thirties who have had only one child. This increase in the age of mothers at their first birth is due both to the postponement of marriage and to the lengthening of the interval between marriage and the first child.

A 1979 survey of the birth experience and expectations of women in Australia aged 45 years or less who had ever been married found that for women married at ages 15–19 the first birth on average occurred 21.4 months after marriage (ABS 1980a). This interval rose to 28.9 months for those married between ages 20–24 and fell to 26.6 months for those women married between ages 25–29 and to 22.8 months for those aged 30–39 (Ruzicka and Caldwell in ESCAP 1982). This deferment of the first birth also influences the timing of the second and subsequent births, delaying them until much later in marriage than was the case for women married in the 1950s and 1960s, although the inter-birth interval may be similar. On average, the interval between the first and second birth in the 1970s was two and a half years and between the second and third child just over three years.

All the measures of fertility considered so far have been cross-sectional. However, much additional light is thrown on fertility change by examining the experience of various cohorts of women over time. Parity Progression Ratios (PPRs) are a useful measure of such changes in fertility over time. They are designed to measure the probability of a woman in a particular age cohort having a certain parity (number of children) going on to have another child. Although parity progression ratios are only really ultimately accurate for those age cohorts who have completed their child-bearing, some distinct patterns are evident in Table 3.1. The table shows the parity progression ratios for women aged 15 and over for the period 1966 to 1981. It is quite evident that there has been a decline in the probability of having an extra child for most age groups at each parity over the 1966–81 period. For example, for the peak child-bearing age groups, 25–29 and 30–34 years, the probabilities of having a second child were fairly high in 1966: 75 per cent and

Table 3.1 Australian parity progression ratios, 1966–81

Age group	Year	Probability of having another child Parity level 0	1	2	3
15–19	1966	554	165	131	185
	1971	170	078	048	077
	1976	209	060	092	067
	1981	185	069	031	–
20–24	1966	620	470	289	247
	1971	468	273	213	189
	1976	480	220	157	151
	1981	426	240	158	149
25–29	1966	859	750	483	371
	1971	713	492	356	315
	1976	684	394	255	237
	1981	624	402	250	203
30–34	1966	930	871	636	496
	1971	859	729	555	466
	1976	807	603	420	363
	1981	767	573	365	290
35–44	1966	921	876	662	562
	1971	891	846	738	662
	1976	843	749	662	599
	1981	799	694	576	514
45+	1966	865	828	629	560
	1971	880	898	844	876
	1976	877	884	879	862
	1981	816	873	855	830

Note: the 1966 census data refer only to married women, whereas subsequent years refer to all women. This of course has a major effect on the comparability of the 15–19 and 20–24 age groups.
Source: ABS (1966 census and *Births Australia* 1971, 1976, 1981)

87 per cent respectively. By 1981 the probabilities for women in these age groups (who had been) born some 15 years later had declined to 40 per cent and 75 per cent respectively. The probability of having three or more children also declined significantly over the time period. It is the probabilities of having three or more children which are particularly important to population growth, for it is only at this parity that populations will, in the long term, grow rather than merely replace themselves or decline. An exception to the above pattern is for those aged 45 and over. For these ages the probabilities of having another child increased up to 1976. This, of course, is due to the fact that women in this age group in 1971 to 1976 passed through their twenties during the high-fertility years of the 1950s.

The most striking feature of Table 3.1 is the considerable reduction in the

PPR between 1966 and 1981 at parity 2 (i.e., the probability of having at least three children, having had two) in the key child-bearing age groups of 20–24, 25–29 and 30–34. The reductions in PPRs at parity 0 and 1 are generally not as great. Hence, these data point toward an increasing dominance among married Australian women, of the two-child family. This is supported by the findings of the 1979 survey (ABS 1980a) mentioned earlier where 49.9 per cent of married women who had not had any children expected to have two children. Of those who already had one child, 39 per cent expected to have only one more; and of those who already had two children, 87 per cent expected no more (Table 3.2). The survey also showed that if the birth expectations of the surveyed women are realized, the families of younger women will be smaller on average than those of women now approaching the end of their reproductive life. The average expected family size of married women in their twenties in 1979 was 2.4 children, compared with 2.9 for women aged 40–44 at the time of the survey. An interesting observation which would appear to point toward some stabilizing of Australian fertility levels, at least in the short term, is that comparison of the results of the 1979 survey with an earlier one conducted by the ABS in 1976 shows that the completed family size expected by all married women under 40 years of age remained stable at 2.5 children per woman over that period. Moreover, the 1981–82 Family Formation Survey of women aged between 25 and 34 years found a mean desired family size of 2.33 (McDonald 1984, p. 27). Some 46 per cent of these women wished to have two children, 7 per cent one child and 8 per cent planned to remain childless. In the 1979 survey, which was of married women only, among those aged 20–24, 3.7 per cent expected to remain childless, 4.1 per cent expected one child only, while 52.4 per cent expected two children. For women aged 25–29 the respective percentages were 3.5, 4.7 and 51.8. The expectations of additional children were partially dependent upon the sex of those children a woman already had. Among married women who had two children of the same sex, 18.4 per cent expected a third child, while of those with a boy and a girl only 9.4 per cent

Table 3.2 Average issue, expected number of children and total expected family size of Australian married women aged 15–44, June 1979

Age	No. of women ('000s)	Average no. of children already born	Average no. of additional children expected	Average no. of total children expected
15–19	26.5	0.5	2.0	2.5
20–24	254.4	0.8	1.7	2.4
25–29	403.8	1.6	0.8	2.4
30–34	421.0	2.3	0.2	2.5
35–39	350.3	2.7	0.1	2.7
40–44	312.9	2.9	–	2.9
Total	1768.9	2.1	0.5	2.6

Source: ABS (1980a, p. 12)

expected a third child. For women aged 15–24, these proportions were 52.9 per cent and 20.2 per cent respectively.

The increase in the time interval between marriage and the first birth and the overall decline in the number of births have meant a continual narrowing of the peak child-bearing age range of mothers in which births occur. In the early 1970s the ages 25–34 accounted for about 50 per cent of total fertility. By 1977 this proportion had increased to 54.5 per cent and by 1982 had risen to 58.2 per cent. The relative contribution of those mothers aged under 25 years to total fertility has declined over this period from around 40.2 per cent in 1971 to 33.9 per cent in 1982.

TRENDS IN EX-NUPTIAL FERTILITY

Although there has been a marked decline in nuptial fertility over the last two decades there has been an increase in fertility outside of marriage. The number of ex-nuptial births has increased consistently over the last two decades. In 1983 there were 35 646 ex-nuptial births, which made up 14.7 per cent of all live births (ABS 1984d). Table 3.3 indicates that the proportion that ex-nuptial births make up of total live births has nearly trebled over the last twenty years.

A large proportion of ex-nuptial births are to young women. In 1983, for example, 29.3 per cent of mothers of ex-nuptial babies were under 20 years of age and a further 35.8 per cent were aged between 20 and 24. This compares with 3.0 per cent and 26.8 per cent respectively in the case of nuptial confinements for these age groups (ABS 1984d). There has however been a decrease in the proportion of ex-nuptial births which are born to very young women. In 1976, for example, 38.1 per cent of ex-nuptial births were to women aged less than 20 years and this proportion had been relatively stable for the previous decade.

The increase in ex-nuptial births is partly due to changes in Australian society's attitudes to cohabitation and child-bearing outside of marriage.

Table 3.3 Numbers of ex-nuptial live births and proportion of total live births, 1951–83

Period	Ex-nuptial births (annual averages)		Year	Ex-nuptial births (annual totals)	
	Number	Proportion		Number	Proportion
1951–55	7 999	4.0	1976	23 064	10.1
1956–60	10 027	4.5	1977	23 314	10.3
1961–65	13 798	5.9	1978	24 744	11.0
1966–70	18 937	7.9	1979	26 110	11.7
1971–75	24 516	9.7	1980	28 076	12.4
1976–80	25 062	11.1	1981	31 200	13.2
			1982	32 958	13.7
			1983	35 646	14.7

Source: ABS (1982h, p. 17; 1984d, p. 17)

Over the years attitudes have become much more liberal. As Ruzicka (1974, p. 1) points out, after the introduction of oral contraception 'social attitudes to premarital sexual experience relaxed and the condemnation of sexual activity outside marriage, predominant in our Judaeo-Christian religious tradition, has lost much of its earlier impact, particularly on the younger generation'. In addition, the legal discrimination against 'illegitimate' children and unwed mothers was removed with the introduction of social security benefits providing financial support to unmarried mothers. This has enabled single women to keep their children instead of placing them for adoption or perhaps being forced into an unwanted, hastily arranged marriage (New Zealand Government Statistician 1981; Ruzicka 1974, 1977, 1979).

In Australia legal marriage still remains the major vehicle of family formation. However, unmarried motherhood and *de facto* marriage are gaining acceptance as modes suited to the rearing of children. For example, a recent survey of a sample of Australian families (ABS 1982e) attempted to distinguish between legally married couples and those 'living together as married'. The latter comprised 4.7 per cent of all families (although the ABS warns that this is almost certainly an understatement of the actual proportion). Nevertheless, as Table 3.4 shows, 35.7 per cent of families in which the couple reported that they were living together as married, or in a *de facto* relationship, had dependent children present. This compares to 53.8 per cent of those 'legally married'. It must be borne in mind, however, that the 'living together as married' category has a much younger age structure than married couples legally married (43.7 per cent of women in the former category were aged under 25 years compared to 8.1 per cent of legally married women) and hence could be expected to include a greater proportion of women who will have children, although they are currently childless.

One feature of the overall fertility decline of the last two decades is that it occurred despite other changes in society which, *other things being equal*, one would expect to be working in the direction of an increase in overall fertility rates. One such element is the rise in ex-nuptial fertility considered

Table 3.4 Australian married couples by form of marriage and number of dependent children, 1982

Number of dependent children present	'Legally' married (per cent)	Living together as married/de facto (per cent)
None	46.2	64.3
One or more	53.8	35.7
One	17.0	16.2
Two	22.4	13.8
Three or more	14.3	5.7
Total number	3 397 400	167 200

Source: ABS (1982e, p. 7)

above, while another is the development of gynaecological and medical techniques of dealing with sub-fecundity: the development of a range of surgical procedures, specialized treatments, a range of fertility drugs and finally in-vitro fertilization have greatly increased the proportion of women who are able to have live births. Despite these developments, however, fertility has fallen and the reasons lie within the major societal changes which have taken place during the last two decades. Some of these questions will be addressed later in this chapter; however, as a preliminary to examination of the causes of Australian fertility decline, it is helpful to examine some major fertility differentials.

FERTILITY DIFFERENTIALS

Aboriginal fertility

Some of the most striking fertility differentials which exist in Australia are those between the Aboriginal and non-Aboriginal populations. As with the mortality differentials considered in the previous chapter, these are a function of the deprived situation of the black population. Aboriginals are demographically a Third World sub-population within a dominant developed-country population. The fertility transition for the Aboriginal population has been quite different from that described earlier. Until half a century ago Aboriginal fertility was lower than the overall Australian levels. Under the catastrophic impact of dispossession, violence and disease associated with European settlement, Aboriginal fertility fell to low levels despite very high mortality (Smith 1980). Table 3.5, which presents some illustrative data for South Australia, shows a gradual recovery in fertility levels during this century up to World War II, in sharp contrast to the pattern in overall fertility described earlier. A peak in Aboriginal fertility was achieved in the 1950s and 1960s when it was twice as high as overall fertility levels. However, as Figure 3.6 shows, the 1970s have seen a sharp decline in Aboriginal fertility (more than 40 per cent in a decade). Gray (1984) in his analysis of the decline has shown that the increased perceived costs in caring for children (especially education costs), the adverse effects on maternal health of child-bearing at older ages, and the physical demands of child-bearing have shifted the balance between perceived costs and benefits of children among Aboriginal

Table 3.5 Indicative estimates of total fertility rates of Aboriginal women in South Australia between 1906 and 1981

Period	Estimated TFR	Period	Estimated TFR
1906–11	3.4	1961–66	6.6
1928–33	4.7	1966–71	6.3
1942–47	5.8	1971–76	3.8
1956–61	7.0	1976–81	3.3

Source: Gray (1982, p. 9)

Figure 3.6 Total fertility rates for Aboriginal and total population, 1956–81

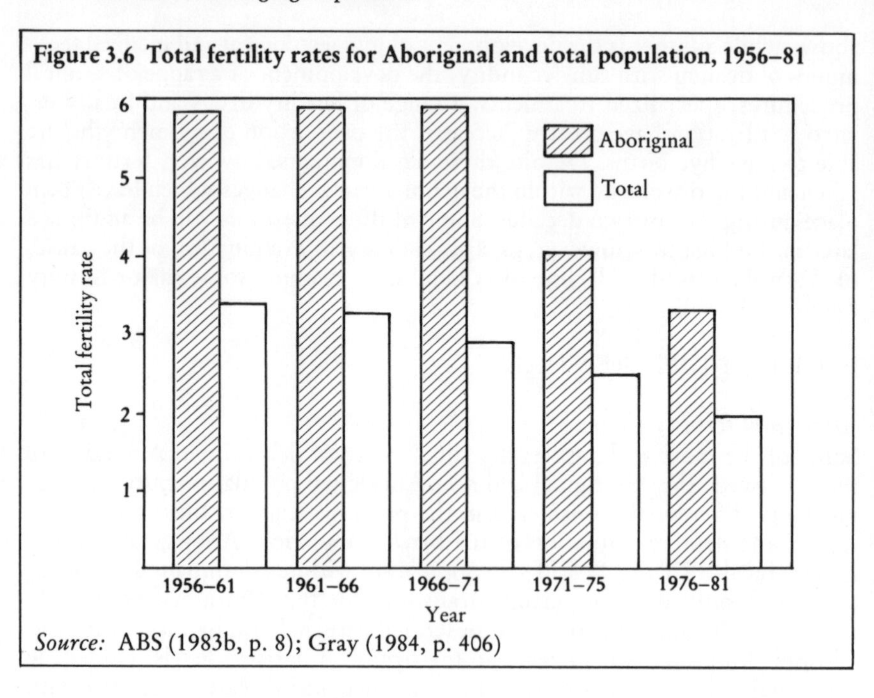

Source: ABS (1983b, p. 8); Gray (1984, p. 406)

women. Consequently, smaller family sizes are now preferred and there is high acceptance of family planning, much of which is provided through the expanding Aboriginal Health Services system.

Fertility differences between immigrant groups

Immigration has been an important component in the post-war growth of Australia's population, not only in the contribution of net migration to growth but also via the fertility of migrant women after their arrival in Australia. A number of studies (e.g., Day 1969, Ware 1975, Yusuf and Eckstein 1980, Yusuf and Rockett 1981, Price, in ESCAP, 1982, Khoo 1984) have established differential fertility among some groups of immigrants. In 1971 the Crude Birth Rate (CBR) for foreign-born Australian women was equal to 26.8 per 1000, while for native Australians it was 20.1. By 1976 the migrant CBR had declined to 19.9, while that of Australian women had declined to 15.8 (Yusuf and Rockett 1981, p. 416). The equivalent rates for 1981 were 18.0 and 15.4, so the differential decline in fertility of the two groups as indicated by the CBR indicates a progressive convergence of the fertility of Australian-born and foreign-born women. However, the CBR is not a very accurate measure of fertility, as it does not account for differences between the two groups in age structure and marital status. Yusuf and Rockett found these two elements varied considerably between Australian-born and foreign-born women when data from the 1971 and 1976 censuses were examined. Not only do most overseas-born populations have an older age structure than the Australian-born, but the proportion of foreign-

Table 3.6 Proportion of women in particular birthplace groups at parity zero and parity three or more, 1981

Birthplace	Per cent parity 0* by age				Per cent parity 3+ by age			
	20–29	30–39	40–49	50–59	20–29	30–39	40–49	50–59
Australia	57	17	15	16	8	37	56	52
UK	59	18	12	13	8	31	49	51
Netherlands	43	12	14	14	16	46	50	54
Greece	25	15	10	12	13	25	43	42
Italy	51	13	13	12	12	46	47	49
Yugoslavia	35	12	8	13	6	28	38	39
Middle East	42	17	21	19	16	53	59	69
Indo-China	45	30	27	–	12	37	64	–
New Zealand	68	27	16	21	6	32	62	33
Total	58	19	14	16	8	39	52	49

*Includes both those reporting parity 0 and 'not stated' category.
Source: ABS (1981 census, one per cent sample tape of individuals)

born women in the 15–49 age group who are married is higher than for Australian-born.

Table 3.6 presents parity information derived from the 1981 census. It shows the proportion of women in particular birthplace-age groups who had no children in 1981 and the proportion with three or more children at the time of the census. Figure 3.7 shows the average number of children born to women in various birthplace-age groups. It indicates patterns of fertility differentials similar to those recognized in studies of earlier censuses, but with an overall downward movement in fertility and convergence of fertility levels when compared to those earlier studies. The main differentials evident in Table 3.6 and Figure 3.7 are as follows:

1 The pattern which has been evident since the 1954 and 1961 censuses (Day 1971, p. 2044), of Dutch-born women having 'unusually high fertility', is still apparent. Table 3.6 shows that the proportions of Dutch women in the 30+ age groups with no children are the smallest of any group and the proportions with more than three children are the highest of any group except the Middle East-born women. It should be noted, however, that there are very large differences in the size of the various age cohorts of Dutch-born, that the bulk of Dutch immigration was in the 1950s and was selective of young adults and their children and the cohort sizes reflect this. Those aged 30 to 39 years in 1981 numbered 11 600; those aged 40 to 49, 8200; those aged 50 to 59, 5700 and those aged 60 and over, 5100 women. On the other hand, Dutch-born women aged 15 to 19 numbered only 700, and those aged 20 to 29, 4900. Hence, the impact of the high fertility of Dutch-born women has virtually no effect on current national fertility.

2 The highest fertility group was women born in the Middle East. More than half of this group in their thirties already had three or more children, as did 16 per cent of those in their twenties, while the average issue for those in their thirties was 2.7 and those in their twenties 1.5. The age structure of

Figure 3.7 Average number of children born according to their mother's age and birthplace, 1981

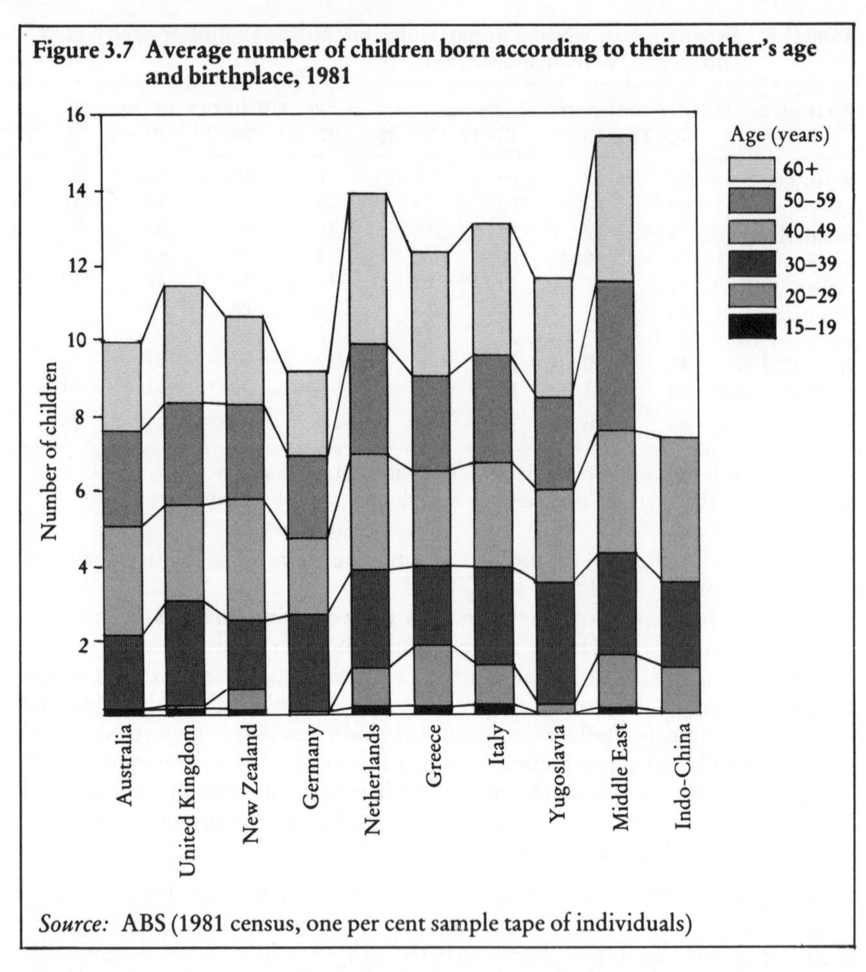

Source: ABS (1981 census, one per cent sample tape of individuals)

Middle East-born women is dominated by those aged between 20 and 39, who comprise 53 per cent of all women aged over 15, compared to 41 per cent for the Australian-born. Fertility rates of the Arab women at all ages were higher than for all other groups—they tended to commence child-bearing earlier and continued later in life. Yusuf and Rockett (1981, p. 421) found that this group also had the highest fertility of any birthplace group in 1971 and 1976. They suggest that Arab fertility is much higher and non-marital fertility is much lower than for other migrant groups because of the 'persistence of the cohesive extended family in this group. It may well be that wealth flows, or is perceived by Arab parents to flow, from offspring to parents'.

3 The most recently arrived of the major birthplace groups studied here are the Indo-Chinese-born. Unfortunately, their very small numbers in the sample increase the probability of error in the parity data presented here, especially in the 15–19 and 40+ age groups. It is clear that their fertility

Table 3.7 Average issue of women aged 30–39 in various birthplace groups, 1981

Birthplace	Average issue
Australia	2.08
United Kingdom	2.10
Italy	2.56
Greece	2.16
Yugoslavia	2.16

Source: ABS (1981 census, one per cent sample tape of individuals)

levels are somewhat higher than those of the Australian-born, although their fertility is much lower than that prevailing in contemporary Vietnam (Jones 1982), reflecting the fact that a large proportion of Indo-Chinese refugees are of middle-class, urban and/or ethnic Chinese background.

4 The fertility patterns of Southern European-born women are especially interesting, given their substantial representation among women aged over 15 years (5.5 per cent in 1981), especially those aged 30–39 (7.3 per cent) and 40–49 (9.8 per cent). The largest group are women born in Italy and a thorough analysis of their fertility (Ware 1981, pp. 83–93) found that if one excludes the 'not stated' category in 1976 the average number of children of Italian wives was 2.69. The figure for 1981 from the census was virtually unchanged at 2.71. Table 3.6 and Figure 3.7 show that Italian-born women generally have slightly higher parity levels than the Australian-born. At the 1966, 1971 and 1976 censuses Italian and Greek women tended to have higher fertility at the younger age groups (15–24). Yusuf and Eckstein (1980) and Ware (1975) suggested this was because a greater proportion of Southern Europeans marry at younger ages than other migrant groups and Australians and are less inclined to postpone pregnancy once married. Italians and Greeks also had relatively higher fertility at the older ages (35–44) and Yusuf and Eckstein suggest this could perhaps be due to their use of less efficient methods of contraception. The Melbourne Family Formation Study, for example, showed a high proportion using withdrawal and other fairly inefficient methods of contraception (Lavis 1975). Table 3.6 shows that at all ages the proportion of Southern European-born women at parity zero in 1981 was less than for the Australian-born. Hence Ware's statement (Ware 1981, p. 83) that 'Italian women who marry almost invariably make a determined attempt to have children, whereas among the Australian-born there was a small but significant minority who deliberately chose not to have children' would appear to still have relevance, not only for Italians but also for other major Southern European groups. Table 3.7 shows the average issue of women aged between 30 and 39 years in the major Southern European birthplace groups and compares them to the Australian-born and United Kingdom-born women in the same cohort. The average-issue calculations, following Ware (1981), exclude women who did not answer the issue question, and hence probably understate the differences a little in that the non-respondents among the Australian-born were probably more likely on

average to be of zero parity than those among the Southern European-born. Nevertheless, higher fertility among the Italian group is evident, as is more marginally higher fertility among the Greek-born and Yugoslavia-born women in this age group. The differentials evident here are smaller than those observed in earlier studies and would seem to indicate that Ware's conclusion that 'Within each successive cohort born since that of 1897–1901 the differentials between the major groups have become more attenuated' (Ware 1975, p. 361) is still valid. The evidence in Table 3.6 showing the proportions of Southern European-born women at parity 3 or above shows generally lower proportions than for the Australian-born. Even allowing for sampling error and differences in reasons for non-response it is difficult to escape the conclusion of Ware (1975, p. 362) based upon her analysis of 1966 census data: '... it is undoubtedly the case that southern European born mothers are no longer more fertile than the Australian born'.

The differential fertility of migrant groups, especially the Southern European migrants, has in the past been partly due to the differences in norms, aspirations and lifestyle patterns (Ware in Burnley 1974; Ware 1975). The majority of Southern European immigrants were Catholic or Orthodox in religion and poorly educated. Because many of the Southern Europeans have immigrated from impoverished rural regions where fertility is high (Yusuf and Eckstein 1980) and because of the high degree of 'ethno-centricity' among some Southern European groups, their attitudes and behaviour towards fertility have been distinctive. With time, however, as assimilation into the Australian society becomes more pronounced, the attitudes, beliefs and behaviour of Southern Europeans have become (and will become) more in accordance with Australian attitudes and behaviour. For example surveys conducted by the ABS in 1976 and 1979 of the birth expectations of women indicate that the expectations of women aged 20–34 from Greece and Italy were marginally lower than for Australian-born women of a similar age (ABS 1979a, 1980a). With the changing attitudes of the younger immigrant women in Australia and the prevailing economic conditions it can be expected that differentials between immigrant groups and Australian-born women will become even smaller and that fertility levels will converge.

5 The patterns of fertility of the major birthplace groups from English-speaking countries other than Australia—the United Kingdom, Republic of Ireland and New Zealand—appear to be fairly similar to those of the Australian-born. This has long been a feature of national fertility patterns. The New Zealand-born have somewhat lower fertility, perhaps because in general they are concentrated in the more highly educated, better-off section of society.

In conclusion, then, the data from the 1981 census would suggest that birthplace differentials in fertility are tending to converge, continuing the trend evident from earlier censuses. Some differentials are in evidence and the explanations for them can only be found from detailed studies such as those associated with the Australian Family Formation Project (Ware in Burnley 1974, Ware 1975). As Ware points out, birthplace fertility differentials can result from one or more of the following: immigrants retaining the distinctive characteristics of their original culture; immigrants representing a balance of basic socio-economic characteristics different from that of the native-born; people who decide to emigrate being themselves distinctive in their psycho-social make-up, and behaviour and attitudes having been affected by the process of migration itself. Ware argues that in the past too much emphasis has been placed on the first of these explanations and shows how the other factors, especially the second, are of importance in explaining fertility differentials in Australia according to birthplace.

Work and fertility

The occupational and workforce status of women is one of the most difficult variables to interpret in analysing fertility differentials. As O'Connell and Rogers (1982, p. 284) point out:

> Without a battery of control variables (such as duration of the woman's previous employment, the husband's employment characteristics and the woman's current or previous wage rate), a causal interpretation of these data is almost impossible.

Nevertheless, despite these difficulties, an analysis of fertility differences between women in various workforce categories can provide some insights into the causes of changes in fertility patterns and, as O'Connell and Rogers suggest (p. 284), 'can reveal patterns of child-bearing that are often integral to planning maternal and child social service programs'.

It is clear that the major decline in fertility which Australia has experienced since the early 1960s has been partly a function of some significant changes in the position and role of women within Australian society. A major element in this has been the increasing participation of women, especially married women, in working outside the home. This is discussed in detail in Chapter 9 but as Hull (1982, p. 8) points out

> Women, whether married or not, have moved into the labour force in a major way since the thirties such that today over half of all women are in the labour force at any given time, and over ninety per cent participate at some time during their lives.

Differences between women in the labour force and those remaining in the home with respect to total issue are shown in Table 3.8. The main comparisons to be made are between the wage and salary workers and those not in the labour force, which have the largest numbers of women. There is a clear pattern of women who are wage and salary earners having substantially lower fertility than women not working outside the home. The proportions of wage and salary earners with zero parity are much higher, and the percentage with three or more children much lower, than for those not in the workforce, especially in the younger, child-bearing years of the twenties and thirties. However, it is precisely in these age categories that interpretation becomes most difficult since, in O'Connell and Rogers' words (p. 284), 'the high fertility rate for women not in the labour force does not necessarily represent births to women who have never worked, since this category includes women who have only temporarily dropped out of the labour force to have a child'.

Table 3.8 Proportion of Australian women in particular workforce status categories at parity zero and parity three or more, 1981

Labour force status	Per cent parity 0* Age (years)				Per cent parity 3+ Age (years)			
	20–29	30–39	40–49	50–59	20–29	30–39	40–49	50–59
Wage or salary earners	81	28	17	20	2	26	47	45
Self-employed	13	10	9	12	16	43	60	53
Employer	30	10	9	13	15	39	56	59
Helper, unpaid worker	33	11	13	11	13	52	62	66
Unemployed	75	26	24	34	3	27	43	43
Not in the labour force	24	10	13	14	16	42	57	51
Total	57	18	14	16	7	36	52	49

* Includes both those reporting parity 0 and the 'not stated' category.
Source: ABS (1981 census, one per cent sample tape of individuals)

Contrasts in the fertility of workforce participants and those not in the workforce are especially marked in Figure 3.8, which shows the average issue for different age groups. If we exclude women not stating their parity level, women in their twenties who are wage and salary earners have an average issue level (0.38) only one-quarter the size of women not in the workforce. Thereafter there is some convergence, with the ratio being three-quarters for women in their thirties and 83 per cent for women in their forties. Nevertheless, these differences are very substantial and do indicate that working outside the home is definitely associated with lower fertility. Nearly a tenth of women aged 15–19 were classified as unemployed in 1981 and half that proportion in the 20–29 age group. These are the ages in which post-war Australian women have traditionally had high levels of workforce participation, often as part of a two-income family. The latter has often been a period of intensive income earning for couples as a prelude to buying a house and establishing a family (Faulkner 1980).

What the implications of high unemployment of women (and for that matter young men) in these ages are for fertility are not entirely clear—will it lead to only a postponement of family formation or will it have a longer-term impact in reducing the average number of children that women have? Bracher (1981) has suggested that the massive increase in unemployment among younger Australians in the late 1970s has been a significant factor in the overall fertility decline of that period. The fertility levels of unemployed women correspond fairly closely to those of women who are wage and salary earners in their respective age categories. On the other hand, women who are in the 'helper, unpaid worker' category have a pattern of fertility close to that of women who are not in the workforce. It is difficult to draw any conclusions regarding this group since their numbers are so small, but it

Figure 3.8 Average number of children born in Australia according to age and labour force status of mother, 1981

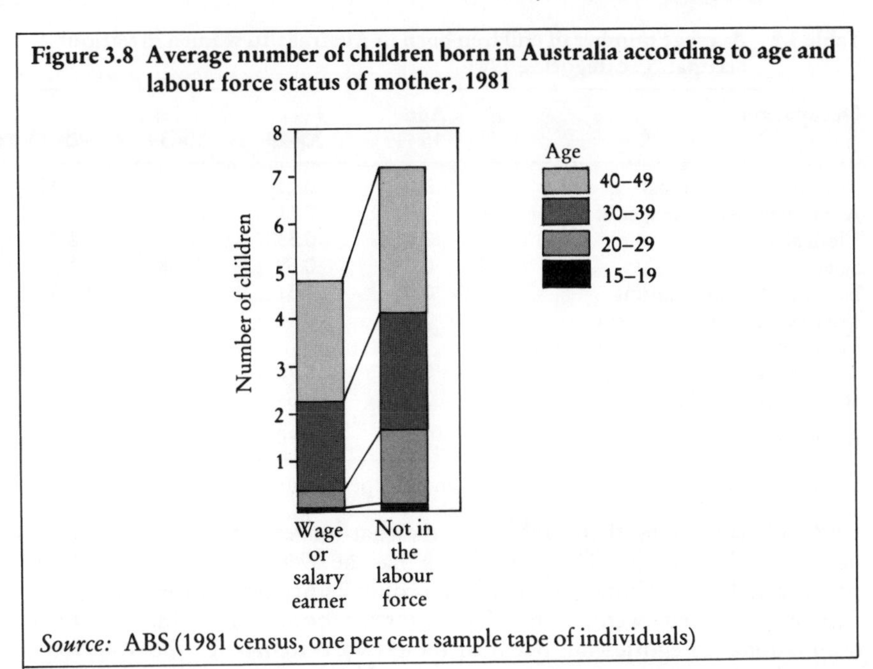

Source: ABS (1981 census, one per cent sample tape of individuals)

is likely that many such women are engaged in agricultural activities on family farms, which may be more compatible with child-bearing than work in a factory or office. Women who are employers or self-employed show somewhat similar patterns and may again reflect large numbers of workers here being in rural sector activities.

The 1981 census one per cent sample allows us to establish whether there are differences in the fertility of women employed in particular occupational categories. Such analyses have been generally lacking in Australian fertility studies. It is perhaps a reflection of the significant changes that have taken place in the position and role of women in Australian society in the last two decades that in Day's analysis of differential fertility in Australia at the 1961 census (Day 1971) the only occupation variable he examined was 'occupation of husband'. Table 3.9 shows that at all ages women employed in agricultural occupations have significantly higher fertility than the next highest group—for women in their twenties their average issue is 49 per cent higher than the average for all women, and twice as large as the next category of employed women (production and process workers). For women in their thirties the difference has closed somewhat but the average issue of women in agricultural occupations is still 23 per cent larger than for *all* women (including those not in the workforce). At the other extreme, the lowest fertility tended to be among professional women, although it will be noted that this pattern is most pronounced among women aged 20–29 and 30–39 and tends to diminish with age. This suggests that professional women tend not only to have fewer children than women in other occupations but also that they

Table 3.9 Average number of children born in Australia to women in various occupation categories, 1981

Occupation	Age 15–19	20–29	30–39	40–49
Professional, technical	0.01	0.21	1.59	2.40
Administrative, managerial	–	0.61	1.92	2.61
Clerical	0.01	0.33	1.70	2.48
Sales	0.02	0.59	2.08	2.63
Farming, fishing, hunting	0.05	1.31	2.71	3.32
Transport, communication	0.04	0.54	2.17	2.69
Tradesmen, production and process workers	0.04	0.71	2.12	2.56
Service, sport and recreation	0.03	0.64	2.21	2.96
All women	0.07	0.88	2.20	2.83

Source: ABS (1981 census, one per cent sample tape of individuals)

tend to delay having their children somewhat longer than women in other occupational categories. The table shows that the average issue for women in professional and technical occupations is only 24 per cent of the average for all women in their twenties and 72 per cent for those in their thirties. Other occupational categories fall between these two extremes. In the 30–39 age group the average issue for women employed in transport (2.17), production and process work (2.12) and services (2.21) was around or above replacement level, whereas that for those in white-collar occupations such as sales (2.08) was below replacement level. This pattern is similar to that found in the United States, where the highest fertility among women employed in non-agricultural occupations tends to be among blue-collar workers. O'Connell and Rogers (1982, p. 284) suggest that this is a function of their having less career orientation than professionals; their marrying earlier than professionals; and having less contraceptive knowledge than professionals, as well as different 'fertility desires'.

Education and fertility

Another major element in the transformation of the position of women within Australia during the post-war years has been a reduction in the inequalities between the sexes in access to higher secondary and post-secondary formal education. For example, Table 3.10 shows the doubling of participation rates in the higher levels of secondary school and the fact that by 1979 female participation rates were higher than those for males. Indeed, between 1967 and 1979 the proportion of females who completed secondary school increased from 19 to 37 per cent while the increase for males was only from 27 to 32 per cent. Over the same period the proportion of twenty-year-olds in university stayed around 7.8 per cent for males but increased from 3.5 to 5.5 per cent for females. The impact of such changes on fertility is complex but it has been the general experience in developed countries that more highly educated women tend to postpone child-bearing to pursue educational and career goals and generally to have lower completed fertility.

Table 3.10 Higher secondary school participation rates in Australia, 1956–79

Age (years)	1956 M	1956 F	1962 M	1962 F	1970 M	1970 F	1979 M	1979 F
15	49	44	67	59	83	79	87	88
16	24	20	39	29	56	48	58	60
17	9	6	17	10	32	24	31	33
18	4	1	6	2	12	6	9	8

Table 3.11 Average number of children born according to age that mother left school, 1981

Age group (years)	Did not go to school	12 or younger	13–15 years	16–20 years	21 or older	Total
15–19	0.14	0.50	0.17	0.07	–	0.07
20–29	1.38	1.92	1.24	0.44	0.56	0.87
30–39	2.20	2.55	2.39	1.97	1.41	2.19
40–49	3.16	2.84	2.92	2.63	2.48	2.76
50–59	3.78	2.85	2.86	2.57	2.90	2.80

Source: ABS (1981 census, one per cent sample tape of individuals)

Table 3.11 shows the average issue of women according to the age at which they left school, and if we take each age cohort in turn there is a general inverse relationship between length of schooling and fertility. Among women in their twenties and thirties there is a clear downward gradient in average issue from those who left school at age 12 years or below to those who left at 21 years or older. As indicated earlier, these women have passed through secondary and tertiary schooling at a time when gender-based inequality has been greatly reduced. Hence, their educational experience differs greatly from that of older women. It will be interesting to observe through the 1980s and 1990s whether or not the differences in fertility evident now among these women are maintained. Nevertheless the inverse relationship between fertility and education is maintained for older women. The shift of many more women into higher levels of education in the last decade or so has undoubtedly been a major contributory factor in the overall reduction in fertility over that period.

There is insufficient space here to fully explore the differences in fertility which exist between socio-economic groups in Australia. We have touched here only upon education and occupation variables which suggest a broad inverse relationship between fertility and socio-economic status. This is confirmed in more detailed analysis of a larger number of socio-economic variables elsewhere (Hugo and Wood 1983).

Fertility and family type

Chapter 7 explores the changes which have occurred in the structure of the Australian family during the 1970s. These changes of course have important implications for fertility change within society, for despite the major social

Table 3.12 Average number of children born by family classification groups, 1981

Age of women	Head only	Head and dependants	Head and spouse	Head, spouse and dependants	Head and other adults	Head, spouse and other adults	Head, spouse, other adults and dependants	Head, other adults and dependants	N.a.	Total
15–19	0.01	0.33	0.05	0.16	0.00	0.02	0.02	0.05	0.06	0.07
20–29	0.04	1.68	0.04	1.83	0.06	0.02	0.60	0.52	0.27	0.88
30–39	0.38	2.34	0.31	2.40	0.54	0.85	2.99	2.99	1.34	2.19
40–49	1.35	2.94	1.83	2.75	2.24	2.67	3.77	3.77	2.22	2.83
50–59	1.96	3.49	2.41	3.15	2.58	3.21	4.26	4.19	2.43	2.81
60+	2.13	3.46	2.44	3.30	2.79	3.36	3.45	3.87	2.09	2.48

Source: ABS (1981 census, one per cent sample tape of individuals)

changes of recent years the family is still the dominant social unit into which children are born and in which they are raised. In this section we will explore the extent to which there are differentials in fertility between women with different living arrangements.

The average issue of women in the various family classification categories are shown in Table 3.12. The 'head only' families of course have the lowest average issue, even in the oldest age categories where a large number of widows are represented. Nearly one-third of women aged 50–59 who are living by themselves are childless. This has important implications, especially since much recent thinking about care of the isolated aged places an emphasis on support from children and other family members. In the case of single-parent families, the average issue figures are similiar to but slightly lower than those of families comprising 'head, spouse and dependants.' However these average figures disguise the fact that a significant proportion of single mothers are at comparatively high parity levels, with 14 per cent of those aged in their twenties having three or more children, 35 per cent of those in their thirties, 54 per cent of those in their forties and 68 per cent of those in their fifties. Hence, a large number of female-headed single-parent families have above-average numbers of children for their age group. Elsewhere (Hugo and Wood 1983, p. 74) it is shown that for each age group over 30 years the proportion of women with parity in excess of two is greater for single parents than for women living with their spouse and dependent children. In the latter family type, women in their twenties have 1.83 children on average and those in their thirties 2.4. This is clearly the family type in which the bulk of present child-bearing is occurring. The families including 'other adults' usually include the grown-up children of the head and/or spouse and hence older women predominate in these groups and relatively high levels of average issue are apparent in the older age groups. The 'not applicable' category is an interesting one in this context, since it comprises non-family individuals—i.e. persons who are not related by blood or marriage to the head of the household. This of course includes persons who are cohabiting (see Chapter 7). Although the average issue of women in this category is lower than for those in two-parent or one-parent families, it is nevertheless significant. Women in this category in their thirties had 1.34 children on average at the 1981 census. Thus while the conventional 'two parents who are married' family remains the main situation in which Australian child-bearing and child-rearing take place, it can be seen that fertility within other 'non-family' types of living arrangements cannot be ignored.

Fertility and marital status

In recent years there have been major changes in marriage and divorce patterns in Australia and these are discussed in Chapter 7. Despite the major social shifts which have seen an increase in divorce and an increasing occurrence of consensual union living arrangements among young people, most child-bearing actually occurs within marriage. McDonald (in ESCAP 1982) in fact argues that the association between child-bearing and marriage has become if anything stronger, since young couples sharing some form of

Table 3.13 Proportion of women in marital status groups at parity zero and parity three or more, 1981

Marital status	Per cent parity 0* Age (years)				Per cent parity 3+ Age (years)			
	20–29	30–39	40–49	50–59	20–29	30–39	40–49	50–59
Never married	91	85	93	92	1	4	3	2
Now married	42	13	8	12	11	40	55	52
Separated not divorced	34	13	13	12	16	37	29	57
Divorced	46	20	17	12	10	30	43	45
Widowed	39	17	10	13	28	37	54	53
Total	57	18	11	16	7	36	52	49

*Includes both those reporting parity 0 and 'not stated' category.
Source: ABS (1981 census, one per cent sample tape of individuals)

consensual union who decide to have children often also decide to become legally married. Nevertheless, substantial numbers of the women who reported at the census that they had never been married had borne children—11.5 per cent of never-married women aged 20–29, 2.5 per cent of those aged 15–19, 14.8 per cent of those aged 30–39, 7.3 per cent of those aged 40–49, 8.8 per cent of never-married women aged 50–59 and 3.6 per cent of those aged 60 years and over.

The broad patterns of fertility differences between women in the various marital status groups are evident in Table 3.13. This shows that although a significant proportion of never-married women have borne children, very few have had three or more. It is perhaps surprising that 42 per cent of women aged 20–29 who are married had no children in 1981. This reflects the pattern of postponing the birth of the first child which has become so prevalent among young Australian couples. Clearly it is of the utmost importance for those trying to anticipate population growth trends of the near future to monitor the fertility experience of these cohorts of women (born 1951 to 1961) during the 1980s, to discover the extent to which they are postponing fertility and the extent to which they are opting to remain childless. The fact that the proportion of married women in their thirties at zero parity is little different to those in older age groups suggests that the 1941–51 birth cohorts, or at least those of them that are currently married, have not opted in large numbers to remain childless. On the other hand, it is clear from the right-hand side of Table 3.13 that this group is extremely unlikely to achieve the same proportions with three or more children as the married women currently aged between 40 and 59. This is of course indicative of the growing dominance of the two-child family in Australian child-bearing within marriage.

It will be noted in Table 3.13 that the bulk of women separated or divorced (even those at relatively young ages) have borne children. Indeed more than a third of such women aged over 30 have three children or more,

Table 3.14 Average number of children per mother according to mother's age, and proportion of children with mother currently married, 1981

Age of mother (years)	Total mothers	Total children	Average number of children		Percentage of children with mother currently married
			incl. 'not stated'	excl. 'not stated'	
15–19	616 900	28 600	0.05	0.07	54
20–29	1 093 600	960 900	0.88	1.01	84
30–39	1 056 500	2 185 700	2.07	2.21	88
40–49	761 900	2 044 300	2.68	2.86	85
50–59	729 700	1 952 100	2.68	2.86	80
60+	1 144 300	2 621 900	2.29	2.53	59
Total	5 402 900	9 793 500	1.81	2.05	75

Source: ABS (1981 census, one per cent sample tape of individuals)

as do a tenth of divorced women in their twenties. There is a clear tendency for divorced and separated women to have fewer children than currently married women but the differentials are not as large as may have been expected. This of course means that a large number of children are growing up in a family in which the mother is not currently married, as Table 3.14 shows. This points to a major change in society—a very large proportion of children are spending a significant period of their childhood in a one-parent family. This is also being observed in the United States, where in 1981 12.6 million children, representing 20 per cent of all children aged under 18, were living in a one-parent family (United States Bureau of Census 1982b, p. 1). This represented a 54 per cent increase over 1970 (despite the overall decline in the number of children in that age group), when some 12 per cent of the under-18s were in single-parent families. The data in Table 3.14 indicate that the situation in Australia is not so extreme, although elsewhere it is shown that around 13 per cent of Australian dependent children at any one time are in single-parent families (Hugo 1983b).

In his study of fertility differentials at the 1961 census, Day (1971) identified *age at marriage* as a most important variable in the examination of fertility differentials. Negative relationships between fertility and age at marriage were found to hold within the religious, residential and country-of-birth groupings he examined. 'The fertility of wives married before age 20 is almost invariably higher than that of wives married at ages 20–21; and fertility of the latter almost invariably higher than that of wives married at ages 22–25' (Day 1971, p. 2049). Table 3.15 shows the average issue for women according to the duration of their marriage at the 1981 census, and some striking differences are in evidence. It is clearly apparent that the negative association between age at marriage or duration of marriage and fertility is a strong one. The relationship is most clear in the 20–39 age group. In the 40–49 and 50–59 age groups the relatively high parity levels of women married for less than five years is of course due to the fact that most of the small

Table 3.15 Average number of children born to married women in various duration-of-marriage categories, 1981

Age of women	Average number of children				
	Duration of marriage				
	0–4 years	5–9 years	10–14 years	15–19 years	20+ years
15–19	0.53	0	0	0	0
20–29	0.31	1.73	2.42	0	0
30–39	1.43	1.89	2.39	2.79	3.11
40–49	2.28	2.31	2.14	2.66	3.13
50–59	2.93	1.88	1.39	1.91	2.70
60+	2.01	1.76	2.48	1.72	2.63

Source: ABS (1981 census, one per cent sample tape of individuals)

number of women in this group have remarried and much of their issue is from a previous marriage. The strength of this negative relationship between age at marriage and fertility has implications for total fertility considering that the average age at first marriage has been increasing in recent years (Chapter 7).

Spatial patterns of fertility

It has been suggested (e.g., Beegle 1966, Spengler 1966), that as society moves through the transition from stable high fertility to stable low fertility, inter-group differentials will become so small that they will diminish or disappear leaving 'the research field [of differential fertility] to the social historian' (Beegle 1966, p. 427). This is said to be particularly true of spatial differentials—it is suggested that what little spatial variation does exist is due to structural factors like variations in age and marital status and not to behavioural and socio-economic factors. But there is still considerable evidence of significant spatial variations in fertility, in Australia at least.

First, there have been some significant variations in the patterns of fertility between the States. Figure 3.9 shows that South Australia has had consistently lower fertility than the other States during the 1970s. This low comparative fertility has been a persistent feature of the State's demographic history and is yet to be adequately explained, although there are two hypotheses for which there is some supporting evidence:

1 A greater percentage of South Australia's population is concentrated in metropolitan areas than is the case in other States. Fertility tends to be lower in large urban areas, hence the very high degree of urbanization and metropolitan primacy means that a greater percentage of the State's population is living in low-fertility sub-areas than in the other States.

2 A comparatively low percentage of South Australia's population is of Roman Catholic religious adherence. One of the clear fertility differentials that exist in Australia is that between the Catholic and non-Catholic population (Day 1971).

Figure 3.9 Total fertility rates in States and Territories, 1971–82

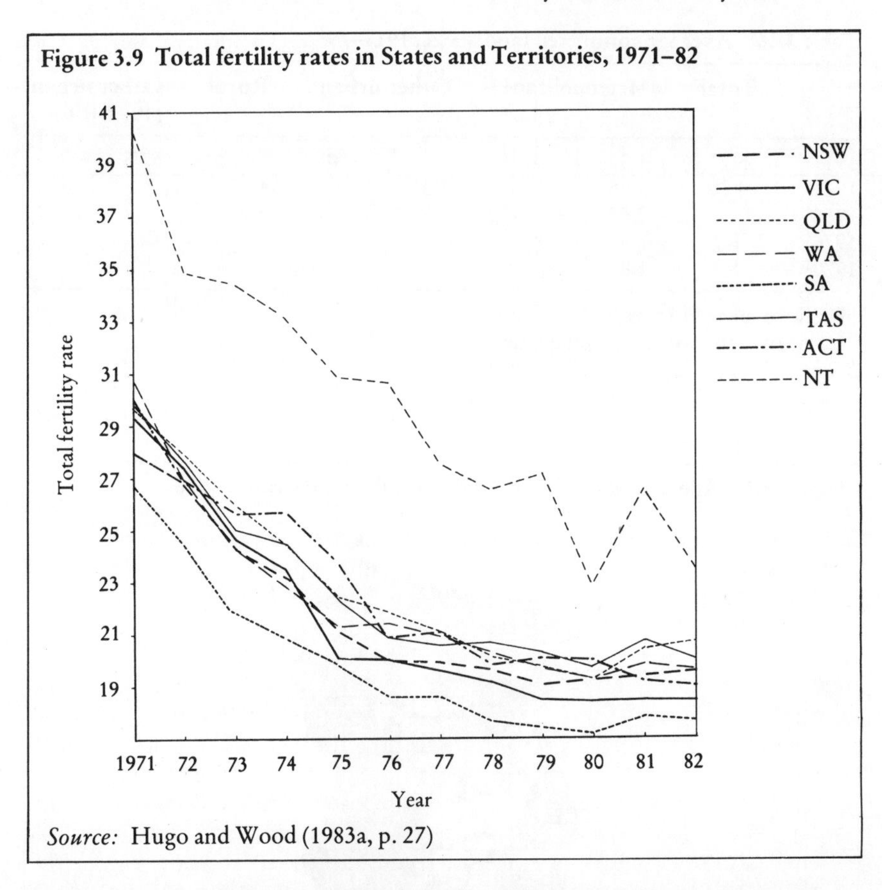

Source: Hugo and Wood (1983a, p. 27)

The other major deviation in the TFR in Figure 3.9 is for the Northern Territory. Consistently throughout the 1970s the Northern Territory has recorded much higher fertility rates than the other States. This is partly a reflection of the age structure of the population and also the high proportion of Aborigines in the population.

There is a persistent pattern all over the world for women living in rural areas to be more prolific than their city cousins. Table 3.16 shows that there have long been differences in family size between urban and rural areas. In fact the pattern shown here of a general upward trend in fertility as we proceed from metropolitan to urban and rural types of areas has been a persistent one. It would appear, however, that the differences have narrowed over time as overall fertility has declined. Rowland et al. (1980), in their anaylsis of the 1976 and 1979 ABS surveys of birth expectations of married women, found that women in metropolitan areas expected an average of 2.5 children, while non-metropolitan women expected 2.7 children.

Analysis of fertility differentials at the local government area level in Australia are few in number and with few exceptions (e.g., Hugo 1983a; Wilson 1971b) concentrate on intra-urban differences (e.g., Wilson 1971a, 1978a).

Table 3.16 Average completed family size, 1911–79

	Total	Metropolitan[2]	Other urban	Rural	Other urban plus rural
1911	5.25	4.57			5.78
1921	4.19	3.65	4.35	4.82	
1966		2.44	2.84	3.22	
1976[1]	1.9	1.8			2.1
1979[1]	1.9	1.8			2.1

[1] For women aged 15 to 39
[2] Comprises the six State capital cities
Sources: NPI (1975); ABS (1980a, p. 4)

Figure 3.10 Adelaide statistical division: total fertility rates, 1976

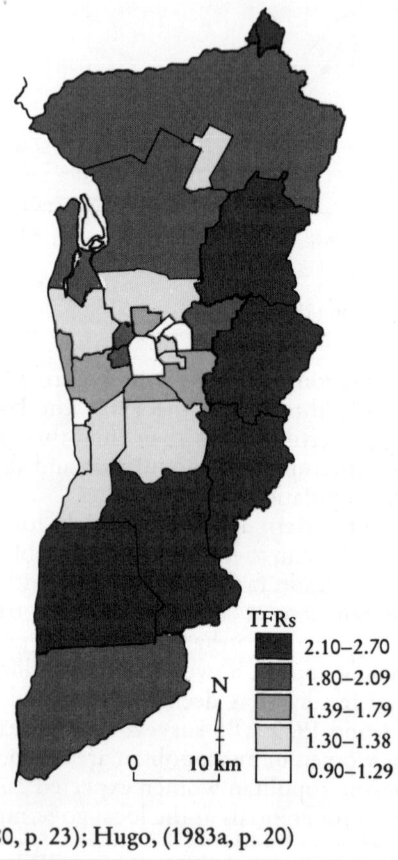

Source: Faulkner (1980, p. 23); Hugo, (1983a, p. 20)

Typical of the pattern of intra-urban differentials is that of Adelaide in the mid-1970s, shown in Figure 3.10. There is an outer ring of local government areas with fertility above replacement level. These are areas of very recent, rapid, low-density housing expansion which are favoured by young couples just beginning to have families. A second group of intermediate metropolitan local government areas with TFRs below replacement level but above the metropolitan average can be recognized. These include two types of area: first, there is a group of outlying suburbs which have not experienced as rapid recent growth as those with fertility above replacement level, either because their peak growth was experienced in the 1960s or because they are so far on the periphery that expansion of the metropolitan area into them has not been great; second, there is a group of older local government areas with generally low socio-economic status. Areas with below-average fertility levels tend to be in the remaining middle and older suburbs, with areas of particularly low fertility being concentrated in inner Adelaide and the areas immediately to the north and east of it and some of the seaside suburbs. The spatial patterns evident in Figure 3.10 are quite distinctive and tend to reflect very different family and lifestyle patterns in the inner areas. Some clue to this can be seen in the fact that Faulkner (1980) found a very strong negative association ($r^2 = 0.8$) between the TFR of a local government area and the percentage of its occupied dwellings composed of flats, units and apartments. There are two possible explanations for this association: women living in high-density housing have decided to have on average fewer children than those living in detached housing; and/or young women spend part of their teens and early twenties in higher-density housing but shift out to lower-density housing areas when they begin child-bearing.

EXPLAINING THE FERTILITY DECLINE IN AUSTRALIA

The explanation of the dramatic fertility decline in Australia since the early 1970s is not a simple task. The examination here of detailed trends in fertility and fertility differentials has shed some light on the causes of the decline. Recent work by Caldwell (1984), McDonald (1984) and Ruzicka and Choi (1981) has made seminal contributions to our understanding of the fertility decline. It is clear that there are a number of elements, both long- and short-term, which have either been underlying causes of the fertility decline or facilitated it. In the space available here it is only possible to summarize briefly these elements.

The impact of short-term economic conditions

Some have suggested that the fall in fertility to replacement level, like that in the 1930s, is related to economic recession. Economic conditions have undoubtedly had some impact. As Bracher (1981) points out, the burden of recession has been carried largely by the young. Unemployment has been strongly concentrated in the ages when Australians have previously begun families, with levels in the late 1970s being over 15 per cent for those aged 15–19, 10 per cent for those aged 20–24 and 5 per cent for those aged 25–29 years. Undoubtedly this has made young couples much more cautious about starting a family. But the reasons for the 1970s fertility downturn are more complex than and different from those which operated in the 1930s.

With respect to the effects of short-term economic conditions upon fertility the Easterlin model (1980) has been put forward in the Australian context by McDonald (1984, p. 19). This model explains oscillations in fertility rates by changes in relative income and posits that there is a negative relationship between cohort size and the success of that cohort in the labour market. Small cohorts will do relatively well in the labour market and have large numbers of children and these large cohorts will do fairly poorly compared to their parents and have fewer births. Hence as McDonald points out (p. 19), the post-war, baby-boom generation who were entering the prime child-bearing age groups during the 1970s 'have, throughout their lives, faced relative deprivation and fierce competition, relative that is to the preceding generations born in the 1930s and early 1940s'.

The changing role of women

This longer-term argument is clearly of absolutely fundamental significance. During the post-war period there has been a sexual revolution associated with major changes in women's access to, and participation in, higher education and employment. As is demonstrated in Chapter 9, there have been major increases in the participation of women, especially married women, in the workforce outside the home. Caldwell (1984, p. 15) points out that this has been the major source of pressure on marital fertility. He concludes that

> the single main reason for not expecting another baby boom is the difficulty in anticipating a reversal in the tendency towards married women spending most of their lives in the workforce. For younger women the social structures for alternative ways of life are disappearing.

The gradual breaking down of barriers to women taking on roles additional to those of mother and wife, together with the support and encouragement to take up these roles given by higher education, have depressed fertility levels, as have the justification and reinforcement provided by the women's movement. Moreover, the lack of societal structures to adequately support women seeking to combine child-bearing with participation in work and other activities outside the home has contributed to lower fertility. These changes have, as Caldwell points out, encouraged women not to give child-bearing 'unqualified priority over all other goals' and indeed, Caldwell forecasts (p. 13) that more than 20 per cent of women married in the mid-1970s will not bear any children at all.

Changing expectations

Another, but less well articulated aspect, of the social changes of recent decades which have undoubtedly influenced fertility, is the changing priorities and expectations of couples both for themselves and their children. Changing levels of education, exposure to mass media, all-pervading pressures to consume in bigger, better ways have contributed to an alteration of the priorities adopted by couples for allocating their time and money. Inter-generational differences in norms regarding housing, motor vehicles, other large consumer goods, travel and entertainment between the young couples of the 1950s and those of the 1970s are enormous. In the United States it has been estimated by Espenshade (1984) that a typical middle-income American family with two children and a mother who works part-time spends $82 400 (in 1981 prices) to raise a child to age 18 and $98 000 if the child spends four years at a public university. A recent Australian study (Lovering 1984) based on 1983 costings arrives at estimates of the costs of children to be fed and clothed at basic survival level. For low-income families the estimates for a year increase from about $870 for a 2-year-old, through $1110 (5 years old), $1370 (8 years old) and $1450 (11 years old) to $2160 for a teenager. There can be little doubt that the perceived costs of clothing, feeding, educating and bringing up a child in a manner expected by contemporary society have increased disproportionately in recent years. Caldwell (1982a) has developed a theory of fertility decline which states that the transition of societies from stable high to low fertility begins because of a shift in the net inter-generational flow of wealth from one favouring parents to one favouring children. There can be no doubt that in recent years the per capita net inter-generational flow of wealth in Australia has moved even more in favour of the child.

Changing patterns of contraception

The beginnings of the downturn in fertility after 1961 in Australia coincided with the introduction of the contraceptive pill and the IUD. Clearly couples must have the motivation to use such technology, so that this must be a 'facilitating' factor rather than an explanation of fertility decline. Nevertheless, as Caldwell (1984, p. 15) points out,

> Social scientists are loath to admit that technology may play a major role in social change.... Such changes in technology interacted in a cyclical way with social attitudes, permitting changes in social mores and allowing new aims to be achieved.

The pill and IUD diffused so rapidly that Australia had the highest per capita use of the contraceptive pill in the world during the 1960s. This technology for the first time gave the two-thirds of Australian women of reproductive age who employed it virtual total control over not only how many children they have, but also when they have them, without modifying their sexual activity. The rapid acceptance of the pill and IUD (Lavis 1975) was clear evidence of the need felt for them by Australian women, and the resultant substantial decrease in unplanned births must have had an influence in depressing overall fertility.

The 1970s, however, saw a second stage in this revolution which Caldwell (1984, p. 15) ascribes a significant role in the steep fertility decline of the last fifteen years. The first element in this has been the liberalizing of access to abortion. In South Australia, for example, broader grounds for abortion were legislated for in 1970 and Table 3.17 shows that not only has there been a substantial increase in the number of legal abortions performed but the incidence of abortions per 1000 live births has more than doubled since 1971.

Table 3.17 Incidence of notified abortions in South Australia, 1970–83

Year	Total abortions	Abortions per 1000 live births
1970	1330	59
1971	2519	109
1972	2672	122
1973	2833	139
1974	2852	141
1975	2916	146
1976	3219	170
1977	3590	189
1978	3819	208
1979	3906	211
1980	4073	220
1981	4096	215
1982	4059	221
1983	4034	203

Sources: Yusuf and Briggs (1979) and ABS (unpublished data)

There is now one abortion for every four live births. The impact of this on fertility levels is such that Yusuf and Briggs (1979) concluded that 'a significant proportion of the fertility decline in South Australia has to be attributed to legalized abortion'.

A second element in this new sexual revolution is the swing away from the pill toward other methods, especially sterilization, the incidence of which trebled in the 1970s (Young and Ware 1979). Caldwell (1984, p. 15) forecasts that 'half of each cohort of couples would move towards sterilization, not because they did so with any particular enthusiasm but because they feared the possibility of dangers arising from spending thirty years on the pill'.

Demographic reasons for the fertility decline

Ruzicka and Choi (1981), in analysing the demographic forces which contributed to the 1970s fertility decline, isolated the contribution of changes in reproductive patterns, marriages and the timing of births. They concluded firstly (p. 117) that three elements of change in reproductive patterns contributed to the decline.

1 There was an overall long-term trend toward fewer women having fourth or higher order births and greater concentration on having two children compared with the earlier post-war period.
2 This was exacerbated by the fact that the cohorts of women in the older reproductive ages in the 1970s had generally married early and had their children at a young age, conforming to the pattern of child-bearing characteristic of the 'baby boom' years. Hence many women of this generation had achieved their desired family size by the 1970s and made little contribution to total fertility.
3 On the other hand, the cohorts of women in the younger reproductive ages in the 1970s did not conform to the baby boom child-bearing pattern

but instead were delaying marriage and postponing first births. Hence the younger women also made a much smaller contribution to total fertility in the 1970s than corresponding preceding cohorts had in the 1950s and 1960s.

Changes in marriage patterns and age at marriage have had a considerable influence on the decline in fertility. These changes are discussed in Chapter 7, where it is shown that since 1974 the post-war trend of declining age at first marriage has been reversed. Ruzicka and Choi demonstrate (p. 124) that significant contributions to the recent fertility decline have been made by a postponement of child-bearing after marriage, a decline in the incidence of premarital pregnancies and the postponement of marriage itself. All of these demographic changes, however, are not so much fundamental causes of the fertility decline but themselves are a product of the wider social and economic changes briefly referred to earlier.

SOME CONSIDERATIONS FOR POLICY MAKERS

Concern with declining fertility has a long history among Australian governments and policy makers, as was demonstrated by the 1904 NSW Royal Commission into the Causes of the Decline of the Birthrate since the 1880s (Hicks 1978) and the 1942 Commonwealth Committee of Inquiry into the declining birthrate (Ware 1973). While one should not understate the significance of the 1970s decline for planning, it should be stressed that this reduction in reproductive rates will not cause a decline in the number of births in the 1980s. As Figure 3.11 shows, the 1980s will see births continue to increase due to the young age structure of the Australian population shaped

Figure 3.11 Total fertility rate and number of live births in Australia, 1970–82

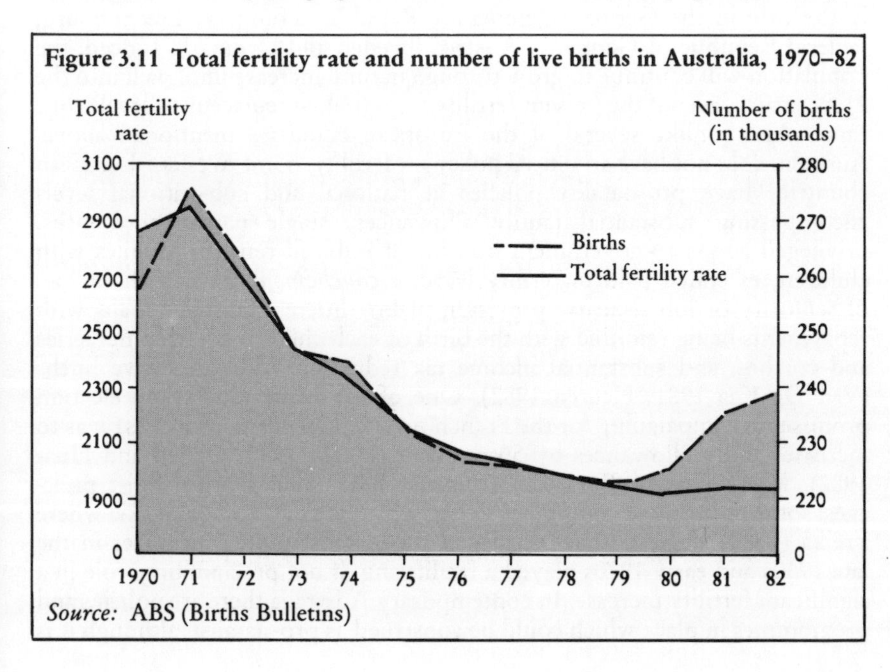

Source: ABS (Births Bulletins)

by the post-war baby and immigration booms. As Caldwell (1984, p. 18) points out:

> even if reproductive rates were frozen at the 1980 level the annual number of births would climb through the 1980s and so, doubtless to public acclaim, would the crude birth rate.... A flattening out of the annual number of births is likely to occur only after 1990.

The fact that the number of women in the prime child-bearing age groups of 25–29 and 30–34 are reaching unprecedentedly high levels in the 1980s is apparent in Figure 3.12. Thus births will increase as the baby boom generation passes through the peak child-bearing years. On the other hand, the diagram also shows that the numbers of women in the 20–24 age group begin to decline in the 1990s as the 'baby bust' generation begins to enter the family formation stage. Some commentators have suggested that the pattern shown in Figure 3.11 represents the beginning of a second 'baby boom' which would see fertility increase until it was once again above replacement level. However, as the National Population Inquiry (1978) suggests in its discussion of the 'echo effect', this upswing in births is unlikely to be anywhere near as large as the post-World War II boom. It has become quite clear over the past decade or so that the attitudes and behaviour of society have changed so that women today on average are having smaller families than their mothers.

Hence Australia, unlike many European countries, is not faced with the immediate prospect of a cessation of natural increase in the population through births being balanced or even outnumbered by deaths, as is presently the case in the German Democratic Republic, Hungary, Luxembourg, Federal Republic of Germany, Austria, Sweden and Denmark. Indeed, the population will continue to grow through natural increase until well into the 21st century, even if the present fertility rates (below replacement level) continue. Also, unlike several of the European countries mentioned above, Australia does not have an official policy on fertility. Some Western European countries have pro-natalist policies at national and sub-national levels encompassing substantial family allowances, single parent allowances, privileged access to government housing at reduced rent for families with children, extended paid maternity leave, *accouchement* leave without loss of seniority or job security, provision of low-interest marriage loans with repayments being remitted with the birth of each child, subsidized nurseries and creches, and substantial income tax reduction with successive births (Van De Kaa 1981; Heeren 1982). One of Mr Mitterrand's key election promises in campaigning for the French presidential elections in 1981 was to increase family allowances by 50 per cent (Hecht 1982; Ogden and Huss 1982). Many Eastern European countries have similar pro-natalist packages, some of the most comprehensive of which are in Czechoslovakia where Frejka (1980) suggests that broadened pro-natalist policy measures in the late 1960s and early 1970s played a facilitating, if not precipitating, role in a significant fertility increase. In contemporary Australia there are policies and programmes in place which could be construed as pro-natalist, although it is only very rarely that pro-natalist statements of the type that are commonplace in European countries are heard from Australian officials. One exception was a past Minister of Immigration and Ethnic Affairs (MacKellar 1980) who stated in late 1979 that

> In a free society there are limits on the extent to which Governments can influence fertility trends. It has been the conventional wisdom that pro-natalist policies will not work in a country like ours. But there are influences and attitudes which have an anti-natalist effect. It is time that we gave thought to means of overcoming these anti-natalist influences. It may be that the cost of pro-natalist policies and programmes will be exorbitant but we do not know whether this is so ... family building patterns might be out of kilter with income patterns and with social security and taxation systems.... The population question in Australia must be approached both in terms of domestic population trends and immigration.

Despite the ex-Minister's final statement, population policy in Australia is frequently considered to be synonymous with immigration policy. Refshauge's (1982 in ESCAP) review of Australian population policy, for example, is overwhelmingly a study of the evolution of immigration policy. An exception, however, is a recent group of papers (in Birrell et al. 1984) which agrees with MacKellar that natural increase should just as much be a matter for public concern and action as immigration. Moreover, they state unequivocally that there are publicly acceptable actions which can be taken to shape fertility decision-making, but definitely part company with the ex-Minister as to what should be done:

> We do however strongly advocate public intervention on fertility issues to ensure that, as far as possible, the rate of natural increase is reduced in the near future, and that there is no upward movement in fertility that could jeopardize the long run achievement of zero population growth (Birrell and Hill, in Birrell et al. 1984, p. 18).

One of the major pro-natalist measures adopted in Europe has been a system of family allowances. The 1984 family allowance rates in Australia are shown in Table 3.18. In addition to those benefits, a family income supplement of $12.00 per child per week is paid to families whose income does not exceed a maximum level. The scale of these allowances is very low when compared to costs of raising a family and does not compare with those offered in the European countries mentioned earlier. Moreover, as Borrie (1979, pp.

Table 3.18 Family allowance rates in Australia, 1986

	A$
Family allowance (per month)	
1st child	22.80
2nd child	32.55
3rd & 4th child (each)	39.00
5th & subsequent children (per month)	45.55
Handicapped child's allowance (per month)	20–85.00
Double orphan's pension (per month)	55.70

Source: Department of Social Security

69–70) points out, the graduation of payments to higher levels for each successive child is ill-adapted to present family building patterns. In contemporary society the most traumatic financial shock is the birth of the first child, which frequently is followed by a period when the family income is halved so that the largest endowment is most needed on the birth of the first rather than the last child. While the Australian family allowance may have had a pro-natalist as well as a social justice origin, it could hardly be defended as having the former function now.

In her survey of Australian population policy Betts (in Birrell et al. 1984, pp. 51–2) argues persuasively that while Australia has not had incentive-based pro-natalist policies, there have been policies of a negative kind which she refers to as 'coercive pro-natalism'. These included

> unequal pay, discrimination against married women and a chronic lack of child care facilities [which] limited women's opportunities in paid employment, and restrictions on the sale and advertising of contraceptives, the absence of birth control clinics and the illegality of abortion [which] limited their ability to control their fertility.

She argues that the removal of a number of these coercive policies over the last decade and a half has been a significant element in the decline of fertility. Betts (in Birrell et al. 1984, p. 52) concludes that the 'policies that affected fertility are to be found not in welfare provisions but in those coercive laws and practices that reinforced traditional forms of family life, female dependency and limitations on freedom of choice'.

There clearly are options available to Australian policy makers to influence fertility. These have been canvassed both in the pro-natalist form common in Europe as by MacKellar (1980) and in anti-natalist terms by Birrell and Hill (in Birrell et al. 1984, pp. 18–22) who advocate better availability of sex education, contraceptive and family planning services; removal of pro-natalist financial incentives (family allowances); reduction of social pressures which are pro-natalist; advocacy of restraint in population growth; and financial disincentives for larger families.

The pro-natalist policies pursued in, for example, Czechoslovakia have been extensive and expensive (Frejka 1980). They incorporated not only direct financial inducements and compensation for the costs of child-bearing but also a range of measures designed to reduce the costs of child-rearing (subsidizing children's clothing, transport, education, health care, etc.). Moreover, the extent to which they actually influenced fertility is debatable. The issue as to whether Australia should have a pro- or anti-natalist policy or even have a birth policy at all is a complex one, and is an important dimension of the confrontation between the population-growth and population-stabilization schools of thought. While this debate continues, however, there should be a heightened awareness of and public attack upon Betts' 'coercive pro-natalism' policies; some of these are still in place (though not because of their effect on fertility) and discriminate against and exploit women. It may also, however, be that there are 'coercive anti-natalism' policies (or lack of policies such as provision of adequate child-care facilities) which force women to forgo child-bearing if they wish to maintain a career outside of the home. Leaving aside their impact upon fertility, the thrust of several aspects of the incentive-based pro-natalist policies of the Eastern European countries is toward a substantial reduction in the inequalities between the sexes. Whatever fertility policy Australia has, whether it be an explicitly articulated policy emerging from public debate or the present set of practices indirectly affecting fertility it must be based upon 'an equitable distribution of costs between the richer and poorer, the childless and the child-bearers and between men and women' as Betts has it (in Birrell et al. 1984, p. 73).

We will now turn from fertility policy *per se* to some of the broader implications of current and impending patterns of fertility to policy makers. Several of the longer-term implications are dealt with in detail in subsequent chapters, especially that concerned with age structure (Chapter 6). However, the following considerations regarding the present fertility regime deserve consideration. An obvious area of major interest in this context is school enrolments. This has been thoroughly studied by Rowland (1983), who points out that total national enrolments in primary and secondary schools have a wave-like pattern produced by peaks and troughs in the age structure. This is readily apparent in Figure 3.13, which shows actual and projected levels of enrolment over the last half of the century. The five-year lagged effect of an absolute reduction in the number of births in Australia is seen in the significant downturn of total primary school enrolments around 1980. However the upturn in births shown in Figure 3.12 will begin to influence primary enrolments in the second half of the 1980s and especially the 1990s when the 'echo effect' described earlier will see primary school enrolments exceed 1.9 million for the first time before the close of the century.

Figure 3.12 The echo effect: trends in the growth and projected growth of the Australian female population in the child-bearing age groups, 1971–96

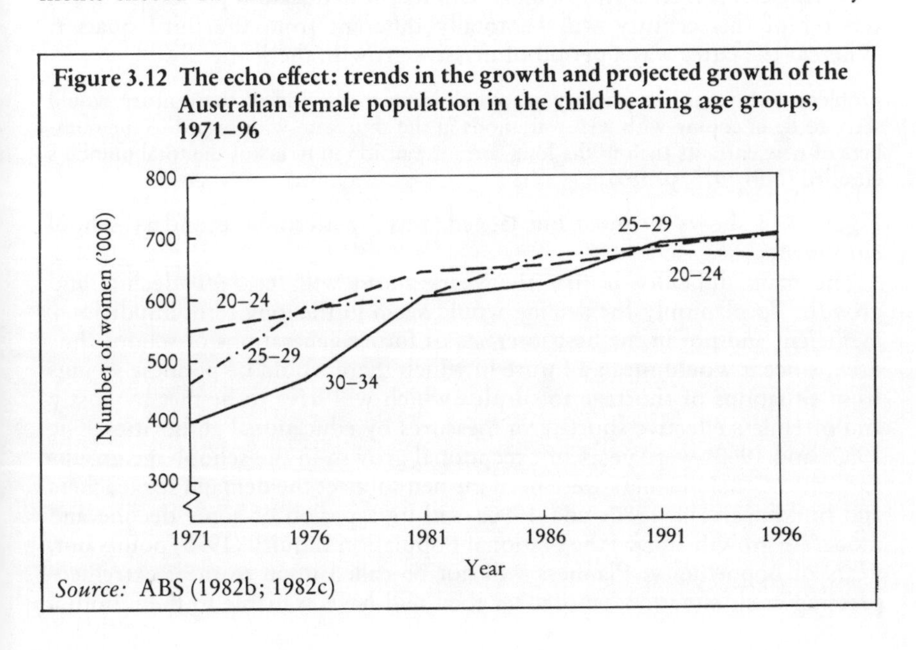

Source: ABS (1982b; 1982c)

Figure 3.13 Primary and secondary school enrolments, 1947–82, and projected enrolments, 1983–2000

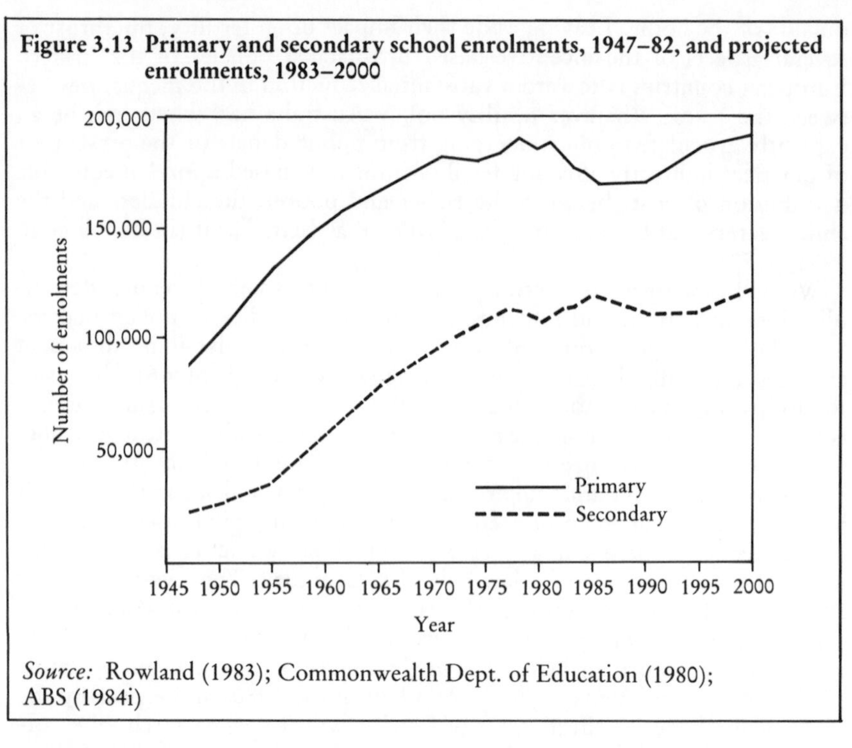

Source: Rowland (1983); Commonwealth Dept. of Education (1980); ABS (1984i)

Nevertheless, it is clear from Figure 3.13 that for education planning the last quarter of this century will be totally different from the third quarter. Whereas the latter was a period of massive growth, the

> problem with regard to primary school children to the end of the century would seem to lie in coping with wide variations in the short-run with regard to the numbers of new entrants than in the long-term expansion in terms of the total numbers enrolled (NPI 1975, p. 385).

Figure 3.13 shows a similar but lagged 'wave' pattern of secondary school enrolments.

The main difficulty is that the years ahead will see *both* decline and growth. To plan only for decline would seem in the long term injudicious, inefficient and not in the best interests of future generations of school children, since it would mean a future in which there would be periodic swings from situations of shortage to surplus which will have to be met by costly and often less effective short-term measures by educational authorities. The 1950s and 1960s were years of exceptional growth in the school-age groups and educational planners were hard pushed to meet the demand for teachers and buildings. The 1980s and 1990s will be a period of some decline and moderate growth and, as the National Population Inquiry (1975) points out, years of opportunity. Planners will not be called upon to meet extremely pressing crisis situations, moreover they will have available to them both a

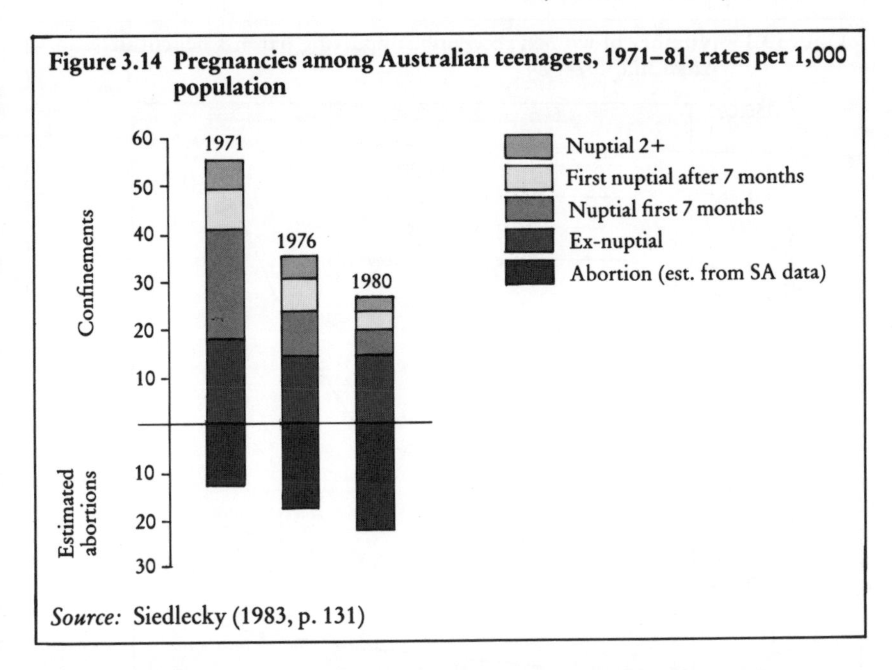

Figure 3.14 Pregnancies among Australian teenagers, 1971–81, rates per 1,000 population

Source: Siedlecky (1983, p. 131)

pool of skilled young people and the time to plan which will give the opportunity to achieve greater quality and efficiency in the provision of education.

While we cannot deal in detail with it here it should be noted that enrolment trends at local levels create the most pressing problems for education planners. As the NPI (1978, p. 94) pointed out,

> More significant for planning than national growth levels will be the very marked changes in growth rates of inner and middle areas of major cities ... flexibility in the location of schools and teachers may replace growth as the most significant problem in the remaining years of this century.

This has been taken up in detail by Rowland (1983).

Although Australian fertility trends are similar in several ways to those of the United States, one area in which there is divergence is teenage pregnancy. In the United States about one baby in six is born to a teenage mother and it is a matter of considerable concern, together with high rates of abortion among teenagers. In Australia the situation is quite different, with only one birth in fourteen being to a teenage mother in the early 1980s. This is not to say that there is no need for concern in this area in Australia. Figure 3.14 shows a 49 per cent overall decline in births to teenage mothers, but all of this decline was in marital fertility, while there has been stability in ex-nuptial births and a significant increase in the number of abortions. The latter point to the need for more and better sex education programmes and greater use of contraceptives since, as Siedlecky (1983) points out, 'neither abortion nor unplanned birth are a "good" introduction to adult life'. Moreover, it is vital that appropriate services and support be available to teenage parents and

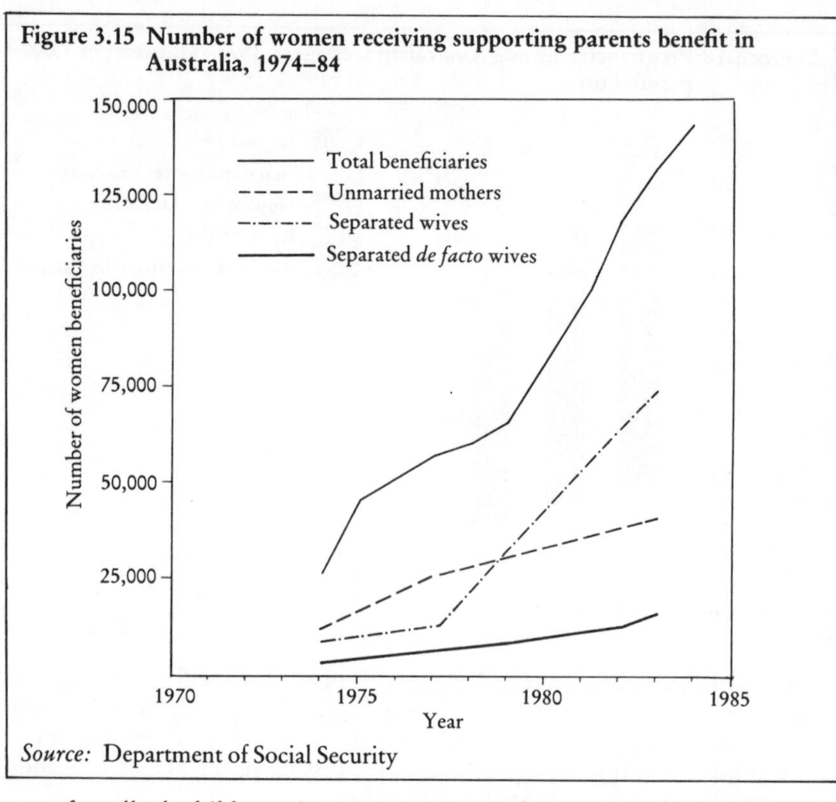

Figure 3.15 Number of women receiving supporting parents benefit in Australia, 1974–84

Source: Department of Social Security

out-of-wedlock children, since past experience has suggested that adolescent child-bearing frequently has long-lasting and adverse social and economic effects on the parents and child, through the inhibiting impact on the occupational mobility of the woman, greater chance of marital instability, etc.

The sharp increase in ex-nuptial births (to women of all ages—see Table 3.3) and in the proportion which they comprise of all births has significant implications in the area of social welfare planning, since it has been established that an ex-nuptial first birth greatly increases the probability that the mother will become a welfare recipient. Australia has had a supporting parents benefit for female single parents since mid-1973 and for males since 1977. Males make up less than 6 per cent of recipients and Figure 3.15 shows the exponential growth in the number of female recipients of this benefit over the last decade. The very rapid growth of deserted wives receiving benefits will be discussed in Chapter 7, but it can be seen that the number of unmarried mothers receiving benefits has been increasing steadily and doubled between 1976 and 1983 to 41 654. Expenditure on supporting parents pensions amounted to nearly $890 million in 1983–84 and its proportion of total pensions paid increased to 10.7 per cent from 2.5 per cent a decade earlier. Clearly, if current patterns of ex-nuptial fertility continue there will be substantially greater pressures on social welfare budgets from this source.

As continued participation in the paid workforce outside the home has become the norm among young women, regardless of whether they are married or not, the need for action in the area of child care is obvious. With the concurrent upturn in births the current shortage of public and private child-care facilities will become even more acute and it may be one element in closing the option of child-bearing to some women.

CONCLUSION

The Australian Bureau of Statistics has two alternative fertility assumptions for their population projections for the remainder of the 1980s. Both assume a linear decline in the TFR from 1.935 in 1983 to 1.93 in 1989, while one assumes constant fertility thereafter and the other a gradual recovery to replacement-level fertility in 1995. These scenarios appear realistic (especially the former) in the current situation but it is extremely difficult to predict future patterns of fertility and one cannot be certain how loud the echo of the post-war baby boom will be during the 1980s. Ruzicka and Caldwell (1977, pp. 366–8) have advanced a number of propositions which should serve as a basis for prediction of future fertility trends in Australia:

1 Fertility levels are not as strongly influenced by economic recession as they were in the 1930s.
2 There will be an intensification of the view that the two-child family is the largest practicable family, because of expense and the extent to which it dictates a different way of life for mothers.
3 We are moving toward a situation where most women work outside the home full-time for most of their lives.
4 Although a major factor in declining fertility in the mid-1970s was deferred rather than cancelled births, a significant proportion of the deferred births will in fact be cancelled.
5 Marital instability will increase and reduce fertility.
6 Where fertility and birth control differentials exist, convergence will take place.

If these propositions are accepted, and it is difficult to argue against them, one can only foresee a pattern of continued low fertility in Australia during the 1980s.

4 A Nation of Immigrants: Recent Immigration to Australia and its Impact

Immigration has played a critical role in shaping the growth and structure of Australia's population during the post-war period. In 1947 only 9.8 per cent of Australians were born overseas but by 1981 this proportion had more than doubled to 20.7 per cent, and a further 18.8 per cent were persons born in Australia who had at least one parent who was born overseas. It is difficult to exaggerate the significance of this immigration, not only in terms of its demographic impact but also in the many ways in which it has influenced wider social and economic change.

The 1970s saw profound changes in Australia's immigration policies which were reflected in a major reshaping of the scale, composition and impact of immigration (Price 1979, Price in ESCAP 1982; Australian Council on Population and Ethnic Affairs 1982a). This chapter will focus particularly on the last decade in which, amid considerable public debate, there have been fluctuations in the levels of immigration as well as shifts in the eligibility criteria applied in the selection of immigrants. As a result of these changes, the profile of immigrant arrivals in recent years has been quite different from that which applied during the era of substantial net migration gains in the twenty-five years following World War II. The aims of this chapter are to examine the changes which have recently occurred in Australia's overseas-born population under the influence of changing patterns of population movements into and out of Australia, to explore some of the demographic, social and economic impacts of immigration and to trace some of the policy implications not only of present and future immigration patterns but of changes which are taking place as a result of past immigration.

RECENT TRENDS IN AUSTRALIAN IMMIGRATION

In this section we are concerned with recent trends in two distinctly different areas. The first is the immigration of settlers to Australia and the second is the net gain of these settlers over former residents departing Australia and hence the contribution of immigration to overall population growth.

The National Population Inquiry (1975, 1978) charted and reviewed the major characteristics of Australia's post-war immigration experience up to the mid-1970s. However, the NPI was undertaken during a major downturn in net migration gains in the early 1970s. The subsequent period has seen

Table 4.1 Population gains in Australia from net migration, 1921–84

Period	Annual average net gain	Year ended 30 June	Total net gain
1921–25	36 654	1976	21 231
1926–30	25 941	1977	57 900
1931–35	–2 177	1978	62 700
1936–40	8 626	1979	55 100
1941–45	1 562	1980	75 900
1946–50	70 617	1981	119 200
1951–55	82 765	1982	129 100
1956–60	81 004	1983	71 200
1961–65	79 978	1984	47 500
1966–70	108 761		
1971–75	68 901		

Sources: ABS (yearbooks and overseas arrivals and departures bulletins), and NPI (1975)

further far-reaching changes in the pattern of immigration, with a major upswing in net gains culminating in 1982 in a net gain larger than for any year since the 1960s. The last decade then has been typical of Australia's immigration history in that there have been wide fluctuations in the numbers of immigrants coming to Australia and in the contribution of net migration to national population growth. This is readily apparent in Table 4.1, which charts Australia's net gains of settlers over the last sixty years. The massive gains following the war are apparent, reaching a peak of 149 785 in 1969. The downswing of the early 1970s is equally evident with a bottom figure of 21 231 in 1976. However, the resumption of an accelerating tempo of net gain by migration throughout the late 1970s eventually brought net annual gains in excess of the average annual gains of the late 1960s. A glance at the figures indicates immediately just how volatile immigration and net migration are as elements of growth—a characteristic which has been underlined by the downswing in 1982–83. During the calendar year 1983, the net overseas migration gain was only 42 200 compared to 102 200 in 1982. Nevertheless for much of the last decade there has been a substantial recovery in net immigration gains; to such an extent that in the early 1980s net immigration gains once again were accounting for nearly half of Australia's population growth, as Figure 4.1 shows.

Changes in the composition of the intake

This pattern of immigration and net migration has led to a considerable swelling of Australia's overseas-born population between the 1976 and 1981 censuses. There were, however, changes in immigration policy which resulted in the composition of the migrant intake being profoundly different from that of the earlier peak immigration years. These changes and their demographic impact have been carefully documented and traced by Price (1979). Figure 4.2 is my updating to 1983 of Price's chart of the major flows

Figure 4.1 Natural increase and net migration to Australia, 1949–83

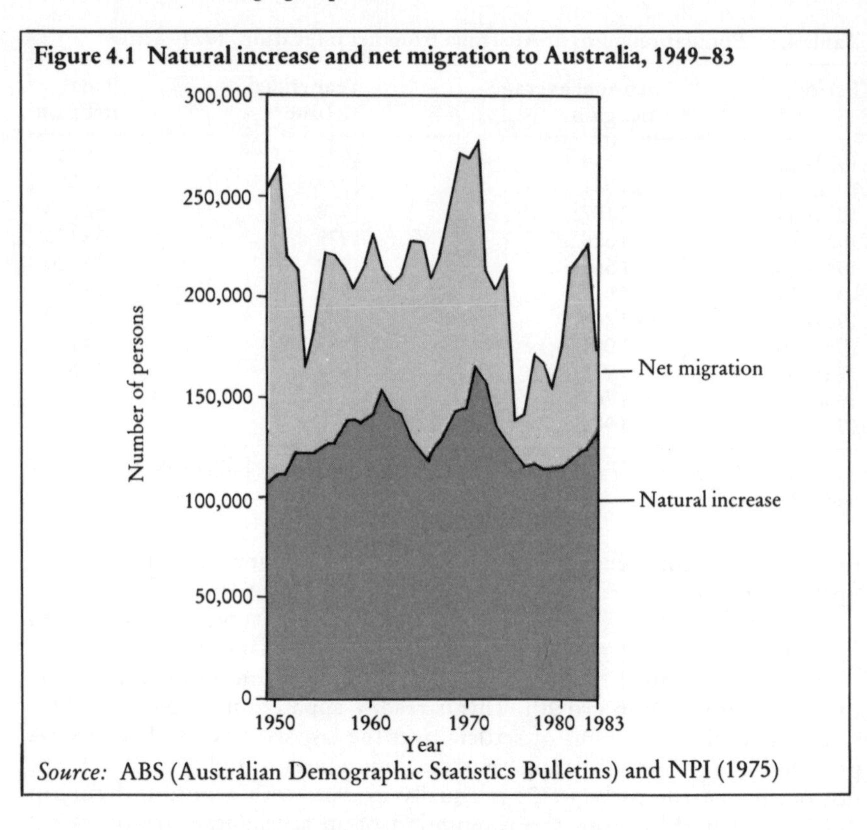

Source: ABS (Australian Demographic Statistics Bulletins) and NPI (1975)

which make up Australia's international migration system. This shows that the overall upswing in total net migration gains and settler arrivals was well above 100 000 in the latter years of the period. However, these are both still well below the 1 per cent of total population which was for many the national target for migration gains in the 1950s and 1960s.

The chart also shows that during the 1976–81 inter-censal period the net losses of Australian-born persons which characterized earlier post-war years were somewhat reduced, with a small net gain being recorded in 1981. Moreover, settler loss also stabilized around 11 000 persons in the late 1970s and early 1980s. Hence, the increasing contribution of overseas migration to population growth in the 1976–81 period reflects not only increased migrant intake but also reduced loss of settlers and Australian-born.

The remaining elements in the graph point to the major changes which have occurred in the country of origin of immigrants during the 1970s. In particular it will be noted that in the 1970s and 1980s there has been a significant decline in the numbers and proportion of immigrants who were born in the United Kingdom and Southern European countries which together contributed a major proportion of the net migration gains of the 1950s and 1960s. With regard to the non-British European sources of migrants, Borrie (Borrie and Mansfield 1982, p. 43) has pointed out that

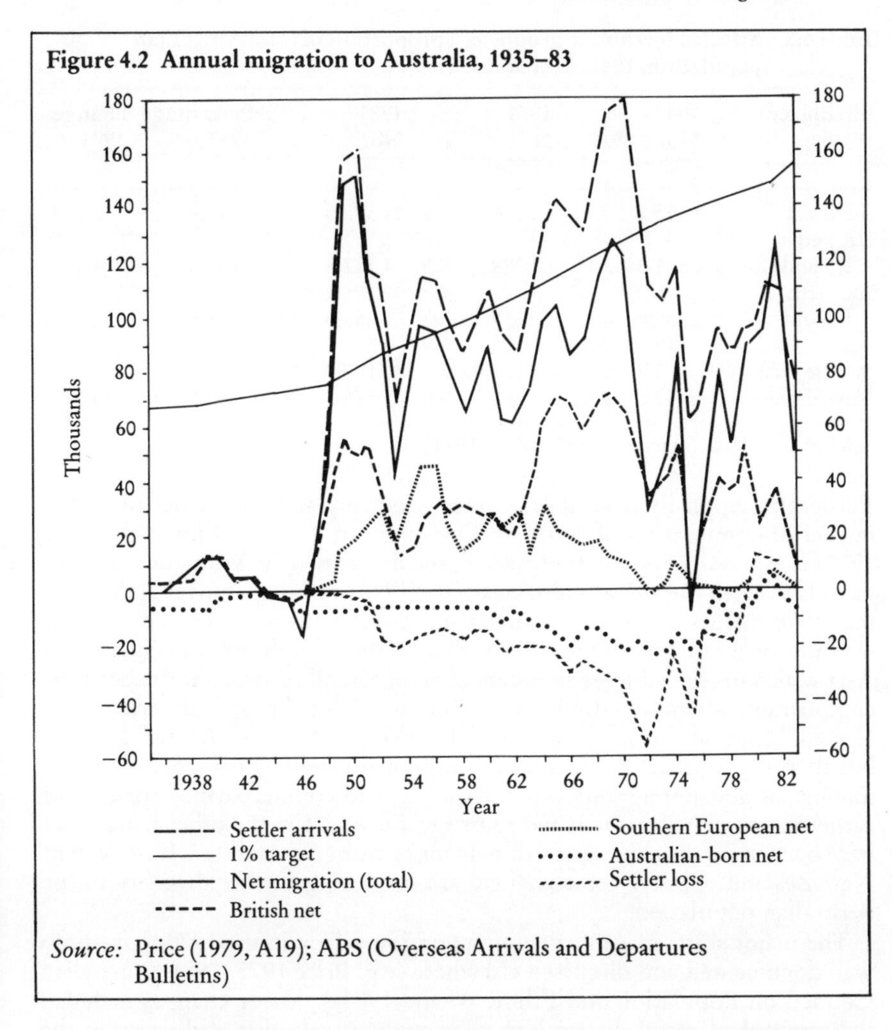

Figure 4.2 Annual migration to Australia, 1935–83

Source: Price (1979, A19); ABS (Overseas Arrivals and Departures Bulletins)

By the mid sixties the numbers from these [countries] had diminished and new groups were building up from Yugoslavia, Turkey and from the Lebanon and Syria. These in turn were followed by increasing numbers from South East Asia supplemented by Indo-Chinese refugees.

The huge impact of the post-World War II immigration programme on the ethnic composition of the Australian population is readily established from the birthplace data shown in Table 4.2. The post-war increase in ethnic heterogeneity within the nation is emphasized if we include British-born and New Zealand-born persons in the same category as the Australian-born (given the similarity in their language, food, institutions and other elements of culture). They comprised an overwhelming 97.3 per cent of the 1947 population but by 1981 were reduced to 88.3 per cent. The main change has been wrought by substantial immigration of non-English speaking

Table 4.2 Selected birthplace groups as a proportion of total Australian population, 1947, 1971 and 1981

Birthplace	1947 No. ('000s)	%	1971 No. ('000s)	%	1981 No. ('000s)	%	Percentage change 1947–71	1971–81
Australia	6835.2	90.2	10 176.3	79.8	11 572.5	79.4	48.9	13.7
UK and Ireland (Rep.)	541.3	7.1	1 088.2	8.5	1 132.6	7.8	101.0	4.1
Southern Europe	59.0	0.8	659.7	5.2	659.6	4.5	1018.1	−0.02
Asia	19.1	0.3	108.6	0.9	255.2	1.8	468.6	135.0
Middle East	5.8	0.08	86.9	0.7	147.0	1.0	14.0	69.2
New Zealand	43.6	0.6	80.5	0.6	176.7	1.2	84.6	119.5

Source: Goddard, Sparkes and Haydon (1984)

Europeans, especially from Italy, Greece, Germany and the Netherlands. The impact of immigration of Southern Europeans in the period up to the early 1970s is especially apparent. However, the downswing in immigration flows from Europe in the 1970s is also clear. The 1970s saw the removal of discriminatory elements of the old immigration policies, some waning of interest in traditional source countries as well as political upheavals in South-east Asia which produced large numbers of refugees, all of which influenced the composition of immigration flows. Not only did the growth rate of the United Kingdom-born population fall below that of the Australian-born but there were actual net losses of Southern European-born persons as the number of new immigrants was not sufficient to counterbalance attrition of earlier immigrants by death and return to Europe. On the other hand there have been substantial net gains of persons born in Asia and to a lesser extent New Zealand. Clearly these changes are producing further diversity in the Australian population.

The major shifts in Australian immigration policy in the 1970s have been well documented and discussed elsewhere (e.g. Price 1975, 1981; Australian Council on Population and Ethnic Affairs 1982a). Major changes included the removal of racial discrimination in migrant selection and entry in the early 1970s, and the replacement of a programme dominated by labour recruitment by one based upon four eligibility categories—family reunion, general eligibility (predominantly people with skills in short supply in Australia), refugees and special eligibility (mainly New Zealanders). In 1983 there was a further change which provides for permanent visaed entry to Australia in *five* categories: family migration (an extension of the old family reunion category), skilled labour and business migration (occupations in demand), independent migration, refugees and special humanitarian programmes and special eligibility. New Zealand settlers do not need visas for travel to and settlement in Australia and are thus considered separately. Moreover, there have been several changes in the selection criteria used, and a gradual reduction in the extent of assisted passage migration to such an ex-

Table 4.3 Categories of settler arrivals to Australia, 1977–85

A Pre-1982 categories

Category of entry	Percentage 1977	1978	1979	1980	1981	1982–83	1983–84
Family reunion	26.2	26.9	25.1	22.6	17.6	29	49
General eligibility	37.2	39.2	28.5	29.7	40.6	41	16
Refugees	11.1	12.7	19.6	24.5	19.6	19	21
Special eligibility	25.5	21.2	26.9	23.2	22.1	12	14
	100.0	100.0	100.0	100.0	100.0	100	100
Total arrivals ('000s)	73.2	75.7	68.7	81.3	111.2		

B Post-1982 categories

Category	1983 No.	1983 %	1984* No.	1984* %	1985* No.	1985* %
Family migration	26 952	28.9	33 957	48.6	42 000	55.3
Skilled labour and business migration	31 831	34.2	11 335	16.2	15 500	20.4
Independent migration	6 494	7.0	283	0.4	500	0.7
Special eligibility	567	0.6	397	0.6		
Refugees and special humanitarian programmes	17 054	18.3	14 769	21.2	14 000	12.4
Total visaed migrants	82 898	89.0	60 741	87.0	72 000	94.7
Total non-visaed migrants	10 279	11.0	9 064	13.0	4 000	5.3
Total arrivals	93 177		69 805		76 000	

*1984–85 expected figures only

Source: Australian Council on Population and Ethnic Affairs (1982a, p. 3).

tent that it is now confined to refugees. Over the 1976–81 inter-censal period the number of refugees steadily increased while, as Table 4.3 shows, other categories fluctuated in their importance. The table shows these changes using both the pre-1982 and post-1982 categories.

The significant changes which have occurred in the origin of immigrants to Australia during the post-war period are apparent in Table 4.4. Throughout the three and a half decades the United Kingdom has been the origin of the majority of migrants, although it is apparent in the table that its dominance has been reduced in the late 1970s. Italy and Greece on the other hand were the next largest contributors up to 1974 but subsequently have been very minor elements in the migrant intake. Thus the vast bulk of the Southern European-born population resident in Australia arrived in this country in the 1950s and 1960s—a significant point that will be taken up later. A similar pattern applies to other European migrant groups, especially the German and Dutch, although the influx of refugees in the early 1980s has

Table 4.4 Net migration to Australia by country of origin of major groups, 1947–74 and 1981–83

Origin	1947–74 No.	%	Rank	1981–83 No.	%	Rank
UK and Ireland (Rep.)	1 005 703	39.3	1	76 793	33.7	1
Italy	271 608	10.6	2	2 839	1.2	16
Greece, Cyprus	173 664	6.8	3	4 799	2.1	12
Yugoslavia	141 866	5.6	4	4 326	1.9	14
UAR/Egypt	109 256	4.2	5	887	0.4	–
Netherlands	107 818	4.2	6	5 224	2.3	11
Germany	83 015	3.3	7	9 253	4.1	7
Poland	82 525	3.2	8	12 012	5.3	4
New Zealand	80 434	3.1	9	21 508	9.4	3
Malta	62 928	2.5	10	2 096	0.9	–
India, Pakistan, Bangladesh	56 929	2.2	11	4 666[1]	2.1	13
China, Hong Kong, Singapore	41 771	1.6	12	11 906	5.2	5
Lebanon and Syria	32 429	1.3	15	3 338[2]	1.5	15
Turkey	18 535	0.7	–	1 809	0.8	–
Papua New Guinea	–	–	–	1 585	0.7	–
Indo-China	–	–	–	29 924[3]	13.1	2
South Africa	–	–	–	8 380	3.7	9
Malaysia	–	–	–	10 290	4.5	6
Philippines	–	–	–	8 543	3.8	8
USA	29 101	1.1	16	7 427	3.3	10

[1] figures for India only
[2] figures for Lebanon only
[3] figures for Vietnam only
Sources: Price (1975, A21; 1979, A23) and ABS (bulletins of overseas arrivals and departures)

seen Poland regain its status among the major countries of origin of migrants. Yugoslavian migration has been more consistent but has also fallen markedly during the late 1970s. Migration from Egypt was significant in the late 1960s and early 1970s but has greatly diminished in recent years. On the other hand, the greatly increased level of immigration from Asian countries and New Zealand during the 1970s is readily apparent in Table 4.4. The impact of refugee migration from Indo-China is clear (in 1981 Vietnamese had become the third largest incoming migrant group). Moreover, there were several other Asian countries among the first ten suppliers of migrants. South African migration has maintained a pattern of steady gains in the last decade or so.

The birthplace composition of immigration to Australia has undergone massive change in the 1970s; but there are other ways in which the characteristics of migrants have significantly changed during the 1970s. It should be noted that the huge upswing in immigration gains in the immediate post-

Figure 4.3 Age profile of immigrants to Australia, 1967–71 and 1980

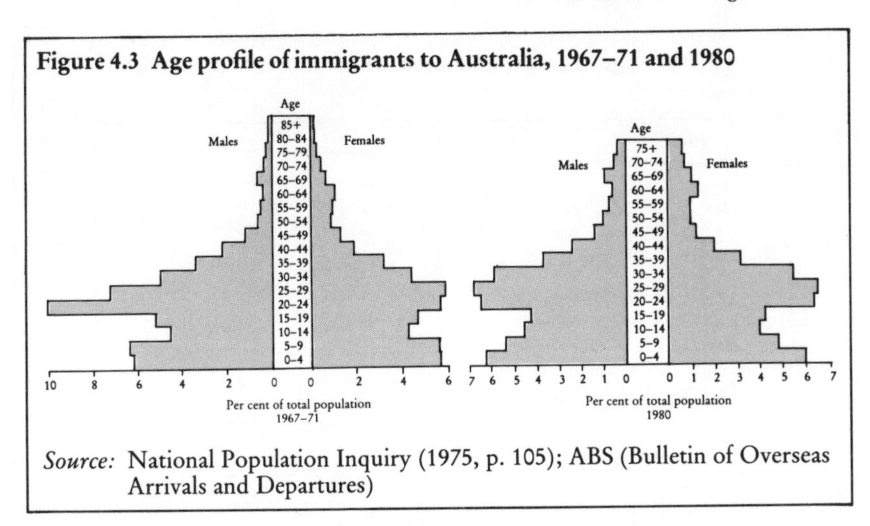

Source: National Population Inquiry (1975, p. 105); ABS (Bulletin of Overseas Arrivals and Departures)

war period (Figure 4.2) was especially selective of particular age groups. The overwhelming purpose of the immigration programme of the late 1940s, 1950s and 1960s was labour recruitment. Hence there was a deliberate selection of persons in their late twenties, thirties and early forties and this concentration can be seen, for example, in the age structure of immigrants to Australia in the late 1960s shown in Figure 4.3. As a result, many post-war migrants were people born in the 1920s and they are swelling the number of Australians currently entering their sixties.

Hence the size, composition and problems of Australia's older population in the latter part of this century will bear the historical imprint of the earlier large-scale immigration waves. The fact that in the mid-1970s net migration gains were reduced somewhat will of course have some effect on the relative size of the aged population, in that it has meant that growth of the younger population is reduced from the levels obtaining in the 1950s and 1960s. Moreover it should also be noted that older people now make up a more significant proportion of immigrants moving to Australia than was the case in the 1950s and 1960s. A quarter of migrants coming to Australia in recent years have come under the family reunion category—which includes substantial numbers of people in the older age groups. Hence the age structure of current immigration is somewhat older than that which prevailed for the first thirty years of the post-war period. This can be seen in the right-hand age pyramid of Figure 4.3. While the migrant intake is still somewhat more youthful than the total Australian population, it would appear that the 'younging' effect of immigration was not as marked in the 1970s as in the 1950s and 1960s. Analyses of the age distribution of the pre-1982 four intake categories by the Australian Council on Population and Ethnic Affairs (1982a, p. 7) show that the refugee, general and special eligibility categories have significantly younger age structures than the general Australian population, with median ages of 20.5, 25.6 and 22.4 years, while that of the family

Figure 4.4 Median age of total population and of immigrant intake,[a] 1949–84[b]

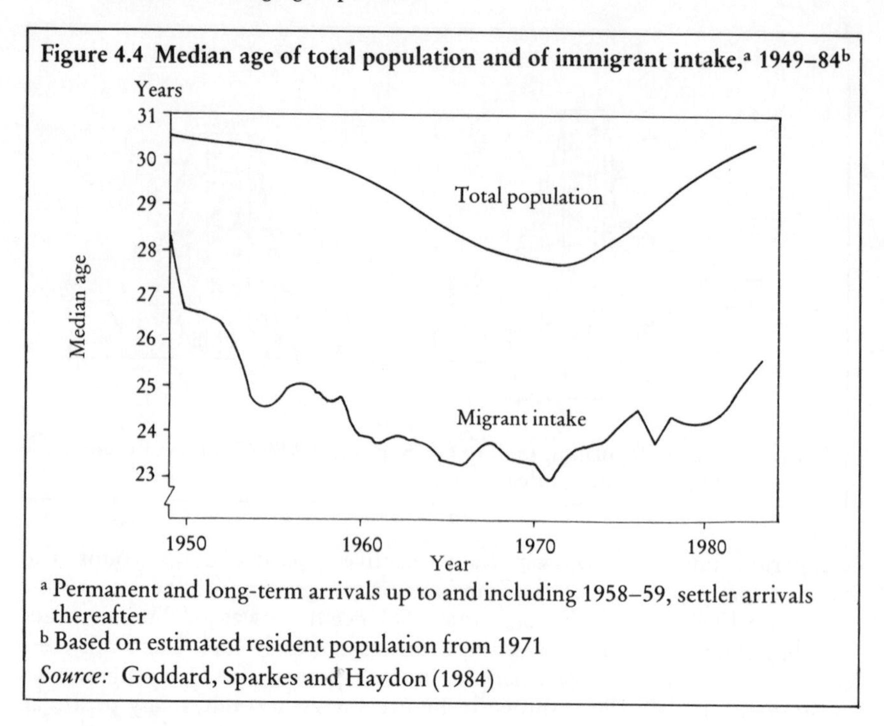

[a] Permanent and long-term arrivals up to and including 1958–59, settler arrivals thereafter

[b] Based on estimated resident population from 1971

Source: Goddard, Sparkes and Haydon (1984)

reunion category was substantially older. Figure 4.4 shows the ageing of the immigrant intake in recent years, as well as a general mirroring of trends in the median age of the immigrant intake and those in the median age of the total population.

CHANGING GEOGRAPHICAL DISTRIBUTION OF IMMIGRANTS

The impact of post-war immigration has not been distributed uniformly throughout Australia's economy and society. Indeed the propensity for post-war immigrants to settle in particular areas has significantly influenced the distribution of Australia's population.

Distribution between the States and Territories

Table 4.5 shows the inter-censal net gains through migration as an annual growth rate in relation to the total population of each State, as well as the total population growth rates through the 1970s. It will be noticed that growth due to net migration gains was above the national average in Western Australia and in the Australian Capital Territory (in 1971–76 only) and Northern Territory (in 1976–81 only), which also had high overall population growth rates. However, above-average rates of net migration gain were also recorded in New South Wales and Victoria despite comparatively sluggish overall growth rates, especially in Victoria. This is due partly to

Table 4.5 Net overseas migration and total population growth rates for Australian States and Territories, 1971–81

State	Growth due to migration 1971–76	1976–81	Total growth 1971–76	1976–81
NSW	0.46*	0.65*	0.98	1.09
Vic.	0.44*	0.54*	1.14	0.71
Qld	0.27	0.42	2.48*	2.31*
SA	0.35	0.26	1.20	0.70
WA	0.67*	0.66*	2.26*	1.97*
Tas.	0.06	0.15	0.70	0.72
NT	0.05	0.71*	2.97*	4.58*
ACT	0.44*	0.15	6.57*	1.81*
Australia	0.42	0.53	1.44	1.24

* above national average
Source: Di Iulio and Choi (1982, p. 4)

Table 4.6 Settler arrivals by State of intended residence, 1978–83

	State pop. as % of national pop.	Percentage of intake 1978 (year ended 30 June)	1979	1980	1981	1982	1983
NSW	34.9	38.5	42.5	40.9	37.6	37.1	34.2
Vic.	26.3	27.4	27.1	26.3	24.1	23.7	24.0
Qld	16.1	10.0	11.6	12.5	15.3	14.1	15.0
SA	8.7	6.5	5.1	6.3	6.5	6.8	7.9
WA	8.9	13.1	10.8	10.7	13.3	15.4	15.8
Tas.	2.8	1.2	1.0	0.8	1.1	0.9	0.9
NT	0.9	2.3	0.8	0.8	1.0	1.0	0.9
ACT	1.5	1.1	1.1	1.7	1.1	1.1	1.4

Source: Goddard, Sparkes and Haydon (1984, p. 26)

Melbourne and Sydney being important ports of arrival of immigrants and also to many of the immigrants being chain migrants attracted by and joining settlers from their country of origin who moved into Victoria and New South Wales in earlier post-war years. In South Australia, Tasmania and the ACT the contributions were lower, reflecting the limited expansion in employment in those areas during the late 1970s (Hugo 1983c). On the other hand, Queensland, a State experiencing rapid overall population growth, recorded below-average net overseas migrant gains. Hence, although the employment situation is significant in shaping the destination of immigrants, the relationship at the State level is by no means a deterministic one.

Indications of more recent patterns of settlement of immigrants can be obtained from examination of the intended place of residence stated by immigrants upon their arrival in Australia. These data for the late 1970s and early 1980s are presented in Table 4.6. The patterns evident in the table reinforce those described above with New South Wales and Victoria attracting a disproportionate share of immigrants. However, it is interesting to note that in the early 1980s there was a decline in their share of the immigrant intake, to such an extent in fact that it was below *pro rata*. A detailed analysis of the intended state of residence data has been made by Goddard, Sparkes and Haydon (1984).

What has been the impact of these net migration gains upon the numbers in particular birthplace groups in each State and Territory? Table 4.7 shows the distribution of each of the major birthplace groups at the 1981 census. Of the more than 3 million overseas-born persons, nearly two-thirds lived in Victoria and New South Wales (63.7 per cent compared to 60.9 per cent of the Australian-born). If we compare the distribution of the overseas-born to that of the Australian-born (Table 4.7) there is an 'over-representation' in Victoria, South Australia, Western Australia and the ACT. Interestingly there is a large difference in Queensland's proportion of the Australian-born and overseas-born populations, which indicates clearly that much of that State's recent rapid growth has been fuelled by interstate, rather than inter-

Table 4.7 Percentage distribution of settlers from selected birthplace groups among Australian States and Territories, 1981

Birthplace	Percentage NSW	Vic.	Qld	SA	WA	Tas.	NT	ACT	Aust.
UK and Ireland (Rep.)	32.4	29.8	44.5	51.6	53.4	54.6	33.8	36.5	37.7
Germany	3.4	3.9	3.9	5.0	2.3	4.5	4.6	5.2	3.7
Greece	4.6	8.3	1.3	4.8	1.2	1.8	5.8	3.1	4.9
Italy	7.4	13.2	5.4	10.6	8.4	3.1	3.4	5.4	9.2
Malta	2.2	3.2	0.7	0.7	0.3	0.2	0.3	0.8	1.9
Netherlands	2.4	3.5	3.9	3.6	3.2	7.1	2.9	3.3	3.2
Poland	1.8	2.6	1.3	2.3	1.4	3.0	0.4	1.8	2.0
Yugoslavia	5.6	6.8	2.0	3.1	3.2	1.9	1.4	6.9	5.0
Total Europe	67.9	77.9	69.3	88.2	77.7	82.3	59.6	73.8	74.3
Vietnam	1.6	1.5	1.1	1.3	0.8	0.5	0.9	1.5	1.4
Total Asia	16.3	12.5	7.3	6.1	10.8	5.7	17.3	12.3	12.4
Total America	4.3	2.4	3.4	1.6	2.4	2.7	6.5	5.2	3.2
Total Africa	3.4	3.3	2.2	1.3	3.3	2.3	2.2	2.2	3.0
New Zealand	6.5	3.3	14.6	2.2	5.3	5.7	11.1	4.5	5.9
Total Oceania	8.0	3.8	17.7	2.7	5.8	7.0	14.5	6.4	7.1
Total overseas born	100.0	100.0	100.0	100.0	100.0	100.0	100.0	100.0	100.0
Percentage of total overseas-born	34.62	29.10	10.99	9.81	11.60	1.42	0.74	1.72	100.0
Percentage of Australian-born	35.31	25.57	16.98	8.56	8.00	3.25	0.87	1.47	100.0

Source: ABS (1981 census)

national, net migration gains. On the other hand, the States which experienced peak growth rates during the 1950s and 1960s (Victoria and South Australia) have a significantly larger share of the overseas-born than of the Australian-born. There are also some interesting differences between the States in their 'mix' of birthplace groups, due to historical differences in the timing of them receiving very heavy net migration gains as well as differences in policies followed by individual States to attract immigrants of particular types. These can be summarized as follows:

1 Persons born in the *United Kingdom and the Republic of Ireland* are the largest overseas-born group in each State but have a low representation in the major immigrant-receiving states of New South Wales and Victoria as well as the two Territories. On the other hand, they account for more than a half of all overseas-born persons in Western Australia, South Australia and Tasmania.
2 *European-born* persons make up more than two-thirds of the overseas-born population in each State and the ACT and accounted for three-quarters of the 1981 Australian population born elsewhere.
3 Among the non-English-speaking European groups there is substantial interstate variation. The *Italian-born* account for 9.2 per cent of all Australia's overseas-born population but their share in the States varies from 13.2 per cent (Victoria) to 3.1 per cent (Tasmania). The Italian-born are most heavily represented in those States taking disproportionately large shares of immigrants in the 1950s and 1960s—Victoria, South Australia and New South Wales.
4 Persons born in *Yugoslavia* represent 5 per cent of the total overseas-born and are most heavily concentrated in Victoria, New South Wales and the ACT. *Greek-born* persons account for a similar percentage and nearly half of them live in Victoria. Victoria's overseas-born have a larger Southern European component than other States and this clearly differentiates that State's stock of overseas-born immigrants from others.
5 The smaller numbers from northern and western continental European countries appear to be more evenly distributed between States and Territories.
6 The *Vietnamese-born* population makes up only 1.4 per cent of the overseas-born and is slightly concentrated in New South Wales and Victoria. The total Asian-born population varies more however, between 17.3 per cent in the Northern Territory and 5.7 per cent in Tasmania. The main concentrations, however, were in New South Wales, Victoria and the ACT as well as in the NT. This reflects predominantly the settlement pattern of persons of Malaysian or Singaporean origin, Filipinos and refugees from the former Indo-Chinese countries.
7 Among other groups there is little interstate variation except in the case of New Zealanders who are strongly concentrated in the States which experienced most rapid economic growth in the 1970s—most notably Queensland and the Northern Territory (McCaskill 1982). The attractiveness of Sydney to New Zealanders has resulted in New South Wales also having an above-average proportion of trans-Tasman immigrants.

Distribution of immigrants within States and Territories
The distinctive patterns of settlement of the overseas-born groups within the States during the post-war period has been closely studied (e.g., Burnley 1974, pp. 165–84, 1975, 1976a and b, 1982; Stimson 1970). Here we shall focus particularly on the distribution of birthplace groups *within* the various States at the time of the 1981 census and establish the extent to which these are different from those identified in studies based on earlier censuses. The spatial distribution of ethnic groups in Australia is of particular interest because, as Price demonstrates in his classic study of Southern European settlement in Australia (1963, p. 140), patterns of settlement are inextricably bound up with a whole range of social and economic elements which impinge upon the well-being of those groups—their means of earning a livelihood, their social contacts within and outside the group, etc.

Until the 1970s, Australia's space economy, like that of the entire developed world, was characterized by a marked tendency toward concentration. Each successive post-war census before 1976 showed an increasing share of both the national population and jobs being concentrated not only in urban areas generally but in the handful of capital cities. Not surprisingly then, immigrants to Australia in this period tended to settle predominantly in these growth centres. Indeed, the net migration gain of overseas-born persons was a major contributory factor to the shifting of the demographic balance toward the larger cities during this period (Burnley 1974). However, the pattern of immigrants settling disproportionately in urban areas predated the post-war immigration boom. At the 1947 census 75.7 per cent of the overseas-born population lived in urban areas as they were defined at that census, compared to only 68.2 per cent of the Australian-born. The arrival of massive numbers of immigrants over the next twenty-five years exacerbated these trends and by the 1971 census some 80.5 per cent of the overseas-born lived in Australia's *capital* cities alone, compared to only 60.5 per cent of the Australian-born.

Table 4.8 shows that whereas in 1981 58.8 per cent of the Australian-born lived in major cities (with more than 100 000 inhabitants), this settlement category accounted for four-fifths of the overseas-born. Moreover, while there was a fall of almost two percentage points between 1976 and 1981 in the proportion of the Australian-born living in major cities, the fall for overseas-born was only one percentage point. Hence, this metropolitan 'turnaround' (which is discussed in the next chapter) has impinged more upon the Australian-born than the overseas-born population. Table 4.8 also shows, however, that the representation of various birthplace groups differs between the settlement categories. Persons born in the United Kingdom and Republic of Ireland, for example, are much more heavily represented in other urban centres (population of 1000 to 99 999) and rural areas than they are in major cities. However, immigrants from non-English-speaking countries are more heavily represented in cities with more than 100 000 inhabitants and their share of the rural population is greater than their share of the 'other urban' population. This pattern is most marked for the Italian-born.

It is important to appreciate that the major factor in the growth of Austra-

Table 4.8 Distribution of birthplace groups between urban and rural settlement categories, 1976 and 1981

Birthplace category	Major urban 1976	Major urban 1981	Other urban 1976	Other urban 1981	Rural 1976	Rural 1981
No. overseas-born	2 185 333	2 389 121	329 825	384 089	193 090	225 545
% overseas-born	25.0	26.0	11.4	11.7	10.3	10.9
% of overseas-born UK-born	38.7	34.8	53.3	50.2	48.9	46.8
% of overseas-born non-English-speaking and European-born	41.1	37.2	30.3	27.2	37.6	33.0
% of overseas-born Greek-born	6.5	5.7	2.2	1.8	1.9	1.5
% of overseas-born Italian-born	10.5	9.7	6.8	5.9	11.8	9.0
No. Australian-born	6 563 178	6 696 907	2 572 155	2 869 585	1 686 060	1 820 982
% Australian-born	75.0	72.8	88.6	87.2	89.6	88.0
% of Australian-born in category	60.7	58.8	23.8	25.2	15.6	16.0
% of overseas-born in category	80.7	79.7	12.2	12.8	7.1	7.5

Source: ABS (censuses of 1976 and 1981)

lia's major cities outpacing that of the non-metropolitan population in the twenty-five years following World War II was not so much the drift from non-metropolitan to metropolitan areas as immigrants from overseas settling in disproportionately large numbers in major urban areas. The reasons for this are not difficult to establish. Above all it was in such centres that employment opportunities were expanding; but the capital cities were also the arrival point of most immigrants, and chain migration had a reinforcing effect on the pattern of settlement in major urban areas.

The issue of the extent to which particular birthplace groups have tended to concentrate in particular areas of Australia is one which has been extensively studied. A useful method which has been used in the analysis of the extent to which ethnic groups have a concentrated pattern of settlement is the Index of Dissimilarity (I_D). This is basically a quantitative statement of the evenness of the distribution of two sub-populations. The index can be interpreted as the percentage of a particular sub-population which would have to change their place of residence if the distribution of that group between sub-areas of the region under study is to be made exactly the same as that of the other sub-group. An index of 0 would mean that the two sub-populations had exactly the same relative distribution while an index value of 100 represents a complete 'apartheid' situation, with no person of one sub-group living in the same sub-area as people of the other sub-group. These two extremes rarely occur. If the index is less than 20 there is little spatial separation of the two sub-populations, if it exceeds 30 there is some significant separation and if it exceeds 50 there is very significant separation.

Table 4.9 Indices of dissimilarity for various overseas-born groups and the Australian-born population in local government areas, 1981

Birthplace group	Total Australia	Non-metropolitan	Metropolitan areas
UK & Ireland (Rep.)	23.76	24.81	18.98
Greece	57.56	46.86	48.45
Italy	46.68	51.36	40.23
Malta	59.56	56.16	53.21
Yugoslavia	49.30	59.66	40.57
Other Europe	25.35	27.95	17.93
Vietnam	67.38	62.12	61.95
Other Asia	39.24	27.74	28.16
New Zealand	30.24	33.65	26.53
US/Canada	31.20	28.82	26.86
Cyprus	55.35	57.29	45.88
Middle East	60.63	53.31	50.83
Africa	34.00	30.67	25.07

Note: an excellent set of maps of the spatial distribution of various birthplace groups at the 1981 census in each of Australia's major cities are included in the series of social atlases produced by the ABS in conjunction with the Division of National Mapping.
Source: calculated from local government area summary file of the 1981 Australian census

Indices of dissimilarity calculated for a range of birthplace groups and comparing their distribution to that of the Australian-born for all local government areas are presented in Table 4.9 and these show some wide variations. The least concentrated groups are those born in the United Kingdom and Ireland (Rep.) and European countries other than the major Southern European source countries. The former is a pattern that has been consistently recognized with each post-war census (Burnley 1976a, p. 184) and is of course a function of linguistic and cultural similarity.

An exception to this pattern is Adelaide, where the I_D for this group is somewhat higher. This is not so much a function of the immigrants seeking to cluster together for mutual support in an alien environment as a function of the housing market in Adelaide during the 1950s and 1960s. In that period immigrant families from the United Kingdom were entering South Australia and more particularly Adelaide in such large numbers that they were a majority among people seeking housing and as a result substantial concentrations developed at the northern and southern edges of the metropolitan area where new housing was being built. This pattern was exacerbated by the fact that the 'assistance package' under which most British immigrants made the journey to South Australia included provision of housing by the South Australian Housing Trust (SAHT).

The 'Other Europe' group in Table 4.9 includes groups born in Poland, Netherlands, Germany and other, especially Eastern European, countries. Most of these groups have been long established in Australia and have not shown marked tendencies toward residential concentration, although some minor concentrations developed such as, for example, the religious-based concentration of Dutch immigrants in the south-eastern and eastern outer suburbs of Melbourne (Burnley, 1982, p. 103).

There is a tendency toward spatial concentration among persons born in Yugoslavia, Malta, Greece, Italy and the Middle East. However the birthplace group showing the greatest separation from the Australian-born is the Vietnamese, the vast bulk of whom arrived in Australia during the last decade.

Table 4.9 also indicates the I_Ds for non-metropolitan Australia at the 1981 census. These broadly reflect the overall patterns but it is interesting that birthplace groups which are well known for their concentrated pattern of settlement within large metropolitan areas also tend to have an even more concentrated settlement pattern in non-metropolitan areas. Moreover, settlement in rural areas is restricted to so few areas that the impact which it has is often more noticeable. The reasons for such concentrations of Southern European populations (to take one group) are very similar to those which operate within the major metropolitan areas (Hugo and Menzies 1980). Greek and Italian non-metropolitan settlement has avoided the extensive wheat-sheep belt and grazing lands and concentrated in the more intensively cultivated areas such as outer-urban market gardening areas, orchard, vineyard and sugar-cane regions. The importance of 'chain migration' in the growth of these communities has been stressed (Price 1963; Burnley 1976a, pp. 82–92; Hugo 1975). A study of Greek settlement in the Upper Murray region of South Australia showed that the most striking feature of the substantial post-war Greek migration into that area was 'the significance of secondary migration—the fact that many Greeks have settled in the region only after spending considerable periods living and working elsewhere, particularly large metropolitan centres' (Hugo and Menzies 1980, pp. 190–1).

How have the patterns of settlement of various immigrant groups within the major cities changed? The patterns, processes and problems from the 1960s up to and including the 1976 census have been comprehensively summarized by Burnley (1982, pp. 91–105). Broadly, the strongly concentrated groups included the Greeks, Maltese, Italians, Yugoslavs; there were moderately concentrated groups, such as the Poles and the Dutch; and slightly concentrated groups, for example, those born in the United Kingdom and New Zealand. These patterns continue to be evident in the 1981 census data summarized in Table 4.9. Burnley (p. 92) notes that the influx of refugees from eastern Europe in the late 1940s and early 1950s produced initial concentrations of Poles, Russians, Ukrainians, Yugoslavs and Czechs in Sydney and Melbourne. However, one of the most striking features of Australian capital cities during the post-war period was the development of concentrations of Greeks and Cypriots in the central city areas and of Italians, Maltese and Yugoslavs in the industrial and inner suburbs. There were also additional significant concentrations in market gardening areas (e.g., along the River Torrens in Adelaide). As Price (1963) and Burnley (1982, pp. 93–101) have shown, small nuclei of these groups developed during the inter-war years. Through chain migration 'these nuclei with their supportive

Table 4.10 Indices of dissimilarity for Australian-born and Greek- and Italian-born persons, Adelaide statistical division, 1961–81

Year	Index of dissimilarity Greek- and Australian-born	Italian- and Australian-born
1961	48.7	33.0
1966	44.6	36.0
1971	42.5	35.2
1976	36.8	38.6
1981	36.2	36.5

Source: calculated from ABS census data

institutions, were important anchors for the much more massive postwar immigration' (Burnley 1982, p. 92). The 1981 census data indicate that these groups have remained relatively concentrated. In Adelaide, for example, Table 4.10 shows that over the last two decades there has been no reduction in degree of concentration of the Italian-born. There has been a movement of Greek-born persons from their original concentration in Thebarton and to a lesser extent other inner suburbs to the west and south of the city; this is reflected in a decreasing I_D although it was still moderately high in 1981.

The influx of more than 50 000 refugees during the 1976–81 inter-censal period has resulted in the formation of 'some strong residential concentrations which in some ways resemble those of the Displaced Person refugees a generation or so earlier' (Burnley 1982, p. 104). Table 4.9 shows that the I_Ds for Vietnamese-born persons in Australian cities were much higher than for any other major group, with nearly two-thirds having to change their local government area of residence to produce a distribution pattern similar to that of the Australian-born population. This is a degree of spatial concentration unprecedented in post-war Australian cities for any significant birthplace group. Even in the early years of post-war Southern European immigrant settlement, these levels of concentration were not approached (Burnley 1976a). The pattern in Adelaide is typical. There were 3416 Vietnamese-born persons enumerated at the 1981 census and more than 30 per cent of them lived in 17 of the 1608 collection districts. These concentrations are in the area near the Pennington Hostel—the initial receiving point for many of the immigrants. This pattern of the locale of immigrant hostels being an important element in concentrating refugee populations was also true for the eastern European refugees arriving in Australia some three decades earlier. To quote Burnley (1982, p. 92):

> The location of the hostels in relation to places of work was a crucial factor in the formation of concentrations of Poles, Russians, Ukrainians and Yugoslavs who were Displaced Persons. The refugees arrived penniless and their means of transport within the city—to and from work and to shops from the hostels daily—was largely by public transport.... Their *activity space* was constrained to territory near where they worked or the hostels where they lived and the public transport routes between. They had become psychologically familiar with their areas and of the housing opportunities within them.

This description could equally apply to contemporary Vietnamese settlements in Australia's capital cities, except that given the high degree of unemployment among recently arrived refugees it may be that the location of the hostel may be even more salient.

The tendency for particular birthplace groups to concentrate in some areas is important in identifying areas and groups in greatest need of particular services. The occurrence of ethnic concentrations does not necessarily indicate the existence of social, economic or political division. As Burnley (1982, p. 105) points out, however, concentrations are 'a natural consequence of the need to adjust to a new and strange environment. There is no evidence that they in themselves inhibit the life chances of individuals or create conflict with the wider society.... The general consensus is that spatial concentration indicates less integration although by no means no learning of the new environment'. However, there can be no doubt that some minority ethnic groups do have particular problems, some of which will be considered in more detail later—language difficulties, social dislocation, reduced opportunity for economic advancement and general deprivation.

MIGRANTS AND THE WORKFORCE

The *raison d'être* of Australia's immigration programme during the 1950s and 1960s was labour recruitment. As a result the National Population Inquiry (1975) was able to report that at the 1971 census immigration had contributed well over half of the growth of the Australian workforce since World War II. Immigrant participation rates in the workforce were higher than those of the Australian-born population, especially among females. At the 1971 census 91 per cent of overseas-born males aged between 15 and 64 were in the workforce, compared to 88 per cent of Australian-born males in that age group. Among females the corresponding figures were 48 per cent and 42 per cent. As has been shown, the thrust of Australia's immigration policy has moved away from a preoccupation with labour recruitment.

Studies by Miller (1982, 1983) have identified the major features of the labour force participation of immigrant groups during the 1970s. His findings, based on the 1976 census, are supplemented here with data from the 1981 census and more recent labour surveys of the ABS. Miller (1983, pp. 31–2) has summarized the major characteristics of male immigrant participation in the workforce as follows:

1 overall immigrant participation in the labour market is similar to that of the Australian-born;
2 the average educational attainment of the overseas-born is similar to that of the Australian-born;
3 the overseas-born are grossly over-represented in the trades occupations;
4 the overseas-born are less likely to be self-employed or an employer;
5 the full-time/part-time job mix is similar to that for the Australian-born;
6 the average income of the employed overseas-born is only 4.7 per cent less than for the Australian-born;

Table 4.11 Major occupations for major birthplace groups, 1981 (percentage distribution)

Birthplace	Professional, technical, executive	Clerical	Sales	Farmers	Tradesmen, process, production	Service, recreation	Unemployed
Australia	18.3	17.8	8.3	7.4	23.6	7.7	5.6
UK/Ireland (Rep.)	20.2	16.9	7.7	1.7	28.5	9.5	6.8
New Zealand	19.7	15.9	8.4	2.8	26.4	10.7	7.1
Germany	18.1	15.2	6.5	2.3	31.8	10.7	5.9
Netherlands	20.3	14.5	7.1	4.7	33.8	8.0	4.8
Poland	15.5	9.1	6.8	1.4	35.5	11.5	7.4
Greece	5.7	4.8	13.8	2.4	47.1	11.5	6.4
Italy	7.6	7.1	6.0	5.4	51.3	9.0	3.8
Malta	5.7	7.9	3.8	4.3	51.6	11.4	4.9
Yugoslavia	5.9	5.0	3.6	1.6	58.6	8.9	8.2
Middle East	6.4	6.8	8.5	1.0	47.8	6.8	12.7
Asia	25.5	17.0	4.5	2.1	22.2	10.4	10.3

Source: ABS (1981 census, one per cent sample tape of individuals)

7 the prestige rating of the typical migrant's job is less than for the typical Australian-born male's job;
8 in each age group, the unemployment rate of the overseas-born exceeds that of the Australian-born.

The pattern for females is somewhat different, with the main features being:

1 the labour force participation rates for immigrants are higher;
2 there is no decline in participation with length of residence in Australia;
3 migrants are over-represented in trades occupations;
4 average income is similar to that of the Australian-born;
5 the full-time/part-time job mix is similar to that of the Australian-born;
6 migrants tend to work in jobs with lower perceived social standing than do the Australian-born;
7 in each age group, the overseas-born experience higher unemployment rates than the Australian-born.

These findings are generalized for the entire overseas-born population, but there are considerable variations among the birthplace groups. For example, in many respects the Southern European-born immigrants are particularly disadvantaged compared to the Australian-born, with especially low levels of educational attainment, low expected income and over-representation in trades occupations with low prestige ratings (Miller 1982, p. 12). This is evident in the 1981 census data presented in Table 4.11, which shows a very low representation of Southern European and Middle Eastern groups in higher-status 'professional, technical and executive' occupations. Conversely, the proportions of these groups in 'tradesmen, process and production' workers categories are more than double those for the Australian-born workforce.

Table 4.12 Unemployment rates by country of birth, May 1984

Birthplace	Workforce ('000s)	Unemployment rate (per cent)
Australia	5264.7	8.4
Born outside Australia	1862.8	10.6
(a) Asia	227.5	16.9
Vietnam	41.9	40.6
Rest of Asia	185.6	11.5
(b) Europe	1360.1	9.3
Germany	71.2	7.6
Greece	89.7	10.6
Italy	162.5	7.3
Netherlands	64.9	9.2
UK & Ireland (Rep.)	684.5	9.0
Yugoslavia	97.0	12.8
(c) Middle East		
Lebanon	28.5	32.7
(d) Oceania		
New Zealand	108.2	8.9

Source: ABS (1984k, p. 16)

The generally greater immigrant participation in the unskilled, blue-collar sectors of the labour market indicates that 'the share of migrant employment in declining occupations was greater than that for Australian born workers' (Bonnell and Dixon, 1982, p. 17). Hence, overseas-born groups have felt the impact of structural change on employment to a disproportionate degree. Stricker and Sheehan (1981, p. 174), for example, concluded that

> During the post 1973 recession the employment position of migrants has deteriorated much more than that of the Australian born population, with the deterioration being spectacular for migrants from the three Southern European countries (Italy, Greece and Yugoslavia) and more marked for migrants from other non-English speaking countries than from the United Kingdom, Ireland and New Zealand. This relative deterioration seems to be largely founded in the change in the occupational structure of the demand for labour in the recession, employment falling heavily in those areas in which migrants are concentrated.

This view is disputed by Bonnell and Dixon, who found that except for the 15–19-year-olds there was little evidence of a deterioration in the labour market position of migrants relative to non-migrants during the 1970s.

It will be noted in Table 4.11 that unemployment rates tend to be higher among overseas-born groups than among the Australian-born. This touches upon one of the most controversial aspects of immigration in Australia—its impact upon unemployment. Table 4.12 shows that unemployment rates vary markedly between different birthplace groups, with above-average rates being recorded among Greek-born and Yugoslavia-born and especially the Asian group, most notably the Vietnamese-born among whom four out of ten workers were unemployed in 1984. (Most Vietnamese are very recent arrivals in Australia and have had to compete for employment in a very depressed job market.) As Hogan (1984, p. 8) points out, 'In this respect they are more akin to the local new entrants to the workforce'. The levels of unemployment among overseas-born are especially high for recent arrivals from overseas, especially among those from non-English-speaking countries, and all groups who have been in Australia less than five years; and the differentials are greater for females among recent arrivals.

THE IMMIGRATION DEBATE

As the component of national population change most amenable to government control and intervention, immigration has been consistently subjected to overt population policies throughout the period of white settlement in Australia (Refshauge in ESCAP 1982). Although the heat and strength of the debate has ebbed and flowed over the years it has usually focused on the total numbers of immigrants and or their ethnic composition. Price (1975, A1) has effectively summarized the situation thus:

> In matters of migration Australia has historically shown two faces: at times the smiling face of encouragement and welcome, silver tongue hard at work enticing new settlers, mainly from the British Isles, for the purposes of population growth, development and defence: at other times, the hard frowning visage of denial, iron voice uncompromisingly rejecting the unsuitable non-Caucasian or restricting the intake of the dubious southern and eastern European. The first voice has called for large scale government programmes of overseas recruitment, assistance with passage, costs and organization of jobs and housing: the second voice brought into being the infamous White Australian Policy with its blanket rejection of most non-Europeans wanting to settle and its strict controls, including rapid deportation, over those temporarily in Australia as businessmen and tourists.

Over the years the debate has taken many forms and only occasionally has involved confrontation between the major political parties, because both tend to contain proponents and opponents of a substantial immigration programme. The arguments marshalled for and against in recent years have been summarized below. The complexity of the issue means that supporters of both sides tend to be very mixed. Thus Betts (in Birrell et al. 1984) has shown that the lobbies which favoured the expanded immigration programme of the early 1980s, with a major emphasis on refugees and family reunion, contained such strange bedfellows as the housing industry, local manufacturers and retailers and land developers, the ethnic community lobbies, humanitarians and liberals advocating an expansion of the refugee intake, and government bureaucracies. The opposition, according to Betts, comprises the 'silent majority' which public opinion polls indicate to be opposed to the present policy, the various lobbies who suggest that the Asian component of immigration is too large, groups concerned with protecting current employment and the conservation lobby. With such internal diversity it is little wonder that bipartisanship has been the rule rather than the exception with respect to post-war immigration policy.

It is not my intention here to comprehensively survey all of the major

Table 4.13 Summary of arguments for and against an expanded immigration programme

For	Against
1 Growth *per se* is a desirable goal (the 'pursuit of numbers'—Betts, in Birrell et al. 1984, pp. 56–7).	1 Puts extra strain on Australia's natural environment.
2 Expands internal market for Australian goods, especially housing—migrants have a greater propensity to consume than the Australian-born.	2 Exacerbates unemployment problems in an economy undergoing structural change and recession.
3 Has multiplier effect on employment.	3 Prevents development of skill training within Australia (Pope, in Birrell et al. 1984, p. 217).
4 Expands skill base of labour force, relieves 'bottlenecks in labour market' (migrant labour force more mobile than Australian-born).	4 Rapid population growth suppresses rather than promotes per capita economic growth.
5 Expansion of refugee programme is a humanitarian act.	5 Ethnic-based social conflict could be encouraged by diversity.
6 Migrants revive decaying parts of cities.	6 Disproportionate costs are carried by poor and disadvantaged.
7 Is good foreign policy.	7 Concentration of migrants aggravates slum conditions, creates ghettos.
8 Ethnic/cultural heterogeneity and diversity enhance quality of life.	8 Pressure for expanded immigration comes from within immigration bureaucracy to ensure its own continued expansion (Birrell 1978).
9 Has a 'younging' effect on age structure.	9 Erodes Australia's export economy (Birrell et al. 1984, p. 194).
10 Enhances defence capability and international political bargaining position.	10 Causes increased competition, conflict and inequality within major urban areas (King, in Birrell et al., 1984).
11 Appeases ethnic lobbies.	11 Places strain on local government and welfare resources.
12 Migrants facilitate structural changes.	12 Migrants act against structural change by concentrating in declining industries.

arguments for and against a substantial immigration programme in contemporary Australia. The arguments cryptically summarized above range from some which can be readily dismissed as spurious or of minimal importance to a few which are widely accepted, but several others are quite complex and there is strong and often heated disagreement about them. This is nowhere more true than with respect to the arguments concerning the economic impact of immigration. Strongly put and well-documented cases for a net positive impact have been made, while others have argued a strong case for the opposite position (see, for example, Douglas 1982, especially pp. 206–7; Birrell et al. 1984, pp. 169–99). A consistent and prolific critic of the existing policy is the sociologist Robert Birrell, who, in a series of papers and books, has argued that concerns about the environment and the social consequences of population growth make it imperative that Australia move as fast as possible toward zero population growth (Birrell 1978; Birrell and Hay 1978; Birrell and Birrell 1981; Birrell et al. 1984). More recently the economic historian Geoffrey Blainey touched off a major public debate when he was reported as saying 'the pace of Asian immigration is now well ahead of public opinion' and the continued entry of Asians at the present rate could 'weaken or explode' the tolerance extended to immigrants over the past thirty years' (the *Age*, 19 March 1984).

There can be no doubt that there has been a significant shift in Australia's immigration policy in the last decade. It was pointed out earlier that one entry category in the current immigration policy is 'Skilled Labour and Business Migration'. It is argued by the DIEA that the new Occupational Share System (OSS), whereby a list is supplied by the Department of Employment and Industrial Relations of expected shortages in the labour market, is responsive to labour market shortages. Nevertheless as Birrell (in Birrell et al. 1984, p. 44) points out 'the past partial nexus between migration and economic conditions in Australia has largely been broken'. Labour recruitment had long dominated immigration policy as Price (1975, p. 1) has described:

> ... immigration has not always been steady or popular; indeed Australia has sometimes been likened to a boa-constrictor, taking huge gulps of immigrants when times are good and immigrants are plentiful, then quietening down for digestion during periods of war and recession.

With the dominance of family reunion, refugee movement and trans-Tasman immigration, internal and international political influences have assumed much greater significance. Birrell goes so far as to state that 'The Australian Government has in effect "lost control" over the migration intake. Migration decisions are not being made on the basis of national economic or manpower needs, but rather reflect the political weight of Australia's ethnic community' (Birrell et al. 1984, p. 43).

The analogy of Australian immigration being a tap to be turned on and off at will as the economic situation dictates is clearly no longer appropriate.

THE FUTURE

The complexity of the immigration debate and the associated volatility in immigration flows due to fluctuations in the economy and changes in the political and social situation in Australia and neighbouring countries make the immigration component the major imponderable in projecting national population growth into the future. A recent DIEA study (Goddard et al. 1984) has produced a set of projections based on six separate immigration scenarios: these are presented in Table 4.14, together with the assumed composition of the immigrant intake. Each scenario has underlying it a set of assumptions regarding economic circumstances: the zero net gain scenario proposed as an appropriate one when the economy is in an extremely de-

Table 4.14 Hypothetical composition of Australia's immigration intake under various immigration scenarios, 1983–2001

Eligibility category	Net migration gain scenario Zero	50 000	100 000	100 000A	150 000	200 000
Family migration	83	48	38	69	43	37
Labour shortage & business	0	21	24	6	21	21
Refugees	0	21	19	19	21	16
Independent	0	7	4	2	5	18
Special	17	3	4	2	2	2
Trans-Tasman	0	0	11	2	8	6
Total	100	100	100	100	100	100

Source: Goddard et al. (1984)

pressed state, although several commentators (see for example Birrell et al. 1984) argue that this scenario should prevail no matter what the situations of the economy. The 50 000 and 100 000A scenarios are seen as applying in an economic situation similar to that which prevailed in the first half of the 1980s, and the remainder in better economic times. Each scenario has a different balance of eligibility categories and hence a distinctive age-sex, skill, birthplace profile. It will be seen from Table 4.14 that it is mainly the balance between the family reunion and labour shortage and refugee categories which varied between scenarios. The high proportions in the family migration category in each scenario are a little problematical in that any modification of the eligibility rules here would undoubtedly affect the number of immigrants from this source. Birrell (in Birrell et al. 1984), for example, mounts a case for dropping the Category C Family Migration sub-category (non-dependent children, brothers and sisters).

The patterns of population growth implied by these various levels of immigration are presented in Table 4.15. In this table the most likely future mortality and fertility scenarios suggested in recent ABS projections (and considered in the previous two chapters) are incorporated with the six sets of immigration assumptions to obtain projections of the total population. It can be seen that there is a very large range in the rates of population growth, such that the total projected populations by the end of the century range from 17.1 million with zero net migration to 18.3 million with 50 000 average net gains through to 21.8 million in the improbable event of average gains being 200 000 per annum. It should be noted that a 50 000 net gain increases the population growth rate by more than 50 per cent while an annual net gain of 100 000 more than doubles the rate of population growth. It will also be noted in Table 4.15 that irrespective of the immigration scenario there will be an ageing of the population, and that in fact immigration is unlikely to have any significant 'younging' effect on the population. The impact of projected immigration on the gender balance is also negligible.

Table 4.15 Patterns of future population change in Australia under various immigration scenarios

Migration scenario	Population 2001	Average annual growth 1983–2001 %	Median age %	Percentage of population aged 0–14	15–19	65+	Males/ 100 females
Zero	17 131 800	0.60	35.64	20.7	66.4	12.9	97.6
50 000	18 279 600	0.97	35.14	21.0	66.5	12.5	97.8
100 000	19 437 800	1.31	34.66	21.3	66.6	12.1	98.1
100 000A	19 442 600	1.33	34.75	21.2	66.8	12.0	98.3
150 000	20 642 700	1.65	34.26	21.5	67.2	11.2	99.3
200 000	21 818 500	1.97	33.77	21.8	67.4	10.7	99.8
1983			30.13	24.4	65.6	10.0	99.6

Source: Goddard et al. (1984)

CONCLUSION

Immigration has been of great significance in shaping Australia's population growth and composition in the post-war period. However, the context in which immigration policy is being determined in the 1980s is quite different from that which prevailed in the early decades of the post-World War II period. The economic situation is entirely different—there is no evidence of significant demand for labour of any type which cannot be met by internal growth of the workforce, for new economic developments tend to be capital- rather than labour-intensive. The social situation is also quite different: the nation is much less homogeneous, culturally and ethnically, than it was three decades ago. Hence, the lobbying power of ethnic groups is a new element in the immigration equation, as is the presence of refugees in neighbouring countries. Immigration will certainly continue, but as to what the scale and composition of the inflow will be we cannot predict two or three years ahead with complete assurance, let alone to the end of the century. At the time of writing, however, it would appear that an intake of around 60 000 to 80 000 persons per annum is likely over the short term, when the existing refugee situation, the influence of ethnic lobbies and employment are taken into account.

5 Australians on the Move: Changing Patterns of Internal Migration and Population Redistribution

Among the most striking and unexpected changes in long-standing demographic trends which occurred in most of the more developed countries of the world during the 1970s were those in population distribution. In the United States, for example, Butz et al. (1982, p. 13) recognized two important shifts in the pattern of migration that emerged clearly during the 1970s:

> First, people are favouring smaller communities over larger ones. Second regional patterns of migration have changed with the South and West gaining at the expense of the North and East.

The objective of this chapter is to find out how far these patterns of population deconcentration and shifts in interstate migration can be recognized in Australia during the late 1970s.

There are several demographic processes which can produce changes in population distribution. The inter-regional variations in fertility and mortality which were discussed in Chapters 2 and 3 made only a minor contribution to regional differences in population growth rates in the 1970s. The most influential element is the pattern of population movement. Changes in this pattern can not only result from increased levels of inmigration or outmigration in those individual regions but also, and this is often overlooked, from *decreases* in movement into some areas and in migration out of others. The latter is important—increased levels of population retention or 'non-migration' relative to earlier periods can be an important element in shaping trends in regional population change.

CHANGING POPULATION DISTRIBUTION PATTERNS

Population change in urban and rural areas

In the early 1970s Burnley (1974, p. 12) succinctly and accurately summarized Australia's changing patterns of population distribution after the war as follows:

> Australia has clearly emerged in the post war world as one of the most urbanized countries in the world, whatever indices of urbanization are used as a measurement. The basic pattern has been the further increase in primacy of the metropolitan capital cities within their respective States; the rapid growth of two industrial non-

metropolitan cities (Wollongong and Geelong) and the very rapid growth of the national capital, Canberra; with a notable absence of any intermediate sized centres in the urban hierarchy of the respective States with the exception of Queensland and Tasmania in which Toowoomba, Townsville and Launceston respectively have had healthy growth rates; and with the exception of a few market towns servicing rural areas, slow growth of a plethora of small country towns and population decline in some.

In developed countries prior to 1970 there was a pattern of increasing concentration of population characterized not only by a growing percentage of national populations living in urban areas, but also by growth in the share of that urban population residing in the largest centres. Australia was the case *par excellence*. Although changes in definition make comparisons over time difficult, the period between the 1947 and 1971 censuses saw the rural areas' share of the national population decline from 31 to 14 per cent and the proportion living in the capital cities increase from 51 to 60 per cent (Burnley 1974, p. 4). In the 1970s however, observers in several Euro-American countries (Vining and Kontuly 1978) and Japan (Kuroda 1977) identified a slowdown of growth in large metropolitan areas and even, in some countries, a reversal of the earlier net migration patterns.

In Australia the existence of a 'turnaround' was recognized soon after the release of the first results of the 1976 census. Stewart (1977), for example, demonstrated a resurgence of non-metropolitan growth between 1971 and 1976. Other studies based particularly upon analyses of internal migration data from the 1976 census identified a change toward deconcentration along the lines of that identified in North America and Europe in the early 1970s. In particular, the work of Jarvie (Jarvie and Browett 1980; Jarvie 1981, 1982, 1984) established definitively the extent of the 'turnaround' in the 1971–76 period, isolated the demographic components of population change on a regional basis and explored the connection between these patterns and structural change in the economy.

Internationally, the 1980 round of censuses have provided confirmation of these deconcentration tendencies. In the United States, for example, Long and DeAre (1982, p. 1111) conclude that the 1980 census results indicate

> that major realignments of the spatial structure of the American population are occurring. At one level of analysis, the data confirm various pieces of evidence and hypotheses that the decade 1970 to 1980 was unique in the degree of deconcentration of population beyond the boundaries of non-metropolitan areas.

In England and Wales results of the 1981 census (Champion 1981, p. 20) indicate that the only local authority districts to increase their rate of population growth over the 1971–81 decade were those identified as 'remoter, larger rural districts'.

The long-term tendency toward concentration of the Australian population is evident in Figure 5.1, which shows a consistent pattern of urban areas increasing their share of the total population up to 1976. At the 1933 census, 37.4 per cent of Australians lived in rural areas but by 1961 this proportion had halved and in 1976 only 13.9 per cent of the population was classified as

Figure 5.1 Changing distribution of population between metropolitan, other urban and rural sectors, 1921–81

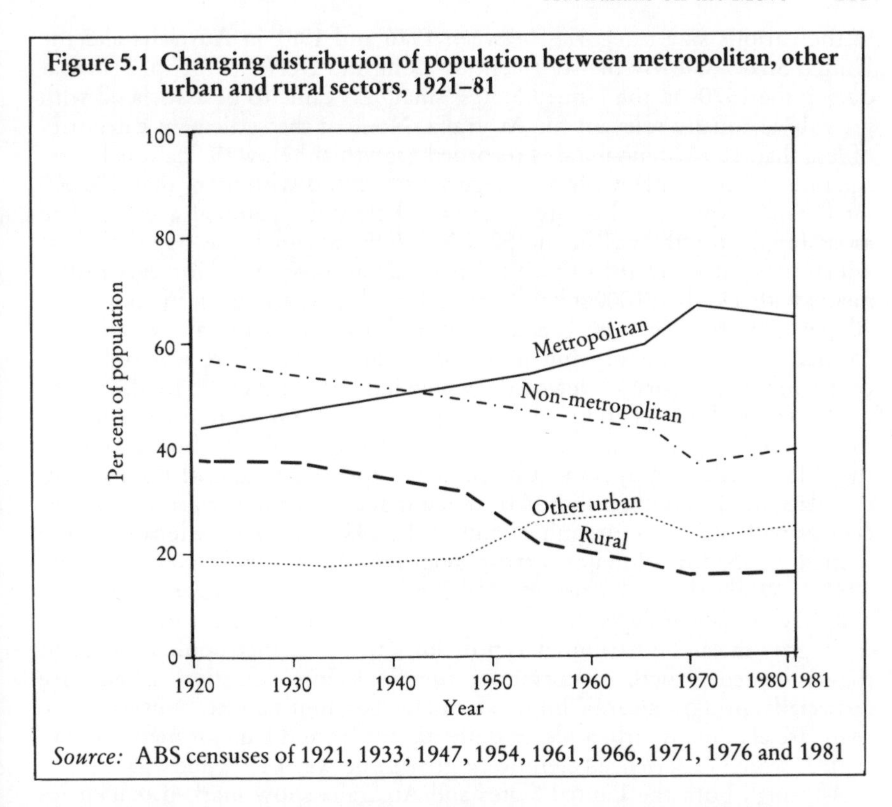

Source: ABS censuses of 1921, 1933, 1947, 1954, 1961, 1966, 1971, 1976 and 1981

rural. The pattern was, however, not just one of concentration in urban centres but of a growing dominance of the largest metropolitan centres. Indeed, the non-metropolitan share of the total national population progressively declined in the half-century following 1921 from 57 to 36 per cent, so that by 1971 nearly two-thirds of all Australians lived in the large metropolitan capital cities. It is apparent in Figure 5.1, however, that the 1970s have seen a change in this pattern. Between 1971 and 1976 the proportion of the population living in rural areas continued to decline (albeit marginally) but there was also a decline in the metropolitan areas' share of the total national population. Hence, in the early 1970s the only sector to gain ground was that of non-metropolitan urban areas. In the 1976–81 inter-censal period, other urban areas continued to increase their share at the expense of the largest metropolitan centres. However, for the first time this century the proportion of the total population living in all non-metropolitan areas increased. In percentage terms these are fairly small changes, but it is clear that they do represent a significant break with past trends.

Elsewhere (Hugo 1983d, pp. 15–24; 1984b) a detailed analysis is made of the types and locations of urban and rural areas experiencing growth and decline. Here I will only examine patterns of population change in various place size categories. Table 5.1 compares the percentage population change in the various size categories between 1976 and 1981 in Australia and the United States. Clearly the statement by Long and DeAre (1982, p. 112) that during the 1970s in the United States 'smallness came to be associated with growth' is equally relevant for Australia. None of the settlement categories of less than 100 000 inhabitants recorded growth at below the national average rate (7.5 per cent) while all categories of centres with more than 100 000 inhabitants experienced a rate of growth below the national average. The most rapid growth was in the 50 000–99 999 category, the population of which grew at more than twice the national average rate. However settlements with less than 1000 inhabitants and rural areas also grew by more than 10 per cent between the censuses. The slowest growth rate was in the 250 000–499 999 category but it should be noted that there was only one centre in this category—Newcastle, which has been influenced by the recent downturn in the steel and ship-building industries. Growth in cities of one to two million people was also very low but it must also be borne in mind that Melbourne and Sydney still accounted for 37 per cent of the national population. Moreover, it should be noted that several rapidly growing urban centres with 5000 or more inhabitants at the 1981 census were located in the immediate shadow of major metropolitan centres, especially Sydney (Hugo 1984c). While these centres are not contiguous with a major urban area and they do have independent functions, it is clear that at least some of their rapid growth can be attributed to proximity to a large metropolitan area and the associated growth of dormitory functions, intensification of land use (especially in agriculture), hobby farming, commuting, etc. Nevertheless, there are also many urban places quite distant from the major metropolitan centres which experienced significant growth between 1976 and 1981.

Although both the United States and Australia show marked tendencies toward deconcentration of population, some striking differences are immediately apparent in Table 5.1:

1 Although both show below-average population growth rates in the largest urban categories, in the United States the major metropolitan areas recorded an overall net loss of population while in Australia the largest cities maintained modest growth.
2 In the United States the deconcentration trend has a bimodal character, with above-average population growth rates being recorded in places with less than 2500 persons and in places with between 50 000 and 3 million inhabitants. In Australia, on the other hand, all settlements with fewer than 100 000 inhabitants experienced population growth at above-average rates.
3 Some of the largest population growth rates for Australian urban areas were recorded in urban areas in the lower-middle level of the urban hierarchy with between 2500 and 50 000 inhabitants, but these were relatively slow-growing areas in the United States.
4 In both nations high growth rates were recorded in the 50 000 to 99 999 size category and in rural areas (bounded rural locality or unincorporated rural areas) at the bottom of the settlement hierarchy.

Table 5.1 Population change in settlements of various sizes in the United States and Australia in the 1970s

Type of settlement	United States			Australia	
	Population (1980)	Percentage change 1970–80	Percentage change 1975–80	Population (1981)	Percentage change 1976–81
Unincorporated (US)/ rural (Aust.)	33 023 000	21.3	10.7*	1 763 982	11.8*
Under 1000	3 390 000	14.1	7.1*	447 319	13.4*
1000–2499	4 018 000	11.8	5.9*	422 115	11.4*
2500–9999	8 936 000	9.7	4.9	1 003 425	11.5*
10 000–24 999	7 182 000	7.2	3.6	799 627	13.1*
25 000–49 999	3 962 000	5.1	2.6	505 761	12.0*
50 000–99 999	3 611 000	20.4	10.2*	606 213	17.5*
100 000–249 999	18 461 000	17.8	8.9*	681 804	5.7
250 000–499 999	24 883 000	16.9	8.5*	258 956	3.0
500 000–999 999	28 640 000	11.6	5.8*	2 634 191	6.2
1 000 000–2 999 999	50 524 000	12.2	6.1*	5 452 942	4.0
3 000 000 or more	39 875 000	–0.8	–0.4	–	–
Total	226 505 000	11.4	5.7	14 576 335	7.6

* above national average rate of growth
Note: population size categories as at 1970 for the United States and as at 1976 for Australia.
Sources: ABS (censuses of 1976 and 1981); Long and DeAre (1982)

Changing regional patterns of population growth

Unlike the United States where there has been substantial redistribution of population between States during the post-war period (Long 1981), the pattern in Australia has been one of 'minor redistributions ... especially as a result of postwar industrialization, the minerals boom, and increased Federal Government expenditure on decentralized urban development, most notably in Canberra' (Rowland 1979, p. 31).

Figure 5.2 shows that since Federation, the only change in the rank order of States according to the size of the population has been Western Australia's recent passing of South Australia. However, during the 1970s the Territories, Western Australia and Queensland have consistently increased their shares of the national population while the other States have lost ground. The inter-censal population growth rates reflect these trends. In the early 1970s the ACT, the Northern Territory, Western Australia and Queensland all grew at well above the Australian average. While this was also true in the late 1970s, the Northern Territory and Queensland had the largest growth rates.

In analysing regional population growth trends as revealed by 1981 census data, Goddard (1983) examined trends in various types of 'settlement' zones, defined according to patterns of land use and associated population density

Figure 5.2 Distribution of population among States and Territories, 1901–83

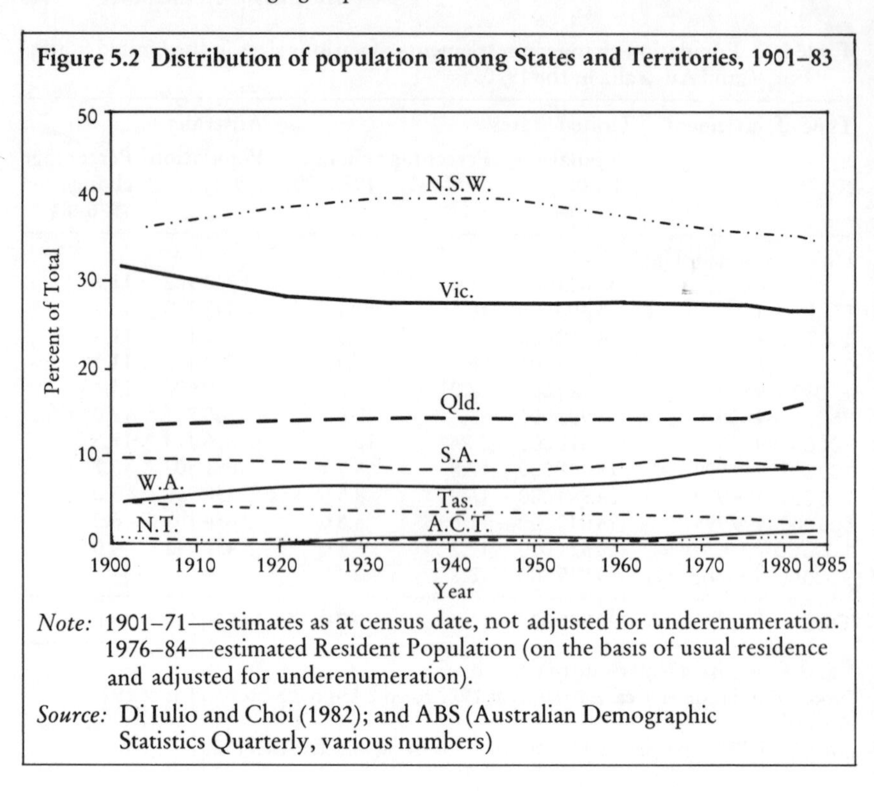

Note: 1901–71—estimates as at census date, not adjusted for underenumeration. 1976–84—estimated Resident Population (on the basis of usual residence and adjusted for underenumeration).

Source: Di Iulio and Choi (1982); and ABS (Australian Demographic Statistics Quarterly, various numbers)

levels. The zones are shown in Figure 5.3. The fastest-growing areas are in the non-metropolitan but closely settled parts of coastal Queensland, New South Wales and south-west Western Australia (Zone IB1). Table 5.2 shows that the population of this zone is growing roughly three times as fast as the major metropolitan areas (Zone 1A), and Australia as a whole. Goddard (1983, p. 16) summarizes the pattern of population change as follows:

> high growth on the peripheries of most major urban areas; strong growth throughout New South Wales and Western Australia zones IB1; perhaps surprisingly, some areas of absolute loss in parts of Queensland zone IB1; pockets of high growth in zone II, particularly in the vicinity of some of the larger regional service centres; areas of appreciable loss in zone II, particularly in areas of marginal cropping; and substantial areas of high loss and high gain in zone III.

There are of course significant within-region variations in these patterns as is shown in detail elsewhere (Hugo 1984b) and summarized below in the discussion of the contribution of internal migration to these patterns of population change. It is important to note here that the 'turnaround' to a pattern of non-metropolitan population growth is by no means a universal one.

Figure 5.3 Land use-population density settlement zones in Australia

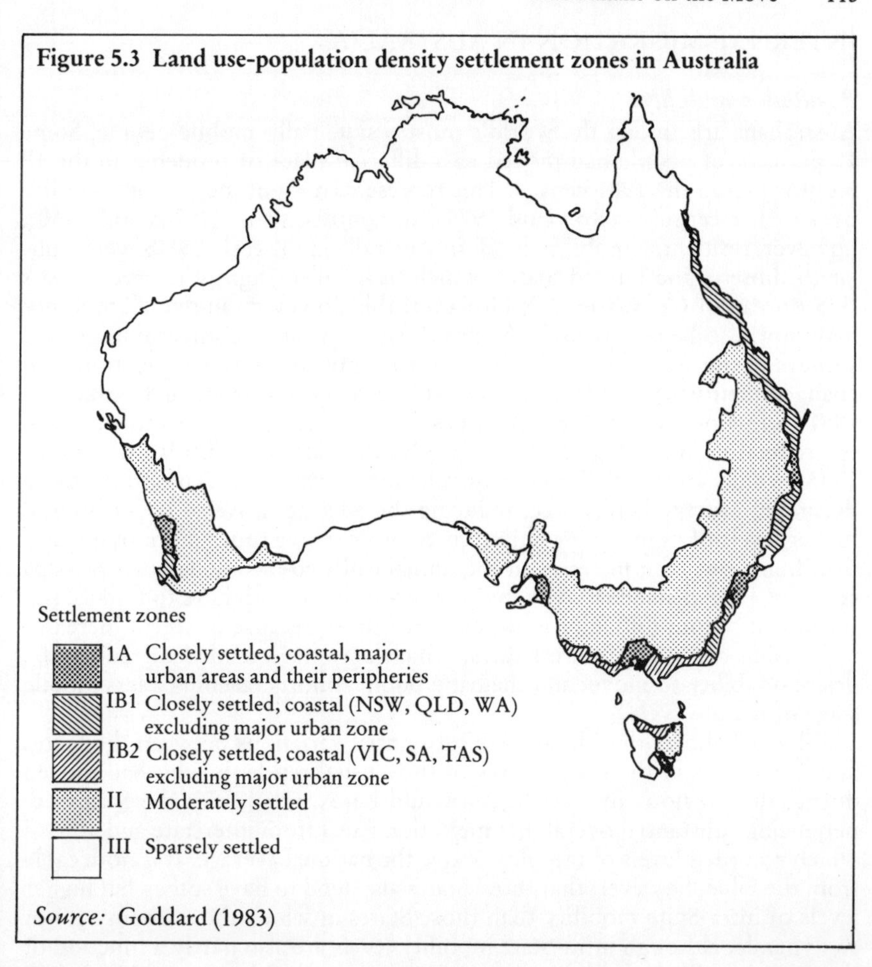

Source: Goddard (1983)

Table 5.2 Population change and net migration by settlement zone, 1976–81

Settlement zone	Average annual change (%)			Inter-censal change in number of persons employed
	From net migration	From natural increase	Total	
IA	0.4	0.7	1.1	8.2
IB1	2.5	0.9	3.3	21.1
IB2	0.2	0.8	1.0	8.6
II	−0.1	0.9	0.9	5.6
III	0.2	1.5	1.8	12.0
Australia	0.5	0.8	1.2	10.2

Sources: Goddard (1983, p. 5); Hugo (1984c, p. 232)

INTERNAL MIGRATION IN AUSTRALIA

Population mobility

Australians are among the world's most residentially mobile people. Some 17 per cent of people had moved to a different place of residence in the 12 months before the 1981 census. This represents a slight increase in mobility over earlier censuses (Rowland 1979). In contrast to the 1970s and 1960s, however, residential mobility levels in Australia in the early 1980s were similar to those in the United States, which have fallen slightly in recent years (US Bureau of Census 1983c). However, this downturn in overall mobility may now also be occurring in Australia, since the annual internal migration surveys of the ABS show a decline in the proportion of the population who changed their usual residence in the last twelve months from 16.8 per cent in 1981 to 15.4 per cent in 1983 (ABS 1984j, p. 4). Certainly the factors causing the reduction in total mobility in the United States (US Bureau of Census 1983) would appear to be equally relevant in Australia. These include: a decline in average family size, reducing the need to move to larger homes; higher levels of home ownership (renters move three times more frequently than home owners); increases in the number of two-income families perhaps reducing long-distance moves, because spouses will both have to find jobs at the new location; difficulty in purchasing homes because of recent increases in housing costs and interest rates, which may have tended to reduce the desire or ability to move; and the baby boom cohorts reaching a less mobile stage of the life cycle.

Table 5.3 shows that there were substantial variations between the States and Territories in the proportions of their usual residents who had moved during the previous five years. As would be expected, it is the States experiencing substantial overall net migration gains from interstate and abroad which recorded levels of mobility above the national average. It is noticeable from the table, however, that those States also tend to have somewhat higher levels of intra-State mobility than those States in which the economy is not so dynamic, although intra-State mobility levels are also partly a function of the geographical size and diversity of opportunities within States. More than a quarter of the usual residents of the Northern Territory had moved in the twelve months prior to the census. When this is added to the more than 10 per cent of the population who were classified as visitors temporarily present on the night of the census and the fact that no migration data were recorded for 5 per cent of persons, it seems that perhaps 40 per cent of the Territory's population had moved in the last year or so. This extremely high mobility is of course a function of the developing frontier character of much of the Northern Territory, which has meant not only that it attracts labour from the other States but that much of this labour will be persons either on short-term transfer with a company or government department or young workers with little intention of establishing themselves permanently in the Territory.

Queensland's and Western Australia's population, too, have very high levels of residential mobility. They do not quite have the frontier character of the Northern Territory, so that more of the migrants they attract are

Table 5.3 Population living at a different place in 1981 compared to 1976

State Territory	Moved during 1976–81[1] (%)				
	Intra-l.g.a.	Other intra-State[2]	Interstate	Overseas	Total
NSW	14.0	21.0	3.5	4.5	43.0
Vic.	10.1	22.6	3.1	3.7	39.5
Qld	11.1	23.9	8.9	3.9	47.8
SA	9.6	22.2	4.3	2.7	38.8
WA	12.2	25.7	5.5	5.6	49.0
Tas.	14.1	18.3	5.3	1.8	39.5
NT	7.2	17.6	28.4	6.6	59.8
ACT	2.0	20.9	19.6	5.7	48.7
Total Australia	11.7	22.3	4.9	4.1	42.9

[1] Persons five years old and over at the census enumeration
[2] The high figures for Qld, NT and ACT may be a little artificial in that Brisbane, Darwin and the ACT have 'pseudo'-local government areas created for census purposes and these tend to be smaller in size and population than those in most metropolitan centres. This has the effect of making more short-distance intra-urban moves into intra-l.g.a. moves in those areas.
Source: ABS (1981 census)

likely to settle permanently. The ACT is strongly influenced by migration of people on employment transfer and this is probably the major factor accounting for its population's high level of residential mobility. New South Wales has a higher level of mobility than other slow-growing States, mainly because of very high levels of intra-State migration associated with the fact that it is the most populous and economically diverse of all the States.

In examining population distribution changes it is more or less permanent changes in place of residence which are of greatest significance. However, we should not totally ignore temporary changes of place of residence, since such movements can lead to substantial seasonal shifts in the distribution of demand for goods and services. Some indication of short-term mobility can be gauged from the extent to which Australians were away from their usual place of residence on the night of the 1981 census. The proportion of the population made up of visitors was highest in the Northern Territory and Queensland. In Queensland 2.4 per cent of the total population enumerated (53 919) indicated that their usual residence was in another State or Territory and 14 750 were overseas visitors. This of course reflects the mid-winter northward exodus of holiday-makers and older people from the southern States of New South Wales (19 874 visitors), Victoria (23 263), South Australia (4705) and Tasmania (2347). The flow to the Northern Territory, where 6.3 per cent were visitors from another State, is partly explained by the seasonal northward flow of holiday-makers and retirees escaping the relatively cold winters of the south. The ACT also recorded relatively high numbers

Table 5.4 Percentage of each age group not at usual place of residence on census night, 1981

Age (years)	Percentage of persons not at usual place of residence	
	Males	Females
0–4	4.2	4.7
5–9	4.2	3.9
10–14	4.2	4.7
15–19	7.1*	6.1*
20–24	8.9*	8.0*
25–29	7.7*	5.6*
30–34	6.7*	5.1
35–39	6.2*	3.8
40–44	5.3	3.4
45–49	5.5	4.0
50–54	5.1	4.3
55–59	5.4	5.5*
60–64	6.6*	6.9*
65–69	7.5*	7.6*
70–74	7.4*	8.1*
75+	6.3*	8.2*
Total	6.1	5.5

* Above the average for all age groups
Source: ABS (1981 census, one per cent sample tape of individuals)

of census-night visitors (2.4 per cent), probably because the 1981 census was conducted on a mid-week night, so that many business travellers were 'captured' as visitors.

There was considerable variation between age groups in the proportion of persons who were not at their usual place of residence on the night of the census. Table 5.4 shows that two groups are disproportionately represented among visitors—young adults and the older segment of the population (including many retired people). It would appear that much of this temporary mobility of the older population resembles the 'snowbirding' phenomenon in the United States whereby older people escape from the frost-belt states of the North-east and Mid-west during winter and travel to the sunnier states such as Florida and Arizona (Krout 1982; Sullivan and Stevens 1982).

Interstate migration

As was shown earlier, there are significant differences between the States in levels of recent population growth. A major determining factor in these differences is population movement between the States, although only 11.7 per cent of Australians moved interstate between the 1976 and 1981 censuses. The major patterns of this movement are shown in Figure 5.4 and are discussed in detail elsewhere (Hugo 1983e) so that only a few main points will be raised here. The most striking features of Figure 5.4 include the

Figure 5.4 Interstate migration, 1976–81

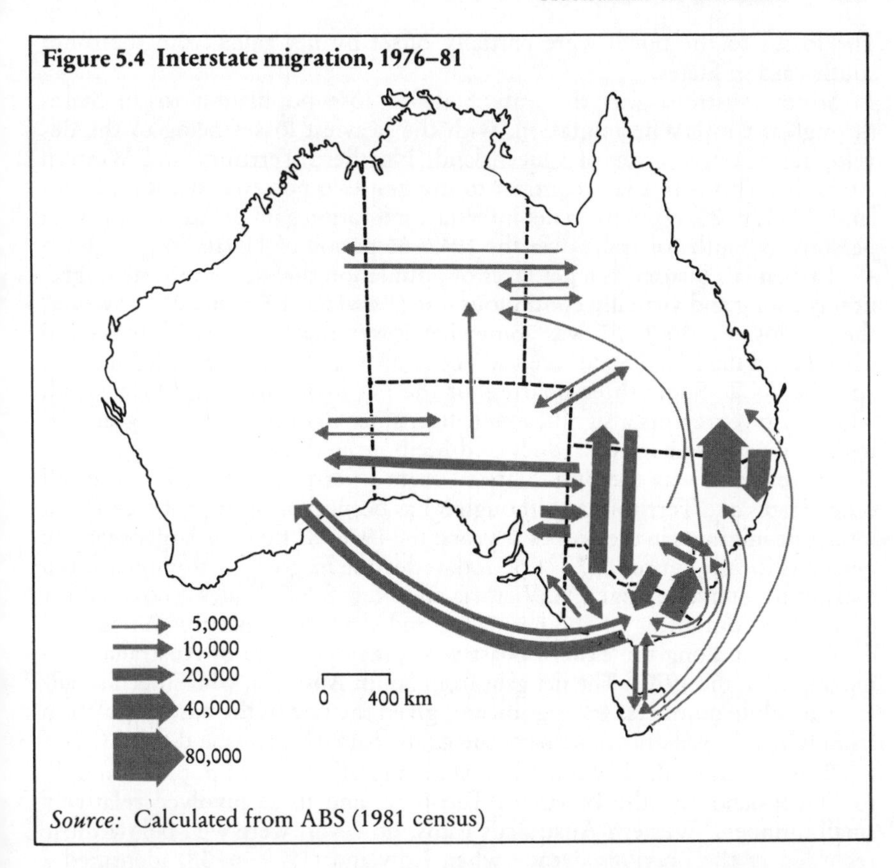

Source: Calculated from ABS (1981 census)

fact that there is a low degree of 'migration effectiveness' in the interstate flows (Hugo 1983e). The differences between the States tend to indicate a close relationship between interstate migration and trends in employment, and can be summarized as follows:

1 The largest net loser of population through interstate migration over the 1976–81 period was Victoria, which lost population to each State except South Australia. Nearly two-thirds of the net migration loss was to Queensland and a fifth to New South Wales. Among the net losses to other States, those to Tasmania are most interesting since they represent a reversal of one of the most consistent patterns in Australian net interstate migration (Scott 1957).

2 New South Wales' net losses were overwhelmingly northward to Queensland, although there was a significant net loss to Western Australia and smaller ones to the Northern Territory and the Australian Capital Territory. (The latter is especially interesting, since it is only a fraction of the net losses recorded in the previous decade. In 1966–71, for example, the net loss to the ACT from New South Wales was 24 times larger than in 1976–81.)

The losses to the north were partially offset by net gains from the other south-eastern States.

3 South Australia was the only State to lose population to all States through net interstate migration, with the heaviest losses being to the developing resource areas of Queensland, Northern Territory and Western Australia. This is in sharp contrast to the first two post-war decades; Rowland (1979, p. 20) estimates a net interstate migration gain of Australian-born persons to South Australia over the 1947–66 period of 11 910.

4 Tasmania's history as a net loser of population through interstate migration is a long and virtually continuous one (Rowland 1979, p. 20). However, the net loss for 1976–81 was somewhat lower than in recent inter-censal periods and the island State received net gains from Victoria, South Australia and the ACT. Some three-quarters of the net losses were to Queensland, which also represents a significant change, since in other post-war years the major losses have been to Sydney and Melbourne (Rowland 1979, p. 44).

5 Queensland was the only State to record net migration gains from all other States and Territories. Although it has been a consistent net receiver of interstate migrants in the post-war years, the 1976–81 figure is larger than the net gains for the entire 1947–71 period, reflecting its growing dominance as a magnet to interstate migrants. Victoria and New South Wales accounted for more than four-fifths of the net gains, and it is clear that this northward displacement along the eastern coast was a major feature of Australia's demography in the 1970s. The net gain from South Australia, while much smaller in absolute numbers, was significant, given the size of the base population from which it was drawn, as were the gains from Tasmania and the ACT.

6 Western Australia had a net interstate migration loss of population only to Queensland and the Northern Territory, and these involved relatively small numbers. Western Australia's gains, however, were well below those recorded in the previous decade when Rowland (1979, p. 38) identified a pattern of westward movement on a scale not achieved since the Kalgoorlie gold rush years.

7 The Northern Territory lost population only to Queensland, but the overall net gain recorded in the census was somewhat lower than in the late 1960s (Rowland 1979, p. 20).

8 The Australian Capital Territory recorded net gains of population by interstate migration only from the south-eastern mainland States, and lost heavily to Queensland. This is in contrast to the previous decade, in which the ACT gained heavily from most States during a period of rapid growth of the national capital.

The broad patterns of interstate migration recognized by Rowland (1979, p. 38) in his analysis of the 1966–71 period are still evident—i.e. of a general westward and northward net displacement of population. There are, however, some differences—the movement has become much more emphatically a northern one focusing upon Queensland and to a lesser extent the Northern Territory, with Western Australia assuming lesser significance. In addition, there has been a substantial reduction in the net gains to the

ACT, especially from New South Wales and Victoria; net losses from South Australia have been stepped up; and the long-standing northward movement from Tasmania is less evident.

Inter-regional patterns of migration

Population redistribution is frequently overlooked in considerations of future demand for services and resources. Projections often unrealistically assume that demand will remain frozen in its present locations. Future intra-State population redistribution and internal migration trends are extremely difficult to predict because of their sensitivity to changing economic and social conditions. With respect to the redistribution of population within Australia, the National Population Inquiry (1978, p. 111) concluded:

> There is little sign of factors that seem likely to lead to any *major* redistribution of population in the near future, or even for the rest of the century. Internal migration is made up of a series of flows and counterflows that tend essentially to keep the distribution system in equilibrium rather than change it.

Interpretation of this statement of course hinges on how one defines 'major'; however, even relatively small percentage redistributions of the total population are likely to have a much amplified impact on the total demand for particular services in particular localities.

In this section we will be focusing especially on the role of internal migration in the 'turnaround' of the long-standing tendency to concentration of the Australian population. This turnaround is the result of three demographic processes (NPI 1978, p. 64) among which redistribution of population from metropolitan to non-metropolitan places is only one. The other processes are:

1 People in non-metropolitan areas who in former years would have migrated to the large cities are showing a greater tendency to stay put (Jarvie 1984). Wright's (1982) case study of a non-metropolitan region in South Australia shows an increasing tendency toward local retention of school leavers. This affects population growth not only in that it reduces net migration loss but also it is likely to have a positive impact on natural increase.
2 The major component in the rapid growth of major Australian cities in the twenty-five years following World War II was not gains from the non-metropolitan sector but from massive net gains of overseas migrants. Burnley (1974, p. 101) estimated that more than half of the 1947–66 population growth in Sydney (55 per cent), Melbourne (59 per cent) and Adelaide (57 per cent), and a third of that in Brisbane (34 per cent), Perth (45 per cent), Hobart (32 per cent) and Canberra (36 per cent) was attributable to net migration gains of the overseas-born. The previous chapter, however, has shown that during the 1970s there was a considerable reduction in migration, so that even if all other things had remained equal the growth of metropolitan areas compared to non-metropolitan areas would have been reduced. Jarvie and Browett (1980) have shown how net migration gains from overseas in the major urban areas of Australia were greatly reduced in the decade 1966–76.

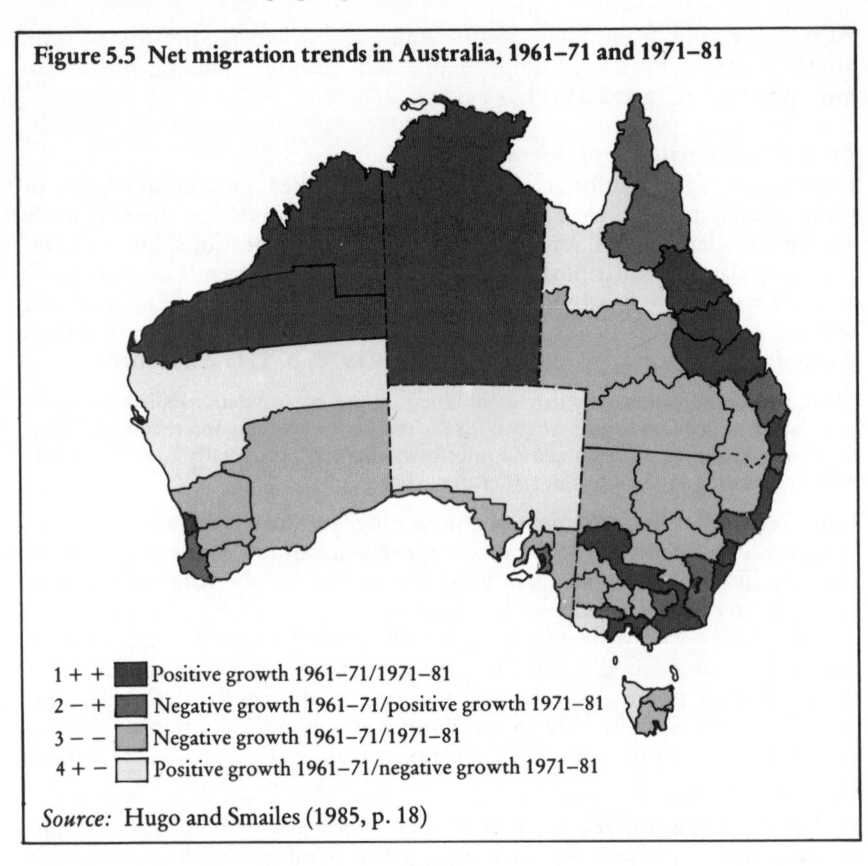

Figure 5.5 Net migration trends in Australia, 1961–71 and 1971–81

Source: Hugo and Smailes (1985, p. 18)

The overall pattern of regional net migration trends in Australia during the 1960s and 1970s is shown in Figure 5.5. Points to note are as follows:

1 Dominant among areas recording an overall net migration gain in both the 1961–71 and 1971–81 decades are the metropolitan centres—Perth, Adelaide, Hobart, Melbourne, Canberra, Sydney, Brisbane and Darwin (but it was pointed out earlier that in recent years these net gains in metropolitan areas have declined somewhat). Most striking, however, is the gain evident in the north-western quadrant of the continent, comprising the northern part of Western Australia and the Northern Territory: however, this is a little misleading, since although the area is a huge one the numbers involved are small. The third area with consistent net migration gains is in central coastal Queensland. There are several other pockets strung along the east coast which have also recorded net migration gains over the past two decades. Several of these adjoin the three largest Australian cities, and in these areas the net gains during the 1970s were much greater than those recorded in the 1960s. The other region recording net migration gains over the last twenty years was the Murray River valley in New South Wales and Victoria.

2 The second category on the map represents areas which experienced a 'turnaround' from net migration losses in the 1960s to gains between 1971 and 1981. Clearly this is confined to a few non-metropolitan regions along the eastern, south-eastern and south-western coasts. As with the areas of consistent net migration gain, several are in those areas near major metropolitan centres (on the margins of, and slightly beyond the commuting zones of those cities). In Victoria there were two inland regions that recorded net losses in the 1960s but net gains in the 1970s, around the growing regional centres of Ballarat and Albury-Wodonga.
3 The third category in Figure 5.5 includes a broad belt inland of the coastal net gains zone. This is an area of consistent net migration losses through both the 1960s and the 1970s, and covers almost the entire wheat-sheep agricultural zone of Australia. It should be noted that the net migration losses in this region were generally smaller during the 1970s than in the 1960s. This zone is particularly extensive in southern Queensland, western New South Wales, western Victoria and southern South Australia and Western Australia. No Tasmanian non-metropolitan district recorded net migration gains in the 1960s and the 1970s, and the eastern half of the island recorded consistent net migration losses throughout the 1960s and 1970s.
4 The final category, of a reversal from net migration gains in the 1960s to net migration losses in the 1970s, covers extensive areas, predominantly in the sparsely settled arid zone of central Western Australia, northern South Australia and central northern Queensland. In the latter area a major element has been the fortunes of Mount Isa, where the expansion of mining activity in the 1960s saw its population double from 13 358 in 1961 to 25 497 in 1971. Population growth based on expansion of mining activity is notoriously fragile, as fluctuations in world markets and/or exhaustion of local ore deposits can produce abrupt reversals—Australia's many ghost towns bear mute testimony to this. The downturn in activity at Mount Isa, for example, has seen its population decline to 24 390 in 1981. This volatility of mining-based population growth must be borne in mind in considering the recent population expansion across the north of Australia. The reversal in central Western Australia and the unincorporated area of South Australia was also partly associated with a decline in mining activity, but in the latter case it was predominantly due to the virtual closure of the Woomera-Maralinga defence research area during the 1970s after it grew rapidly during the 1960s. The reversal of net gains in western Tasmania was also associated with a downturn in mining activity. The south-west of Victoria was the only district recording this type of population change which was not in an arid and/or mining zone.

We will now turn to focus more closely on the most recent inter-censal period. The distribution of non-metropolitan local government areas which recorded net migration gains during the 1976–81 period is shown in Figure 5.6. Compared with the general pattern of net outmigration from most rural areas during the 1960s (except in a few areas such as resource frontiers, urban peripheries, etc.) net gains are relatively widespread throughout the continent.

Nevertheless, some spatial concentration of net migration gain areas is in evidence. These are particularly within closely settled areas adjoining the major urban centres, but also in some sparsely settled areas where among other things mining developments have initiated inmigration. This is especially so in northern Western Australia, the Northern Territory and parts of northern and western Queensland. There has been net migration gain in many coastal districts too, and in central Victoria and around major provincial centres.

When we aggregate net migration estimates for the various settlement zones, a number of interesting patterns are evident (Table 5.5 shows the results for Australia as a whole).

1 The closely settled coastal areas adjoining the major urban centres in New South Wales, Queensland and Western Australia grew most rapidly and in these areas 78 per cent of inter-censal population growth was attributable to net migration gain and only just over a fifth of the growth was caused by natural increase. The net migration gains were clearly most dramatic in New South Wales, where the total population in the zone grew by a quarter

Figure 5.6 Non-metropolitan local government areas recording net migration gains, 1976–81

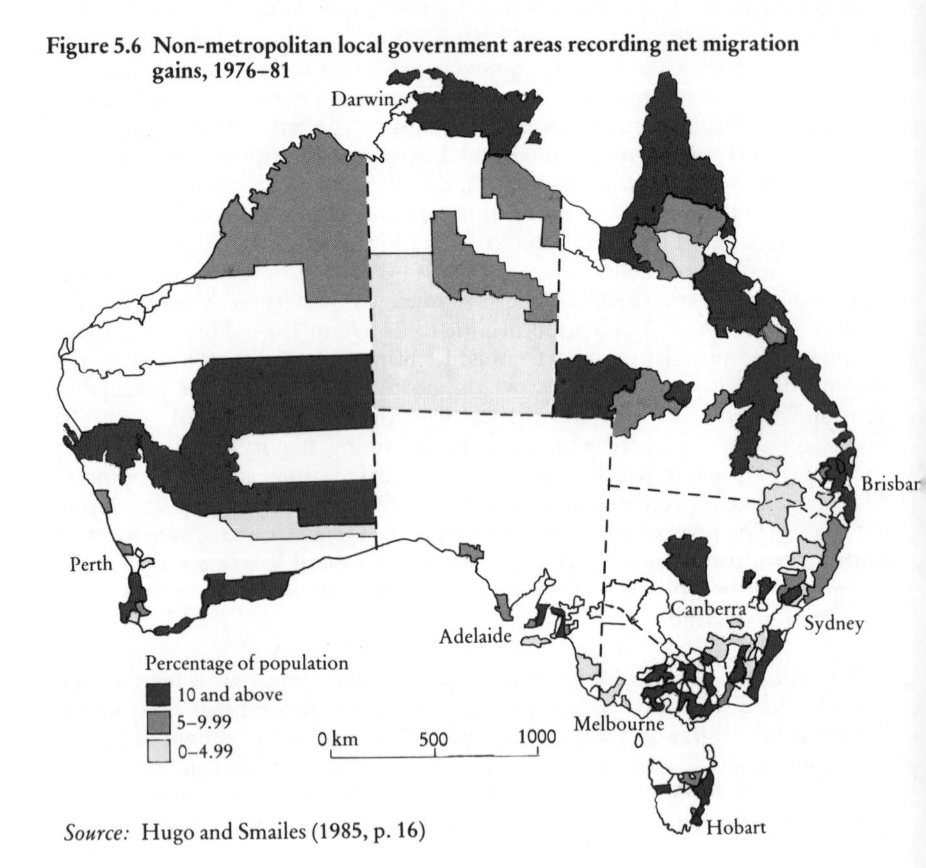

Source: Hugo and Smailes (1985, p. 16)

over the five-year period. This zone includes the areas favoured by 'rural retreaters' seeking more rustic alternatives to city living, as well as resorts and retirement centres. The growth of large regional centres in this zone was less spectacular but, in most cases, above national average growth rates.

2 In the major urban centres (IA) there was a net migration gain of around 3 per cent, contributing around half of the overall population growth. This was especially concentrated in Brisbane and Perth.

3 In peri-urban areas in the low-growth states of South Australia, Victoria and Tasmania, overall net migration gains amounted to only a quarter of the overall growth, but the contribution of natural increase to growth was higher in these zones than in major urban centres, suggesting a younger age structure associated with inmigration of young families. It should be noted that Victoria's peri-urban areas received significant net gains of migrants and South Australia's recorded net losses.

4 The moderately and sparsely settled zones both recorded overall net losses of migrants, although it is clear from Figure 5.6 that in both zones, especially the sparsely settled areas, there were localities recording gains.

Table 5.5 Population growth and its components by settlement zone, 1976–81

Settlement zone	Population increase as percentage of 1976 population	Natural increase as percentage of 1976 population	Net migration as percentage of 1976 population
IA (Closely settled, coastal, major urban areas and their immediate peripheries)	6.95	3.95	3.00
IB1 (Closely settled, coastal NSW, Qld, and WA excluding major urban areas)	21.1	4.64	16.4
IB2 (Closely settled, coastal Vic., SA and Tas., excluding major urban zones)	6.21	4.66	1.55
II (Moderately settled)	4.85	4.87	−1.88
III (Sparsely settled)	4.41	6.32	−2.22
Total	7.46	4.28	3.17

Source: calculated from data supplied by ABS

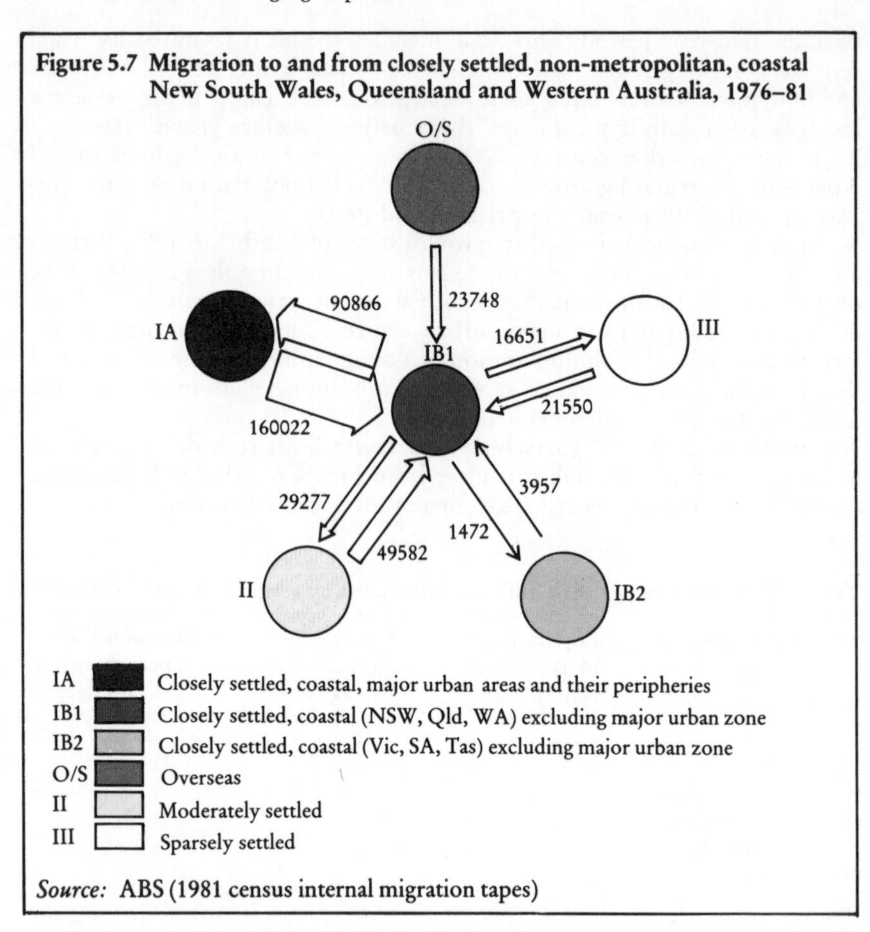

Figure 5.7 Migration to and from closely settled, non-metropolitan, coastal New South Wales, Queensland and Western Australia, 1976–81

Source: ABS (1981 census internal migration tapes)

The so-called 'turnaround' and the net migration gains associated with it are thus spatially concentrated in particular ecological zones and this should be borne in mind in analyses of causes and implications. This pattern of population deconcentration is as yet little studied and understood in Australia, but it is of obvious importance and significance to the planning of Australian urban and rural areas during the next decade.

The net migration patterns considered so far indicate the areas which have experienced population growth and decline due to migration, but do not give any indication of the origin of inmigrants and the destination of outmigrants. Here we will examine the exchanges of population between the major settlement zones over the 1976–81 period. Figure 5.7, using the zones defined by Goddard (1983), focuses on the IB1 zone which was shown above to account for the majority of non-metropolitan net migration gains and shows, among other things, the reciprocity of the migration relationship between zones—net migration indeed is only the tip of an iceberg, with the bulk of migration being hidden. It is clear from Figure 5.7 that the major

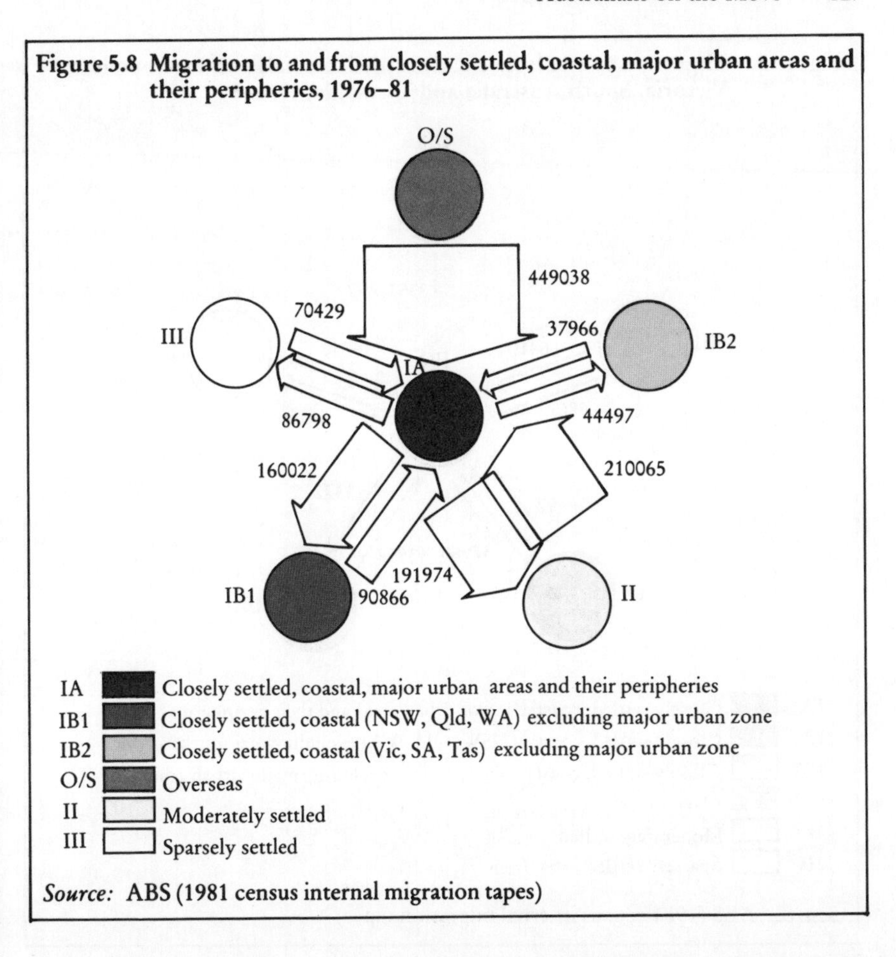

Figure 5.8 Migration to and from closely settled, coastal, major urban areas and their peripheries, 1976–81

Source: **ABS (1981 census internal migration tapes)**

source of inmigrants to the closely settled non-metropolitan coastal areas of New South Wales, Queensland and Western Australia is the major metropolitan areas of those States, which provide some 60 per cent of all inmigrants. It is important to discover the extent to which these migrants still go to work in the metropolitan area. In this context however, it should be noted that the IA zones were deliberately 'over bounded' beyond the built-up metropolitan area to include adjoining local government areas in which the bulk of extra-urban commuters would be found, so long-distance commuting from the IB zones is unlikely to be massive. It is also important to note the relative smallness of the inflow of persons from overseas to zone IB1, especially since against it we should put an unknown number of residents of the zone who have subsequently moved overseas.

The pattern of 1976–81 migration to and from the major urban areas and their peripheries (Figure 5.8) is very different. In contrast to zone IB1, where the growth was dominated by internal inmigration from other parts of Australia, in zone IA the dominant flow is from overseas. The diagram

Figure 5.9 Migration to and from closely settled, coastal, non-metropolitan Victoria, South Australia and Tasmania, 1976–81

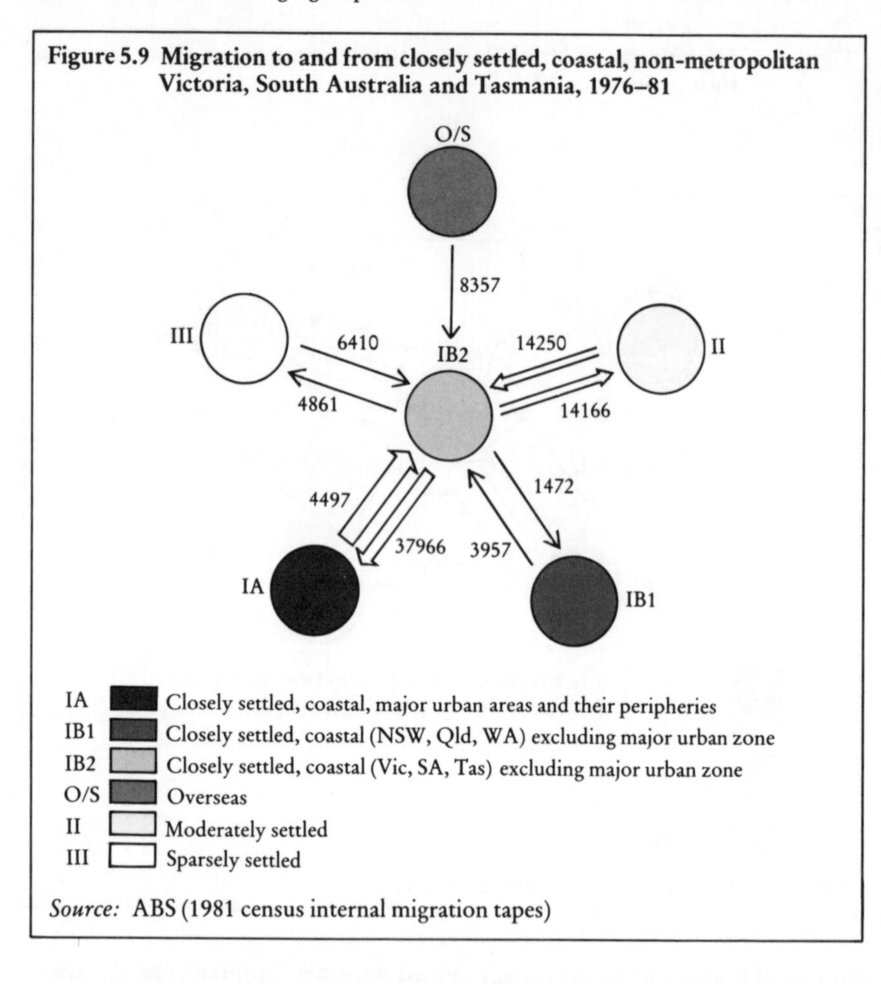

Source: ABS (1981 census internal migration tapes)

exaggerates the dominance of the inflow from overseas since we have no information on 1976 residents of the major cities who were overseas in 1981: nevertheless, it is clear that the major cities continue to be the main recipients of immigrants, as they have been in the entire post-war period. It also should be noted that the major metropolitan centres are continuing to receive more inmigrants from the moderately settled areas than they are sending outmigrants.

The dominance of the coastal areas of Queensland, New South Wales and Western Australia in non-metropolitan net migrant gains is underlined when we compare Figure 5.7 with Figure 5.9, which shows the migration exchange pattern in the equivalent areas in Victoria, South Australia and Tasmania. The inflow from the metropolitan centres is only one-quarter that in the IB1 zone, although again we should note that in both IB zones the dominant source of inmigrants is the capital cities—there is a significant net inflow from this source. It is apparent too that the net inflow from the sparsely and

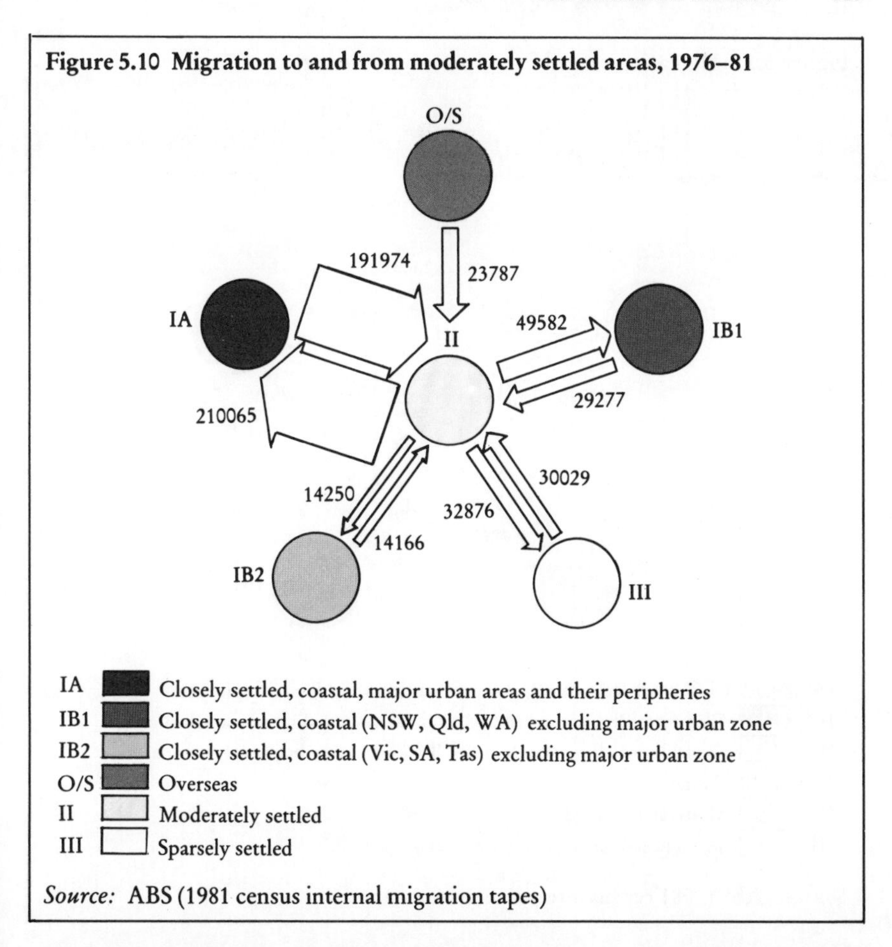

Figure 5.10 Migration to and from moderately settled areas, 1976–81

Source: ABS (1981 census internal migration tapes)

moderately settled agricultural zones to the IB2 zone are small in comparison to those received in the IB1 and IA zones.

The moderately settled zone sent more migrants to each other settlement zone than it received from those zones (Figure 5.10). However, the dominance of the linkages between this zone and the major urban areas is readily apparent. This general pattern is repeated on a smaller scale for the sparsely settled zone (Figure 5.11).

Space limitations prevent a more detailed consideration here of the patterns of migration and population change in non-metropolitan areas. These patterns are elaborated elsewhere (Hugo 1983d, 1984b) and at the time of writing were the subject of a major study based in the Geography Department at Monash University (McKay and Maher 1984, Maher and Goodman 1984, McKay 1984), so we shall proceed to a brief examination of net migration patterns within Australia's major cities before proceeding to consider the various explanations which have been put forward to explain the population 'turnaround'.

Figure 5.11 Migration to and from sparsely settled areas, 1976–81

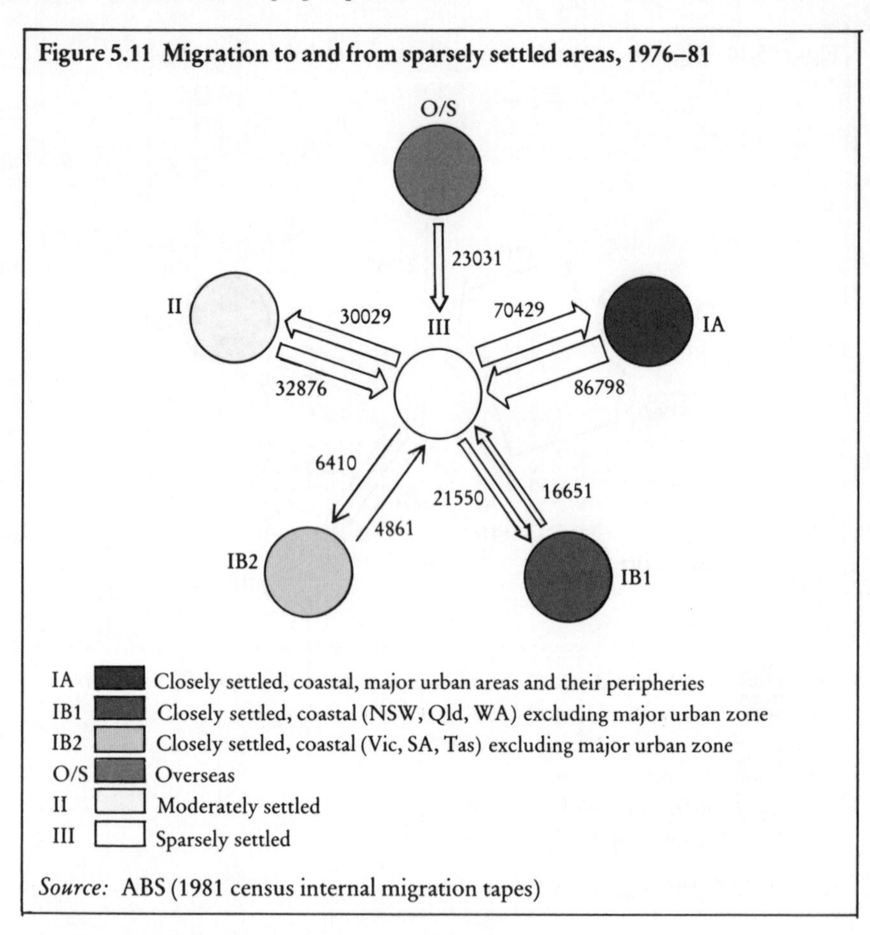

Source: ABS (1981 census internal migration tapes)

Intra-urban migration

The turnaround notwithstanding, a majority of Australians still live in the major capital cities, so the redistribution of population *within* those cities is of major importance to urban planners and policy makers. The typical post-war pattern has been one of spatial separation, with a roughly concentric pattern usually evident, with a ring of outer suburbs in which most new low-density residential development takes place experiencing sustained population growth. There is also a ring of middle suburbs which experienced growth as recently as the early 1970s but declined in 1976–81: these are predominantly areas which underwent massive growth in the 1950s and early 1960s, since these suburbs were at that time on the fringes of the built-up area and absorbed most of the post-war baby and immigration booms. Finally, areas which had a continuous pattern of population decline throughout much of the post-war period are particularly clustered in the central part of the metropolitan area. These inner suburbs have been built up for more than fifty years, and many of the original settlers have died and their children have moved out, while expansion of non-residential land use has continued apace. In some parts of the inner suburbs, however, there has been population growth associated with the process of 'gentrification'.

The most common residential moves in Australia are within the major cities. This accounts for some 57 per cent of all moves (Maher 1984, p. 5). As with the flows considered in the previous section, however, the bulk of the movement is compensated for by moves in the opposite direction, and net displacement due to migration is small in relation to the total volume of movement. Nevertheless, when one examines the patterns of net migration by local government area, there is an even sharper pattern of regionalization and spatial separation than was the case for patterns of population change. Areas of net migration gain tend to be clearly separated from the areas of net loss. The data suggest that the population growth effects of 'gentrification' have been somewhat exaggerated: few inner suburban local government areas recorded net migration gains during the 1976–81 inter-censal period. For example, Figure 5.12 shows net migration patterns in Melbourne, where in all the inner and most of the middle suburbs more people moved out than moved in between the censuses. The same applied in Adelaide, but in Sydney the central areas of North Sydney and Sydney both recorded small net gains as did the north coastal local government area of Manly. This may in fact be a harbinger of things to come in Australia's largest city since a 1981 ABS survey found that a greater number of people expressed a wish to move to the inner area from the outer areas than wished to move to the outer areas from the inner (Newman et al. 1984, p. 16). Moreover, in Brisbane where the local government areas which are artificially created for the census are much smaller than those in other metropolitan centres, a somewhat different pattern emerges, with some central areas recording net migration gains. Nevertheless, in spite of the considerable evidence of gentrification and a return to vogue of inner suburban living in Australia's largest cities this does not show out in a significant net inflow of population to such areas. Despite the increasing costs of commuting, the dominant pattern remains one of young couples entering the family formation stage moving to the outer suburbs. Indeed, as was shown in the previous section, many are going beyond the boundaries of the metropolitan area to settle down.

Intra-urban migration is clearly all-important in determining spatial differences in population growth within Australia's metropolitan areas. This form of migration differs greatly from inter-regional migration in the non-metropolitan sector in that it is generally less dependent on job search and job transfer and more on the urban housing market, life and career cycle changes, status considerations and local environment factors (Maher 1984). An ABS survey of housing intentions in South Australia (1980c) found that 39.8 per cent of 'dependency units' planned to move in the next decade and that the area which is likely to receive the largest proportionate gain of migrants is the environs of Adelaide. This suggests that the substantial migration of persons into the Outer Adelaide statistical division which occurred in the 1970s (Menzies and Bell 1980) appears likely to continue, the energy

Figure 5.12 Melbourne metropolitan area: net migration by local government area, 1976–81

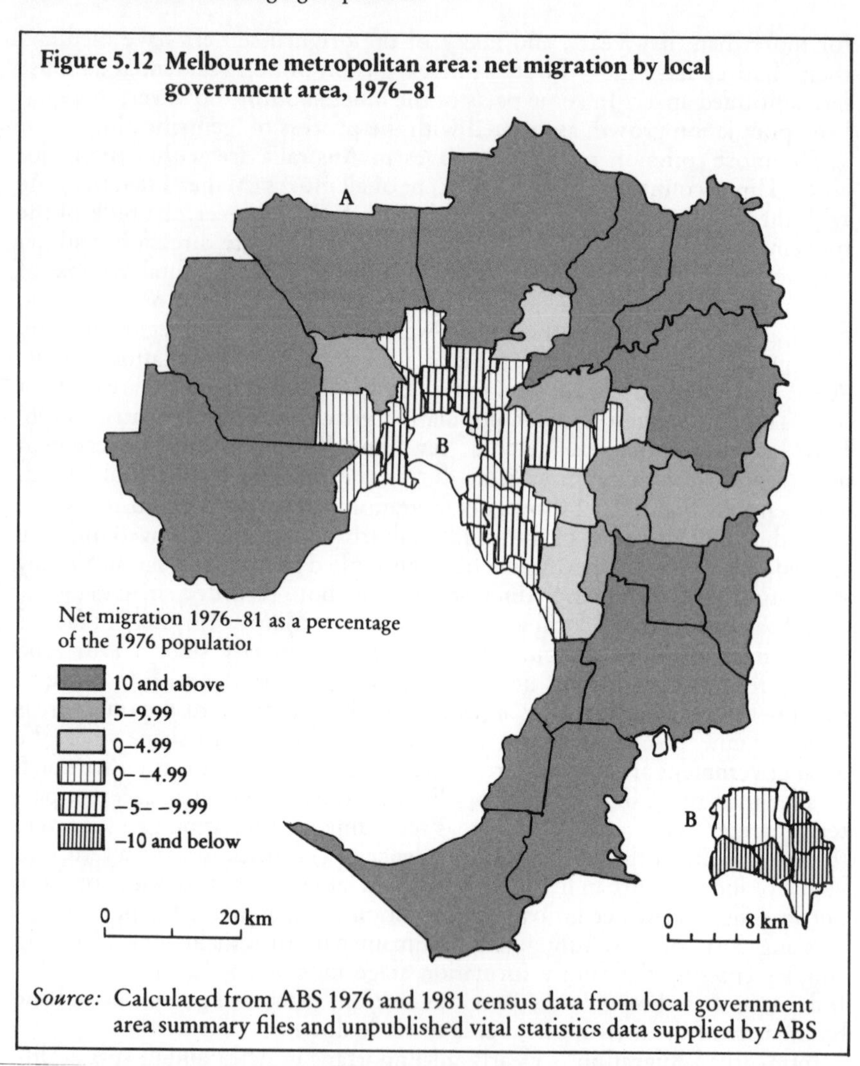

Source: Calculated from ABS 1976 and 1981 census data from local government area summary files and unpublished vital statistics data supplied by ABS

crisis notwithstanding. Outmigration from the established suburbs will remain high. A similar survey in Sydney statistical division (ABS 1978) found that 64 per cent of dependency units which planned a move intended to move into the outer suburbs.

EXPLAINING CHANGING INTERNAL MIGRATION PATTERNS

The causes of population movement are complex and all that can be attempted here is an outline of the main explanations which have been put forward. We will concentrate upon inter-regional movements rather than intra-urban flows which, as was indicated earlier, tend to be influenced by a number of different considerations. Maher (1984) has made a comprehensive study of population mobility within Australian cities which provides an excellent treatment of the magnitude, nature, composition, impact and causes of that movement.

Explaining interstate migration

Despite the growing significance of migrations which are little influenced by economic conditions, such as the movement of retirees to seaside, mountain or riverside areas, the changing pattern of longer-distance inter-regional and interstate migration is strongly related to variations between regions' economic-development. But there is debate as to whether inter-regional migration is employment-led or whether capital investment follows or accompanies changes in the distribution of population, or whether both processes occur. The processes of structural change and technological innovation which create employment in some sectors of the economy and destroy jobs in other sectors will impinge unequally upon different groups in society and upon different regions and local economies. Such changes have been occurring apace in Australia since the early 1960s and they are discussed in Chapter 9. All that will be attempted here is to show some of the major shifts in employment which occurred at the State level over the 1976–81 inter-censal period and to relate these changes to the patterns of interstate population redistribution examined earlier.

One aspect of the changing employment situation is indicated in Table 5.6. Altogether some 504 466 more Australians were employed in 1981 than in 1976; but this increase was very unevenly distributed between the States and Territories. The most striking figure is that for South Australia, where between the censuses there was an increase of a mere 578 jobs while the total population increased by 40 281 persons. Tasmania and Victoria were other States to receive less than their pro rata (by population) share of the number of new jobs created, although they fared somewhat better than South Australia. These were of course the three States which experienced the most significant net migration losses and the lowest relative gains of migrants from overseas. On the other hand, Queensland, Western Australia and the

Table 5.6 Net increases in number of employed persons, 1976–81

State	Net no. of jobs created	Percentage of Australian total	Percentage of national population
NSW	202 133	40.1	35.1
Vic.	96 409	19.1	26.5
Qld	115 270	22.8	15.7
SA	578	0.1	8.8
WA	61 192	12.1	8.7
Tas.	6 456	1.3	2.9
NT	12 809	2.5	0.8
ACT	9 631	1.9	1.5
Total	504 466	100	100

Source: ABS (1976 and 1981 censuses)

Table 5.7 Changes in employment in manufacturing and construction sectors in States and Territories, 1976–81

State	Manufacturing		Construction	
	Number	%	Number	%
NSW	−13 460	− 3.2	+14 289	+11.4
Vic.	− 9 964	− 2.6	−16 953	−15.3
Qld	+ 7 987	+ 6.9	− 8 568	−10.7
SA	− 9 550	− 8.4	−14 261	−32.3
WA	+ 2 647	+ 4.0	− 360	− 0.9
Tas.	− 1 546	− 5.6	− 1 629	−12.9
NT	+ 695	+36.7	− 914	−15.1
ACT	− 671	−15.5	− 3 152	−38.1
Total	−23 863	− 2.1	−31 575	− 7.4

Source: ABS (1976 and 1981 censuses)

Northern Territory, which together account for only one-quarter of the national population, attracted 37.4 per cent of the new jobs and, along with that, significant net interstate migration gains. Although New South Wales generated a disproportionately large share of the new jobs, it experienced a net migration loss as a result of interstate movements. However, this was more than counterbalanced by the fact that it absorbed more than 40 per cent of Australia's net gain from overseas migration over the 1976–81 period.

The sector which has borne the brunt of job loss associated with structural change in Australia during the last decade is manufacturing. In all, New South Wales, Victoria, South Australia, Tasmania and the ACT recorded a net reduction of 35 191 jobs in manufacturing, while Queensland, Western Australia and the Northern Territory gained 11 329 jobs. This represents a net loss of 2 per cent of manufacturing jobs, although in South Australia the loss was four times as high. The major net loss of jobs occurred in the construction sector, and this again was spread unevenly between States, with South Australia and the ACT losing a third of their construction workforce during the inter-censal period. In fact, only New South Wales expanded its labour force in construction during the inter-censal period (Table 5.7).

The main areas of employment growth were in tertiary activities of wholesale and retail trade, finance, public administration, community services, entertainment and recreation. In these areas there was a total net increase of 394 879 jobs between the censuses. More than a quarter of that net gain was in Western Australia, a quarter in New South Wales, with Victoria and Queensland having more than a fifth each. Hence, even in this sector the growth in the other States was very small. Similarly in the growth sectors of utilities, transport and communication, New South Wales and Queensland accounted for nearly two-thirds of the growth in jobs. There was also a 22 per cent net increase in mining employment, with most of it being in New South Wales, Western Australia and Queensland.

The examination of census employment data, especially at the gross scale

Table 5.8 Persons aged 15 years and over who moved interstate in year ended 30 June 1982 and their reasons for moving (percentage distribution)

Reason for in/ out migration	NSW In	NSW Out	Vic. In	Vic. Out	Qld In	SA Out	WA In	NT In	Aust.
Housing	13	13	12	13	10	16	19	8	12
Employment	40	38	38	41	44	44	38	54	42
Change in marital status	7	4	*	*	3	*	*	*	4
Retirement	*	4	*	*	6	*	*	*	3
Other	34	35	34	36	33	31	33	33	34
Unspecified	*	5	11	*	*	*	*	*	5

* = estimate with standard error of more than 35 per cent
Source: ABS (1984j, p. 18)

of analysis of the State or Territory, can do no more than point to some very broad tendencies. Nevertheless, there is clearly a close correspondence of employment and net migration patterns, indicating that structural economic change remains a primary force shaping the broad pattern of population movement to and from Australian States and Territories.

A recent ABS internal migration survey (ABS 1984j) showed that there were some distinct differences between the reasons given for intra-State and interstate moves. In the case of the former, 51 per cent gave 'housing' as their reason for moving, compared to only 12 per cent of interstate movers. This reflects the short distance and intra-urban nature of the bulk of intra-State movers. On the other hand, employment was the main reason given for interstate moves, accounting for 42 per cent of responses compared to 15 per cent for intra-State moves. There are some problems with the survey data—there is a high probability of sampling error, and the breakdown of reasons is a little cryptic with the catch-all 'other' category being quite large. However, the survey does indicate the relative importance of employment in interstate migration. Table 5.8 shows the dominance of employment in migration to the northern States and migration out of the south-eastern States. Retirement accounts for only 3 per cent of all moves and is represented in numbers with an acceptable standard error only among inmigrants to Queensland (6 per cent of total) and outmigrants from New South Wales (4 per cent of total). The retirement factor thus has approximately the same proportion as that reported by Long and Hansen (1979, p. 6) in the United States. However, the fact that a third of responses remain masked in the 'other' category prevents us from making an unequivocal judgement on the degree of employment bias in reasons for movement. Other findings of the internal migration survey (ABS 1984j) provide some evidence supporting the contention that the bulk of interstate movement is employment-related. For example, mobility was strongly concentrated in the working age groups, especially young adults in the early stages of their careers who can be expected to have a greater need (in that they are looking for their first job), and are perhaps less bound by home ownership and more ready to move. At the time of the survey the annual interstate mobility rate for Australia was 18 per 1000, but for persons aged 20–24 it was 37 per 1000 and for those aged 25–29, 27 per 1000. Moreover, mobility was especially high among the unemployed—in fact more than twice as high as for the population as a whole—above all, the young unemployed. Among the unemployed aged 20–24 years, 44.1 per cent of males and 52.9 per cent of females had changed their place of residence in the year prior to the survey.

Although interstate migration in Australia is dominated by members of the workforce, the ABS internal migration surveys have shown an upswing in movement of older people. There is no doubt that retirement migration has increased in scale in Australia, but much of this movement is intra-regional and certainly intra-State. This is being corroborated by new analyses at the local government area level of internal migration data from the 1981 census. Among long-distance retirement migration the outstanding pattern is a 'northward shift [which] is dominated by the loss of migrants from Sydney and Melbourne apparently to the coastal areas of southeast Queensland and northern N.S.W.' (Cook 1980, p. 10). However, retirement migration has only a limited impact on the overall interstate migration pattern. The migration of the aged is considered in more detail in the next chapter.

Long and Hansen (1979) have analysed stated reasons for interstate migration in the United States, and found that the predominant reasons were job transfers, taking a new job, looking for work or accompanying a person moving for one of those job-related reasons. However, they suggest that these reasons have declined in importance and that non-economic factors and quality of life considerations have assumed greater significance. The latter is only partly attributed to the growing proportion of retirees among interstate movers. Long and Hansen suggest (p. 28) that in the United States there is an 'enhanced locational freedom [which] implies a rise in the degree to which jobs follow people, as opposed to the somewhat more traditional process whereby the creation of jobs more clearly preceded the movement of individuals'. As yet, however, there is little evidence that non-economic factors are having anything other than a minor influence in shaping the pattern of interstate migration in Australia.

Explaining population deconcentration in Australia

A number of explanations have been suggested for the deconcentration in population distribution in Western countries during the 1970s and early 1980s. These are reviewed in detail elsewhere (e.g., Bell 1978; Jarvie 1981). Hugo and Smailes (1985, p. 12) have listed them in approximate order of increasing relevance to the Australian situation as follows:

1 The turnaround is only a temporary fluctuation in the general trend toward urban concentration in response to the economic recession of the 1970s.
2 It is a demographic effect of changes in the particular age and life cycle population mixes of metropolitan/non-metropolitan populations.

3 It is a result of successful public regional development and decentralization policies, particularly those promoting deconcentration of manufacturing industry from large cities.
4 It is an area-specific effect traceable to employment growth in particular, localized industries (e.g., mining, defence), in favoured non-metropolitan regions, rather than a general broad-scale phenomenon.
5 The turnaround is a result of the gradual emergence of scale diseconomies in large urban areas, which combined with growing social problems encourage people to leave urban areas.
6 Reduced 'distance friction' associated with new transport and communication technology has allowed a further rapid extension of urban commuting fields into widely dispersed but still metropolitan-focused economic networks.
7 There has been a basic change either in people's values and lifestyle preferences or in their ability to act on such preferences, in favour of residence in rural or small town environments and against large cities.
8 The turnaround is primarily a result of structural change in modern Western economies as the proportion of tertiary and quaternary employment increases relative to secondary employment, while the decline in primary employment has almost run its course.

Hugo and Smailes suggest that it is necessary to adopt an eclectic approach to explain recent changes in patterns of migration and regional population change in Australia, using elements of several of the hypotheses listed above. In particular, however, the last three explanations appear to gain some support from the Australian evidence and these will be considered briefly here.

The expanding urban fields approach

> postulates a scaled-up continuation of the same basic processes of suburbanisation and extension of metropolitan commuting hinterlands as occurred in the 1950s and 1960s, with the metropolis exerting a perhaps more tenuous but still dominant influence on the location of new employment opportunities and residential choices (Hugo and Smailes 1985, p. 12).

The fact that, as has been demonstrated above, much of the non-metropolitan population growth and net migration gain has been recorded in the IB1 and IB2 densely settled zones, must lend some support to this theory. There can be no doubt that the rapid development of transport and communication systems has greatly extended the distances over which businesses and people can maintain linkages with the city centre and greatly expanded their options for location. Nor can there be any question that much of the population growth in areas on the margins and immediately beyond the limit of daily commuting has led to the establishment of enterprises and households the location of which is still strongly influenced by proximity to the major centre (Hugo and Smailes 1985). Nevertheless, this technological factor is a 'facilitator' of the population growth in this zone rather than a fundamental explanation of it. Hence, even within a zone of 100 to 200 km around each major city it is likely that more fundamental causative processes are at work. Moreover, it is clear from the material

Table 5.9 Changing employment patterns in rural and urban areas, 1976–81

	Total persons employed			
	Major urban	Other urban	Bounded rural locality	Rural
1976	3 830 365	1 121 946	142 913	885 123
1981	4 074 588	1 298 271	147 748	765 307
Percentage change	6.38	15.72	3.38	11.7

Source: Hugo (1983d, p. 48)

presented earlier that there are many non-metropolitan areas experiencing the turnaround that are well beyond such a radius and for which this 'explanation' is ruled out.

There is considerable debate, especially in the United States, as to whether deconcentration of population is occurring due to the movement of employment-creating enterprises out of large cities and into smaller places, or whether it is a process led by people moving out for lifestyle considerations and the enterprises following them. Jarvie (1981) has argued forcefully on the basis of her analysis of the 1971–76 period in Australia that the process is predominantly 'employment-led'. Some support for this position can be gained through examination of changes in the employment characteristics of people residing in metropolitan, urban and rural areas between the 1976 and 1981 censuses. There was a greater increase in the number of employed people living in non-metropolitan locations (261 344) than in cities with more than 100 000 inhabitants (244 523), in spite of the fact that in 1976 two-thirds of all employed persons lived in large cities. Table 5.9 shows that there was a 15.7 per cent increase in employed persons in cities with 1000 to 99 999 inhabitants in 1981, compared to only 6.4 per cent in larger cities and 11.7 per cent in rural areas. From an examination of the changing mix of industry types providing employment in the metropolitan and non-metropolitan areas, we can establish what kind of jobs are being created and lost in those areas. Table 5.10, for example, shows changes between the 1976 and 1981 censuses with respect to employment in the urban and rural sections of Australia. The structural changes occurring in the economy as a whole are immediately evident in that although overall there was a 6.9 per cent increase in the total number of jobs there were declines of 6.2 per cent in agriculture, 2.1 per cent in manufacturing and 7.3 per cent in construction. The latter were offset by gains of 22.2 per cent in mining, 15.7 per cent in utilities and transport and 9.3 per cent in trade, finance, administration, retailing and services. However, the table shows some wide variations between the four urban and rural categories. These can be summarized as follows:

1 In cities of more than 100 000 population the following changes were of particular note: there was a net loss of 40 000 manufacturing jobs; there was a net loss of 28 000 jobs in the construction sector; there was an increase of 193 750 jobs in tertiary activity.

Table 5.10 Changes in employment patterns in urban/rural categories, 1976–81

		Total	Percentage			
			Major urban	Other urban	Bounded rural locality	Rural
Agriculture	1976 no. employed	404 188	0.5	3.7	11.7	47.9
	1981 no. employed	379 211	0.5	3.7	10.6	38.5
	Percentage change	−6.2				
Mining	1976 no. employed	72 594	0.5	3.4	4.4	1.2
	1981 no. employed	88 693	0.6	3.6	4.6	1.4
	Percentage change	+22.18				
Manufacturing	1976 no. employed	1 138 403	23.3	15.3	12.7	8.1
	1981 no. employed	1 114 321	21.4	14.2	11.7	8.3
	Percentage change	−2.12				
Construction	1976 no. employed	429 522	7.0	9.6	9.5	5.8
	1981 no. employed	398 045	6.0	8.2	6.5	5.7
	Percentage change	−7.33				
Electricity, gas, water, transport, storage, communication	1976 no. employed	499 567	8.9	10.2	10.2	4.4
	1981 no. employed	578 113	9.5	11.1	10.8	5.5
	Percentage change	+15.72				
Trade, finance, property, business services, public administration, defence, community services, recreation	1976 no. employed	2 845 257	53.2	50.9	43.3	25.5
	1981 no. employed	3 136 820	54.7	51.2	46.1	30.8
	Percentage change	+9.30				
Not classified or not stated	1976 no. employed	390 577	6.6	7.0	8.3	7.2
	1981 no. employed	482 305	7.3	8.0	9.6	9.8
	Percentage change	+23.49				
Total	1976 no. employed	5 780 056	100	100	100	100
	1981 no. employed	6 177 508	100	100	100	100
	Percentage change	+6.89	+4.25	+13.36	+3.33	+11.70

Source: ABS (censuses of 1976 and 1981)

2 In other urban areas there was growth in all employment categories except construction where there was a net loss of 3275 jobs; there was a net gain of 8000 mining jobs; the economy is increasingly dominated by tertiary activity, with an inter-censal increase of 80 428 jobs; there was a net gain of 26 551 jobs in transport and utilities.
3 In rural areas there was a net loss of 33 995 jobs in agriculture, so the revival of rural population growth occurred despite a continuation of the long-standing labour displacement from agriculture; the main increase was of some 67 000 jobs in the trade, finances and services sector.

Employment change data from the census are a little misleading in that they relate to the place of residence of the worker and not the location of the job, so that an important question remains as to the proportion of workers living in rural or other urban localities but commuting to jobs in major urban areas. Indeed, it is certain that in many of the non-metropolitan local government areas recording net migration gains and located in zones IB1 and IB2 there is an increasing blurring of the distinction between urban and rural populations. Similarly, an important research question is the extent to which tertiary-sector jobs in rural areas are providing services for the local population and hence catering to demand generated by the farms and manufacturing and mining population and the multiplier effect of retirement centre and resort developments. Little is known of the extent and degree of employment deconcentration which has occurred in Australia. In the United States Long and DeAre (1982, p. 1115) have identified several reasons for the trend toward employment deconcentration:

> strictly cost benefit calculations (lower taxes, land costs, and wage rates in less urban locations), manufacturing techniques that require large amounts of land, and simply changes in the basic nature of the economy (for example a shift from bulky output toward lightweight, high technology products that can be transported by truck or air rather than rail).

The extent to which similar forces are operating in Australia is not readily apparent.

Goddard (1983, p. 12–15) has analysed the changing patterns of employment in the settlement zones used earlier in our analysis of population growth and internal migration trends. He shows (Table 5.11) that between 1976 and 1981 employment growth in zone IB1, that experiencing the most rapid net migration gains and population growth, far outstripped that in zones IA, II and III. However, it must be borne in mind that the percentage of all workers employed in major urban areas declined only marginally between the 1976 and 1981 censuses from 70.6 to 70.3 per cent. Goddard also shows that in all zones there was a substantial decline in employment in agriculture and that the patterns of employment gain in the non-metropolitan zones heavily favour tertiary industry and tend to point towards a deconcentration of employment in Australia.

Another approach to explaining the turnaround is a behavioural one emphasizing changing patterns in people's residential preferences away from

Table 5.11 Employed population in various settlement zones, 1976 and 1981

Zone	1976 No.	1981 No.	Inter-censal change %
IA	4 082 140	4 414 261	8.2
IB1	359 147	434 878	21.1
IB2	175 892	190 995	8.6
II	937 716	989 873	5.6
III	225 195	252 116	12.0

Source: Goddard (1983, p. 14)

those dominated by job-related factors to a range of quality of life considerations. In Australia there is evidence of migrations to non-metropolitan areas which are increasingly less influenced by economic conditions and more by environmental and lifestyle considerations—the growing volume of movements of retirees (Murphy 1979a and b; Prinsley et al. 1979; Cook 1980; Wait 1979; Hugo, Rudd, Downie, Macarper, Shillabeer 1981), hobby farmers (McQuin 1978; Menzies and Bell 1981), long-distance commuters (Paterson et al. 1978) and people seeking alternative lifestyles (Lindblad 1976) all testify to this. While Jarvie (1984) rejects net migration of the aged as a significant element in the turnaround at the statistical division level for the 1971–76 period, there can be no doubt that the growth of the older population in non-metropolitan areas is having a significant impact in particular local areas (Hugo and Wood 1984). It has been shown that there is a strong positive correlation between the proportion of the population in non-metropolitan local government areas aged over 60 years and their growth rate between the 1976 and 1981 censuses. Moreover, there are growing net migration gains of the elderly in particular types of non-metropolitan ecological niches (Hugo and Wood 1984).

Case studies in non-metropolitan areas experiencing the turnaround also provide some support to the behavioural hypothesis: one study in rural South Australia (Smailes and Hugo 1985), for example, concludes that there is strong evidence of migration arising from a desire to improve lifestyles (this is not to deny, of course, that the bulk of inter-regional migration is strongly shaped by the availability of job opportunities). Nevertheless it would seem that no single hypothesis can be unequivocally pressed to explain inter-regional variations in population growth and net migration patterns. As is concluded elsewhere (Hugo and Smailes 1985, pp. 27–8),

> The structural change hypothesis on the turnaround is seen as providing the key motive force and affecting the largest and oldest and/or most specialised industrial cities adversely, reducing rural-metropolitan migration streams and increasing metropolitan migration to the larger and middle sized country centres in regions offering cost savings. The behavioural hypothesis, on the other hand, has favoured the open countryside and the smallest centres disproportionately, particularly in the more attractive and densely populated rural areas and especially within the expanding commuting fields of major metropolitan areas. These elements are much interconnected.

SOME CHARACTERISTICS OF INTERNAL MIGRANTS

The economic and social impact which migration has upon communities is partly a function of the relative volume of migration, but also of the extent to which migration causes net gains and losses of particular *types* of people. An examination of migration differentials at the 1981 census has been attempted elsewhere (Hugo 1984c) and there is only sufficient space here to mention a few of the more striking patterns which provide some helpful clues to the causes and impact of internal migration within Australia. Age selectivity is of particular significance since the pattern and level of demand for jobs, education, housing and services vary with age and stage of the life cycle. The pattern of age-selectivity of migration for the 1976–81 inter-censal period follows the typical pattern of Euro-American societies, with very high proportions of young adults moving (Figure 5.13). This period of peak mobility is associated with the stage of the life cycle where young people are leaving the parental home to establish separate households, are entering higher education and/or seeking employment and are very likely to receive regular transfers in employment. The smaller secondary peak among young dependent children suggests that some of this high mobility of young adults involves young families. From peak mobility in the mid- to late twenties there is a regular fall-off in the mobility rate, although even among the elderly (the least mobile group) a fifth moved house between the censuses.

While the pattern shown in Figure 5.13 holds generally throughout Australia, there are distinct inter-regional variations in the age-sex distribution of *net* migration gains and losses. Figure 5.14, for example, shows age-sex net migration profiles for three selected regions over the 1961–71 and 1971–81 periods. They are drawn from a more detailed analysis of regional growth

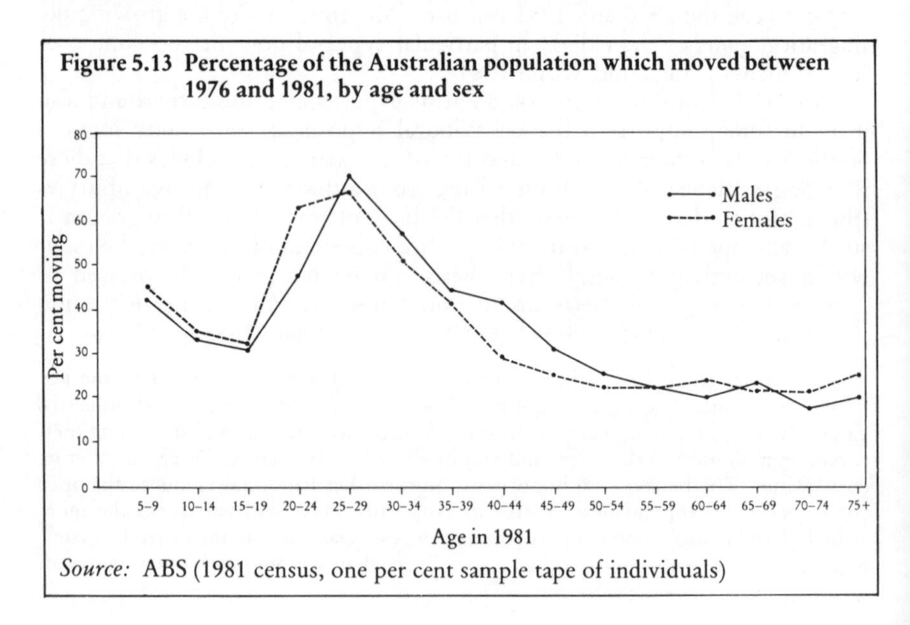

Figure 5.13 Percentage of the Australian population which moved between 1976 and 1981, by age and sex

Source: ABS (1981 census, one per cent sample tape of individuals)

Figure 5.14 Age–sex net migration profiles for three areas, 1961–71 and 1971–81

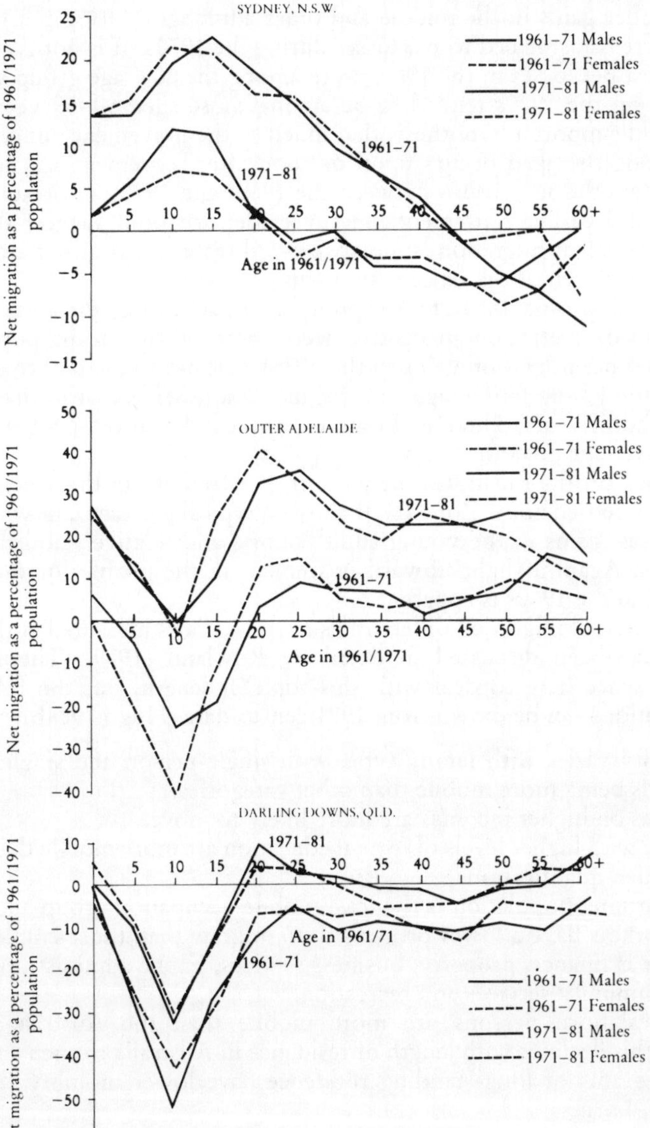

SYDNEY, N.S.W.

Net migration as a percentage of 1961/1971 population

Age in 1961/1971

1961–71 Males
1961–71 Females
1971–81 Males
1971–81 Females

OUTER ADELAIDE

Net migration as a percentage of 1961/1971 population

Age in 1961/1971

1961–71 Males
1961–71 Females
1971–81 Males
1971–81 Females

DARLING DOWNS, QLD.

Net migration as a percentage of 1961/1971 population

Age in 1961/1971

1961–71 Males
1961–71 Females
1971–81 Males
1971–81 Females

Source: Hugo (1984b)

trends and the role of migration in those trends (Hugo 1984b). The profile of Sydney shows an overall reduction in net migration gains during the 1970s (the 'turnaround' again). Net gains are concentrated heavily in the young adult age groups, much of which is attributable to overseas migration. The much smaller gains in the middle and older adult ages during the 1961–71 period were transformed to net losses during the 1970s. It is noticeable that the heaviest net losses in the 1960s were among the 60+ age group whereas those during the 1970s tended to be among those aged 50–59 years. This shift would support a hypothesis that much of the movement out of capital cities among the aged occurs upon or soon after retirement and has thus moved down the age groups between the 1960s and 1970s as a result of the trend toward earlier retirement. Survey evidence would suggest that this type of retirement migration is mostly toward resort areas or toward places where the children of the retirees are living.

The second profile illustrates the point made earlier, that the areas adjoining the major metropolitan centres were areas of significant population growth and net migration gains in the 1970s. Clearly the latter are concentrated in the young family age cohorts and to a lesser extent in the middle and later adult years. There is, however, a sharp dip in the profile for the school leaver age groups.

The third profile illustrates the pattern of selectivity in the wheat-sheep moderately settled zone (Zone II). It shows a typical pattern of heavy school leaver losses, gains in the young adult cohorts and relative stability in the other ages. Again a slight upward movement in the profile for the 1970s compared to the 1960s is apparent.

Other internal migration differentials in Australia as measured at the 1971 census have been discussed in detail by Rowland (1979). There is insufficient space here to deal with this topic at length, but the following generalizations can be drawn from 1981 census data (Hugo 1984b):

1 Mobility varies with family type, with single-person and single-parent households being more mobile than other categories.
2 Persons on higher incomes are more likely to move.
3 People with higher levels of formal education are more mobile than those without such qualifications.
4 The farming population is the least mobile occupation group and 'blue-collar' workers have a lower propensity to migrate than those employed in areas such as finance, property, business services, public administration, defence, community services and recreation.
5 Overseas-born persons are more mobile than the Australian-born, although this declines with length of residence in Australia to such an extent that immigrants of long-standing residence have lower mobility than the Australian-born.

SOME POLICY IMPLICATIONS

There is a tendency in much planning to assume either that the spatial distribution of demand for particular goods and services changes very slowly or

Figure 5.15 Geographical patterns of internal migration in Australia, 1976–81

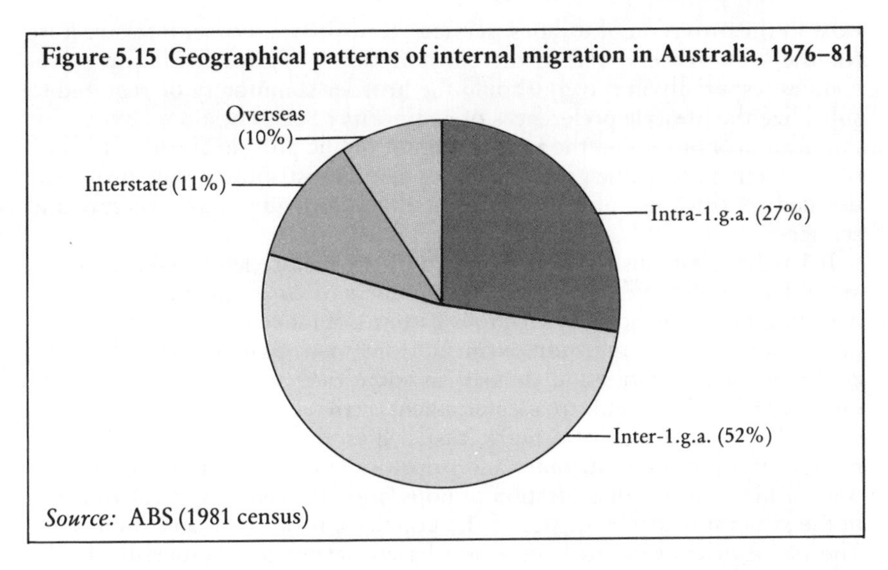

Source: ABS (1981 census)

that any changes will be in the direction of those observed in the recent past. This 'equilibrium' view is given apparent credence by the facts that although Australia has some of the highest levels of residential mobility in the world much of that movement occurs within communities (Figure 5.15), and that in most cases the ratio of net migration to total in- and outmigration tends to be small. Moreover, at the broader level, interstate shifts of population are not on the scale of those in, for example, the United States. Nevertheless it has been established in this chapter that the status quo of population distribution has been changing in new directions during the 1970s. This applies especially to the deconcentration of population. While the scale of the phenomenon should not be exaggerated, it does appear to have significance across a wide front of policy concerns. At the broadest level, any shift in population distribution will require responses from public and private sectors to provide infrastructure and services in areas of growth and to cope with problems of reduction in economic and social potential in the areas of decline. There can be no doubt that much of the existing structure for planning and providing services and infrastructure is strongly metropolitan and may need some restructuring if the existing tendencies toward population deconcentration gather pace.

Several important questions arise as to which groups are participating in the population deconcentration and what costs and benefits accrue to the community as a result of it. For example, it was shown earlier that the bulk of non-metropolitan net migration gains have been recorded in Zone IB1 which also contains a significant part of the nation's limited area of well-watered fertile agricultural land. The extent to which this 'rural renaissance' is taking prime land out of production should be addressed. Similarly the comparative community costs associated with non-metropolitan and metropolitan living need to be assessed. If differentials of significant dimensions exist in the provision of utilities, services, transport and other infrastructure for the 'new settlers' and in the consumption of scarce fossil energy resources (especially in travel), should the broader community be required to subsidize the lifestyle preferences of a minority? Such questions have major implications not only in the formulation of public policies aimed at guiding or redirecting economic growth and population distribution, but also in the detailed specification of priorities for publicly provided infrastructure and services.

It has been established here that two of the major elements in the turnaround are first, the retention of large numbers of young people who would have migrated to major cities if 1960s patterns of movement had been maintained, and second, the outmovement from metropolitan areas of young adults in their twenties and thirties (in some cases as conventional family units with children) and, to a lesser extent, retirees. As a group these 'new settlers', although seeking a more 'rustic' lifestyle, usually have a different pattern of aspirations, attitudes and priorities from the established populations. Indeed the deconcentration of population is producing a convergence in the structural characteristics of the populations of urban and rural areas. The new settlers tend to have urban-based occupations, especially in the tertiary and quaternary sectors, and have higher-than-average levels of formal education. In all, there is a reduction in differences between metropolitan and non-metropolitan districts in income, occupational status, educational attainment, household size and labour force participation (Zuiches and Brown 1978, p. 71). On the one hand, this produces major changes in the potential of communities so affected but also creates the possibility for conflict between the needs and aspirations of the existing population and those of the newcomers (Lumsdaine 1983).

Most of the present generation of public policy makers and planners in both the private and public sectors have spent their working lives in a period of overall rapid population growth, and the problems faced have been those posed by rapid growth of population. However, our experience of dealing with stability and decline has been extremely limited. This is true not only at a national level but also at the regional and local scale, and this chapter has demonstrated that while the renaissance of population growth in non-metropolitan Australia is substantial, it is spatially concentrated and there are many areas experiencing significant population decline. Whereas in the 1950s and 1960s population decline was confined largely to dry farming areas, especially in the wheat-sheep zone, there have been some significant changes in the 1970s. In particular, the structural changes in the Australian economy which have reduced employment in manufacturing have fallen disproportionately heavily upon regional cities which have been highly specialized in one or two such activities. Cities such as Wollongong, Mount Isa, Broken Hill and Whyalla, which grew rapidly in the early post-war years, are now faced by heavy losses of employment opportunities and population decline. Such declining communities present a whole range of seemingly intractable problems. The litany of problems of 'local shrinking pains' listed by Morrison (1979, p. 15) have their Australian equivalents:

problems of obsolescence, most notably in vacant and abandoned housing, underused schools, outmoded public facilities and an ageing inventory of stores, offices and factories. Selective outmigration also adds to a locality's burden of dependency by increasing the relative number of elderly and low income citizens remaining after the younger and more mobile people have left.

While Australia is not faced with a spectre of the 'rustbowl' of the industrialized north-eastern United States, we have been less successful in developing policies for declining regions than for growing regions.

In the United States the turnaround has resulted in a net outmigration of population from most of the largest cities. This has not occurred to a significant extent in Australia. A majority of Australians still live in a State capital and these continue to grow, with only Hobart experiencing an absolute decline between 1976 and 1981. Nevertheless, the rate of growth has slowed substantially and this, on the surface at least, would suggest that urban planners will be released from the pressure of keeping up with exponentially increasing demand, so that there is a chance for developing more equitable, efficient and innovative policies and programmes of service provision in such areas. Within these cities, redistribution of population is occurring and for the first time in the post-war period there is not a simple monotonic correlation between population growth rates and distance from the city centre—because of the gentrification trends in sections of the central and inner suburbs of all the major cities. Nevertheless, the bulk of growth is still in the outer suburbs, and it is in these areas, especially those of lower socio-economic status, that the greatest challenges in provision of housing infrastructure and services will be faced.

In Australia the issue of decentralization of economic activity and population growth away from the south-eastern metropolitan centres has been the subject of much rhetoric but little action. Pryor (1978) compiled an impressive list of State and Federal authorities and specific policy measures with which they have been charged to effect this decentralization. He concluded that the programmes have failed to redirect internal migration streams or to markedly improve non-metropolitan job opportunities. This was in spite of significant proportions of Sydney and Melbourne residents professing a preference for living outside those large cities (Pryor 1977). The 1981 census results would suggest that there is at least some evidence of a tendency toward the long hoped-for decentralization. It is unlikely, however, that the present deconcentration is a direct result of government policies suddenly becoming effective, and it remains for directed research to clearly identify the processes responsible for the change, measure the full social and economic impact of the changes and establish the likelihood or otherwise of a continuation of the deconcentration trends.

It is clear that the deconcentration of population and employment is part of, and a reflection of, wider social and economic processes occurring within Australian society, especially the major structural changes which are occurring in the economy. As yet an understanding of these changes is limited and more research is needed into the population distribution implications of those economic and social forces. Only then will we be able to assess whether the 'turnaround' demonstrated here is an initial phase of a new era of population redistribution or a temporary aberration in a longer-term spatial concentration of population.

CONCLUSION

In common with other developed nations, Australia underwent significant shifts in the patterns of population distribution and internal migration during the 1970s. The present chapter has summarized some of the major dimensions of these changes, although space limitations have prevented a detailed consideration of the patterns and their causes and consequences. Unfortunately, our understanding of the fundamental causes of internal migration in Australia is limited, as is that of its effects on the migrants themselves, the areas they leave behind and the communities in which they settle. However, such an understanding is a major prerequisite for all forms of spatial planning and further research in this neglected area is urgently needed.

6 The Greying of Australia: Changing Age Composition and its Implications

In 1982, 142 308 Australians celebrated their 60th birthday and 88 925 people aged 60 years or older died, representing an overall net gain of 53 383 persons to the older population of the nation. The 60+ population in Australia is currently growing at a rate of 2.5 per cent per annum, while the total population is growing at only 1.5 per cent. The older section of the population is the fastest-growing age group in our society and this clearly has many significant socio-economic implications. Nevertheless, the extent of ageing of the population has in fact been exaggerated and misinterpreted in some quarters and it is important to clarify the demographic dimensions of the phenomenon—and such a clarification is one of the aims of this chapter.

While the 'greying' of Australia has gained a great deal of recent attention from policy makers and the public generally, there are other shifts occurring within Australia's age structure during the 1980s which also are of significance for planning. In this chapter these changes will be outlined and explained. The level of demand and need for most goods, services and infrastructure among individuals tends to vary with their age, so that shifts in the age structure changes at local, regional and national levels are basic to planning in both the private and public sectors.

AGEING IN AUSTRALIA IN WORLD PERSPECTIVE

In 1950 there were 200 million persons in the world aged 60 years and over, by 1980 this had nearly doubled to 375 million and the United Nations projects an increase to over 590 million in the year 2000 and to over 1.1 billion by 2025—an increase of 224 per cent over 1975 (Salas 1982, p. 4). The distribution of the world's older population aged 65 years and over between developed and developing nations in 1980 was approximately equal (Myers 1982, p. 16). However, in developing countries it is expected to increase by 77 per cent in the last two decades of this century compared to 30 per cent in developed countries. While the number and proportion of aged persons in Australia are increasing, Australia's population, as Rowland (1982c, p. 764) states, is transitional between the demographically 'young' populations of developing regions such as South Asia where only 3 per cent of the population is aged and the 'old' populations of Europe where the aged population represents 14 per cent of the population. Figure 6.1 shows that compared to

Figure 6.1 Percentage of the population aged 65+, Australia and selected countries 1941–80

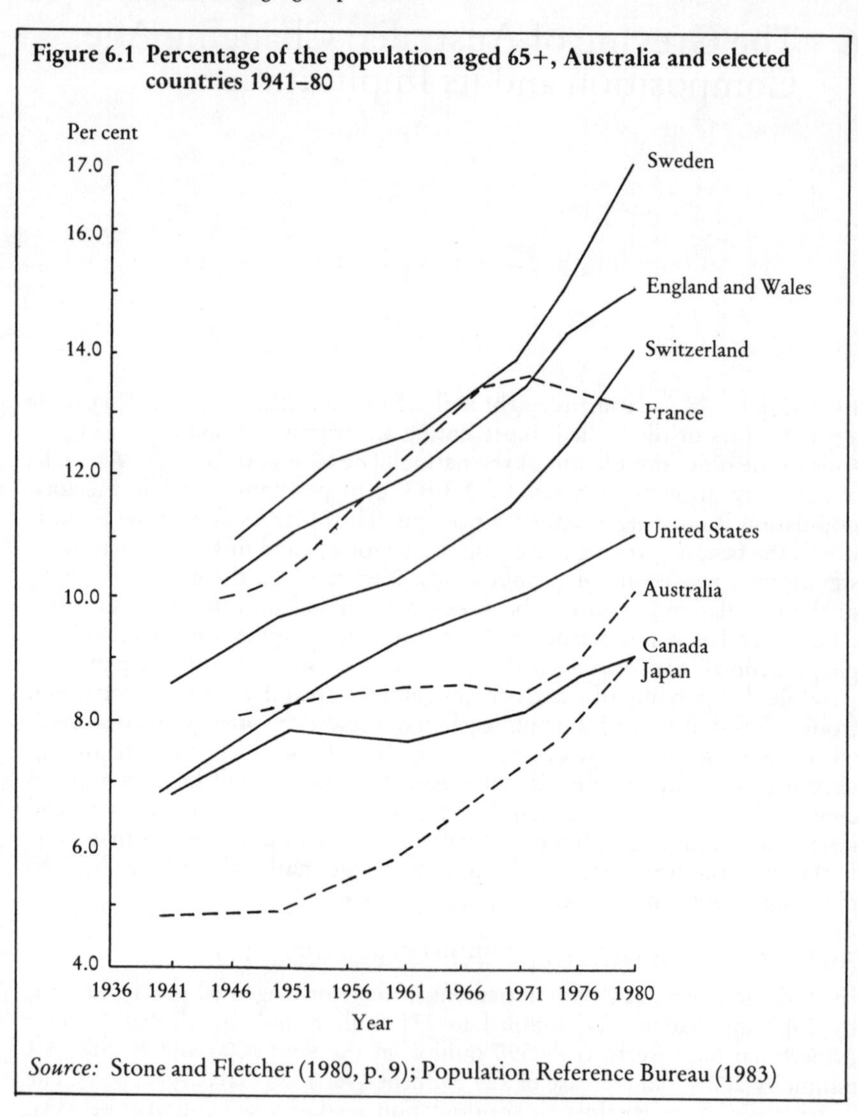

Source: Stone and Fletcher (1980, p. 9); Population Reference Bureau (1983)

most European countries Australia still has a relatively young population similar to that of the United States and Canada. However, in recent years the rate of increase in the population aged 65 years and over has been steeper in Australia than in North America although less rapid than in Japan.

THE CHANGING AGE COMPOSITION OF THE AUSTRALIAN POPULATION

The age structure of a population is a critical factor influencing population growth. In fact, the nature and significance of past and impending demo-

Figure 6.2 Age structure of the Australian population, 1961, 1981 and 2001

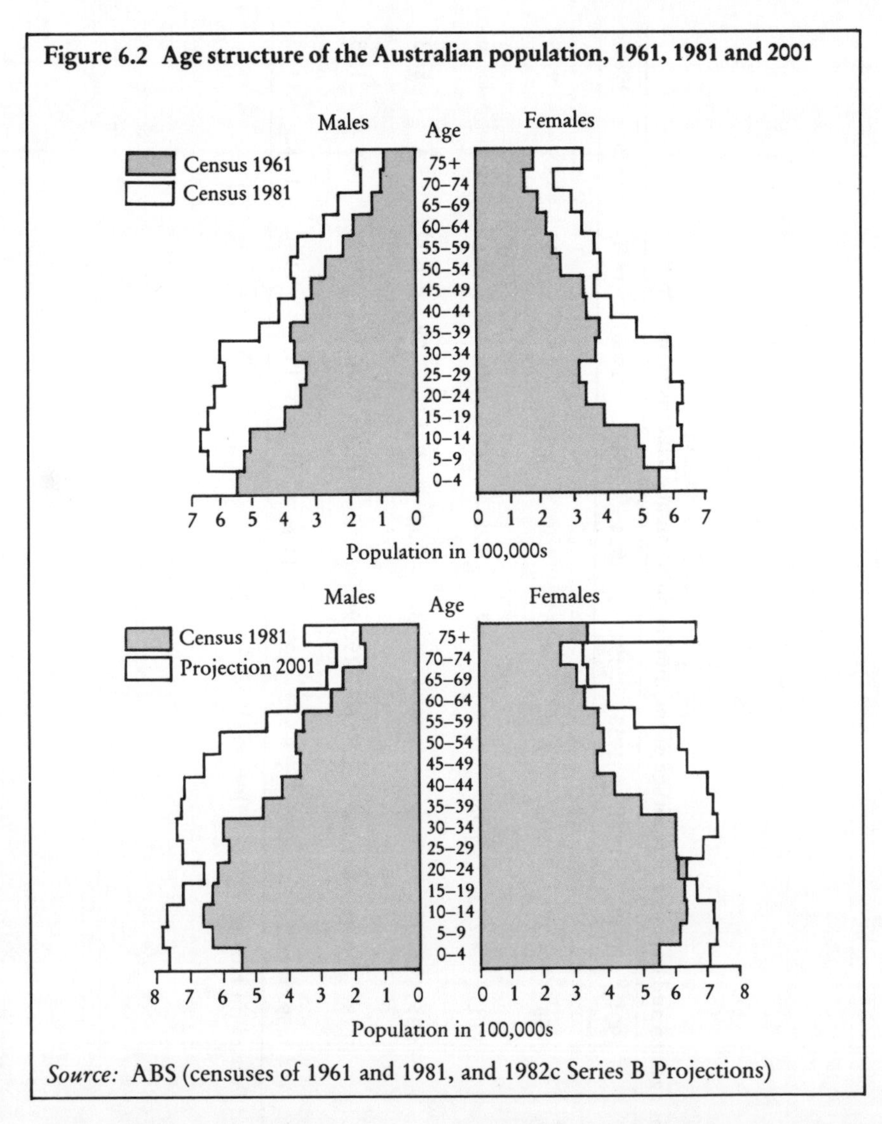

Source: ABS (censuses of 1961 and 1981, and 1982c Series B Projections)

graphic change in a region can be traced from the age profile of its present population. Take, for example, the age pyramids for Australia in 1961, 1981 and 2001 shown in Figure 6.2. It will be noticed that the profiles do not follow an even pyramidal shape and that there are several bulges in them reflecting past fluctuations in fertility and migration. For example, the low fertility and zero net migration from overseas of the Great Depression years are evident in the relatively low proportion of persons in their twenties in 1961 and in the early forties age groups in 1981. Due to such unevenness in age pyramids, different age groups will grow at different rates over time. Persons born in the post-war baby boom years (1947–61) have formed such

Table 6.1 Persons aged 65 and over as a percentage of the total population at each census since 1901

	1901	1911	1921	1933	1947	1954	1961	1966	1971	1976	1981
Persons 65 and over to total persons	3.98	4.27	4.43	6.48	8.05	8.30	8.51	8.54	8.35	8.9	9.75
Females 65 and over to total females	3.61	4.20	4.38	6.59	8.67	9.25	9.82	10.01	9.75	10.3	11.26
Males 65 and over to total males	4.31	4.34	4.48	6.38	7.43	7.37	7.23	7.09	6.97	7.4	8.23
Persons 65 and over to total workforce	9.29	9.91	10.46	15.66	19.09	20.15	21.17	20.31	19.98	19.9	21.75
Persons 65 and over to persons 15–64	6.59	6.72	6.92	9.81	12.03	13.14	13.89	13.75	13.40	13.8	14.93

Source: Pollard and Pollard (in Howe 1981, p. 14); ABS (1982b, p.35)

a bulge that their impact can be seen in Figure 6.2 progressively moving up the age pyramid from birth to maturity. In the process they have firstly overcrowded maternity hospitals, then primary schools, then secondary schools and tertiary institutions, then the job market, then the housing market and eventually they will place a strain on pensions, old age homes, cemetery space, etc. Similarly, the hollow developing at the base of the age pyramid in 1981 has consequences which are equally inevitable in terms of an absolute reduction in demand levels as it follows the bulge of persons born between 1946 and 1971. The inevitability and unavoidability of such a pattern must be stressed. The young adults of the late 1980s and early 1990s have already been born.

It will be noted in Figure 6.2 that in the 1981 age pyramid there is a 'bulge' which is on the verge of entering the older age groups. This is a result of not only high Australian fertility in the early twentieth century, but also the swelling of the size of these birth cohorts by the influx of large numbers of young adult overseas-born migrants in the two decades following World War II. It is this group which is primarily causing the current much publicized increase in the population aged 65 years and over. Between 1971 and 1981 the number of Australians in this age group increased by a third to 1 455 234 and from 8.3 to 9.8 per cent of the total population. In fact, as Table 6.1 shows, the Australian population has been steadily ageing throughout the present century. In 1901 only 3.98 per cent of the total population was aged 65 years or over. By 1947 this proportion had almost doubled and the total number of aged persons was 504 900. Since then, however, there has been a 141 per cent increase in the number of Australians aged 65 years and over.

Figure 6.3 Projected population growth in broad age groups, 1982–2021

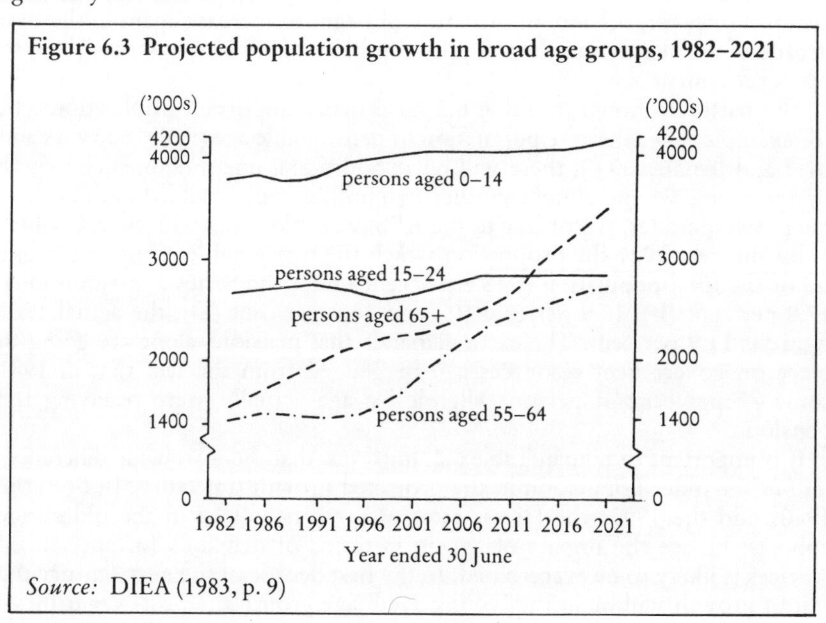

Source: DIEA (1983, p. 9)

Table 6.2 Projected numbers of persons aged 60+ in Australia, 1981–2001

Age group	Population ('000s) 1981	1991	2001	2011	Percentage increase 1981–91	1991–2001	2001–2011
60–64	613.9	718.8	768.2	1 145.2	17.1	6.9	49.1
65–69	535.8	654.5	629.8	853.0	22.2	–3.8	35.4
70–74	401.2	502.9	590.6	636.2	25.3	17.4	7.7
75–79	261.1	384.4	475.5	463.2	47.2	23.7	–2.6
80–84	154.6	234.1	302.4	359.4	51.4	29.2	18.9
85+	102.5	162.5	256.8	348.1	58.5	58.0	35.6
65+	1 455.3	1 938.4	2 255.3	2 659.9	33.2	16.4	17.9
Total pop.	14 926.8	17 008.6	18 916.7	20 557.1	14.0	11.2	8.7

Note: These are the Series A–B projections (see Chapter 1) which assume net immigration gain of 75 000 persons annually and an improvement in mortality
Source: ABS (1982c, pp. 27–8)

ABS projections suggest that by the year 2001 there could be an additional 858 466 aged persons and by 2021 the aged population could number 3 678 000 or 14.9 per cent of the population (ABS 1982c). It is clear from Figure 6.3 that during the 1980s the 65+ population will be the fastest-growing segment in the total population, expanding at double the rate for the total population. The growth rate of the 65+ group will halve in the 1990s (but will still be significantly higher than that for the total population), as the smaller cohorts born in the 1930s and early 1940s enter the older age group. However, the rate of growth will begin to increase again in the first decade of the next century as the post-war baby boom birth cohorts begin to reach retirement age.

The patterns shown in Table 6.2 have many important implications. If, for example, one takes the population of pensionable age (males 65 years and over and females 60+), there will be an additional one million such people by the year 2001 and almost another two million will be added in the subsequent two decades. According to the ABS projections introduced in Chapter 1, by the year 2021 the proportion which the pensionable group will make up of the total population is 18.8 per cent under the Series A assumptions, 17.8 per cent (B), 17.9 per cent (C) and 16.9 per cent (D); the actual 1981 figure is 11.9 per cent. The extra demands that pensions alone are going to place on government resources can be gauged from the fact that in 1981 some 77 per cent of persons eligible by age actually were receiving the pension.

It is important to note in Table 6.2, however, that there are wide differences *within* the older population in the projected growth trajectory. In both the 1980s and the 1990s the fastest rates of growth will be in the oldest age cohorts. Hence the impact of ageing in terms of demands for specialized services is likely to be exacerbated. In the first decade of the next century the fastest growth will be in the 'young aged' age group (the post-war babies);

however, growth of the oldest age group will still be very high. The rapid growth of the 'old-old' group especially in the 1980s should be stressed—the 75+ population will more than double between 1981 and 2001! Some of the effects of such a growth of the oldest age groups are already being seen in the United States. In June 1983 the US Bureau of Census announced that the nation had more than 32 000 people aged 100 years or more. It is no longer uncommon in the United States to have two generations in a family receiving age pensions.

The fact that it is the oldest segment of the aged population that is growing fastest should be stressed—the age structure of those over 65 is altering and in itself is ageing. In 1901, 75 per cent of those over 65 were aged between 65 and 74 and only 10 per cent were more than 80 (Graycar 1981, p. 282). By 1981 the proportion of those over 65 and under 75 had declined to 64.4 per cent while the proportion 80 and over had increased to 17.7 per cent. These differences in the age structure of the elderly population will continue to increase over the next forty years. In the last two decades of this century the fastest growth rates will be in the oldest age groups such that by 2001 the proportion of the aged population 80 years and over will have increased to over 24 per cent.

The ageing of the population is differentiated only not by age but also by sex. Although the proportion of the aged has increased from nearly 4 to 10 per cent over the last eighty years, the rate of increase for females has been greater than for males and more consistent. The proportion of the male population aged 65 and over fell slightly at every census from 1947 to 1971. In comparison the proportion of the female population aged 65 and over rose continuously from 3.61 per cent in 1901 to 11.26 per cent in 1981. By the year 2001 the proportion of the male population aged 65 and over could increase to 9.6 per cent while for females the proportion could be as high as 13.6 per cent (ABS 1982c). Hence in each age grouping of the 65+ population, the percentage of women increases with age. While 54 per cent of those aged 65–69 in 1983 were women, over 73 per cent of those over 85 were women.

THE DEPENDENCY DEBATE

One of the major issues or areas of concern as the population ages is the changing 'balance' between various age groups (Figure 6.4). Much attention has been focused upon the so-called 'dependency ratio'—defined as the ratio of the population under 15 and 65 years and older to those between the ages of 15 and 64. It has been feared that over the next twenty to thirty years the economically active age groups (generally taken as those aged 15–64) will not be able to supply a large enough tax base to support the dependent age groups, especially the elderly. Ageing, however, does not mean the total burden of dependency is likely to increase. In fact, Table 6.3 shows that up to 2011 the dependency ratio will undergo little overall change and in fact the proportion of the population of working age will rise and not decrease. For example in 1901 there were 64.5 people under 15 or over 65 for every 100 in the

Table 6.3 Actual and projected dependency ratios for Australia, 1978–2011

	No. of persons per 100 aged 15–64				
	1978	**1983**	**1991**	**2001**	**2011**
Total dependency ratio (less than 15, more than 65)	55	52	51	50	48
Aged dependency ratio (65+)	14	15	17	18	19
Young dependency ratio (<15)	41	37	34	32	29

Source: ABS (Series A Projections 1982c, 1982b)

Figure 6.4 Projected distribution of population among broad age groups, 1982–2021

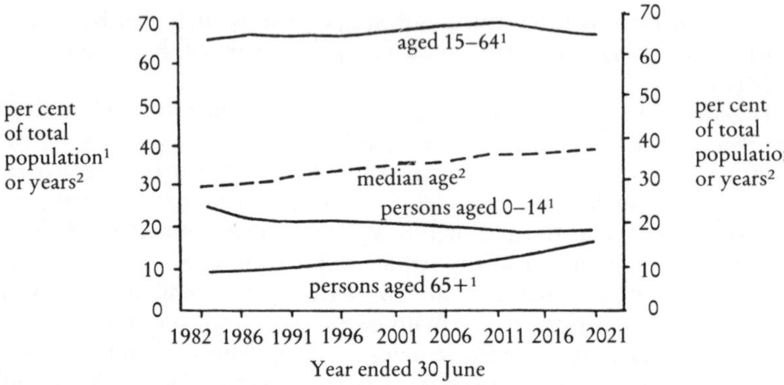

per cent of total population[1] or years[2]

70 60 50 40 30 20 10 0

aged 15–64[1]

median age[2]

persons aged 0–14[1]

persons aged 65+[1]

1982 1986 1991 1996 2001 2006 2011 2016 2021

Year ended 30 June

Source: DIEA (1983, p. 10)

'working age' groups. By 1981 this had fallen to 52.9 and ABS projections suggest that it will continue to fall over the next twenty years (Table 6.3). However, it is also evident that there will be a gradual shift away from a dependency ratio heavily skewed in favour of children. Over the next thirty years aged dependants will be far more numerous relative to young dependants. Some have interpreted this to mean that increased expenditure for the elderly can be offset by lower public costs for educating and maintaining the young. However, it has been estimated that Australian government spending is 2.3 times greater on the aged than on young people (Dixon and Crompton 1983, p. 6). It should be borne in mind, as Betts (in Birrell et al. 1984, p. 64) points out, that such accounting procedures are biased since while the greater part of costs of supporting the elderly such as pensions, etc., show up in the government ledger, the costs of bringing up children are borne predominantly by parents, especially by women. Thus, for the government the problem is that while parents share the major economic burdens of their

Table 6.4 Changes in the participation rates of the older population in the workforce, 1969–84

Age group	Percentage participation (males and females) 1969	1976	1978	1982	1984	Percentage change 1969–84
55–59	59.6	59.3	57.8	52.6	52.5	–11.9
60–64	46.1	40.8	35.3	28.1	27.3	–40.8
65+	11.8	8.8	6.8	5.3	4.6	–59.3

Source: ABS (labour force surveys)

dependent children with government, the elderly are largely supported through government expenditures. Hence, a shift in the age distribution of dependants from the young to the old in itself is going to place a great strain on the tax base.

The difficulties of increased aged dependency are being exacerbated by dramatic reductions in workforce participation in the 60–64 age group, which Table 6.4 shows to be well over 40 per cent over the last fifteen years. Moreover, the table shows significant reductions in the 55–59 age group. Early retirement occurs for a number of reasons but it has been advanced by the fact that a high proportion of men ageing into their 60s in recent years are returned soldiers from World War II and hence eligible for full pension benefits at age 60 rather than 65 as is the case for other males. This trend of course affects the size of the tax base available to the government and in the United States such patterns are causing great concern (e.g. see Clark and Spengler 1980). Davis (in Lipset 1980) points out the paradox that United States society still encourages people to retire early even though this forces fewer workers to support more non-workers and many people desire to work past the present retirement age. Some United States commentators argue that the trend toward early retirement must be reversed and the retirement age raised if retiree benefits are to be continued at anywhere near the levels needed for retirees to live on. Indeed the mandatory retirement age has been raised to age 70. It should be noted, though, that this whole argument depends on the continued validity of the present system of redistribution of economic surplus in the face of automation and structural unemployment.

It can be seen in Figure 6.5 that it is in the older age groups that the most dramatic increases in numbers have occurred in recent years, while there has been a decline in the numbers of children aged less than five years, and overall stability in the dependent-child age groups (the implications of this were referred to in Chapter 3). The other major change apparent in Figure 6.5 is in the 15–24, 25–34 and 35–44 age groups which show the impact of the post-war baby boom cohorts, a phenomenon which has been extensively studied in Australia (e.g., NPI 1975; Rowland 1983; McDonald 1984). Before proceeding to an examination of Australia's aged population I will briefly discuss some implications of the maturing of the baby boom generation.

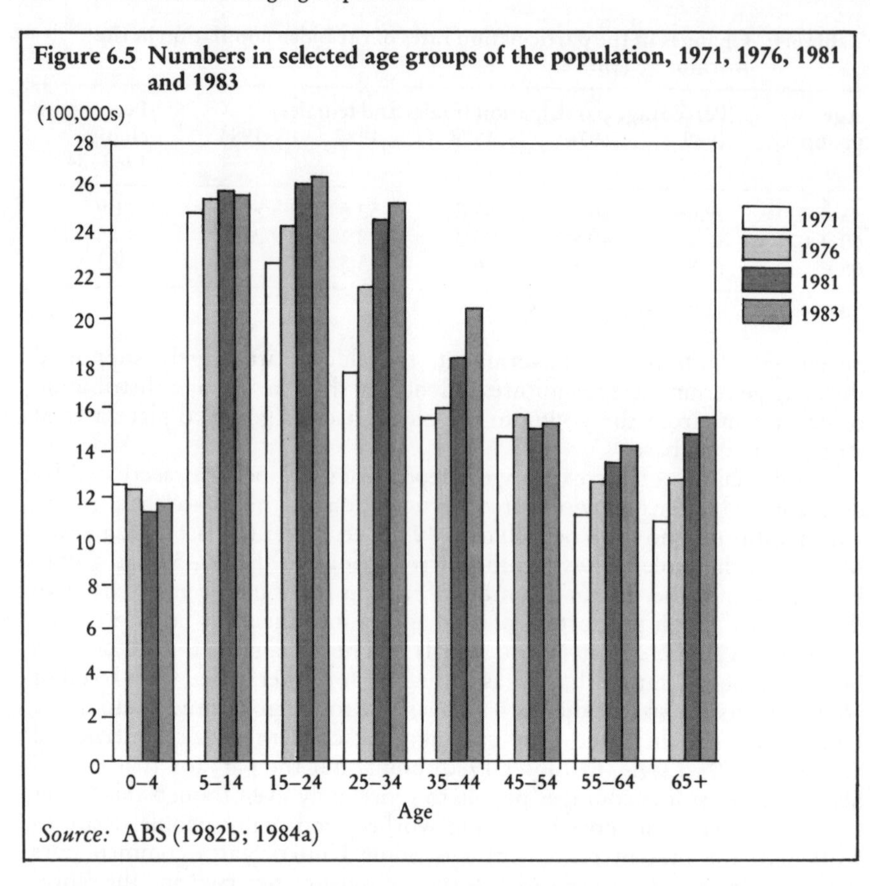

Figure 6.5 Numbers in selected age groups of the population, 1971, 1976, 1981 and 1983

Source: ABS (1982b; 1984a)

THE MATURING OF THE BABY BOOM GENERATION

No generation in Australia has caused more surprises and more problems for educational planners than the baby boom generation, born between 1946 and 1961. Formerly their progress through childhood created unprecedented demands for school accommodation. Now their debut as adult members of society has reversed this trend: their tardiness in child bearing as well as their alacrity in departing from many of the places of their upbringing, has often left schools without pupils.

This lament (Rowland 1983, p. 104) on behalf of the educational planners could be echoed in equally heartfelt fashion by planners in a wide array of areas; the 'swollen generation' has also placed stresses of one kind or another on tertiary education, various types of housing, social welfare services, health services and the job market. Their passage into adulthood has been blamed for societal ills as disparate as high inflation, an explosive increase in crime, skyrocketing unemployment and escalating costs of accommodation. The baby boomers are likened to a pig passing through a python—it seems explosive because the cohorts immediately preceding it (those born in the Depression and World War II years) and following it (born in the 'baby bust' of the 1970s) are comparatively small. Their impact will continue to be felt not only as they pass into successively older age groups which have demands for new and different sorts of services, but also through the echo effects created by their children and grandchildren.

In the United States Taeuber (1979, p. 9) has suggested that the size of the baby boom generation is such that it dominates the total population and strongly influences the general character of that total population—'It created a child-centred society—which is becoming an adult-centred society as the boom generation grows up'. There are elements of such a pattern evident in Australia. What are the impacts that the baby boomers will have in the next decade or so as they pass through the middle years of adulthood? The stabilization of education enrolments has already been considered, as have its demographic echo effects (Chapter 3). Bouvier (1980, p. 16) has listed some of the impacts on non-demographic variables of the maturing of the United States baby boom generation, and most of these are relevant to Australia. They are:

1 reductions in unemployment and crime rates as the baby boom cohort ages out of the highest-risk age groups;
2 increases in consumer spending on homes, expensive durables such as appliances, furniture and automobiles and, associated with this, high levels of consumer debt;
3 major shifts in the business world, with companies shifting the balance of their activities (Bouvier quotes a baby food manufacturer moving into life insurance) or shifting the orientation of their advertising (many advertisements previously oriented to the young are now pitched at a wider age range).
4 divorce remaining high;
5 decreasing overall residential mobility.

In fact the baby boom may now be entering a period where it will cease to be labelled as troublesome. The final years of the 1980s will see the last of the baby boomers pass out of the 'difficult' ages of leaving the parental home, seeking a first job, forming a family, etc., and into the more stable and settled middle adult years. Bouvier suggests (p. 32) that the baby boom is on the verge of its most productive and economically active phase of life and sees this as a reason to be optimistic about the future. Of course such optimism should be tempered by the knowledge that the baby boom generation will begin to enter the pensionable ages a decade into the next century. Clearly, however, whatever else happens to Australian society over the next decade or so, planners will have to take the baby boom generation into account. Samuelson (1979) goes so far as to suggest that 'You cannot understand economics or politics today without understanding the impact of the "baby boom"'.

SPATIAL VARIATION IN AGE STRUCTURE

It is important for planners to realize that there are wide regional variations in age structure—the national age distribution is an averaging out of these variations. At regional and local levels age structures can vary substantially from the national age pyramid, and knowledge of the spatial concentration of particular age groups is basic to planning the location of many services and facilities. Rowland (1983, p. 60) for example has identified and mapped nine main types of age structure within Australian metropolitan local government areas, ranging from an 'old' structure in which around 15 per cent of the population are aged over 65 to a 'very young' structure with over 15 per cent aged less than 5 years of age. Not only is age structure more variable at the local level, but it is also more volatile. Local age structures are subject to very rapid change, since selective in- or out-migration of particular age groups can and does dramatically change not only the total population of small areas but also the age distribution of the resident population.

Rowland's study of age structures of Australian metropolitan local government areas established a pattern of successive concentric rings of progressively younger age structures with increasing distance from the city centre. This pattern has been disrupted somewhat by the process of 'gentrification'—younger people (especially young families) settling in older inner and central parts of the major cities, especially Sydney. There is a general pattern within particular localities, especially those within large cities, for a clustering to occur of people at particular stages of the life cycle. When new areas are first opened up for suburban development they tend to be settled by people within a particular stage of the life cycle—i.e. young families—hence a heavy concentration of a few stages of the life cycle occurs in particular areas. In fact we can recognize a series of stages in the development of Australian suburbs as these initial groups of settlers age their way through the life cycle. These are presented in simplified form in Figure 6.6. This essentially cyclic nature of the changes in age structure of suburbs in Australia's major cities has important implications for planners. It means there will be a periodic (and cyclic) shifting of the focus of demand for services like schools, sports and recreation facilities, aged care, etc. It should not come as a surprise to planners in 'a middle suburb' which developed during the post-war baby boom years that the huge demand for schools and recreation facilities for children in the 1950s and 1960s has been transformed into one for meals-on-wheels, home handyman services, domiciliary care, senior citizens clubs, bowls clubs and the like in the 1980s. Given this knowledge we should be able to plan our physical fixed structures so that with minor expenditures they can be modified to accommodate changes in the age structure of suburbs. There is also a need for more research to establish the nature and extent of the mismatch between the 'life' of facilities oriented to particular age groups and the length of time these particular age groups tend to be dominant in a suburb.

Although we can recognize some cyclic tendencies in the age structure of non-metropolitan localities, they generally are not subject to such extreme variations in age structure or to the rapid changes in those structures which characterize metropolitan local government areas. There are exceptions to this, where there has been a major influx of inmigrants concentrated in specific age groups (such as the movement of retirees into coastal resort

Figure 6.6 A simplified model of the life cycle of a suburb in an Australian city

Stage and Characteristics	Typical age structure[1]
1 Initial Development Rapid population growth occurs, due to the inmigration of large numbers of young couples living with their parents in older suburbs or in medium- and high-density housing in the inner suburban or city area.	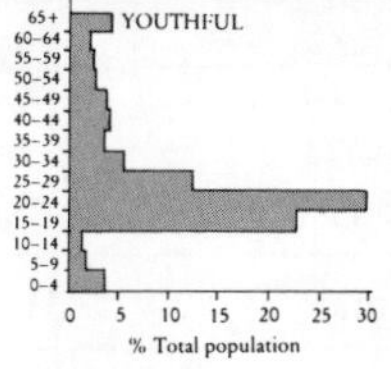
2 Family Building Rapid population growth continues as these couples establish themselves and have children and there is continued inmigration as remaining vacant land is infilled.	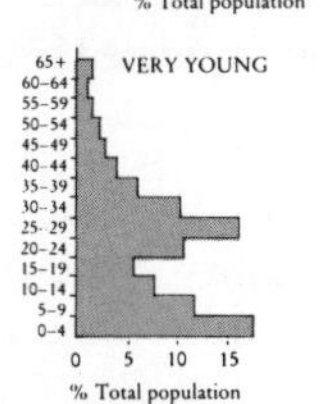
3 Consolidation Population growth levels off as couples complete child-bearing and most vacant land is taken up for housing.	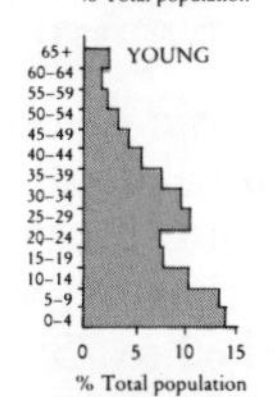
4 Maturing Population begins to decline as children leave home to set up separate households in inner-suburban flats or in outer suburban low-density housing areas.	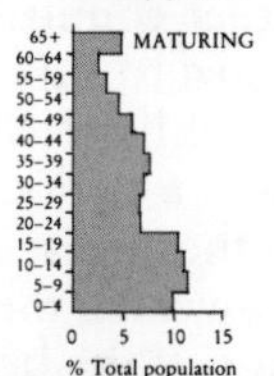
5 Child Launching Population decline accelerates with outmigration of children and the deaths of settlers from Stage 1.	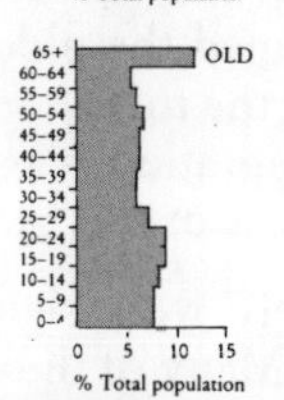
6 Rejuvenation By this stage the population decline is halted and in some cases reversed, due to inmigration of young couples into the houses vacated by original settlers who have died or moved out. In many areas in which accessibility to the city centre is good there is flat and home unit development, which attracts groups of young people who have left home for the first time, such as students and newly married couples. In some areas the process known as gentrification occurs.	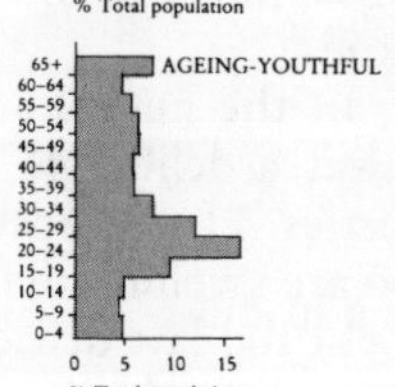

[1] These age structures are based on Rowland (1983, p. 60)

Table 6.5 Net migration gains of persons in older age groups, 1971–81

Age group	Net gain by 1981	Total population in 1981	Percentage due to net migration
60–64	9142	613 948	1.49
65–69	9407	535 777	1.76
70–74	7471	401 247	1.86
75+	5584	518 210	1.08
Total	31 604	2 069 182	1.53

Source: calculated from unpublished statistics supplied by ABS

areas), or alternatively a massive selective exodus out of a non-metropolitan community. The dynamics of local changes in age structure are taken up later in this chapter, with special reference to the older population.

DEMOGRAPHIC PROCESSES AND AGEING IN AUSTRALIA

All the basic demographic processes—fertility, mortality and migration—have contributed, albeit unequally, to the current rapid growth in the number of older Australians. The size of the older population at any single point of time is going to be determined by, first, the number of births that occurred 60 to 75 years earlier in Australia; second, the number of migrants from other countries who were born 60 to 75 years ago and subsequently immigrated to, and settled in, Australia; and third, the extent to which these two groups have suffered mortality in the intervening period. The 1910s and 1920s was a period of relatively high fertility in Australia so that persons born in those years have formed a bulge in the contemporary age pyramid, and are swelling the numbers of aged Australians in the 1980s. The 1970s by contrast saw the beginnings of a substantial decline in fertility and if this is maintained the older age groups will become more significant as a proportion of the total population.

Immigration was covered in some detail in Chapter 4. What are the implications of this pattern of immigration for the ageing of the population?

1 There were significant gains, averaging over 30 000 per annum, in the 1920s. Many of the children born to those immigrants are now entering their sixties.

2 In the huge upswing in immigration immediately after World War II it was a deliberate procedure to select young adults in their twenties and thirties. Hence post-war migrants were people born in the 1920s and they too are swelling the number of Australians currently entering their sixties.

3 In the last decade a shift in immigration policy to one in which family reunion predominates has meant that incoming immigrants are generally older than in the earlier post-war years. Hence, as Table 6.5 shows, immigration has made a small but significant contribution to the growth of Australia's older population over the 1971–81 period. In sum, 1.53 per cent of the population aged 60 years and over in 1981 was attributable to net migration

Table 6.6 Percentage of the total population aged 65+ in Australian States and Territories, 1971 and 1981

State/Territory	1971	1981	Change	No. of persons aged 65+ in 1981
NSW	8.5	10.1	+1.6	528 468
Vic.	8.6	10.0	+1.4	393 118
Qld	8.8	9.7	+0.9	226 711
SA	8.5	10.6	+2.1	139 196
WA	7.4	8.7	+1.3	112 980
Tas.	8.1	9.9	+1.8	42 463
NT	2.1	2.2	+0.1	2 727
ACT	2.7	4.2	+1.5	9 571
Australia	8.3	9.8	+1.5	1 455 234

Source: ABS (1971 and 1981 censuses)

gains over the preceding decade. The largest contribution was in the group aged 70–74 years at the time of census.

We often hear that the reason our population is ageing is because we are all living longer. This is, however, only a part of the story, although it is one which has assumed greater significance in recent years. It was shown in Chapter 2 that in the 1970s for the first time in Australia's demographic history there were major improvements in the life expectancy of older persons. Clearly this unanticipated increase in longevity among older Australians is contributing to the overall ageing of the population. The extent of this contribution can be gauged from the fact that projections of growth of the 65+ population made in the mid-1970s under-predicted the 1981 aged population by 11 per cent and 91.3 per cent of this discrepancy was due to the improvement in mortality among older people (Hugo 1984a).

THE SPATIAL DISTRIBUTION OF THE AGED POPULATION

Like most minority groups, Australia's elderly are concentrated in particular areas. An appreciation of the pattern of distribution of the aged and of how they are constantly changing is clearly important in planning the location of services for them, especially since many older people are not very mobile.

Table 6.6 shows that there is considerable variation between the States in the proportions of their population who are aged 65 years or over and that the extent of ageing during the 1970s has also varied. The greatest degree of change is evident in South Australia, which overtook the three mainland eastern States during the 1970s to have the 'oldest' population in 1981. This was a function not only of a very large reduction in fertility and significant outmigration of young adults in the 1970s but also of a comparatively heavy inmigration of young adults in the 1950s in that State (Hugo 1983e). Despite Queensland's popular image as a focus of retirement migration, the increase in the proportion of the total population in the 65+ age group was substantially less than the average for all of Australia, so that during the 1970s it went from being Australia's oldest State to being the 'youngest' of the eastern and southern States.

Within States there is a slight 'over-representation' of the elderly in urban areas, with 64.3 per cent of persons aged 65 years and over living in cities with more than 100 000 inhabitants, compared to 63.2 per cent of the total population. The difference is even more marked in smaller cities which contain 25.1 per cent of older Australians but only 22.6 per cent of the total population. The rural sector has an under-representation of the aged, as is to be expected given the tendency for older persons to move from rural areas to urban areas either at retirement or to find specialized accommodation.

An analysis of the detailed spatial distribution of the aged population has been undertaken elsewhere (Hugo and Wood 1984) and only the main patterns will be outlined here.

1 There are concentrations in non-metropolitan coastal resort areas, particularly along the northern and southern coast of NSW and in south-eastern Queensland with retirees migrating toward the attractive environment and equable climate (Murphy 1979a and b). The growth of seaside retirement communities is a well-established phenomenon throughout the Western world (Kain 1977); in Australia it is clear that with early retirement, portability of pensions, greater participation in superannuation schemes and greater longevity that a larger proportion of older people have both the financial means and the health to move to such locations upon retirement. In some States similar retirement developments have occurred along rivers, especially the River Murray in South Australia and Victoria.

2 Another pattern is the growth of retirement communities in hills areas

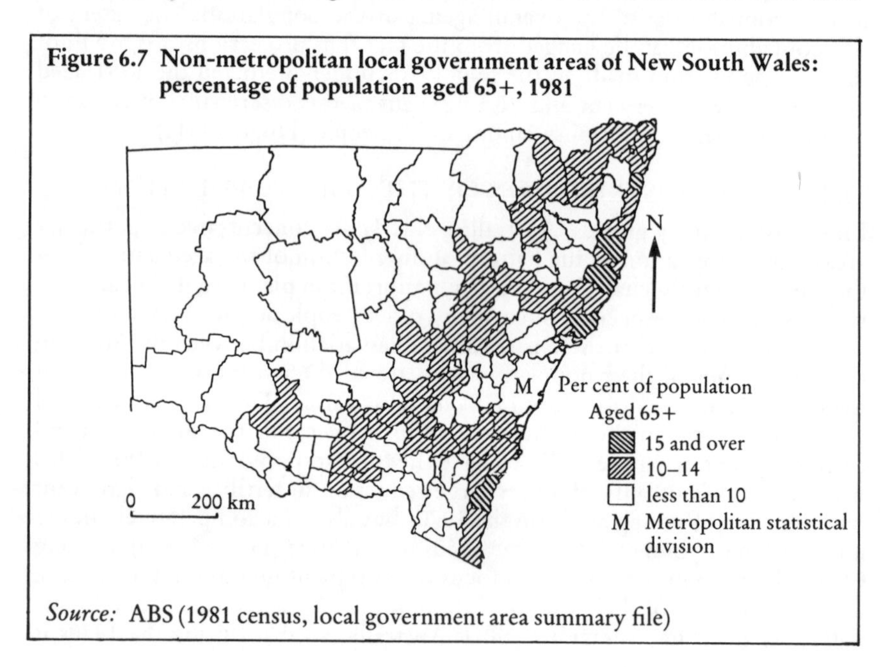

Figure 6.7 Non-metropolitan local government areas of New South Wales: percentage of population aged 65+, 1981

Source: ABS (1981 census, local government area summary file)

near the larger cities. Such patterns are evident around Sydney (e.g., the Katoomba and Moss Vale areas), Melbourne (parts of the Dandenongs) and Adelaide (e.g. Mt Pleasant, Tanunda, Angaston and Strathalbyn).

3 Many country towns have an above-average concentration of older people. This often reflects a pattern of older people retiring from farm properties into nearby towns which allows them to maintain (and perhaps even enhance) existing social networks and 'keep an eye' on their children who have taken over the farm.

4 Other districts with above-average concentrations of older people are found in the more closely settled agricultural areas located beyond the commuting zones of the largest cities—mostly a function of the heavy outmovement of younger adults.

Figure 6.7 shows the non-metropolitan pattern as exemplified by New South Wales and it is possible to recognize several 'types' of concentration.

Within the major cities it is also possible to identify a number of 'types' of areas with above-average concentrations of older people and the pattern in Melbourne shown in Figure 6.8 is typical.

1 As in most Western cities there is a concentration of population aged 65 years and over in the central and inner suburbs (exaggerated by a selective

Figure 6.8 Melbourne local government areas: percentage of population aged 65+, 1981

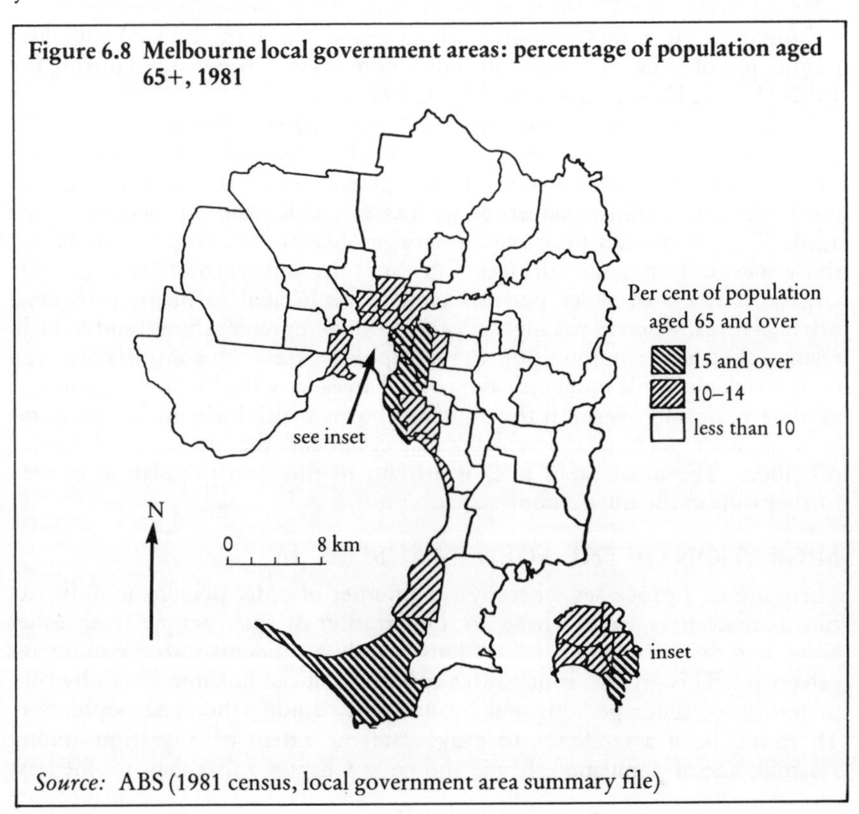

Source: ABS (1981 census, local government area summary file)

out-movement of younger people). Many of the institutions for aged persons are here too. For example, in Adelaide more than 40 per cent of the population aged 65 years and over living in non-private dwellings (mainly aged care institutions) at the 1981 census were located in the inner suburbs. These suburbs together contained only one-fifth of the aged population living in private dwellings, however.

2 Also typical of Australia's major cities are the high proportions of elderly people in coastal suburbs. These tend to be relatively old, well-established suburbs which developed initially because of their function as resorts. Recent home unit and flat development associated with the congenial seaside location has attracted substantial numbers of retirees.

3 The 'middle' suburbs of Australia's major cities tend to have above-average proportions of their populations in the 65+ age group. These are the suburbs which absorbed much of the very rapid population growth of Australia's major metropolitan areas in the 1950s and 1960s. Between the end of World War II and the early 1960s there was a huge influx of young families into these suburbs, including not only young adults moving out from the inner-suburban homes of their parents to establish homes of their own, but also many young immigrants newly arrived from European countries. Many of the people who moved into these suburbs in their young adulthood are now approaching retirement or are already in the post-retirement phase of the life cycle. It is these suburbs which already have the bulk of the older population of large cities and this will become even more marked during the 1980s (Hugo, Downie and Rudd 1981, 1984).

So far we have looked at the aged as a percentage of the resident population of an area. However, it is an obvious but strangely overlooked point that it is changes in the *numbers* of older persons in particular areas that is of most relevance to those concerned with assessing demand for services for the aged. There is often a poor match between places with large numbers and those with large proportions (see Table 6.7). In non-metropolitan areas the largest numbers of older persons tend to be located in major provincial urban centres, whereas the highest proportional representations tend to be in resort-retirement communities. In metropolitan areas the contrasts are even more marked. While inner city and coastal areas have the highest percentages aged 65 years and over, it is the middle suburbs which have the largest numbers of older persons and which must command the attention of service providers. The most rapid rate of growth of the aged population is even further out, in the outer suburbs.

MIGRATION OF THE AGED IN AUSTRALIA

There are two processes whereby the number of older persons in a district can increase over time. These are inmigration of such people from other areas, and the 'ageing in place' of long-standing residents into the older age categories. This growth is of course counterbalanced to some extent by out-migration of older persons and by mortality among the aged population. There has been a tendency to exaggerate the extent of migration among Australia's aged population. It was shown in Chapter 5 that they are the least

Table 6.7 Metropolitan local government areas with the largest numbers and highest percentages of persons aged 65+, 1981

Largest numbers				Highest percentages			
L.g.a.	State	Number	%	L.g.a.	State	Number	%
Warringah	NSW	16 821	9.7	Glenelg	SA	3578	26.9
Stirling	WA	16 746	10.4	Flinders	Vic.	5821	23.0
Camberwell	Vic.	15 011	17.5	Nedlands	WA	4273	21.1
Randwick	NSW	14 560	12.5	Kensington Norwood	SA	1832	20.5
Gosford	NSW	14 268	15.1	Claremont	WA	1611	19.7
Canterbury	NSW	14 261	11.3	Burnside	SA	7207	19.2
Perth	WA	13 457	17.0	Brighton	SA	3722	19.1
Rockdale	NSW	13 131	15.7	Payneham	SA	3126	18.9
Caulfield	Vic.	12 906	18.5	Unley	SA	6719	18.7
Sutherland	NSW	12 868	7.8	Gawler	SA	1135	18.6
Bankstown	NSW	12 839	8.4	Cottesloe	WA	1252	18.6
Parramatta	NSW	12 796	9.8	Brighton	Vic.	6242	18.5

Note: Brisbane is not included because its artificially created local government areas are much smaller than those in other major cities and hence, have a greater chance of containing high percentages of aged persons (e.g. Karawatha, 70.4 per cent) but have very small numbers of old people
Source: ABS (1981 census)

residentially mobile age group in the Australian population although they tend to have relatively high rates of seasonal, non-permanent migration. The latter phenomenon is of some interest. The presence of some 60 700 visitors aged 55 years or older in Queensland (13.6 per cent of the total) on the night of the 1981 census is a reflection of the seasonal northward movement of older persons away from the winter chills of the south.

Seasonal mobility of the aged has been neglected among students of the aged in Australia. However, it is of increasing scale and is of significance for several reasons.

1 It may produce quite substantial seasonal shifts in demand for various goods and services for the aged population in both the areas of origin and destination.
2 It may be the first stage of a move which ultimately becomes permanent.
3 Such mobility may in fact constitute a compromise between moving permanently and staying at the place of origin permanently whereby the 'snowbird' maximizes benefits at both origin (maintenance of links with family, friends and relatives, etc.) and destination (escaping the cold climate, enjoying the environment, climatic and recreational resources of a resort area, etc.).

In fact a greater proportion of older persons were not at their usual place of residence on the night of the census than were classified as having migrated during the last twelve months.

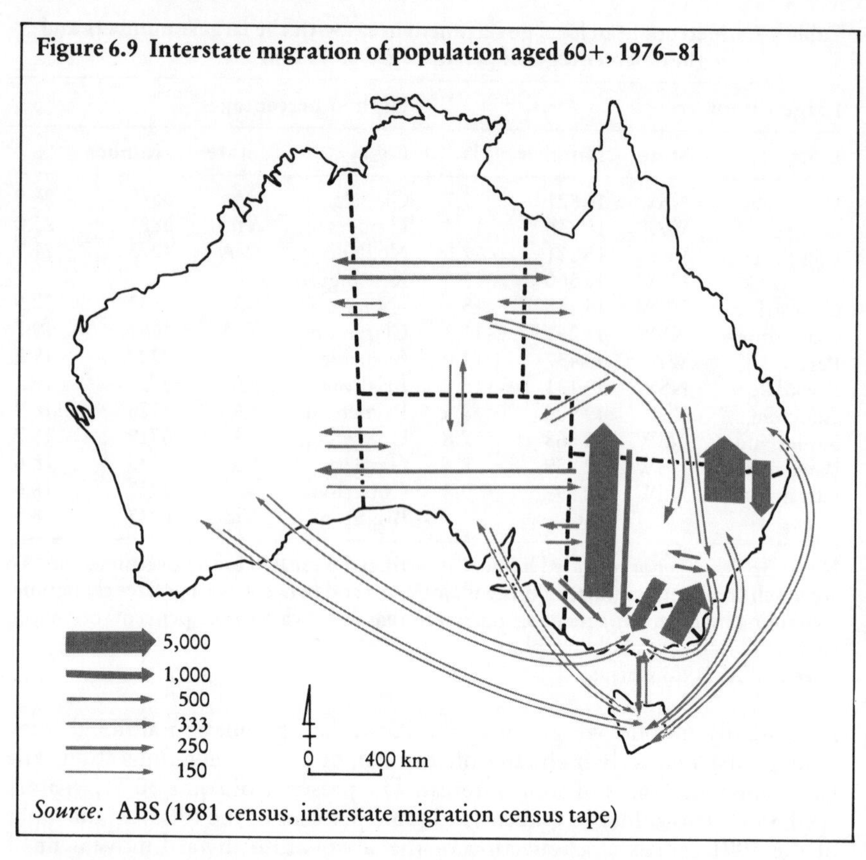

Figure 6.9 Interstate migration of population aged 60+, 1976–81

Source: ABS (1981 census, interstate migration census tape)

Turning to a consideration of the more permanent migrations among the aged, we find that at the 1981 census some 40 267 Australians aged 60 and over reported having moved interstate since 1976, representing only 2 per cent of all persons in this group. Figure 6.9 shows that the whole pattern is dominated by movement from New South Wales and Victoria to Queensland, accounting for a third of all interstate moves. If the reciprocal flows are included, the proportion increases to 44 per cent of all interstate movements of the 60+ population. In the previous chapter it was shown that there is an increasing tendency for Australian interstate migration to be toward the north, especially Queensland. However, a comparison of Figure 5.4 with Figure 6.9 shows that Queensland's dominance is even more emphatic in the inter-censal migration of the older population. Nevertheless, it should also be noted that there are significant reciprocal flows of older people from Queensland to New South Wales and Victoria.

With respect to *net* interstate migration of the aged, Queensland dominates with a net gain of almost 10 000 older persons between the censuses. Western Australia, South Australia and the ACT also experienced net migration gains of persons aged 60 years and over. These patterns are somewhat surprising and it is interesting to speculate on the causes of that movement. There is some anecdotal evidence that the low housing costs in Adelaide and the mild Mediterranean climate may be attracting small numbers of retirees from interstate. The net movement to Western Australia and the ACT is more difficult to explain but may be an 'echo' effect of their large net gains of young families during the 1960s and early 1970s. The parents of this group may have subsequently followed their children (and grandchildren) upon their retirement in order to live closer to them. Downie (1980) found in his study of an outer suburb of Adelaide that there was a significant amount of this type of movement among older people.

Among the four States that recorded net losses Victoria stands out, with especially heavy net migration to Queensland (–4333) and New South Wales (–1358) and net losses to all other States and Territories except the Northern Territory. In New South Wales the net loss was half as large as Victoria but was overwhelmingly to Queensland (−3378). The reciprocal nature of the flows shown in Figure 6.9 would suggest that there may be a pattern of older people subsequently returning to their State of origin after spending some time at a destination like Queensland. This pattern of circularity has been observed in studies of retirement migration to resort areas which have shown that people may subsequently return to their long-standing place of residence, especially if chronic illness is experienced or a spouse dies. Such patterns of course have important implications for provisions of specialized services for the aged—there may be more demand for the kinds of services used by the 'young old' than for those commonly used by the 'old old'.

Interstate migration represents only 10 per cent of all moves made by Australians aged over 50 years (Hugo and Wood, 1984, p. 69). This compares with 12.4 per cent of moves made by all Australians, so that not only do older people have a lower propensity to move but that when they do move they are slightly less likely to move interstate than the remainder of the population. The main patterns of intra-State migration of the aged are as follows:

1 The main net migration losses of older persons were sustained by metropolitan capitals especially Sydney and Melbourne, which over the last two decades had losses among over-50s of 41 078 and 38 409 respectively. This movement is mostly toward resort areas or toward places where the children of retirees are living. In the capitals of the smaller States, however, small net gains of older persons were recorded.

2 Districts which are essentially non-metropolitan in character but which adjoin large cities and are partially penetrated by the commuting fields experienced significant net gains of older people in the 1970s. Moreover, the gains were much larger than those recorded in the 1960s (Hugo and Wood 1984, p. 75). These areas have long been favoured by retirees seeking a more congenial environmentally situation but retaining access to the facilities, family and friends in the city in which they previously lived and worked.

3 It is clear also that there has been significant migration of older persons

Table 6.8 Population aged 65+ in the Adelaide statistical division—components of growth, 1971–76, 1976–81

Suburban sector	1971–76			1976–81		
	Net migration	Net ageing	Total change	Net migration	Net ageing	Total change
Inner	–1917	1229	–688	–373	879	506
Coastal	68	–63	5	–109	1725	1616
Middle	–1314	7008	5694	–185	8772	8587
Outer	1121	2505	3626	1909	4055	5964
Total	–2042	10 679	8637	1242	15 431	16 673
% of total change	–23.6	123.6	100.0	7.5	92.5	100.0

Source: Hugo, Rudd and Downie (1984, p. 21)

to environmentally favoured areas further away from the major cities, but still within the closely settled belt along the south-eastern and eastern coasts. The general pattern is for these areas to have coastal locations but there have been some inmovements to scenically attractive mountainous areas and townships along the River Murray like Mildura.

4 More remote non-resort areas of Australia are still experiencing significant net migration losses of older persons.

5 Within metropolitan areas, net migration plays only a minor role in the growth of aged populations. A typical pattern is that shown in Table 6.8 for Adelaide. During the 1970s only the outer suburbs had significant net migration gains of older persons, while most of the established suburbs (including those with very rapidly growing aged populations in the 'middle' suburbs) experienced net losses.

The general patterns of aged migration in Australia are fairly clear, although our knowledge of the causes, selectivity and implications of that migration is very limited. It would appear that overall rates of movement are similar for both the young-old and the old-old, although the two groups tend to move for different sets of reasons:

1 Among the 'young old' the main types of movement are those of a strongly voluntary nature, and disproportionately occur among the better off. The main influences are as follows:

(a) recreational opportunities, climate and other environmental considerations;

(b) unforced housing adjustments—to be closer to relatives or friends, or to move to what is perceived as more appropriate types of housing (e.g. from houses to flats or units); and

(c) forced housing adjustments—e.g., renters may be forced to trade down the housing market because of income reduction.

2 Among the 'old old' the moves are less often voluntary and are influenced more by widowhood or onset of disability or chronic illness requiring an adjustment in location and/or type of housing.

However, little is known about this mobility and even less of why the older people of Australia who do not move opt to stay (or are forced to stay) in residences which may not be appropriate to their needs and capacities. This need for understanding is made even more urgent since it has been suggested by some authors that the rate of elderly migration will increase in the near future. Hence Wiseman (1979, p. 35) states that in the near future

> as a group the elderly are expected to be relatively more affluent, and therefore, more able to afford the financial costs of migration. They will have had more frequent travel and vacation experiences, have higher levels of educational attainment, and consequently will have greater awareness of relocation opportunities. Furthermore, their social networks will be more diffused regionally as a result of earlier migration of their peers and family members.

Although levels of mobility among the older population (especially among those leaving the workforce upon retirement) may have risen in recent years, the dominant demographic process in the growth of the elderly population in most sub-regions is that of the in-situ ageing of middle-aged residents of long standing. The significance of this frequently overlooked 'ageing in place' is amplified in many Australian contexts by the uneven age structure at local, regional, state and national levels—the product of substantial fluctuations in fertility, inmigration and international migration over this century. For example, an analysis of Sydney (Hugo and Wood 1984, pp. 92–4) found that net ageing in place was positive for all local government areas in the 1976–81 period. In only four areas was net migration a more significant contributor to growth of the older population than ageing in place, and these were the specialized resort/retirement areas—the Blue Mountains, Gosford and Wyong and the outer suburb of Campbelltown.

Overwhelmingly then, ageing in place is the major factor in the *local* growth of the older population. The concentration of particular age groups in particular places caused by city development processes has meant, moreover, that the net ageing-in-place can be substantial, even in the brief five-year period considered here. A quarter of all Sydney local government areas experienced an inter-censal net ageing-in-place of their 60+ populations in excess of 1900 persons. When this is considered as an increase in numbers of people requiring specialized services the enormity of the impact of ageing-in-place can be appreciated. The largest numerical increases due to ageing-in-place occurred in the middle suburbs—those which absorbed much of the rapid population growth of Sydney in the 1950s and early 1960s.

The dominance of net ageing-in-place in the local growth (or decline) of the aged population is a powerful planning tool (Hugo, Rudd and Downie, 1984). In such situations cohort-component method population projections with soundly based mortality assumptions will give fairly accurate indications of future growth of the aged population in most metropolitan local government areas. Hence, in most areas we have five to ten years lead time to plan provision of services for the aged. The vital point is that except for areas attracting or losing large numbers of older people by migration (and it must be remembered that the elderly are the least residentially mobile adult age group in the population), we can have much greater confidence in the accuracy of our short-term local projections of the aged population than we can of any other group. In such areas we should never be surprised by the rapid growth of the aged population.

THE LIVING ARRANGEMENTS AND CONDITIONS OF THE AGED

A crucial element in the degree of well-being felt by older people is the nature of their living arrangements and the family context within which they live. Considering firstly the marital status of older people at the 1981 census the following patterns have been identified (Hugo and Wood 1984, p. 99):

1 The proportions of older males who were married at the time of the census were much higher than for older females, especially in the 70+ age group, in which two-thirds of males but only slightly over a quarter of women were currently married. This pattern is of course a result of the wide sex differentials in mortality. However, the planning and policy implications are of major significance. Most older men spend their final years in their own homes with the companionship of a spouse—thus men with chronic illnesses are more able and likely to be cared for at home than older women with such illness, whereas women more often are forced to move into an institution.
2 The obverse pattern of the above is that the number of older women who were widowed at the time of the 1981 Census—423 622 over 65—was more than four times those of widowed men.
3 More than 7 per cent of older men have never been married and this must be borne in mind in all discussions of the general move to place more responsiblity for the care of the aged back on the family—a significant proportion may have no immediate family because they have never married. Nearly a tenth of women aged over 70, over 50 000 individuals, have never been married due to the low marriage rates which prevailed in the 1930s and early 1940s, years of economic depression and war. The policy implications are clear—there is a large minority of older women (and to a lesser extent men) who not only do not have a spouse to call upon for assistance and companionship during old age, but also do not have children or grandchildren. As the younger cohorts move into the older age groups the proportions never married will decrease but certainly for the 1980s and 1990s Australia is faced with a significant proportion of its aged population who do not have a spouse or children. This group is obviously at high risk of experiencing the syndrome of psychological, social and physical problems associated with isolation.

Much recent discussion about services for the aged places stress on individuals taking more responsibility for the well-being of their older dependent family members much as they do for their younger dependants. This raises the question of just how many children do older people have whom they can potentially call upon for assistance of various kinds as well as with whom they can interact? The census collects data on the number of children that women have borne during their lifetime (Table 6.9). If we follow the

Table 6.9 Total issue for women according to their age in 1981

Total issue	Percentage distribution 40–49 years	50–59 years	60+ years
0	9	9	15
1	7	11	14
2	26	24	22
3	25	21	17
4	15	14	10
5	7	6	5
6	3	4	3
7+	3	4	4
Not stated	6	6	10
Average issue A*	2.58	2.62	2.23
Average issue B*	2.76	2.80	2.47

*A includes not stated who are regarded as zero parity
*B excludes not stated
Source: ABS (1981 census, one per cent sample tape of individuals)

ABS and regard the 'not stated' category as being childless, Table 6.9 shows that for women aged over 60, a quarter have not had any children. It may well be that there has been some mis-reporting exacerbated by recall problems, but the main source of error is probably associated with women not including children who have predeceased them. Even making generous allowance for such factors, one would conclude that at least a fifth of older women do *not* have any children whom they can call upon for assistance. This clearly should be recognized by policy makers and planners of aged care services. The proportions are clearly smaller among women in their forties and fifties but certainly well in excess of a tenth would not have any children at all during their old age. The table shows that more than a third of older women have had only one or two children, and among these there are bound to be a significant number whose child or children live a considerable distance from them and thus only be of limited assistance.

At the 1981 census 638 309 Australians (4.4 per cent of the total population) were counted as living in non-private dwellings, and a fifth of this population were aged more than 70 years of age. Table 6.10 shows the considerable differences between the proportion of older males and females living in non-private dwellings at the 1981 census, with higher proportions of males in the category below age 70 and high proportions of females above age 70. Although a fifth of persons aged 75 years and over were living in a non-private dwelling on the night of the 1981 census, this should not be interpreted as this proportion of the 'old-old' being institutionalized. The number of persons aged 75 years and over enumerated as living in a nursing home was 9920 males and 34 766 females. This represented 5.54 per cent and 10.92 percent of all males and females aged 75 years and over respectively. Hence slightly less than 9 per cent of the 'old-old' were enumerated in nurs-

Table 6.10 Older persons living in non-private dwellings, 1981

Age group (years)	Males Number	Percentage of total male population	Females Number	Percentage of total female population
55–59	19 173	5.3	12 541	3.5
60–64	17 118	6.0	13 272	4.3
65–69	15 768	6.5	13 829	4.9
70+	38 925	10.9	85 111	15.6
Total	364 991	5.0	292 893	4.0

Source: ABS (1981 census)

ing homes—the remaining 10 per cent in non-private dwellings were in hospitals, hostels, vacationing at hotels, etc. Thus, there is an enormous complexity among the living arrangements of the 'old-old' and it is extremely difficult to determine levels of institutionalization from census data.

The vast majority of older Australians live in private dwellings and we shall now briefly examine their living situations. Figure 6.10 shows the distribution of family types of older persons. Chapter 7 shows that one of the major changes in Australian family structure in recent years has been the large increase in 'head only' families, which by 1981 had become the second most common type of family. A major element in this increased importance of single-person households has been the tendency for older persons to stay in independent separate households much longer, even after the death of a spouse, than was previously the case (partly because of greater financial security but also because of changing societal attitudes towards aged relatives). Table 6.11 shows that a third of older women live alone, compared to less than a fifth of older men. There is no way of determining from the census how many of these have family members living near by with whom they are in regular contact, nor can we determine how far the absence of family is compensated for by close interaction with neighbours and friends. Nevertheless, the survey evidence shows a strong relationship between living alone and incidence of loneliness and problems of social isolation (Rowland 1982a).

The older (60+) population accounted for 42 per cent of single-person families at the 1981 census and their number increased by 19 per cent between 1976 and 1981; moreover, we can expect this to accelerate in the 1980s. Australia's older population in 1981 was overwhelmingly concentrated in the 'young aged' categories, so as they age and their partners die, the numbers of old people living alone will increase. The progressive increase in the proportion of persons in single-person households with increasing age is apparent in Figure 6.10.

The predominant family type among the older population is the 'head and spouse' structure. Among persons aged 65–74, 48 per cent live in this type of household as do 28 per cent of those aged 75 years or more. The small

Table 6.11 Proportion of older persons living alone, 1981

	65–74 years No.	Percentage	75 years and over No.	Percentage
Males	56 087	13.4	35 702	19.5
Females	159 769	31.9	122 552	37.5

Source: ABS (1981 census, cross-classified tables)

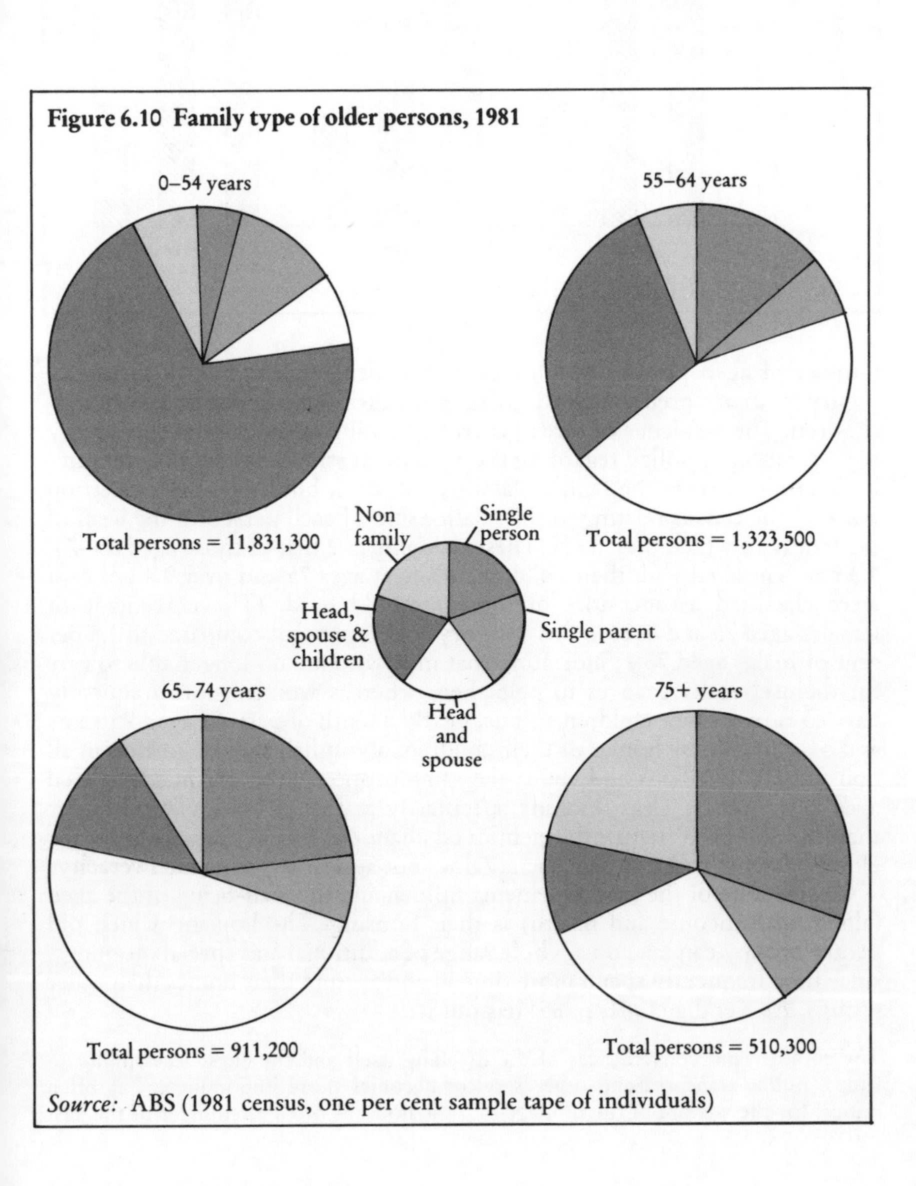

Figure 6.10 Family type of older persons, 1981

Source: ABS (1981 census, one per cent sample tape of individuals)

Figure 6.11 Mean weekly income of population by age, 1982

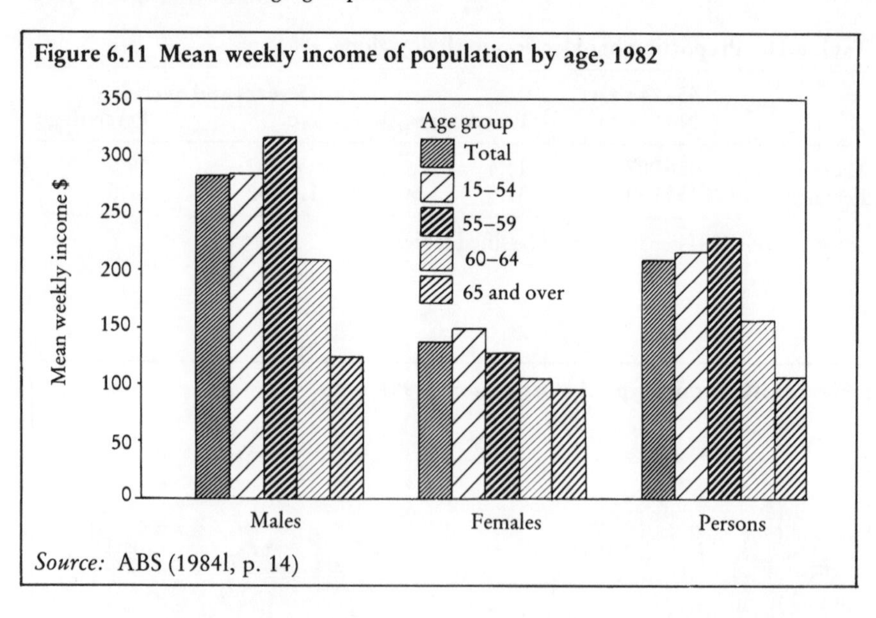

Source: ABS (1984l, p. 14)

number of aged persons in families with dependent children in them (see Figure 6.10) are predominantly living with their adult children and grandchildren. The incidence of three-generation families—very important in any consideration of policy regarding the aged in Australia—cannot be definitely determined from the family classification data, but there was a question asked at the census relating to the relationship of each person to the head of the family in which they lived. These data indicate that of those aged 65–74, 4.3 per cent lived with their children, while at ages 75 and over 9.4 per cent were classified as ancestors of the household head. (The percentage of females aged 75 and over in this category is 12.1 per cent compared to 4.4 per cent of males aged 75+, indicating that men who are no longer able to care for themselves have wives to help them whereas women more frequently have to turn to their children.) Thus, nearly a tenth of persons aged 75 years and over live in the homes of their children, about half the proportion in all non-private dwellings and about the same proportion as are in specialized aged care homes. Thus, looking specifically at the 75+ population rather than the 65+, the frequently mentioned abandonment of responsibility for elderly parents in Australian society does not appear to have much veracity.

Clearly, one of the major elements influencing the well-being of the aged (along with income and health) is their housing. The housing which old people occupy can take on a whole range of additional and special meanings, since they frequently spend more time in and around their homes than other groups. As Kendig (1981, p. 85) has put it:

> The comfort and conveniences of the dwelling itself and the close accessibility to shops, public transport and other services becomes more important and is often critical for the welfare of the frail aged ... the house is often a reminder of the past

Table 6.12 Structure of dwelling of older household heads, 1981

Structure of dwelling	Age (years) 0–54	55–64	65–74	75+	Total (all ages)
	Percentage				
Separate house	71.5	77.3	71.1	54.8	71.1
Semi-detached house	2.5	2.6	3.5	2.7	2.7
Row or terraced house	1.1	1.0	1.2	0.9	1.1
Flat	13.7	11.4	15.6	17.5	13.8
Other	0.6	0.4	0.4	0.4	0.5
Not applicable*	9.3	6.2	7.3	22.8	9.6
Not stated	1.4	1.1	1.1	1.0	1.2

*i.e., not living as part of a family in a private dwelling
Source: ABS (1981 census, one per cent sample tape of households)

and a help in maintaining a sense of identity and purpose as adjustments have to be made in their later years.

The housing situation of the aged is extremely complex since the financial, physical, social and psychological changes associated with ageing put increasing pressure on older people to make adjustments to their residential circumstances. This pressure tends to build up progressively with age due to increasing frailty, decreasing mobility, death or illness of a spouse etc. and create difficulties for aged people. Among older people there are a greater variety of living arrangements than any other major life cycle group in the population. This is reflected in the type of housing structures that they occupy. As Table 6.12 shows, a number move into institutions (covered by the 'not applicable' heading), while others move from separate houses to flats. This pattern has become more pronounced over the last two decades (Hugo and Wood 1984, pp. 130–1). Nevertheless, the fact that the majority of older persons living as a couple or alone occupy detached, separate dwellings has led some commentators to designate such housing as 'underutilized'. However, it should be also borne in mind by policy makers and planners that an aged persons housing survey (DHCD, 1976) found that less than 30 per cent of older people could think of anything they disliked about their current dwellings and only one in five wanted to move. As Kendig (1981, p. 89) has noted, 'Considering the high housing satisfaction of older owners, any policy proposals for shifting them to other dwellings must be considered cautiously'.

Housing inequalities, as Kendig (1982, p. 2) points out, tend to accumulate over the life span and assume their greatest force in old age. Differences with respect to house ownership are particularly important, since the capacity to pay rent is generally greatly reduced after retirement.

Home ownership over the post-war period has been the key mechanism by which economic advantage early in life has been accumulated, multiplied and transferred into financial security in old age ... economic wellbeing among the aged depends as much on this principal source of wealth as it does on income.

Census figures show that the rates of owner-occupancy among older household heads living in private dwellings (78% in 1981 for those 65 and over) are higher than for the population as a whole (70%).

The advantages of home ownership for the aged are manifold as Kendig (1981, p. 87) shows—low cost, security, it is a substantial financial asset and constitutes 'a sense of pride and accomplishment in looking back on one's life'. Primarily because of their advantageous housing situation, fewer aged home owners are in poverty than other groups such as renters, boarders and lodgers (Commission of Inquiry Into Poverty, 1975). Surveys undertaken by the ABS (1982d, p. 47) show that housing costs are more than twice as high among aged renters as among aged home owners. Even so, the 1981 census data on amount of rent paid showed a concentration of older age groups in low-rent categories, reflecting both their low capacity to pay high rents and their access to low-rent State authority housing. The burgeoning demand for the latter can be illustrated by the fact that over the last seven years applications to the South Australian Housing Trust from aged persons increased by 166 per cent, more than twice the overall increase in applications (74 per cent). Those who are unable to gain access to low-rent or subsidized public housing and rely completely upon the pension for income can only obtain housing at the lower end of the private rental market, and even then pay extraordinarily high proportions of their income in rent (Kendig 1981, p. 92). The private housing sector has been slow to respond to the ageing of the population, still orienting the overwhelming bulk of its activity to three- and four-bedroom homes, and at the upper end of the aged market, with the building of high-cost units and apartments in prime locations. In his comprehensive synopsis of the housing of Australia's aged, Kendig (1981, p. 92) concludes his discussion of renters as follows: 'Some of the difficulties of aged renters are offset by their residence in the inner suburbs. These areas offer a diverse choice of dwellings and proximity to public transport and shops'. However, as was demonstrated earlier, the locational centre of gravity of the aged population in Australian cities is moving outwards, while many of the services for the aged are within the areas where formerly most of the aged lived—the inner suburbs. Moreover, in the middle and outer suburbs not only are housing densities lower but average distances to convenience shops and public transport also tend to be greater and this can create difficulties for the less mobile aged. This lower mobility arises not only from greater incidence of disability among the aged, as will be discussed in a later section, but also from substantially lower access to private motor vehicles (41 per cent of those aged 75 and over have no access to one).

SOCIO-ECONOMIC AND ETHNIC DIFFERENTIATION AMONG THE AGED

Too often the aged in our society are thought of as a more or less homogeneous group. Too often service provision is not based upon need but upon a simple population distribution basis or, even worse, upon the force and strength of lobbying or submissions made by regional groups. Such models of planning are based upon an assumption that need is uniformly distributed among the aged, and this is patently not so.

Table 6.13 Principal source of income for persons aged 65+ in 1978–79 and 1981–82

Principal source of income	Percentage 1978–79	1981–82
Wage or salary	5.3	1.0
Own business	3.6	3.0
Government cash benefits	78.6	79.9
Superannuation	4.6	10.6
Interest, dividends etc.	6.5	4.8
Other	0.6	0.6
Total	100.0	100.0

Source: ABS (1982d, p. 35, 1984l, p. 14)

Table 6.14 Persons receiving the aged pension, 1971–83

	1971 (June)	1981 (June)	1983 (Dec.)
Number of aged pensioners	758 700	1 327 900	1 557 296
Percentage of total population	5.9	9.0	10.1
Percentage of workforce	13.5	19.7	22.3
Percentage of those aged 65–69 receiving pension	54.6	66.4	77.3
Percentage of those aged 70+ receiving pension	70.2	93.1	97.2

Sources: Department of Social Security (1983, p. 2); ABS (1982d, pp. 40–1)

In any consideration of the well-being of older persons, their wealth and/or income levels must loom large. For most people their personal income is cut by one-third to one-half upon retirement and this results in households headed by aged persons having considerably lower incomes on average than those headed by younger persons, as Figure 6.11 shows. Some 80 per cent of persons aged 65 years and over in 1981–82 quoted the government age pension as their principal source of income. Table 6.13 shows that in recent years there has been a marginal increase in the proportion dependent upon pensions but a doubling of the proportion dependent on superannuation funds. Hence the expansion of superannuation funding in Australia in the 1960s and 1970s is starting to have an impact. The large reduction in workforce participation is also evident in the dramatic fall in the proportion of older persons dependent upon a wage or salary for income.

There has been much recent debate about the stress being placed on the social security system by the demand for aged pensions. Table 6.14 shows that the increase in the number of persons receiving the aged pension has been well in excess of the rate of increase of the aged population discussed earlier. The number of aged pension recipients has doubled since the 1971 census; the proportion that they make up of the total population has increased by about three-quarters, as has their ratio to the workforce. The annual expenditure on age pensions has increased by 448 per cent between 1973 and 1983, from $888m to $4868m (figures not adjusted for inflation). This represents 3 per cent of Gross Domestic Product, 7.1 per cent of all government outlays in Australia and 10.6 per cent of Commonwealth government expenditure. This increase occurred partly as a result of a widening of the eligibility criteria for the age pension. In addition, there have been substantial increases in the 'take-up' rate among those aged persons who are eligible, following a major shift in societal attitudes toward the pension; fewer people regard receipt of it as 'charity' and more consider it a right earned by a lifetime of paying taxes. These trends clearly are of major concern and the community must confront them in the immediate future.

With the drop in income that follows retirement, some older Australians encounter poverty for the first time. The Commission of Inquiry into Poverty (1975) attempted to identify major groups in Australian society living in poverty and found that the aged were disproportionately represented. Income data from the 1981 census show that for those aged 75 and over, over 70 per cent in 1981 had an income of $8000 or less. In relation to the rest of the population, therefore, the income of the aged is very low (Hugo and Wood 1984, p. 151). Aged women are especially disadvantaged.

Because access to education, especially at higher secondary and tertiary levels, has greatly improved in Australia in recent decades, the current generation of older people is not as well educated formally as those that follow them (Hugo and Wood 1984, p. 153). In the United States it is estimated that one-tenth of the elderly population is functionally illiterate (Soldo 1980). We don't know the Australian figure, but it almost certainly is at a significant level. Low levels of education can be, and often are, a handicap—for example, in finding out about service and benefit programmes. Also, even if they find out about them poorly educated old people often find it difficult and frustrating to deal with the paperwork and bureaucracy built into many such programmes. Again, there are clearly some cohort effects apparent here. The sex differential is much greater among the older population than the younger groups. Women in the present generation of older Australians faced greater barriers than their brothers in seeking out higher secondary and tertiary education in the pre-World War II period.

The 1980s, for the first time since white settlement, will see Australia having an aged population characterized by a significant degree of *ethnic* heterogeneity. In particular, for the first time in more than a century the aged population includes significant numbers of persons from non-English-speaking backgrounds, as the first waves of post-war migrants from Eastern and Southern Europe enter the retirement age groups. In 1981 some 220 000 persons, or 11 per cent of Australia's population aged 60 years and over, were born overseas in non-English-speaking countries. However, by 2001 it is projected that the ethnic aged population will be three times larger and will comprise one in five of all aged Australians. The implications of these changes are considerable, especially since it must be borne in mind that most policy makers and administrators of services for the aged have gained their experience in dealing with an aged population which is fairly homogeneous in language and culture.

Table 6.15 Projections of change in numbers of persons aged 60+, by birthplace, 1981–2001

Birthplace	Persons 1981	2001	Percentage change 1981–2001
Australia	1 535 510	1 889 558	+ 23.1
UK & Ireland (Rep.)	264 433	355 770	+ 34.5
New Zealand	17 278	33 350	+ 93.0
Germany	14 064	42 819	+204.5
Greece	14 139	64 900	+359.0
Italy	45 779	120 873	+164.0
Lebanon	2 512	18 589	+640.0
Malta	6 036	19 362	+220.8
Netherlands	16 447	35 097	+113.4
Poland	21 695	30 027	+ 38.4
Yugoslavia	12 946	58 139	+349.1
Asia	27 549	125 718	+356.3
Other Europe	47 243	85 882	+ 81.8
Other Oceania	2 214	11 550	+421.7
Africa	10 732	34 150	+218.2
America	7 287	30 906	+324.1

Source: Australian Institute for Multicultural Affairs (1983b, pp. 242–57)

In Chapter 8 the characteristics and problems of Australia's growing ethnic aged population are discussed in some detail. What should be pointed out here, however, is that the very rapid recent growth of overseas-born aged persons in Australia is only the harbinger of a much more marked expansion of numbers which will occur over the next two decades. The magnitude of this impending change is evident in Table 6.15, which shows an impending surge of growth of all overseas-born aged groups, but especially the Southern European groups, and to a lesser extent Asian. Moreover, it should be pointed out that while the present ethnic aged population is still predominantly a 'young-old' one, in the late 1980s and 1990s the 75+ group will grow very rapidly so that the numbers making intensive use of health welfare and other services will be growing especially rapidly.

HEALTH OF THE AGED POPULATION

Consideration of the health of the elderly Australians is rendered difficult, first because, as Ehrlich (in Howe 1981) has pointed out, the health of aged persons is influenced significantly not only by physiological considerations but also by their psychological and social well-being; second, study of health and illness among the aged in Australia is, as was shown in Chapter 2, greatly hampered by the lack of representative and accurate data. The data which we do have available confirms that as is the case elsewhere, 'the health needs of older persons are greater than those of other age segments of the population, as is their utilization of services. These health needs include many that are not met even now' (Siegel and Hoover 1982, p. 175).

Table 6.16 Most common reported chronic conditions among the population aged 65+, 1977–78

Type of chronic condition[1]	Incidence per 1000 population			
	65 and over		Under 65	
	Males	Females	Males	Females
Diseases of circulatory system	444	586	93	136
Diseases of musculo-skeletal system	321	457	98	122
Diseases of nervous system	301	272	91	102
Diseases of the respiratory system	226	164	174	173
Diseases of the digestive system	108	71	39	29
Endocrine, nutritional and metabolic diseases	86	68	19	18
Diseases of skin and subcutaneous tissue	56	46	49	67
Diseases of genito-urinary system	42	28	7	18
Total all chronic diseases	1735	1832	662	756

[1] Provision was made for respondents to report up to five chronic conditions.
Source: ABS (Australian Health Survey, 1977–78)

In the Australian Health Survey (1977–78) conditions which had been present for more than six months were identified as chronic. More than three-quarters of the 65+ population reported having at least one chronic condition compared to 42 per cent in the under 65 population. There is a slightly higher incidence among women which is, on the surface, in conflict with our knowledge of greater female longevity. Perhaps more women who experience illness survive it, perhaps women are more likely to report chronic illnesses.

The most commonly reported chronic conditions among the aged are reported in Table 6.16 and show that nearly half of the 65+ population suffers diseases of the circulatory system. These include heart disease (with an incidence of 165 per 1000 for males and 156 for females) and hypertensive disease such as high blood pressure (134 for males and 262 for females). More than a third suffer diseases of the musculo-skeletal system, especially arthritis. In all the diseases shown (with the minor exception of skin disease) the incidence is much higher among the older population than those aged less than 65 years.

These very high incidence rates present a major challenge to the health delivery system as the numbers in the 65+ age group increase rapidly. Moreover, the Australian system is predominantly set up to deal with episodic illnesses that may require expensive intensive attention for a short period, and the treatment usually results in total curing of the patient. However, the diseases listed in Table 6.16 are chronic continuing conditions which require less intensive (and less expensive per unit of time) treatment. Ehrlich (in Howe 1981) suggests that this mismatch has tended to produce unnecessary hospitalization of the aged not only adding to the costs but also providing inappropriate care that results in the patient deteriorating physically and mentally. Ehrlich maintains that older people in such circumstances comprise up to 40 per cent of the patients in some New South Wales hospitals, especially those in non-metropolitan areas.

The data presented in Table 6.16 do not show the severity of the condition experienced by the aged persons reporting them. In the Australian Health Survey, however, a separate definition of a '*limiting*' chronic condition was also used—this referred to conditions which resulted in a person being confined to bed, confined to the home or needing help in getting out of the house. The survey found (ABS 1982d, p. 14) that of the 950 700 aged persons reporting chronic conditions, 17.2 per cent described them as having a limiting effect. This constituted 13.4 per cent of all aged persons. Moreover there is a major increase in the incidence of limiting chronic conditions as people age further: while only 6 per cent of persons aged 65–69 reported having one or more limiting chronic conditions, more than a quarter of those aged over 75 had such a condition. In Chapter 2 it was shown that over the next three decades there will be a doubling of the numbers of older persons with chronic conditions and of those with handicaps, if current levels of incidence are maintained. However, it was also pointed out that these rates of incidence may in fact increase, in association with the decline in mortality.

The ABS survey of handicapped persons of 1981 identified handicaps as limitations in relation to five areas of activity—self-care, mobility, communication, schooling and employment. This found that of 1 331 100 aged persons living in private households, 27.7 per cent were handicapped to some degree, while of the 81 500 in institutions (handicapped person homes and hostels, hospitals, nursing homes, retirement homes and villages), 89.1 per cent were handicapped. In total, a third of all persons aged 65 years and over have disabilities which restrict their daily activities.

The 1977–78 Australian Health Survey confirmed that aged persons consult a doctor more frequently on average than other groups. The ABS (1982d, p. 14) found that on average persons aged 70 years and over received 11.5 medical services per head per year. Some 13.4 per cent of respondents aged 65 years and over reported that they had travel problems in getting to a doctor, which was more than twice the proportion for the non-aged population. The study also showed very low use of district or community nurse services, with only 2.7 per cent of persons aged 65 years and over reporting consultations. One feature of the 1977–78 survey was the very high usage of medicines and drugs by older people, with 74.7 per cent reporting having taken some form of medication in the two days preceding the interview compared to 47.4 per cent for the rest of the population. One especially neglected area of attention among the aged is psychiatric illness. In particular there is little understanding not only of the causes and effects but also of the incidence of various types of dementia among the aged. In the United States it is known that Alzheimer's Disease affects between 5 and 10 per cent of the population aged 65 years and over, but we know little about its incidence in the Australian population.

Clearly the ageing of the Australian population raises a major policy question of the funding of health services. In Chapter 2 it was shown that annual government health expenditure on the 75+ population was more than three times per head that on any group aged less than 65. Clearly with the doubling of the numbers of persons aged 75 years and over by the end of the century, the pressure on health costs is going to be great. Cost pressures will almost certainly force radical reforms on the health care delivery system. This will partly involve the provision of less expensive (and often more effective) home-based health care through various programmes of home care, day care, respite centres, community health centres, community health workers, outpatients services, etc. The funding of medical services will probably also transfer some responsibility away from the public sector, back to the family and the individual.

CONCLUSION

The main task here has been to summarize some of the demographic aspects of ageing in Australia. In closing, however, a few brief observations regarding the social and economic implications will be made. First, while many of the media stories of the 'greying of Australia' and forecasts of a future Australian society dominated by geriatrics are false and misleading, there can be no question that the older segment of the population will assume greater demographic significance in the coming decades. There will be an increase of significant dimensions both in their total numbers and in the proportion which they make up of the total population.

Perhaps the most discussed issue is that of the financing of pensions and of other services which are intensively used by our older citizens. It is clear that there should be some redistribution of financing, resources and effort away from the youth who have dominated our thinking during the post-war years of rapid population growth. It is not simply a question of redistribution however, since the young population will continue to grow, albeit at a slower rate than in the early post-war years. Moreover, the needs of the elderly are obviously quite different. These needs must be clearly identified and resources deployed selectively to most benefit those with the greatest needs. The demographic pressures of ageing may mean that our traditional ways of approaching provision of services for the older population will have to be modified. In the United States, where the ageing of the population has occurred somewhat earlier than in Australia (because of the large immigration waves of the early 1900s and 1910s producing a bulge in the United States age pyramid of people currently aged in their late sixties and seventies), it is clear that there is renewed interest in developing better ways of sharing responsibility for the elderly between public and private sectors. There are major attempts to formalize and enhance the existing, but weak and often overlooked, partnerships between all levels of government, the elderly themselves and their families and private agencies, church groups and neighbourhood associations.

In many areas there is much greater scope for innovative approaches in providing services for the aged and for the older population themselves to be involved in deciding what services are provided where and how. With younger retirement ages, increased longevity and people able to have more active and mobile years of retirement, there is clear scope for involving the 'young aged' more in the care of the older more dependent aged population. This is already done in organizations such as 'Meals on Wheels' and the principle could be used more widely with benefits to all concerned.

As was discussed earlier, public sector expenditure on the aged has undergone massive increases. There are a myriad of State government departments, local authorities and private and charitable organizations contributing to the support of the aged. Dominant in the public sector, however, is the Commonwealth government in which there are five departments with explicit concerns with the aged (Social Security, Veterans Affairs, Health, Housing and Construction and Immigration and Ethnic Affairs). Figure 6.12 shows the breakdown of Commonwealth expenditure on the aged. Clearly the pensions dominate this expenditure. There is also currently much debate about a domination of Commonwealth non-pension expenditure on the aged by institutions. In 1981 about 90 per cent of this expenditure was on persons being cared for in institutions ($334 million) while only $34 million was targeted toward non-institutional community and family-based care services such as day care, domiciliary care, home help programmes, etc. Many have argued that there is a pressing need to reallocate resources toward community and family-based service provision (e.g., Parliament of the Commonwealth of Australia 1982). Gibson and Rowland (1982, p. 12), for example, argue for

> a reallocation of the resources toward community based care, and not only for more domiciliary services, but for more variety and flexibility in their provision. Prospective increases in the numbers of the handicapped aged, emphasises the need for restraint in the use of institutional care. The development of more varied and flexible domiciliary programmes will not only contribute to the solution of this problem, but also ensure that greater attention is given to the wishes of the elderly for personal autonomy.

The Henderson Inquiry into Poverty in Australia in the early 1970s identified the elderly as being one of the main groups in Australian society with high incidence of poverty and need, and this important and frequently overlooked problem is likely to increase with the demographic changes outlined here. Housing of the elderly is often inappropriate to the social and physical needs of the elderly. More consultation with the elderly themselves, the provision of intermediate accommodation between detached homes and the senior citizen homes (thus allowing our older population to stay in their own neighbourhood and maintain important social relations as long as possible) need more investigation. The substitution of premature admittance to nursing homes with domiciliary care services of various kinds is an urgent priority—not simply to keep costs down in the face of rapidly increasing demand but mainly for the social and emotional well-being of the older people themselves.

The demographic changes identified here will mean that the needs of the elderly will account for a larger share of our total health care effort, re-

Figure 6.12 Commonwealth expenditure on the aged, 1965–66 and 1978–79

	1965–6	*1978–9*
Expenditure ($m)	561.6	5269.3
% of total government outlay	11.2	18
% of GDP	2.7	5.2

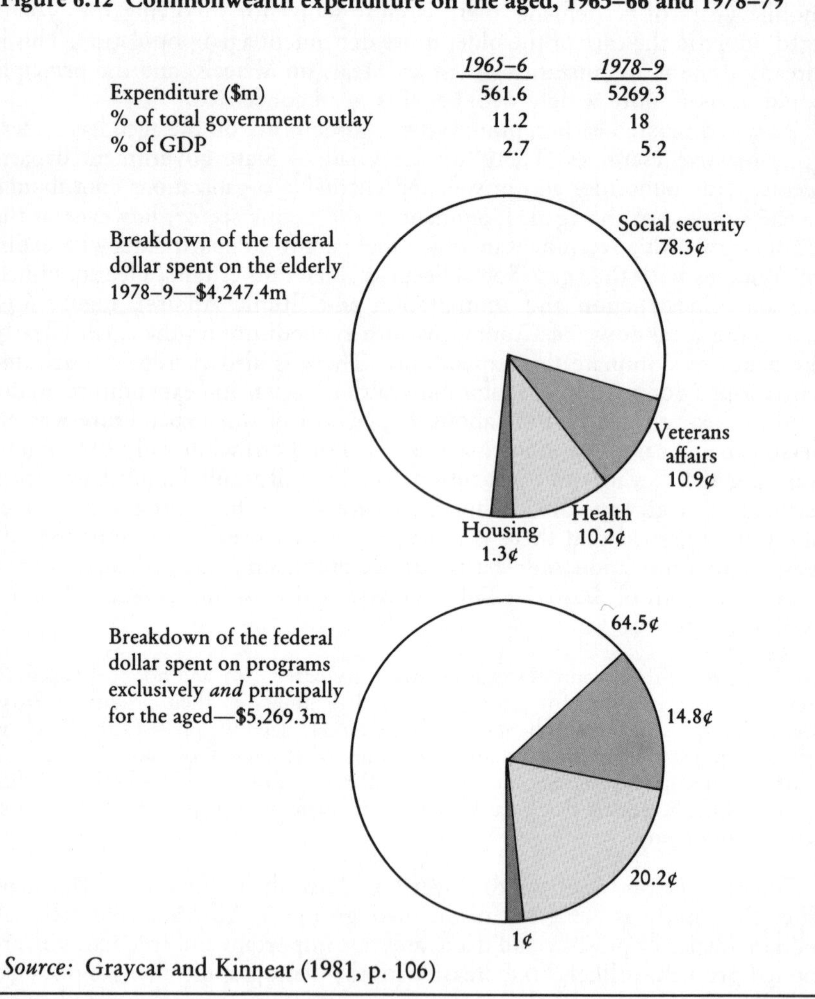

Source: Graycar and Kinnear (1981, p. 106)

sources and budget. The elderly currently make more visits to doctors per person and use hospitals more frequently than younger age groups. The necessity of re-orienting our health care system more toward treatment of chronic rather than acute illnesses is self-evident. Increasingly, too, we are recognizing high incidence of emotional disorders among the elderly—perhaps related to the small family system that has come to dominate in our society and the reluctance of Australians to take the elderly into their homes and create three-generation families. As increasing numbers of people survive to older ages, the relative frequency of persons with chronic, seriously debilitating conditions in later life will increase. This suggests the need for more widespread confrontation of the complex bio-ethical issues relating to life with dignity and the right to die and for exploration of these concepts in relation to the general issue of basic human rights.

A point which must be stressed is that the projections of the older population up to the early part of the next century are not hypothetical. We can predict the future numbers of our aged population up to the end of the century with some confidence, because the persons who are in the age cohorts which will be entering old age over the next few decades have, as Uhlenberg (1977, p. 202) points out, 'completed much of their life course and hence possess a variety of relatively fixed characteristics'. This is information which we must use to anticipate the problems of the aged and the demand for services. Davis (in Lipset 1980) has criticized policy makers in the United States for not even making use of short-term projections in their planning. He asserts that we are needlessly surprised by social change which forces individuals to adjust as best they can while institutions lag behind, making this adjustment even more difficult. Davis cites ageing of the population as a prime example of this and shows that 'industrial nations have failed to make an adjustment to it even after it has happened'.

The ability of elderly persons to adapt and thrive is contingent upon their physical health, personality, earlier life experiences and the societal support they receive in the way of adequate finances, shelter, medical care, social roles and vocation. These critical latter factors of societal support depend not only on older people themselves but on the rest of society committing resources to this end—i.e. not only public financial resources but family and private social investments of interest, time and caring. The demographic changes of the next two decades will place more pressure on society for this commitment than has been the case at any time in our history, and it represents a most significant challenge.

7 The Death of the Family? Changing Patterns of Family and Household Formation

In the myriad changes which have impinged upon Australian society during the post-war period, few institutions have been so fundamentally reshaped as the family. However, the demography of the family, defined by Bongaarts (1983, p. 27) as the branch of the subject 'which deals with the quantitative aspects of the size, composition and changes of families and households', remains little studied in Australia. Knowledge of trends in the numbers and composition of families and households, their causes and implications is not only of practical and policy significance but also constitutes essential background to an understanding of many social, demographic and economic changes occurring within contemporary Australian society.

Although the family is a basic and universal unit of social organization there is considerable debate concerning the definition of family and how this differs from the concept of household (Bongaarts 1983, p. 27). This debate, however, is somewhat academic in the context of this chapter, since most of the data used here are from secondary sources and definitions are thus imposed externally. In the 1981 Australian census of population and housing the concepts of family and household used were as follows:

1 A *household* consists of a person or persons who consider themselves to form a separate household or who have common eating arrangements. Boarders are treated as part of that household and lodgers as separate households.
2 *Family* structure was imputed during processing from replies to questions concerning the relationship of each person in the household to Person 1 in that household. However, individuals in the household who were not related by blood or marriage to Person 1 in the household were not considered family members but were classified as non-family individuals.

Our concern here is predominantly with that section of the population which resides in private dwellings. Persons living in hotels, gaols, religious and charitable institutions, defence establishments, other communal dwellings and caravan parks are considered as being in non-private dwellings for census purposes. Such persons are not deemed to be members of a household or a family, and they do not appear in the household and family statistics. This is usually overlooked in studies of census family and household data, yet in 1981 some 638 309 persons (4.4 per cent of the total) were counted in 22 516 non-private dwellings.

CHANGING PATTERNS OF HOUSEHOLD FORMATION AND HOUSEHOLD SIZE

In Australia rates of household formation have outpaced rates of population growth over the last half-century (Hugo 1983b). Between 1966 and 1976 the rate of household formation was twice that of population growth, while during the last inter-censal period (1976–81) the number of households increased at 2.5 per cent per annum compared to 1.5 per cent per annum growth in population. This differential was somewhat smaller than that in the United States during the 1970s (Norton and Glick 1979, p. 19). While population growth slowed dramatically during the 1970s, the growth rate in the number of new households remained at a high level.

Associated with this pattern is a shrinking in the size of Australian families and households. This is apparent in Figure 7.1, which shows the average number of persons per occupied dwelling in Australia at each census since Federation. The consistent trend of a decrease in the size of households evident for a century has accelerated in recent years. Over the fifteen years since the 1966 census the average size of the Australian household declined by 12 per cent from 3.53 to 3.1 persons. During the 1976–81 period alone there was a 6 per cent decline. The average number of persons per occupied dwelling was still higher than in the United States, however, where the 1980 census results indicated that the average household size declined from 3.11 to 2.75 during the 1970s (Russell 1981, p. 28). Figure 7.2 shows that over the last two decades the proportion of one- and two-person households has increased by nearly 15 per cent at the expense of larger households. It can also be seen that the most commonly occurring household size is of two persons. However, the fastest-growing category is that of single-person household, which increased by 452 per cent between 1947 and 1981 and 29.2 per

Figure 7.1 Changes in average household size, 1911–81

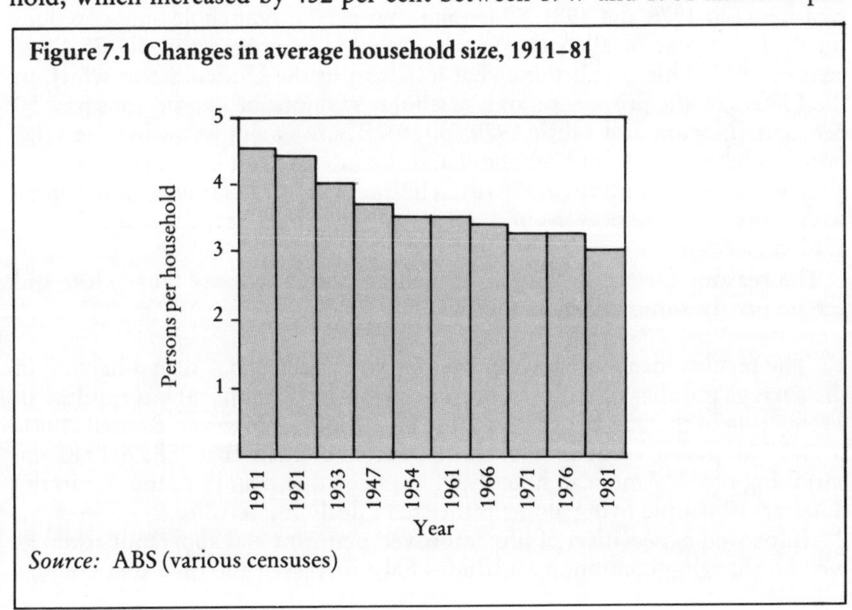

Source: ABS (various censuses)

Figure 7.2 Households by size, 1961 and 1981

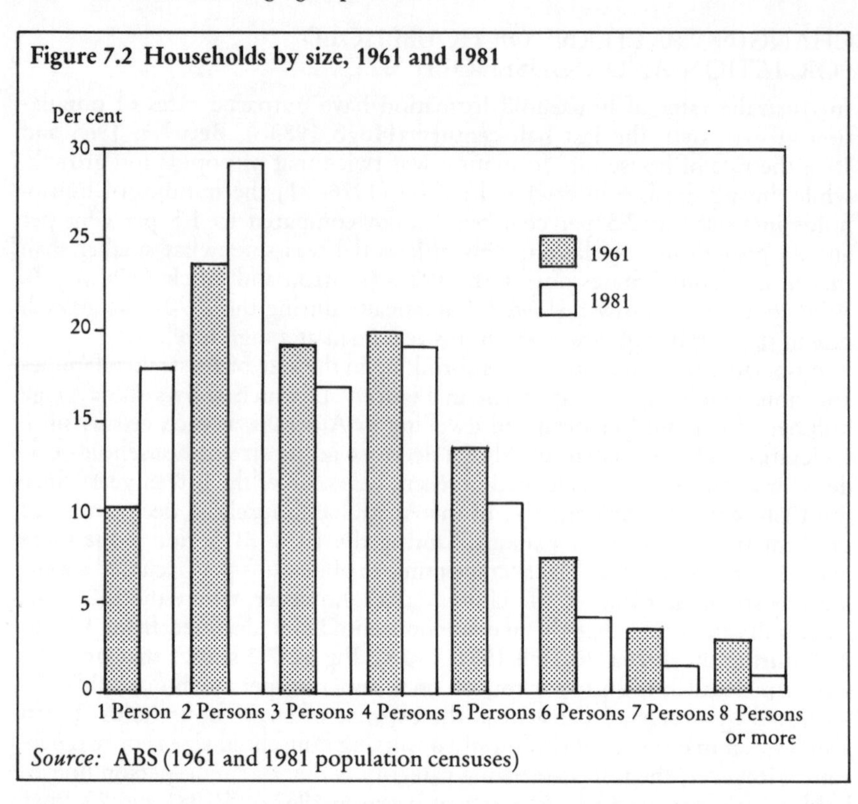

Source: ABS (1961 and 1981 population censuses)

cent between 1976 and 1981. One- and two-person households now account for 47.1 per cent of all Australian households compared to only 28.4 per cent in 1947. This is still somewhat less than in the United States which in the 1970s saw the proportion of households with one or two persons pass 50 per cent (Norton and Glick 1979, p. 19). There is almost an inverse relationship between size of household and the rate of growth of that size category of households (Hugo 1984d). The number of Australian households with more than five persons in them actually declined between the 1976 and 1981 censuses.

The reasons for the decline in household family size are fairly clear and can be briefly summarized as follows:

1 The fertility decline which in the last two decades has seen a halving of the average number of children born per woman (Chapter 3) has resulted in a reduction in the number of very large households. However, Russell (1981, p. 28) has pointed out in the United States context that 'Since 1940 the shrinking of the American household has been due mainly to the rise in the numbers of people living alone, rather than declining fertility.'

2 Improved expectation of life, improved pensions and superannuation, as well as changing community attitudes have increased the time that couples

and widowed persons can maintain themselves as an individual family—prolonging the 'empty nest' stage of the life cycle (Brown 1981, p. 13).

3 Divorce, which usually splits a family into two separate households, has increased.

4 The post-war baby boom cohorts have passed into the household formation young adult age groups (Chapter 6).

5 There is an increased tendency for young people to leave the parental home at a younger age and establish separate households (Hugo 1979a, p. 12).

CHANGING PATTERNS OF HOUSEHOLD HEADSHIP

To understand the causes of this rapid growth in the number of households we need to disaggregate the components of change, those elements adding to the stock of households and those subtracting from it. The former includes new households migrating in from elsewhere (Chapter 4) but also the splitting of existing households, either through the divorce or separation of cohabiting couples or by adolescent and young adult children leaving the parental home and establishing new, separate households. On the other hand, the number of households will be reduced to the extent that members of those households die or that they combine with another household (as when an aged woman moves in with the family of one of her children, for example). During the 1970s we have seen an acceleration of the splitting processes but a slowdown in the combining processes, especially because older people are maintaining themselves in separate housing for a longer period than was the case previously.

It is self-evident that the probability of individuals forming new households varies considerably with the life cycle stage that they are in. At each such stage the numbers of households will depend, first upon the number of persons in that age category and second, upon the headship rate among people of that age—i.e., the probability that a person of that age will form a separate household. Growth can occur either through people entering that age group outnumbering those leaving it, or through an increase in the propensity of people of that age to form a separate household.

To a large degree the rate of new household formation is going to depend upon the rate at which the adult population is being expanded. The major source of such expansion of course is in the younger adult ages, either through young Australians leaving their parental homes to set up a new household or through net gains of migrants (who also are disproportionately concentrated in the young adult ages). This can be seen in Figure 7.3, which shows a very steep increase in male headship in the young adult ages and stabilizing at a very high level for males after the mid-thirties. For females there is a steep increase in headship in the late teenage years, steadying around 20 per cent in the middle adult years, then a steady increase after age 60 as a greater proportion of women are widowed.

The ageing of the post-war baby boom generation (Chapter 6) into the young adult ages during the late 1960s and 1970s gave the major impetus to household formation outpacing population growth. Households with heads

Figure 7.3 Household headship rates for males and females, 1961, 1976, 1981

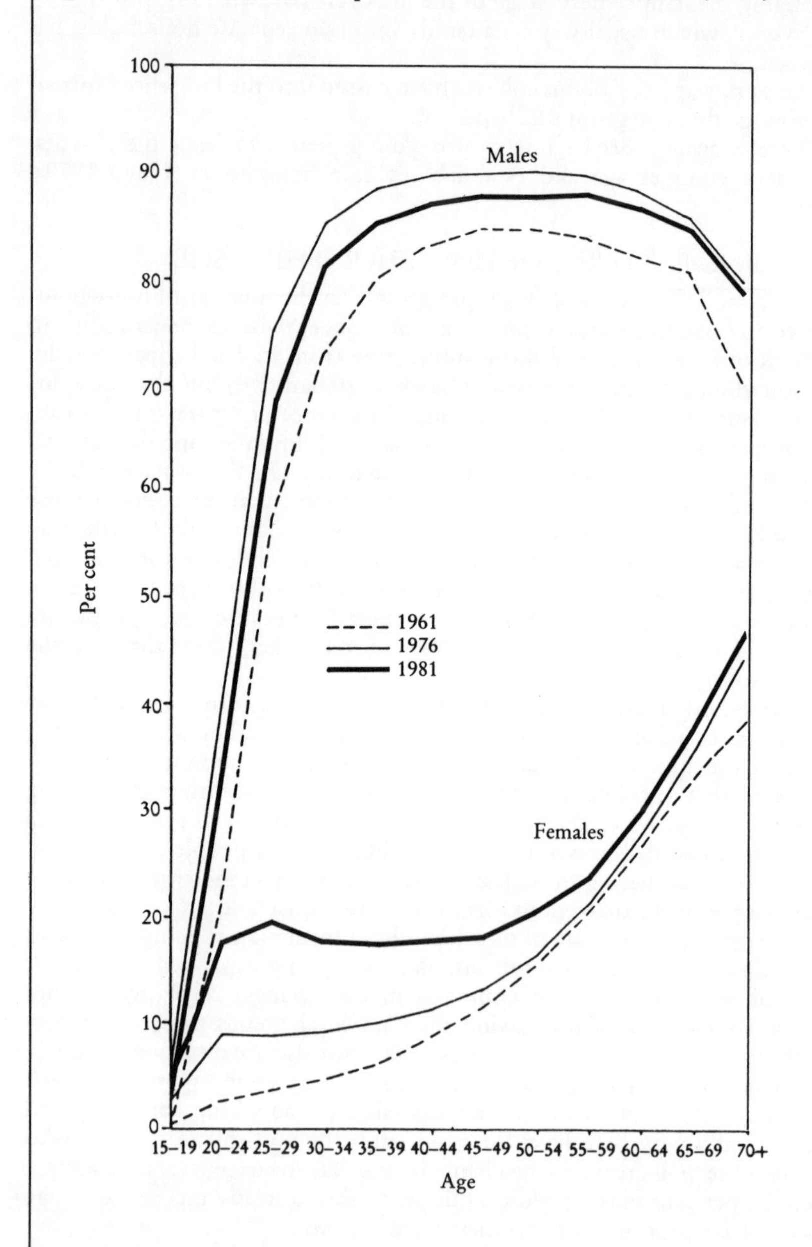

Source: Boundy (1980); ABS (1981 census)

Table 7.1 Changing household headship rates in major age groups, 1976 and 1981

Age group	1976	1981
15–24	12.9	14.7
25–34	44.4	46.8
35–44	50.4	52.5
45–54	52.6	54.0
55–64	55.1	56.2
65+	57.1	58.9

Source: ABS (censuses of 1976 and 1981)

aged less than 25 increased at around 10 per cent per annum during the 1960s, or more than three times the rate at which all households increased, and five times the rate of population growth (Hugo 1979a). The undercutting at the base of the 1981 age pyramid (Chapter 6) means that toward the end of the 1980s there will be a major reduction in the numbers of people entering the prime new household formation ages. Another striking feature is the increasing growth in recent years in household headship among the population aged 65 years and over.

It is not only the increasing numbers of people in the 'high risk' age groups which have caused a substantial increase in households. It is clear from Figure 7.3 that headship *rates* for males and females of all ages have increased significantly over the last two decades. It will be noted that there is a significant difference between that for males and females between the 1976 and 1981 censuses, with a general reduction in 'headship' rates for males and substantial increases for females, especially in the young adult ages. This pattern is partly a reflection of the shift in societal attitudes concerning family headship and partly the changed concept adopted by ABS for the 1981 census, leading to a greater incidence than in earlier years of women being reported as head of the family where both husband and wife are present.[1] The important point in this context is that *total* levels of headship (for both sexes combined) have continued to increase for all ages between 1976 and 1981, and this is clear from Table 7.1. In the youngest age category there was a continuation of the trend toward higher headship rates which was evident in the previous two decades. Throughout the post-war period more and more children have been leaving their parents' home, and at a younger age than in the past. This was not only a result of the major post-war decline in average age at first marriage up to the mid-1970s and the almost universal ability of those young marrieds to establish a separate household

[1] The concept of a head of household was employed in Australian censuses up until the 1976 census and this historically tended to mean that a husband was considered the head of a household which he and his wife maintain jointly. To eliminate this implicit sexism in 1981 the ABS abandoned this concept and replaced it with that of 'person one', i.e. the person in respect of whom the first column of the census schedule was completed.

straight after marriage, unlike many of their parents, but also of the growing trend for young men and women to establish households in so-called 'non-family living situations'. This created a considerable upswing in demand for housing—for flats and apartments as well as detached houses. It is extremely difficult to predict whether or not these trends for higher headship rates among young adults will continue or change. It may be that very high rates of unemployment among younger people and the growing popularity of communal living arrangements will alter the trend. There is also some evidence in the United States of a growing tendency for unmarried young adults to return to the parental home after spending a period of time in a separate household, because of increased unemployment and costs of housing (Cary 1980, p. 90). The projections of headship rates made by the National Population Inquiry (Di Iulio 1976, p. 15) assume that an increase in the headship rates will occur over the projection period (1976–2001) among the 15–19 age group. More recent projections by the Indicative Planning Council for the Housing Industry (1984, p. 62) have an increasing headship rate scenario (associated with high levels of economic growth) and a decreasing rate scenario associated with low levels of economic growth.

Another demographic element shaping the rate of household formation, and hence housing demand, is the rising incidence of divorce. The proportion of household heads made up of permanently separated and divorced persons rose from less than 1 per cent in 1947 to 5 per cent in 1971 and the liberalization of grounds for divorce by the 1975 Family Law Act further increased this proportion to 11 per cent in 1981.

A further demographic trend which must be considered is the ageing of the Australian population (Chapter 6) and the tendency for people to maintain separate living quarters not only after their children have formed households of their own but also after attaining retirement age and following widowhood. The essential point here then is that separate households are 'surviving' longer than in the past and hence requiring separate housing units for a longer period.

CHANGING PATTERNS OF HOUSEHOLD AND FAMILY STRUCTURE

Household composition and family structure have undergone fundamental demographic and sociological changes in Australia during the post-war period. The sociological underpinnings of these changes are not fully understood but the demographic influences are fairly readily identified. Figure 7.4 shows that since the 1966 census significant shifts have taken place in the relative importance of different types of family structures. It is apparent that the conventional stereotype of the typical Australian family being a wife, husband and dependent children is one which needs some revision, since it accounted for 30.7 per cent of families in 1966 but only 26.6 per cent by 1981. This remained the most common of the family types but it will be noted that the gap between this 'typical' composition and single-person households in 1981 was only one-third its size in 1966. It will be shown later that a substantial number of the 'other adults' in the categories of family type

Figure 7.4 Changing distribution of family types, 1966–81

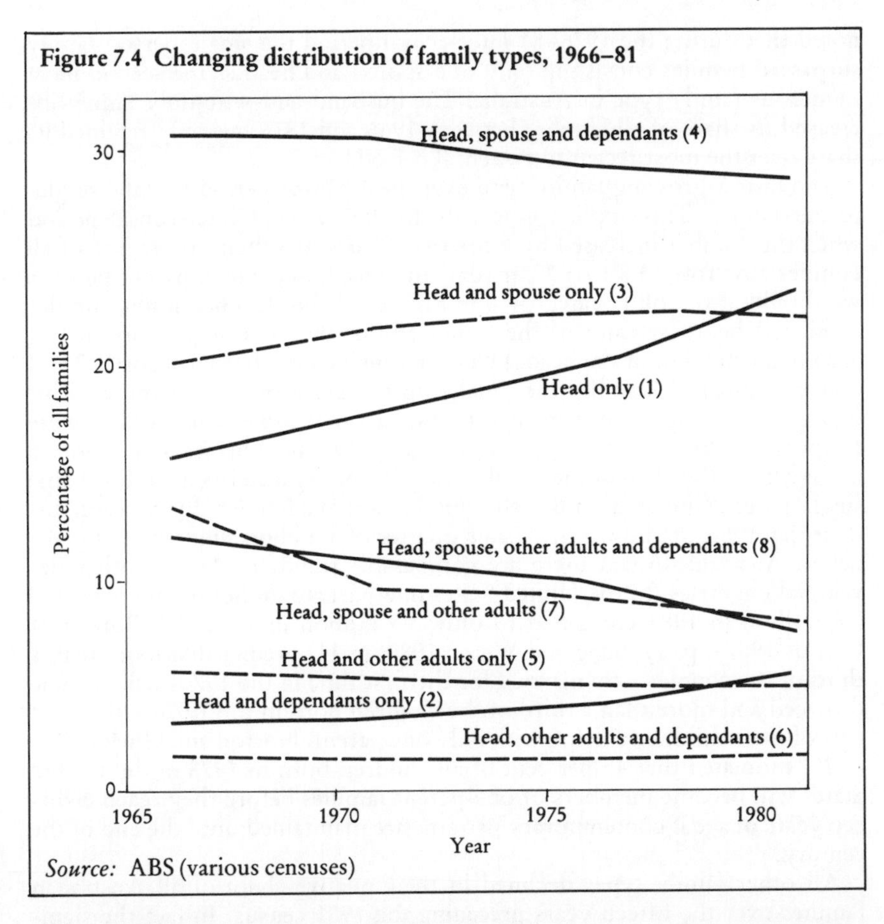

Source: ABS (various censuses)

given in Figure 7.4 are in fact children of the head and spouse of that family who have reached adult age. Hence, if we add categories 4, 7 and 8 together, all families with head, spouse and children (whether dependent or not) will be involved except for those not residing in private households (e.g. those in caravans on census night). Obviously since the 'other adults' category also includes other adult relatives of the head of the family (e.g. elderly parents or parents-in-law), this figure will exaggerate the actual number of families comprising only the head, spouse and their children. In 1966 these three categories together accounted for 53.1 per cent of all families, but by 1981 there had been a major decline to 43.6 per cent.

Over the fifteen years covered in the diagram, the number of one-person families more than doubled while the total population increased by only 28.6 per cent. This has been a pattern characteristic of most developed countries. In Canada, for example, between 1951 and 1976 the number of people living alone increased from one-quarter of a million to 1.2 million, while the total population increased by only 64 per cent (Harrison 1981, p. 9). It will be noted that during the 1976–81 inter-censal period the single-person family surpassed families consisting only of a spouse and head as the second most numerous family type in Australia. The husband-and-wife-only family increased its share of all families between 1966 and 1976 but only retained its share over the most recent inter-censal period.

The fastest-growing family type over the 1966–81 period was the single-parent family. This applied especially to the 1976–81 inter-censal period when the number increased by more than 90 000 and their proportion of all families rose from 3.8 to 5.2 per cent. In considering single-parent families we should also look at category 6 in Figure 7.4 (head, other adults and dependants) because many of the 'other adults' in this category are in fact grown-up children of the head. Hence, if one includes both categories 2 and 6 as single-parent families they make up 6.6 per cent of all families. This figure may be slightly exaggerated by the fact that some householders were temporarily absent on the night of the census. On the other hand, category 5 in Figure 7.4 (head and other adults) can also be regarded as including some single-parent families although the children are of adult age. In any case, it is clear that there are now more than a quarter of a million single-parent families in Australia. Again there are comparable trends evident in other developed countries. In the United States one-parent families numbered some 6.6 million in 1981 compared to only 3.3 million in 1970 (US Bureau of Census 1982a, p. 1). Bane and Weiss (1980, p. 11) predict that more than a third of the couples who married for the first time in the 1970s will become divorced and more than a third of the children born in the 1970s will spend part of their childhood living with only one parent. Norton and Glick (1979, p. 20) estimated that 45 per cent of all children born in 1978 in the United States will become members of one-parent families before they reach eighteen years of age if contemporary patterns are maintained until the end of the century.

All other family types declined in their relative share of all Australian families over the fifteen years preceding the 1981 census. In fact the significance of families made up of head, spouse, other adults and dependants decreased to such an extent that the number of such families actually was less in 1981 than in 1966. Much of this absolute decline was recorded in the 1976–1981 inter-censal period. This type of family is of particular importance and interest since it includes many of those households where a parent (or parents) of the household head or spouse are living with them. If the decline in this category indicates a reduction in the propensity of householders to take in aged parents, it is a matter of considerable policy interest and concern given the substantial increase in the Australian aged population which is going to occur during the next decade. But, as noted earlier, the 'other adults' category also includes adult children of the head and spouse of the family, so the decline in this category may also reflect the increased propensity for young adults to leave the parental home at a younger age than in the past and to set up separate households of their own.

We should also note some differences between males and females in the headship of the various family types considered above. Table 7.2 shows the

Table 7.2 Changes in family type by sex of head of family, 1976–1981

Family type	Males			Females			Ratio M:F	
	1976	1981	Percentage change	1976	1981	Percentage change	1976	1981
1 Head only	364 197	507 196	+39.2	475 842	606 844	+ 27.5	0.77	0.84
2 Head, children only	23 325	34 887	+49.5	137 321	217 170	+ 58.1	0.17	0.16
3 Head, spouse only	922 846	987 996	+ 7.0	28 599	75 315	+163.3	32.27	13.12
4 Head, spouse, children	1 215 543	1 323 207	+ 8.8	17 370	55 222	+217.9	69.98	23.96
5 Head, other adults only	64 603	70 549	+ 9.2	136 078	152 820	+ 12.3	0.47	0.46
6 Head, other adults, children	13 260	12 343	− 6.9	47 821	52 491	+ 9.7	0.28	0.24
7 Head, spouse, other adults	373 030	355 396	− 4.7	6 511	14 518	+122.9	57.29	24.48
8 Head, spouse, other adults, children	414 127	335 996	−18.8	5 399	10 920	+102.2	76.70	30.77
Total	3 390 931	3 627 570	+ 6.9	854 941	1 185 300	+ 38.6	3.97	3.06

Source: calculated from ABS censuses of 1976 and 1981

number and proportions of Australian household heads who were males and females in 1976 and 1981. It will be noticed that there was a large increase in the proportion of households headed by women between 1976 and 1981. In addition to the different concept of household headship used in 1981 which was explained earlier, the causes of these trends in Australia are similar to those listed by the US Bureau of Census for the large growth in the number of families maintained by women. These were as follows:

1 an increase in child-bearing outside marriage;
2 the dissolution of families through separation, divorce and widowhood;
3 contemporary women's inclination and ability to establish and maintain independent families rather than live with parents and other relatives;
4 the disproportionately large segment of the population in the young adult stage and living as singles.

In Australia between 1976 and 1981 the ratio of male to female heads declined from 4:1 to 3:1. It is clear from Table 7.2 however that this change was not evenly distributed across all types of families. In fact, among single-person families, which accounts for more than a half of all female family heads, the inter-censal increase was not as great as it was for males. The number of males living alone increased by 39.2 per cent between the censuses compared to 27.5 per cent for women living alone, although there were still nearly five women living alone for every four men in that living situation. This may be a function of increased divorce rates resulting in more men living alone and perhaps more young men leaving home and setting up independent single-person households.

One of the most interesting trends evident in Table 7.2 is the dominance of single-parent families by female heads. The very rapid increase in the number of single-parent families between 1976 and 1981 has been greater for those headed by women. In 1981 there were 217 170 single-parent families headed by a woman compared to 34 887 single-parent families headed by a man. In the United States in 1981 some 90 per cent of one-parent families were maintained by women (US Bureau of Census, 1982a, p. 1). It should also be noted in Table 7.2 that there were 52 491 families comprising a female head, other adults and children which also could be classified as single-parent families.

It is interesting to compare patterns in the United States and Australia with respect to the proportions of primary family units being maintained by married couples, single males and single females. This is attempted in Table 7.3, which also utilizes the United States Bureau of Census concept of 'family' and 'non-family' (i.e., households comprising one person or two or more unrelated persons). It can be seen that the split between family and non-family households is similar in both nations but there are some significant differences in the distribution between different types of family households. In the United States the proportions of such households maintained by single parents is double that in Australia. Hence it may well be that single-parent families in Australia will continue to increase rapidly. This has important implications for planners, since such families constitute intensive users of welfare services and are often poor (Hugo 1983b).

Table 7.3 Various household types as a percentage of all households, Australia and United States, 1981

Household type	Australia	United States
Family households		
Maintained by a married couple	66.8	59.8
Man—no wife present	0.93	2.3
Woman—no husband present	5.5	11.0
Non-family households		
Maintained by a man	10.94	11.3
Maintained by a woman	15.9	15.5

Sources: ABS (1981 census); Population Reference Bureau (1982, p. 13)

Anticipating future changes in family composition is even more problematical than projecting future household formation rates. However, there is little or no evidence to suggest that the trends of change in the structure of Australian households during the 1970s which have been identified here will be drastically redirected during the rest of the 1980s. In the United States context Reynolds et al. (1980, p. 15) have made the following prediction for households through to the end of the decade:

> even quite conservative projections show the number of individuals living alone increasing and the average household size declining through the end of the decade. Non-family households and single parent households are likely to grow more rapidly than husband-wife households.

Such a prognosis would appear to apply equally to the Australian situation.

The major changes in the composition of families and in living arrangements briefly outlined above are the product of wider demographic, social and economic forces. It is with an examination of some of these forces, insofar as they can be discerned from census data, that this chapter is particularly concerned. Accordingly we will now turn to a brief analysis of recent trends in marriage and divorce, since these obviously have a basic influence upon changes in family formation and dissolution as well as upon the changing structure and composition of the family.

CHANGING MARRIAGE AND DIVORCE PATTERNS

McDonald (in ESCAP 1982) recognized two major eras in the demography of marriage in Australia. Before 1900 both age at marriage and proportions marrying were similar to those prevailing in England at that time. However after 1900 there was a movement away from this pattern whereby both 'men and women married at younger ages and a much lower proportion remained unmarried' (ESCAP 1982, p. 186). Figure 7.5, for example, shows the consistent decline in the proportion of men and women aged 45–49 who had never married over the years since the 1921 census.

Figure 7.5 also gives some indications of changing patterns in age at marriage via the proportions of persons aged 20–24 who were unmarried at each census since 1921. After the increase in age at marriage during the depression of the 1930s there were two major periods of downward movement in the

Figure 7.5 Percentage of males and females never married in particular age groups, 1921–81

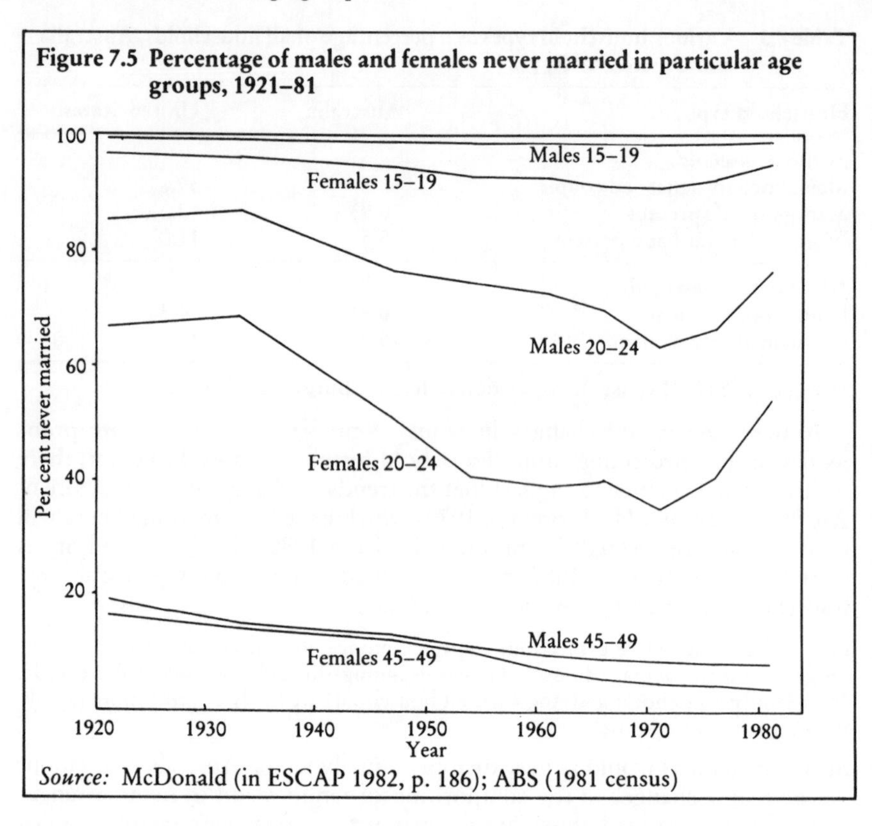

Source: McDonald (in ESCAP 1982, p. 186); ABS (1981 census)

age at marriage which are clearly evident in the middle two graphs. These were during the Second World War and in the latter half of the 1960s. McDonald (ESCAP 1982, p. 190) concludes that from the 1930s onward (or at least until the early 1970s), the conservatism that had surrounded marriage from initial white settlement was dissipated and Australians displayed much greater readiness to marry.

If we turn to the 1970s, however, Figure 7.5 shows that whereas in 1971 36 per cent of females and 64 per cent of males aged 20–24 years had never married, this had increased to 54 per cent and 77 per cent respectively by 1981. This clearly indicates that in the 1970s Australians had begun to marry at much later ages. It is interesting to note, however, that a reverse pattern exists among women aged 55 years and over where there has been a decline in the proportion never married during the 1970s (Hugo 1983b, pp. 26–8). This of course reflects the high marriage rates among young women in the 1940s and 1950s who are entering the older age categories during the 1970s. However there are still large numbers of women, and to a lesser extent men, in the 70+ age category who have never been married. Indeed, among women there is a regular pattern of increase in the proportion who have never married with increasing age; from 4.1 per cent in the 45–54 age group to 9.1 per cent of those aged over 70. The latter is significant from a policy viewpoint. It means that nearly a tenth of older women and 7.6 per cent of men aged over 70 *do not* have daughters and sons whom they can call upon to help them, or any grandchildren. One would expect some of these to be lonely people. This pattern has existed for all of the 1970s; but as the younger cohorts move into the 70+ age category the proportions never married will decrease.

In examining the proportion married it is as well to bear in mind that at the censuses of 1976 and 1981 no distinction was made between *de facto* and legal marriages. Hence, it would seem that most people in a form of consensual union would have been reported as 'now married'. We have very little information on the extent of incidence of various forms of consensual union. However, the survey of families undertaken by the ABS in 1982 (ABS, 1982e) does give some indication of the incidence of '*de facto*' and 'living together as married' unions. The survey asked respondents to indicate whether their marriage relationship was either *de facto*/living together as married or one of legal marriage. However the survey report points out (p. 2) that 'some respondents may have chosen not to reveal that they were "living with someone as married" and therefore the number of couples "living together as married" may have been understated'. The survey showed a significant incidence at all ages between 15 and 54, although the proportion of *de facto* marriages falls off steadily with age. Half of unions involving women under 20 were such unions, while 17 per cent of those of women 20–24 and 7 per cent for women aged 25–29 were reported as 'living together as married'. Among the *de facto* married women 64.4 per cent had no children present and 16.2 per cent had one child present.

McDonald (ESCAP 1982, p. 190) in his discussion of changes in age at marriage points out that there has been a broadening of the age at marriage. He concludes that 'While Australians in the 1970s have moved rapidly to delay marriage, it seems that most ultimately will marry'. He makes the point that the current move toward later age at marriage is a return to earlier conservatism, despite it being frequently seen as a liberal change in behaviour patterns. He argues that it represents a change in the pattern of decision-making regarding marriage whereby couples are delaying marriage until the 'economically' and psychologically proper time. This is greatly facilitated by modern contraceptive methods. He suggests that the significance of marriage as a life cycle event has declined and that the birth of the first child has assumed greater significance:

> The distinction between two young couples, one legally married without children, the other living together in a defacto union has become small. Marriage takes place, therefore, when a couple feel they have reached the economically proper time to have children or, if they plan to delay their first child after marriage, when they feel that they have reached the psychologically proper time to marry.

Since marriage patterns generally have undergone significant and major changes it is important to establish whether there are variations between groups in these patterns. McDonald (1974) found in his analysis of the period of the 'marriage boom', for example, that education was a major factor influencing age at marriage. In the key child-bearing age groups from 20 to 34 years the proportion of women with tertiary qualifications who remained unmarried was substantially higher than for all women in those ages. Indeed, this pattern is maintained for all subsequent ages. On the other hand, the proportion of women with no post-school educational qualifications who remained never married was below the average for all women at all ages. Wide educational differences therefore exist in marriage behaviour patterns and as McDonald (ESCAP 1982, p. 192) points out these differences may be widening:

> it appears that the decline in this level of conformity [in marriage patterns] in the 1970s may be related to the emergence of a more hard headed approach to marriage among educated and career oriented women, whose proportion of the younger population increased rapidly during the late 1960s and the 1970s.

Some support for this view of widening differentials in marriage behaviour is provided by analysis of differences between occupational groups. McDonald's (1974) analysis of 1961 census data found few such differentials, but 1981 census data show some substantial differences between groups in the proportions married, especially in the key 20–34 age groups (Hugo 1983b,

Figure 7.6 Percentage of women in particular occupational groups never married at the 1981 census, by age

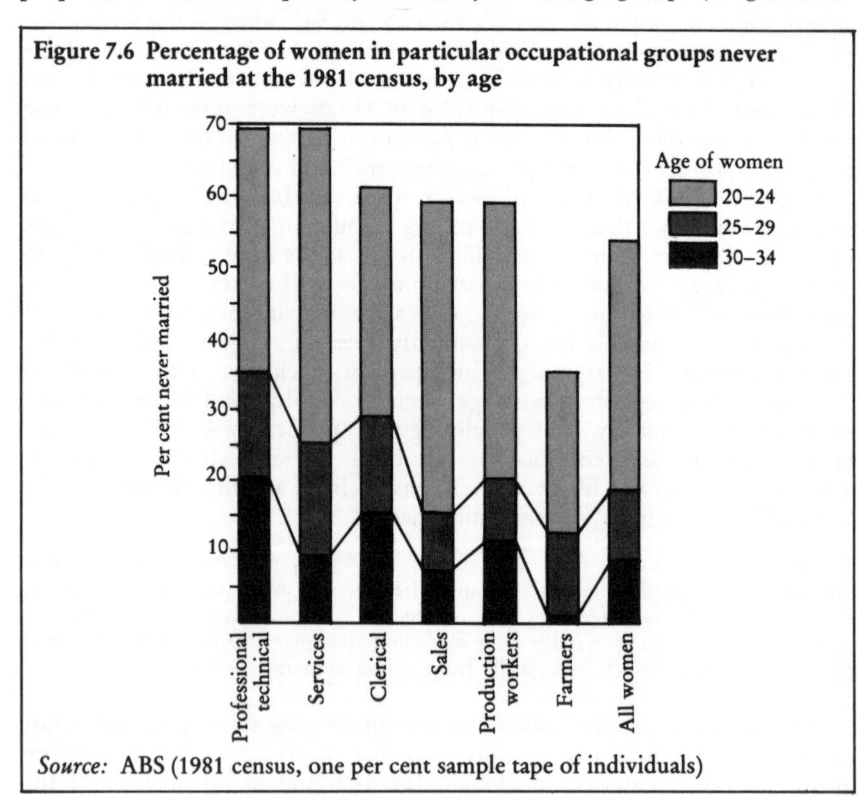

Source: ABS (1981 census, one per cent sample tape of individuals)

pp. 31–2). Figure 7.6 shows the proportions remaining unmarried are consistently well above average among women employed in professional and technical occupations. In fact for most employed women these proportions were above the average for all women, albeit to a lesser extent than for professional women. The major exception is women employed in agricultural occupations for whom marriage is nearly universal and tends to occur at an early age. There have been substantial changes in the two decades since McDonald's work and differentials in marriage patterns according to occupational status and different types of occupation are now of some significance.

McDonald's (ESCAP 1982, p. 191) analysis of the marriage behaviour of different birthplace groups as revealed by the 1966 census concluded that 'no matter what the pattern at arrival or in the country of origin, all immigrant groups moved towards the pattern for the Australian born'. Table 7.4 shows the proportion of women in various birthplace groups who were classified at the 1981 census as never having been married. Although the numbers are small and the chance of sampling error in some groups is significant, there are some large differences in evidence. For most age groups the proportions of Australian-born women remaining unmarried were greater than those for United Kingdom-born and Southern European-born women of equivalent age. The pattern reported by McDonald of UK-born women's marriage behaviour closely approximating that of the Australian-born is apparent. The high proportions of Australian-born women aged 50 years and over in 1981 who had never been married underline the fact mentioned earlier that a large proportion of our aged popluation in the 1980s and 1990s will not have husbands, daughters and sons to interact with or rely upon for support of various kinds. This pattern is much less in evidence among immigrant women. The data relating to younger Southern European-born women suggest that they have been less affected by the patterns of delaying marriage than have the Australian-born.

Contemporaneous with the downturn in marriage has been a rapid increase in divorce. In 1961 there were 2.8 divorces per 1000 married women

Table 7.4 Percentage of women in particular birthplace groups never married, by age, 1981

Age group	Australia		UK		Greece		Italy		Yugoslavia	
of women	No.	%	No.	%	No.	%	No.	%	No.	%
15–19	5037	96.0	367	96.5	19	82.6	48	94.1	44	88.0
20–24	2740	55.0	227	47.9	16	26.2	28	43.1	13	19.6
25–29	893	19.0	69	15.4	3	4.6	8	10.8	5	6.5
30–34	373	9.1	40	7.6	6	6.1	10	7.6	2	2.2
35–39	192	6.0	21	4.1	2	2.0	0	0.0	0	0.0
40–49	135	2.6	25	2.8	0	0.0	5	1.4	2	1.4
50–59	304	5.7	15	2.1	1	1.1	3	1.1	0	0.0
60+	669	8.1	78	5.4	3	4.2	1	1.4	1	1.7

Source: ABS (1981 census, one per cent sample tape of individuals)

Figure 7.7 Numbers and percentages of women divorced or separated, by age, 1971 and 1981

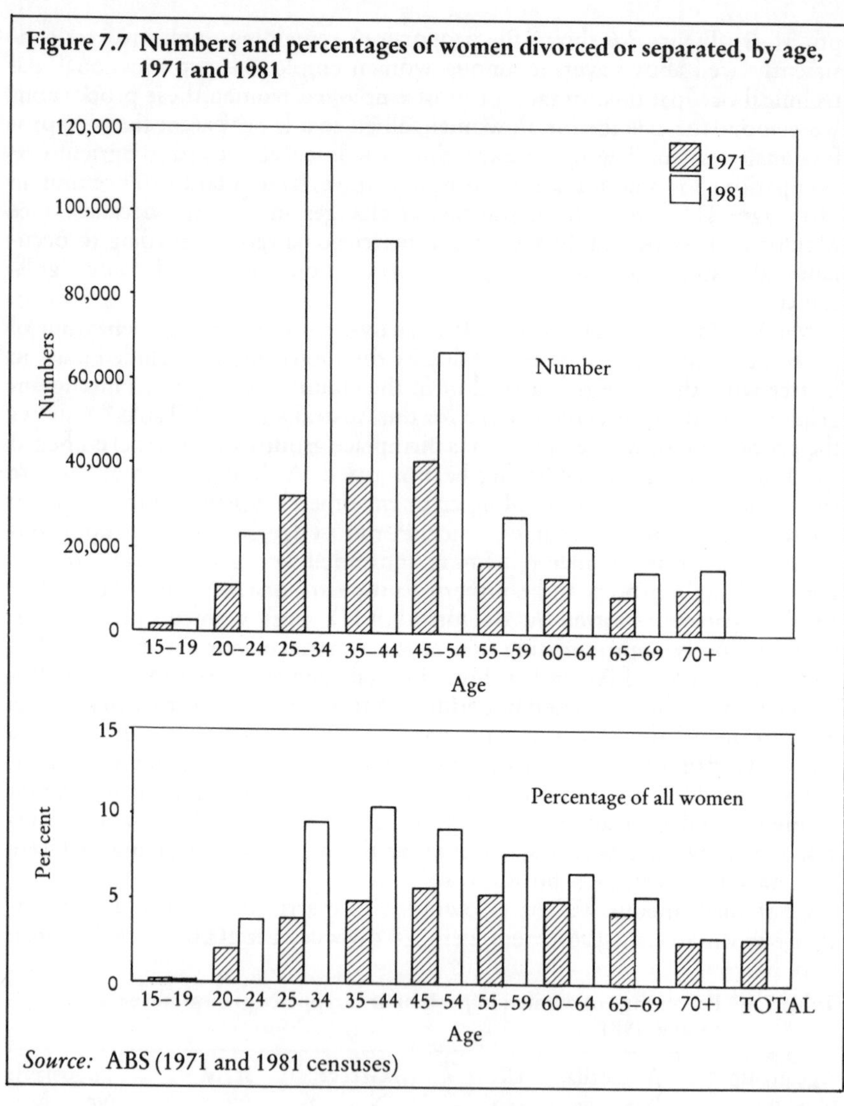

Source: ABS (1971 and 1981 censuses)

but this increased to 4.3 in 1971 and 12.7 in 1981. The highest rate yet achieved was 19.2 in 1976 following the promulgation of the Family Law Act. Moreover there has been a substantial increase in the proportion of women whose first marriage ends in divorce. In fact Figure 7.7 shows that in 1981 a tenth of all women aged 25–34, 35–44 and 45–54 were divorced or separated. McDonald (in ESCAP 1982) found that in the 1960s the extent of remarriage following divorce in Australia was surprisingly high, with virtually all divorced persons remarrying within six years. In 1982 some 30 per cent of Australia's 117 275 marriages involved at least one divorced person and in 10 per cent of cases both participants were previously divorced. More than a half of all marriages of women aged over 30 were of previously divorced women. At the 1981 census the proportion of women who had been divorced or separated by their early thirties was over 12 per cent. This is still substantially lower than in the United States where it was estimated during the 1970s that between 25 and 29 per cent of women in their late twenties will end their first marriage in divorce some time during their lifetime (Brown 1981, p. 11), while the equivalent proportion in Australia is about a fifth (Day 1979, p. 31). Hence, it would seem that rates of divorce will continue to rise in Australia for some time yet. This pattern is seen in some quarters as a sign of social malaise and a symptom of breakdown of the Australian family. In such quarters the 1975 Family Law Act, which provides only one ground (irretrievable breakdown) for dissolution of marriage, is seen as 'encouraging people to look on marriage as a temporary arrangement to be withdrawn from at the slightest provocation' (Day 1979, p. 26). Most commentators, however, see it as an appropriate and reasonable method of resolving poor marriages.

NON-FAMILY MEMBERS OF HOUSEHOLDS

The ways in which individuals in Australia are grouping themselves into households have become increasingly more complex during the post-war period; it is difficult to chart the detailed demography of these patterns because official data collection, coding and publication procedures and concepts have not always kept pace with the constant changes in these patterns. A basic distinction made at the 1981 census is between family and non-family members of households. The various categories of persons regarded at the census as being non-family members of private households include the following (ABS, 1983f, p. 15): related non-family members (relatives belonging to a family unit outside the household); boarders; and other non-family members (e.g., friends, guests, foster children, employees).

At the 1981 census there were some 477 816 non-family members of private households. It is clear that many of these are cohabiting in households with persons who were classified as single-person *families* at the census. This can be inferred from the fact that, whereas the census identified 1 113 136 *family* units consisting of only one person, only 839 301 *households* were reported as having only one person. It would appear that this pattern has been established through most of the 1970s since at the 1976 census 842 405 family units consisting of one person were identified but only 649 646 households were counted as having one person.

The 1981 census one per cent sample of individuals identified some 486 600 persons as non-family members of households. Of these, 57 700 were related in some way to the household head and 52 500 were boarders. We will concentrate here on the remaining 376 400 (or 2.6 per cent of the total population). An examination of the distribution of sizes of households in which there were non-family individuals shows a clear concentration of non-family individuals in two-person households, with 42 per cent of non-family people being in such households compared to only 19 per cent of family individuals (Hugo 1983b). Two-thirds of cohabiting unrelated persons are in two- or three-person households compared to around a third of family individuals. Whereas 2.6 per cent of the total population was classified as not being related to the head of the household in which they were living at the time of the census, this applied to 6 per cent of people in two-person households and 4 per cent of persons in three-person households.

Persons residing in non-private dwellings on the night of the census made up 4.5 per cent of the population and nearly two-thirds were in dwellings with more than sixty residents and 84 per cent were in dwellings with twenty or more inmates. This reflects the predominance of institutional populations in this group. Prominent among these are those in aged care institutions, with nearly a quarter of the non-private dwelling population being aged over 65 (Hugo 1983b). On the other hand, 77 per cent of the 'non-family' individuals were aged between 15 and 34.

The population living in situations in which they are not related to the household head are overwhelmingly young adults living in pairs or groups of three. Indeed 5 per cent of all Australians aged 15–19, 10 per cent of those aged 20–24 and 4 per cent of those aged 25–34 were classified in this way at the 1981 census. In addition, the percentages of these groups in institutions, caravan parks, etc. (i.e. in non-private dwellings) were also relatively high—5 per cent, 6 per cent and 4 per cent respectively. However, the highest proportions of Australians enumerated in non-private dwellings were among the older age groups, with 6 per cent of those aged 65–74 and 19 per cent of the 75+ group living in this category of dwellings, predominantly various types of aged care institutions.

Some further information regarding non-family individuals can be discerned from the 1982 survey of Australian families (ABS, 1982e) which recognized a special category of 'non-family individuals' defined as 'persons living alone or who are not related to any other member of the household'. This survey identified some 1 495 500 persons (10.2 per cent of all Australians) as non-family individuals. The majority of these were persons living alone—numbering 1 009 200 persons (58.9 per cent of them females)—and a further 74 500 were living with other family members (e.g., brothers or sisters-in-law). Hence 411 800 persons were living with other non-family individuals. Some 55.3 per cent of these were males, whereas only 41.1 per cent of persons living alone were males. Young adults dominated among persons living with people to whom they are not related—78 per cent of males and 77 per cent of females being under the age of 35. On the other hand, among people living alone, older persons dominate with 63 per cent of women and 32 per cent of males living alone being aged over 60. Unfortunately we do not have comparable census data for 1976 and 1981 to establish the amount of increase in the number of unrelated people living together, but it is clear that this has become a pattern of living arrangements of considerable importance especially among the young. This of course is also occurring in other Euro-American societies. In 1982 in the United States there were 1.9 million households shared by two unrelated adults of the opposite sex and 81 per cent of these included a partner under the age of 35 (US Bureau of Census, 1983a).

AGE COMPOSITION OF DIFFERENT FAMILY TYPES

The age structure of families is a vitally important determinant of many services required by those families. Hence, it is important to establish whether there are significant differences between the various family types with respect to their age composition.

Before examining the age structure of families we should note the age characteristics of the 1 135 701 Australians (7.8 per cent of the total population) who were not considered to be family members by the definition adopted at the census. Non-family individuals living in private households, who make up some 44 per cent of persons not included in families, are predominantly young adults aged 15 to 34. Figure 7.8 shows the age structure of the 638 309 (4.4 per cent) of Australians living in non-private dwellings on the night of the census. As indicated earlier, this group is dominated by older persons (especially females), with a fifth being aged over 70 years. However, there is also a large representation of young adults, especially males, many of whom would be living in barracks, tertiary education colleges, etc., as well as others who were travelling at the time of the census.

Figure 7.9 shows the age-sex distribution of household heads (i.e. those designated 'person one') of the eight major family types identified earlier and graphically points to differences between the various types of families.

For the single-person family, as is the case in North America (e.g., Harrison 1981, p. 177), there are two distinct bulges in the age pyramid—'one at young adult ages (20–29) and another among the older age groups (particularly 60–79) ... the pyramid compresses at old ages'. Hence, living alone tends to be concentrated among people in both the earliest and latter stages of separate household formation. The differences between the sexes are of

Figure 7.8 Age–sex structure of the populations living in private dwellings and in non-private dwellings, 1981

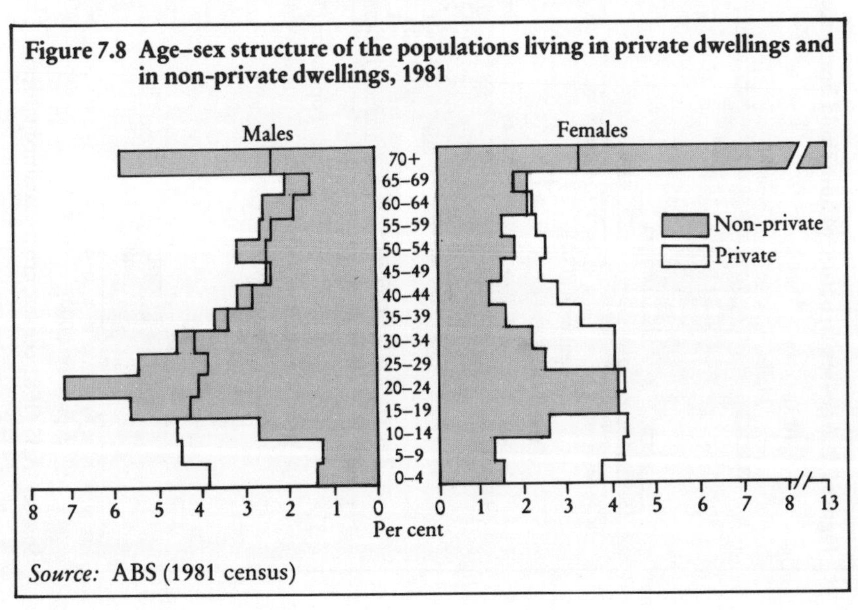

Source: ABS (1981 census)

Figure 7.9 Age–sex structure of household heads according to family type, 1981

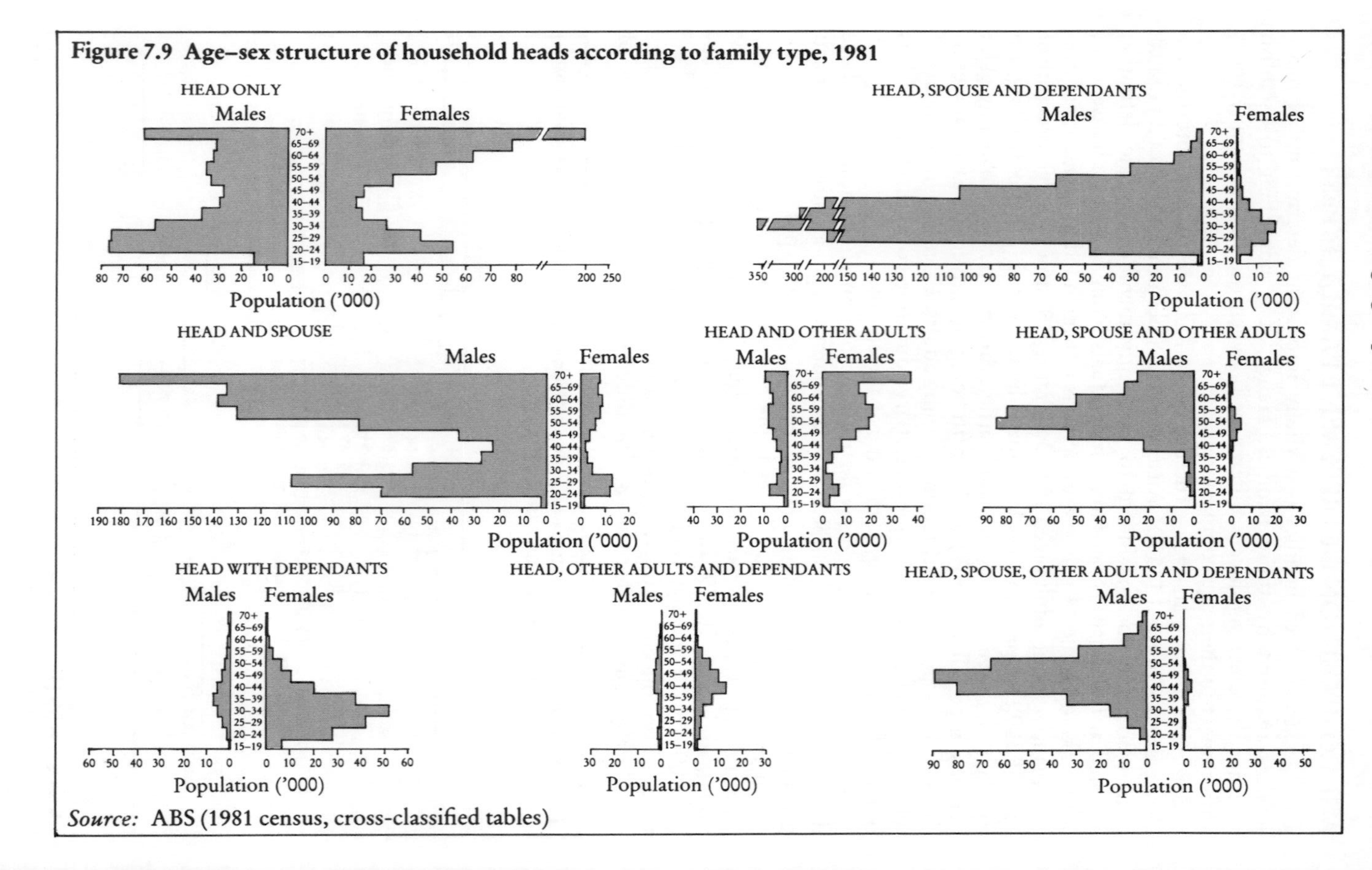

Source: ABS (1981 census, cross-classified tables)

Table 7.5 Single-person families—changing age structure, 1976–81

Age	1981 Males	Percentage change 1976–81	1981 Females	Percentage change 1976–81	1981 Total	Percentage change 1976–81
<30	165 743	+50	111 828	+ 68	277 571	+57
30–44	122 883	+71	56 301	+ 79	179 184	+73
45–59	94 744	+20	93 977	+ 11	188 721	+15
60+	122 892	+18	344 697	+ 17	467 589	+18
Total	506 291	+38	606 844	+227	1 113 135	+32

Source: ABS (censuses of 1976 and 1981)

interest, with males living alone outnumbering females in all age groups under 55 and females being overwhelmingly dominant in the older ages, especially among the over-70s. This age distribution has several important policy implications. For young people, living alone is frequently an assertion of independence and a prelude to marriage and family formation; but among older people, living alone is too often associated with loneliness, disengagement from society and need for services.

Given that single-person households are among the fastest-growing of all household types, it is important to establish whether there is any difference between the two major age groups of such families in their rates of growth. Table 7.5 shows that during the 1976–81 inter-censal period the young adult bulge in the age pyramid of single-person householders grew considerably faster than that in the 60+ age group. Although the under-thirties age group accounts for only a quarter of single-person families, the numbers of these young single-person families grew by 97 per cent during the 1976–81 period. Much of this growth of course is not of single-person *households*, since many of these single-person families have one or more non-family individuals cohabiting with them. The overall growth is a function of the post-war baby boom cohorts moving through the ages where they leave the parental home for the first time to set up their own households as individuals or cohabitors with other people to whom they are not related. The other fast-growing age group among people living alone, however, is in the middle working age groups between 30 and 44 years, where there was a 73 per cent increase in the numbers of single-person families. This group still, however, makes up only a relatively small proportion of the total number of single-person families (16.1 per cent). The reason for this rapid growth is, of course, the increase in the incidence of divorce during the 1976–81 inter-censal period, which has had the effect of not only creating a large number of single-parent families but also inflating the number of single-person families. The older (60+) population accounted for 42 per cent of single-person families and, although their numbers grew much faster than the total population between the censuses (by 19 per cent), it was by no means as rapid as that at the other end of the age spectrum.

The second family category to be considered is that of *single-parent fami-*

Figure 7.10 Age-sex distribution within family types, 1981

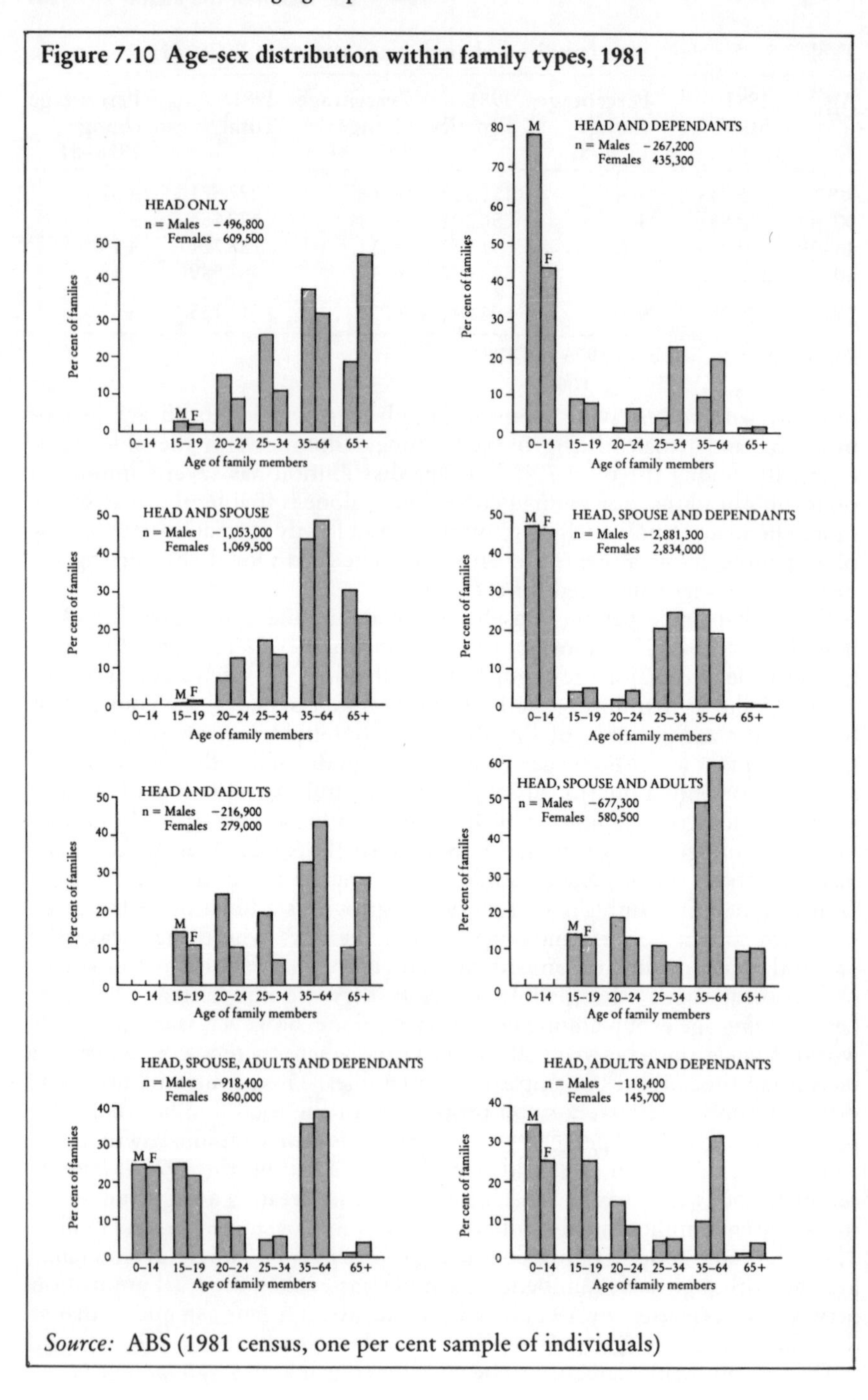

Source: ABS (1981 census, one per cent sample of individuals)

Table 7.6 Children in single-parent families, 1981

Type of single-parent family	Age group (years) 0–14 No.	Percentage	15–19 No.	Percentage
Head and dependants	399 300	10.9	56 900	4.6
Head, other adults and dependants	78 500	2.1	79 400	6.4
Total	477 800	13.0	136 300	11.0

Source: ABS (1981 census, one per cent sample tape of individuals)

lies. Figure 7.9 shows that there is an overwhelming predominance of females among the heads of those families and in the 25–34 age group. However, if we consider the entire population living in single-parent households shown in Figure 7.10, we see that this family type's age structure is dominated by young dependent children. This indicates that a substantial proportion of Australian children now spend part of their childhood living with only one of their parents. At the time of the 1981 census in Australia, as Table 7.6 shows, some 13 per cent of children aged less than 15 years and 11 per cent of those aged 15 to 19 lived in single-parent households. These figures are very high, especially when it is borne in mind that they refer only to a single point in time so that the proportion of all children who have spent or will spend at least part of their childhood in a single-parent family situation will be considerably higher. The significance of these figures for a whole range of social policies and programmes is obvious. Bane and Weiss (1980, p. 11) in reporting findings of a longitudinal study of the experience of 5000 families in the United States concluded the following:

> To note simply the trend to more single parent families is to understate the succession of changes a family undergoes. Most single mothers eventually remarry—after an average of 4.5 years. This may be a relatively brief interval for an adult, but is a significant one in a child's life.... Single parent status is an indicator of a chain of abrupt changes in family status, which not only cause significant psychological stress, but also produce other disruptions that add to the burden of stress. These include, especially, relocation and a reduction in income.

It is sometimes tacitly assumed that the vast majority of single-parent families are formed as a result of the divorce of the parents. However, the ABS 1982 sample survey of one-third of one per cent of Australian families found that of the nation's 263 700 single-parent families, only slightly over one-third (36.7 per cent) of the parents were divorced, while 30.3 per cent were separated, 18.7 per cent had never married and 14.4 per cent were widowed.

It is difficult to establish change over time in the proportion of Australian children living in single-parent households due to changing conventions and definitions used in the censuses. An attempt to compare changes over the 1971–1981 period is shown in Table 7.7 and although the data are not directly comparable, it is apparent that there was a major increase in the chances of

Table 7.7 Changes in the number and proportion of children living in 'head and dependants' families, 1971–81

Children in head and dependants families Year	No.	Percentage	Inter-censal change
1971	328 424	8.3	–
1976	397 070	9.9	+20.9
1981	614 100	12.5	+54.7

Note: For 1971 and 1976, data is for children aged under 16 only, whereas data for 1981 is for children aged less than 20. For 1971 and 1976, ratio of children in head and dependants families to those in head, other adults and dependants assumed to be same as in 1981
Source: ABS (censuses of 1971, 1976 and 1981)

a child being in a 'head and dependants' family during the second half of the 1970s.

Not all Australian single-parent families are included in the 'head with dependant' category; some single parents live with other adults in addition to their dependent children, and such families make up 1.35 per cent of all families and a fifth of all single-parent families. Figure 7.10 shows that the heads of such households are usually women, but women somewhat older than those heading 'head and dependants' families. This would suggest that in these families the 'other adults' may frequently be grown-up children of the head who are no longer classified as dependants. This is further supported when the entire age structure is examined in Figure 7.10.

The rapid growth of single-parent families has major policy and planning implications, especially in the area of social security. In 1983 more than 90 000 Australian women were receiving a separated wives supporting parents benefit. This represented an increase of 14 per cent over the previous year and a doubling over the previous five years. Figure 3.15 shows that it is the divorce/separation component of supporting parents which has grown most rapidly over the last decade, so that in 1983 there were 139 156 non-widowed persons receiving a supporting parents benefit. Analysis of 1981 census data supports the findings of earlier studies (Jordan 1979, pp. 6–7) that Australian 'single parent families, especially those headed by women, had lower per capita incomes on average, were less adequately housed and reported worse physical and mental health than two parent families'. The exponential growth of this group is thus a matter of major concern for the planning of future social security provision.

It was shown earlier that until recently families consisting of 'head and spouse only' had long been the second most common Australian family type. They were made up, first of older couples at the 'empty nest' stage of the life cycle when their children have grown up and left the parental home to set up a separate household, and second, of recently married young couples establishing themselves before beginning child-bearing. The age-

Table 7.8 Families comprising a head and spouse—changing age structure, 1976–81

Age	1981 Males	Percentage change 1976–81	1981 Females	Percentage change 1976–81	1981 Total	Percentage change 1976–81
<30	181 878	−13	25 016	+160	206 894	− 5
30–44	106 133	+29	9 094	+210	115 227	+35
45–59	247 317	+ 1	17 830	+160	265 147	+ 5
60+	452 662	+16	23 374	+152	476 036	+19
Total	987 995	+ 7	75 315	+163	1 063 310	+11

Source: ABS (censuses of 1976 and 1981)

sex structure of 'heads' of this type of family (Figure 7.9) and that of all members (Figure 7.10) reflect this pattern.

Given the bimodal nature of the age distribution of this important family type, we should establish if there is any significant difference between the two modal age categories in the rates of growth of 'head and spouse' families. Table 7.8 shows that over the 1976–81 inter-censal period growth was well above average in the oldest age categories, but the greatest rates of growth in 'head and spouse' families were in the 30–44 age group. This was partly an age structure effect, since this was the age group into which the post-war baby boom cohorts moved during the late 1970s. However, it is also indicative of the increasing number of couples in the baby boom cohorts who have decided to postpone having children until the woman is in her thirties or who have decided to remain childless. In fact this dominance of the *growth* of 'head and spouse' families by young adults in concert with the dominance of younger adult age groups in the recent *growth* of single-person households should be stressed. One- and two-person families have increased in recent years such that they now account for over half of all Australian families and it is sometimes suggested that this rapid growth is predominantly a function of the ageing of the population. However, it is clear from the 1981 census data that, while the importance of the older population among such families should not be overlooked, young adults are a major and *faster*-growing element in one- and two-person families. Hence, while our housing industry is making some belated moves away from an overwhelming emphasis upon three- and four-bedroom houses for young families to more appropriate housing for the aged population, there is little evidence of policies and programmes oriented toward younger singles and couples.

The above notwithstanding, it should be pointed out that nearly half of the families comprising a head and spouse are aged 60 years and over, and Table 7.8 shows that they too have grown rapidly through the late 1970s as the bulge in the age pyramid of people born in the 1910s and 1920s moves into the retirement ages. With improved longevity for older men it is certain that the number of households of this type will continue to increase significantly during the rest of the 1980s.

Turning to the stereotypical Australian family-type of 'head, spouse and dependants', the age-sex distribution of household heads in Figure 7.9 is, not surprisingly, dominated by males on the younger side of the middle working years. The structure of the total population in Figure 7.10 also contains no surprises, with two distinct bulges—that of parents in the young to middle working age groups and that of school-age and infant children. Although we usually think of children growing up in such a family situation, it is worth mentioning that only 73.1 per cent of Australian children aged under 15 years were enumerated in this type of family. While considering this family type we should also consider that comprising 'head, spouse, other adults and dependants'. Figure 7.9 shows heads of this family type to have a similar age-sex structure to that of head, spouse and dependants. It is apparent that the bulk of 'other adults' in this category are children of the head and spouse who have grown up and ceased to be dependants but not yet left the parental home. It is perhaps surprising in Figure 7.10 that there is such a small representation of persons aged 65 years and over since households which have taken in the aged parents or parents-in-law of the household heads (and still had their children at home) are included in this category. An ABS survey conducted in 1975 (ABS 1975b) found that only 2.6 per cent of two-parent Australian families had an aged person sharing their accommodation. As indicated earlier, older people are tending to remain in independent living units much longer than was previously the case. The pattern of living arrangements among the Australian aged has become one of maintaining an independent living unit (often an inappropriately large one) as long as is possible and, when the onset of disability prevents this, entering some form of institutionalized accommodation without an intermediate stage of living within the family of a son or daughter.

The 'head, spouse and other adults' category is the other family type that could include aged persons living with their adult children. Figure 7.9 shows that the age-sex distribution of heads of such families closely approximates that for 'head, spouse, other adults and dependants' except that it is slightly older. However, the age-sex structure of the total population living in this type of family situation (Figure 7.10) shows a much greater representation of the 35–64 and 65+ age groups than in the latter family category. This suggests that the incidence of older people living with their adult children is somewhat greater when those children no longer have dependent children living with them.

The final family category is that of 'head and other adults'. Figure 7.9 shows that this category has an age structure of heads which is dominated by women, especially older women, although the age distribution of the total population (Figure 7.10) living in these families has a considerable representation of young adults. This would suggest a high representation of single parents (especially mothers) living with grown-up children.

Hence each of the family types and the heads of those family types tend to have a distinctive age-sex structure. This has significant implications for the demand created by families for a range of goods and services, especially housing. It is to a consideration of the type of housing that these family types occupied at the time of the 1981 census that we now turn.

HOUSING OCCUPIED BY DIFFERENT FAMILY TYPES

The 1981 census data provide some interesting insights into the differences between family types in the type of housing which they occupy. Table 7.9 shows that more than half (55 per cent) of all single-person families occupy detached, separate dwellings. In addition, 81 per cent of families comprising only a wife and husband also lived in separate houses. This has led to some commentators suggesting that there is a considerable pool of 'under-utilized' housing in Australian cities. Nearly one and a half million of Australia's 'separate house' dwellings are occupied by families consisting of one person or a married couple. This represents 39 per cent of the total 'detached house' dwelling stock. Most of these occupants are in the older age groups and the house which they currently occupy is the same one in which they brought up their children who have since grown up and moved elsewhere (Hugo 1983b). The school of thought which designates such housing as 'under-utilized' often over-simplifies the situation. Before we contemplate any policy measures to encourage such families to move into more compact housing in order to free up larger homes for families, we need to answer the following questions:

1 How far is this perceived mismatch of family size and housing structure a function of policies and practices in the private and public housing sectors which have failed to produce sufficient and suitable alternative independent housing for older persons? The housing industry more than many others seems to be guided and preoccupied by the needs of the stereotypical Australian family, comprising wife, husband and dependent children, although such families now account for only slightly more than a quarter of the total families.
2 How much is the attachment of older single people and couples to their present dwelling specific to that dwelling, and how much to the local area in which social contacts are maintained? If the latter is significant, the provision of reasonable, appropriate higher-density housing in the 'middle suburbs' of Australian cities may free up lower-density housing for younger families and take some pressure off the housing market. It may also produce a greater age-mix in suburbs—a matter of considerable concern to many local governments.

There is a real need for research into this area to establish the housing preferences and needs of older people. It is clear that premature admission to aged care institutions is rife in Australia, and survey work would seem to point to many older people suffering from isolation and experiencing difficulty in maintaining large houses and gardens. Consideration of greater and more equitable provision of a range of intermediate housing possibilities which are within the reach of all older people is needed, as are policies which

Table 7.9 Distribution of family types by structure of dwelling, 1981

Family type	Separate house	Semi-detached house	Row or terrace house	Other medium density	Flats over 3 storeys	Caravan, houseboat etc.	Improvised home	Dwelling non-dwelg. combined	Not stated
Head only	55.16	4.39	2.55	30.07	3.78	0.65	0.30	1.07	2.00
Head with dependants	74.27	4.86	1.44	14.71	1.76	0.37	0.37	0.81	1.37
Head and spouse only	80.70	2.88	0.98	11.37	1.43	0.41	0.15	0.67	1.37
Head, spouse and dependants	89.86	1.89	0.49	4.51	0.49	0.34	0.19	0.84	1.26
Head and other adults only	77.24	3.89	1.51	13.48	1.77	0.14	0.13	0.67	1.13
Head, other adults and dependants	83.77	3.87	1.03	7.77	1.10	0.19	0.29	0.68	1.25
Head, spouse and other adults	91.76	2.01	0.56	3.28	0.49	0.12	0.07	0.61	1.05
Head, spouse and other adults and dependants	93.10	1.64	0.46	2.16	0.35	0.13	0.17	0.83	1.12
Total	78.70	2.95	1.21	12.67	1.58	0.38	0.20	0.83	1.43

Source: ABS (1981 census)

attempt to meet the housing needs of other groups in the city who are discriminated against in the existing housing market. The data in Table 7.9 as well as income and tenure data from the census point to several such groups. The lowest representation among families occupying detached houses is for single-parent families. This is a reflection of the general pattern of deprivation among this group as will be demonstrated later.

Consideration of the issues raised here, albeit in an over-simplified way, is imperative. The ageing patterns discussed in Chapter 6 will mean that the proportion of the 'detached dwelling' housing stock occupied by aged singles and couples will increase substantially in the 1980s. It is made even more urgent by the fact that such trends of the 1980s as increasing unemployment, increases in the number of highly vulnerable groups like single-parent families etc., mean that younger families are having increasing difficulties in gaining access to appropriate housing.

INCOME DISTRIBUTION AMONG FAMILY TYPES

In assessing the well-being of families, a paramount consideration is their income. Table 7.10 summarizes differences between family types in the level of weekly income at the 1981 census. Again, it is the single-parent family which shows up as being the least well off, with half earning less than $115 per week in 1981. This applies to less than 3 per cent of two-parent families and less than a quarter of husband-and-wife households. The highest family

Table 7.10 Weekly family income, percentage distribution by family type, 1981

Family type	Weekly family income None	<$77	$78–154	$155–288	$289–500	$501+	Not stated
Head only	2	17	14	41	12	1	1
Head and dependants	3	14	58	19	4	1	2
Head and spouse only	1	1	21	23	32	16	5
Head, spouse and dependants	1	1	10	37	32	10	10
Head and other adults only	3	38	16	34	6	1	2
Head, other adults and dependants	3	16	53	21	3	1	3
Head, spouse and other adults	1	1	23	31	29	8	7
Head, spouse, other adults and dependants	1	1	17	37	31	8	9
Total	1	4	20	34	20	6	5

Source: ABS (1981 census, one per cent sample tape of households)

Figure 7.11 Percentage of women in the workforce for two family types: head and spouse, and head, spouse and dependants, 1981

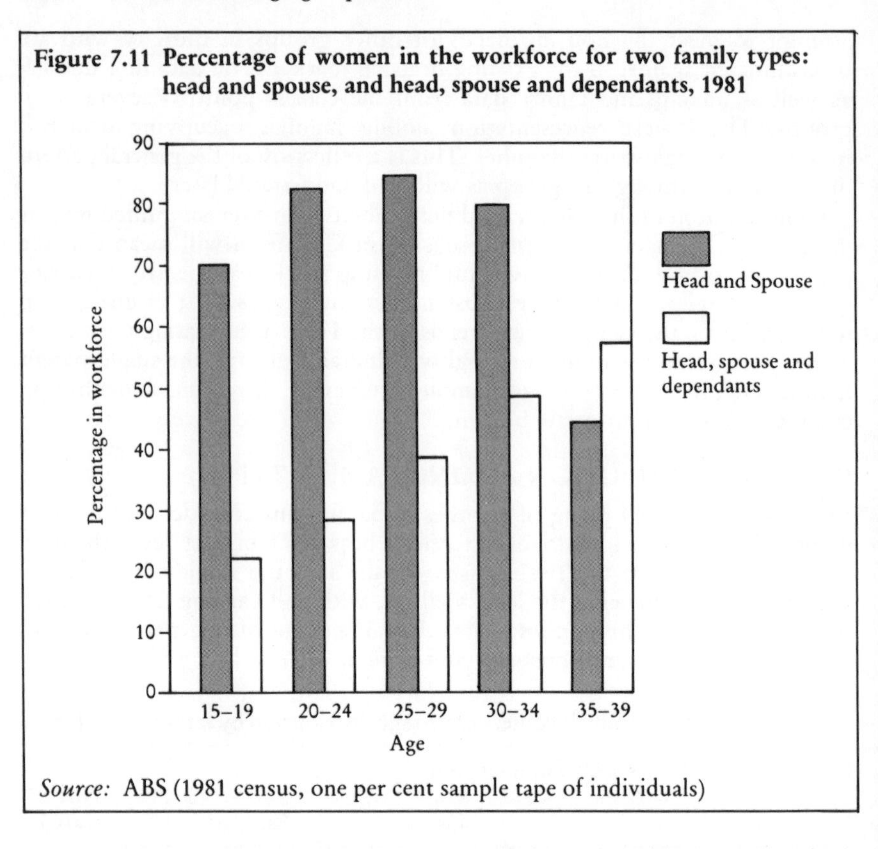

Source: ABS (1981 census, one per cent sample tape of individuals)

income levels occur in the head, spouse and dependant category, in which more than two-thirds of families earned over $232 per week. There were also relatively high average income levels in families in which there were several adults—obviously there is a high incidence of multiple income earners in such families.

One of the most important social changes which has impinged upon the structure and function of Australian families during the post-war period has been the major rise in women's labour force participation (see Chapter 9). Figure 7.11 indicates the proportions of young women in 'head and spouse' and 'head, spouse and dependants' families who were in the workforce in 1981. This shows that around 80 per cent of women aged 20 to 34 living with a spouse and with no dependants were in the labour force. This fell to only half for women aged 35 to 39, which would seem to suggest a significant number of women of that age group dropping out of the workforce, perhaps to have their delayed first child. For women living with a spouse and dependants the pattern is quite different, with a gradual increase in the proportions working outside the home in each five-year age group until more than a half of such women aged in their late thirties are in the workforce. This of course reflects the now dominant situation in Australia of young women postponing child-bearing and extending the period after marriage when they participate in the workforce and also of women returning to the workforce after temporarily leaving it to have their children.

Associated with these changes in labour force participation among women has been a major shift in the ways families derive their economic support. In the bulk of single-parent families and the majority of single-person families, women are of course the major (and usually only) breadwinners. However it is clear from the above that they also contribute to the incomes of the majority of families in which there is a husband present. The extent and significance of this contribution is discussed elsewhere (Hugo 1983b, p. 61). In the case of women living with a spouse only, 28 per cent earned an individual income which was in the same income category as the total family income, so that the contribution of their spouse to the total family income was little or nothing. In the case of women in head, spouse and dependants families, the proportion was considerably smaller, with only 6 per cent of husbands contributing little or nothing to total family income. However, if one adds the number of women whose individual income is in the next lowest category to their families' total income, the proportion rises to 24 per cent of all 'head, spouse and dependants' families. In this group, the women are definitely the major breadwinners in the family, although there are significant, albeit smaller contributions from other sources. It will also be noted that the dominance of the female income in the family income is greatest in the lowest family income categories. Among families reporting incomes lower than $15 000 per year (about one-third of all head, spouse and dependants families in 1981), two-thirds were families in which women were the only or dominant breadwinner. These data should help lay to rest any lingering attachment to the stereotype of families in which there is a husband and wife present as being where 'family income is synonymous with the male's income, occupational status with the male's occupation, commuting preferences with the male's journey to work' (Stapleton 1980, p. 1105). Only in 30 per cent of 'head, spouse and children' and 21 per cent of 'head and spouse' families do women not contribute income earned outside the house. Hence we should be thinking in terms of 'dual-headed' households not only in collection of statistics but in any social or economic analysis or theory which relates to households or families (Stapleton 1980, p. 1102).

DEMOGRAPHIC ASPECTS OF HOUSING DEMAND AND HOME OWNERSHIP

The National Population Inquiry (1978, p. 88) has demonstrated the fundamental influence of demographic factors on housing demand. While it is clear that there are many 'intervening variables' such as changing levels of real income, distribution of wealth within the community, institutional constraints, government housing policy, changing housing preferences of young people before marriage or those of elderly people, changing preferences in choice of residential areas, etc., the nature and rate of formation of new households continues to be the major determinant of overall housing requirements. The extent to which this demand is met by home ownership as opposed to other forms of tenure is, however, much more strongly shaped by those factors referred to above as intervening variables than by the direct influence of demographic changes. This is especially so given the long-standing and very high value placed upon ownership of one's place of residence by most Australians. Nevertheless, changes in population structure can be influential in changing overall patterns of home ownership.

Housing demand

It was shown earlier that due to age structure and several other demographic and societal influences, the rate of increase in the number of households has been greater than that of overall population growth. The degree of this difference has varied considerably from one period to another, as Table 7.11 shows. Moreover, as was mentioned earlier, rates of household formation will almost certainly continue to outpace growth rates for the total population for the rest of this century. Several aspects of this are of particular significance to housing planners in the private and public sectors. Australians' changing age structure not only strongly influences overall total demand for housing but it has a major impact on the nature of that demand. It is instructive, therefore, to look at not only overall growth in household numbers but also in growth trends of households with heads of particular ages. An examination of recent and projected trends in the growth rates of households classified according to the age of the household head suggests the following trends:

1 The number of households with heads aged less than 25 will grow only slowly after 1981, after two decades of rapid increase. In fact, projections

Table 7.11 Growth of population and households, 1947–81

Census	Population Number ('000s)	Growth[b] rate %	Households[a] Number ('000s)	Growth[b] rate %	Mean household size[d]
1947[c]	7579	–	1874	–	3.75
1954[c]	8987	2.46	2343	3.25	3.55
1961[c]	10508	2.26	2782	2.48	3.55
1966	11600	2.00	3155	2.55	3.47
1971	12756	1.92	3671	3.00	3.31
1976	13550	1.21	4141	2.44	3.12
1981	14576	1.47	4668	2.43	2.98

[a] Heads of private occupied dwellings.
[b] Average annual percentage growth since previous census.
[c] Full-blood Aboriginals were excluded from census in 1947, 1954 and 1961, and they were not included in official results until 1971. At that time the average number of persons in households with Aboriginal heads was 5.5, well above the Australian average.
[d] Population in private occupied dwellings divided by the number of private occupied dwellings.
Sources: censuses quoted in Boundy 1980, p. 7; ABS (1981 census)

which assume zero net migration indicate that there would be an absolute decline in the number of households with heads aged less than 25 in the 1990s. This has clear implications for the demand for housing favoured by these younger age groups (flats in inner suburban areas, etc.).

2 A similar, although not so dramatic, reduction in the rate of increase of households headed by persons aged 25–34 is to be expected.

3 There will be an upswing in the increase of households with heads aged 35–44 and 45–54, as the post-war baby boom surge reaches these ages.

4 We can expect a fall in the rate of increase of household heads aged 55–64.

5 There will be a slow but steady increase in household heads aged 65 and over.

Clearly there are readily observable differences in preferences for various types and locations of housing between groups at different stages of the life cycle. Thus it would appear that the widely dissimilar rates of increase at various ages outlined above would, as Morrison (1977b, p. 207) has pointed out in the United States context, foreshadow significant shifts in the composition of future housing demand. As will be shown later, changes in age structure can not only affect the overall level of housing demand but also exert some influence on the proportion of that demand which will involve owner-occupation of a dwelling. Other factors influencing housing demand and which have been dealt with earlier include levels of immigration and a range of factors which impinge upon headship rates—marriage and divorce trends, the conventional time at which children leave the parental home and policies toward the aged (see also Hugo 1979a, 1980a).

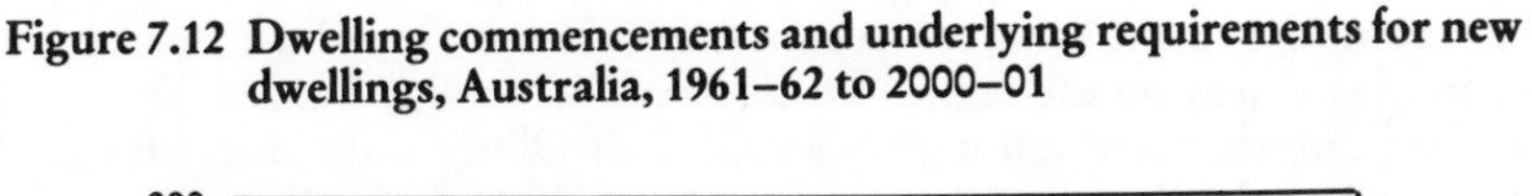
Figure 7.12 Dwelling commencements and underlying requirements for new dwellings, Australia, 1961–62 to 2000–01

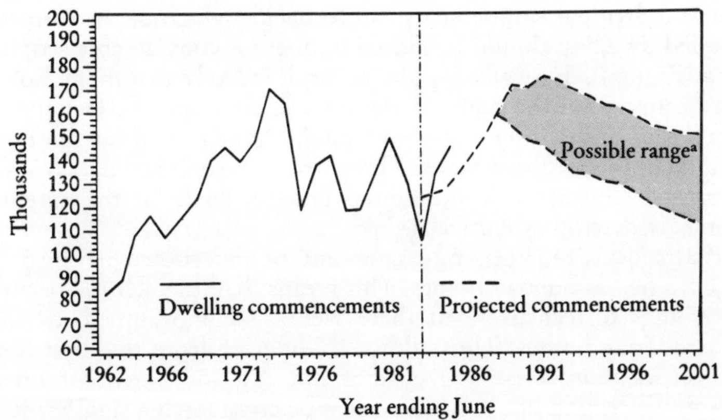

[a] Range of longer-term projections under alternative economic and demographic scenarios.

Source: Indicative Planning Council for the Housing Industry, 1984

The Indicative Planning Council for the Housing Industry (1984) has produced a series of long-term projections of housing demand and these are depicted in Figure 7.12. These projections are based on ABS population projections and assumptions concerning headship rates. The likely future scenario is thus as follows:

1 Up to 1988 there will be an increase in demand for new dwellings from around 125 000 in 1983–84 to 160 000 in 1987–88. This is due to the continued passage of baby boom generation cohorts into the prime household formation ages, and an assumed economic recovery and associated increase in headship rates.
2 From 1988 to 2000 there will be a decline in annual average dwelling requirements to a figure between 115 000 and 150 000, depending upon levels of immigration and economic growth. The expected decline in demand is due to the passage of 1970s deficit birth cohorts into adult ages, and less scope for increased headship.

The second home phenomenon
One of the most striking aspects of the housing information collected at recent national censuses in Australia is the spectacular increase in the number of *unoccupied* private dwellings which is shown in Table 7.12. The table shows that in 1976 there were four times as many unoccupied private dwellings for each occupied private dwelling as in 1947. The unoccupied private dwelling category includes all structures built specifically for living purposes and capable of being lived in but not occupied on the night of the census (30 June). These can include dwellings vacant because they are newly completed, those vacant for demolition or repair, dwellings to let, those where the household is absent on the night of the census, or holiday homes. The latter have been differentiated among unoccupied dwellings only since the 1961 census. Since individual enumerators had to decide which of the categories an unoccupied dwelling should be placed in, there is considerable scope for error in classifying such dwellings. Moreover, it is likely that many holiday homes are occupied on the night of the census, although the fact that the count is taken in mid-winter outside of public holiday periods minimizes this likelihood in the southern States. Hence the holiday home data from the census must be considered a substantial underestimate of the extent of second home ownership in Australia.

At the 1981 census, 113 911, or 24.3 per cent, of unoccupied private dwellings were classified as holiday homes. This means that for each 100 occupied private dwellings on census night there were 2.44 unoccupied dwellings classified as holiday homes. Thus, although differing from the 'first home' market in its location, type and cost of housing and extent of owner-construction, the second house market must be considered a significant one within the total housing scene. There are many imponderables in considering the future of holiday homes in Australia; however, if we examine the changing age structure of household heads some trends of particular relevance can be discerned. The large groups of young adults born in the

Table 7.12 Growth in number of unoccupied private dwellings in Australia, 1947–81

Year	No. of unoccupied private dwellings ('000s)	Ratio to occupied private dwellings	Growth rate per annum over previous inter-censal period Unoccupied	Occupied
1947	47	0.025	− 2.8	+1.6
1954	113	0.048	+13.6	+3.2
1961	194	0.070	+ 8.0	+2.4
1966	258	0.082	+ 5.9	+2.5
1971	339	0.092	+ 5.6	+3.1
1976	431	0.104	− 4.9	+2.4
1981	469	0.101	+ 1.7	+2.4

Source: ABS (various censuses)

post-war baby boom who have been recently (and are still) passing through the prime household formation ages (20–30) will lead to a surge in the number of household heads in their thirties and early forties in the 1980s. Households at this 'early-middle' stage of the family life cycle could create a considerable potential demand for holiday homes. They constitute a major element among those seeking second homes, since holiday homes offer recreation possibilities highly favoured by families comprising adults with school-going children. Moreover, households at this stage of the family life cycle will have passed beyond the financially onerous early years of primary home ownership, so that in most cases mortgage and bank loan repayments and purchase of major furnishings, household appliances, etc. will be absorbing a progressively decreasing proportion of family income. This, together with the high incidence of households in which both husband and wife are salary earners among this group, means that such family units could have more disposable income to invest in second homes than many other groups. It is possible then that these 'massive cohorts of young adults born during the postwar baby boom' (Morrison, 1977a, p. 5) could create a third 'wave' of upswing in demand for a distinctive particular type of housing in the Australian market of the late 1980s. Previously, as young single individuals and couples, they had initiated a surge of demand for flats, units and other rental accommodation in the inner and middle suburban areas of Australian cities; subsequently, as they entered the family formation stage, they put considerable pressure on the market for detached and semi-detached houses in the outer suburbs of the major cities; and it may be that they will have a third major impact on the housing market by creating a substantial demand for holiday homes. Clearly, however, whether or not such a 'third wave' eventuates will depend on much more than demographic factors. Declines in the level of affluence and level of employment currently enjoyed by many in this age group would of course greatly reduce the demand for second homes. The extent and nature of the changes which the consciousness of limited oil supplies causes in population mobility within

Australia will also be important. Substantial increases in the cost of travel between primary and secondary residences could reduce the demand for holiday homes. Alternatively, the fact that the high cost of fuel will make motoring vacations prohibitively expensive may make the possibility of holidaying regularly at a fixed location, especially if it is not too distant from the family home, a more attractive proposition.

Demographic trends and changing patterns of home ownership

Although changing patterns and rates of home ownership are primarily functions of income levels and distribution within a society, institutional factors, housing market constraints, government policy and community preferences, demographic changes do have some impact on such patterns and an analysis of them is essential if one wishes to work toward a comprehensive understanding of trends in home ownership. Boundy (1980, p. 17) has pointed out that ownership of one's dwelling place has long been a highly valued element in Australian society because of 'the security of tenure and

Table 7.13 Rates of home ownership (owner-occupancy) by age, 1966–81

Age of head (years)	1966	1971	1976	1981
15–24	28.6	25.8	25.2	24.5
25–29	51.6	49.5	53.6	51.3
30–34	64.9	62.6	66.6	65.9
35–64	75.7	74.9	75.4	75.7
65+	80.6	79.9	75.2	74.8
All ages	71.4	68.7	68.3	68.1

Source: ABS (1966, 1971, 1976, 1981 censuses)

Table 7.14 Number of households and household members by nature of dwelling occupancy, 1976 and 1981

Nature of occupancy of dwellings	1976 census		1981 census	
	Number of households	Percentage	Number of households	Percentage
Owner	1 306 293	31.5	1 548 873	33.2
Purchaser	1 437 770	34.7	1 542 882	33.0
Owner/purchaser undefined	17 434	0.4	87 110	1.9
Tenant—housing authority	204 627	4.9	228 938	4.9
Tenant—other	839 873	20.3	935 543	20.0
N.e.i.	232 477	5.6	190 647	4.1
Not stated	102 047	2.5	134 916	2.9
Total	4 140 521	100.0	4 668 909	100.0

Source: ABS (1983c, p. 21)

the ability to develop and alter the property to meet individual needs... [and] the ownership of a dwelling is for many households their major form of acquiring and holding wealth'. The almost universal acceptance among Australian householders that home ownership is a goal of primary importance, together with supportive policy measures and increases in levels of disposable income among a large segment of society, brought the achievement of this goal within reach of a broader range of society in the two decades following World War II—to such an extent, in fact, that the proportion of household heads owning their homes increased from 52.6 per cent in 1947 to 71.4 per cent in 1966. Table 7.13 shows recent changes in rates of home ownership (or owner-occupancy of dwellings) which is measured as the proportion of all *household heads* who are owner-occupiers. The table indicates that after 1966 the overall home ownership rate fell to 68.1 per cent in 1981. There is some debate about the accuracy of these data, since ABS surveys tend to give higher levels of ownership (Boundy 1980; Hugo 1980a). The apparent decline in rates of home ownership has also been disputed by Gordon (1977) who suggests that there is a clear difference in trends depending on whether one regards home owners as a subset of householders (a decreasing trend) or as a subset of the total population (an overall increase).

Table 7.14 shows that between 1976 and 1981 there was little change in the overall balance of tenure types, with owner-purchaser (i.e. owner-mortgagee) occupancy accounting for around two-thirds, around a fifth being in privately rented accommodation and 5 per cent in housing authority accommodation. Figure 7.13 shows how this mix varies considerably between various groups. The gradual transition from rental through purchasing to owning with age of household heads is apparent for married couples. However, for one-parent income units, renting of various types is dominant.

CONCLUSION

The changing demography of Australian families and households has profound implications in a wide range of areas. Identification and analysis of shifts in the number of families and households, their composition, structure and distribution are basic to the academic study of many elements of change in our society. Moreover, they are also of use in providing indications of changing levels of demands and need for a range of services and goods within both the private and public sectors. As Norton and Glick (1979, p. 19) point out, these trends are important indicators

> to consumer marketers and a guide to public service planners. Many large purchases—homes, appliances, furniture and automobiles and the like—are made on a household unit basis rather than a one person basis. Additionally different kinds of households have different economic patterns.

The aim here has been a modest one, to utilize analyses of 1981 census results to chart where possible recent trends in the size, characteristics and structure of Australian families and households in the last decade or so, and to point to some of the implications for policy makers. These changes have

Figure 7.13 Nature of accommodation occupancy of various family types, 1982

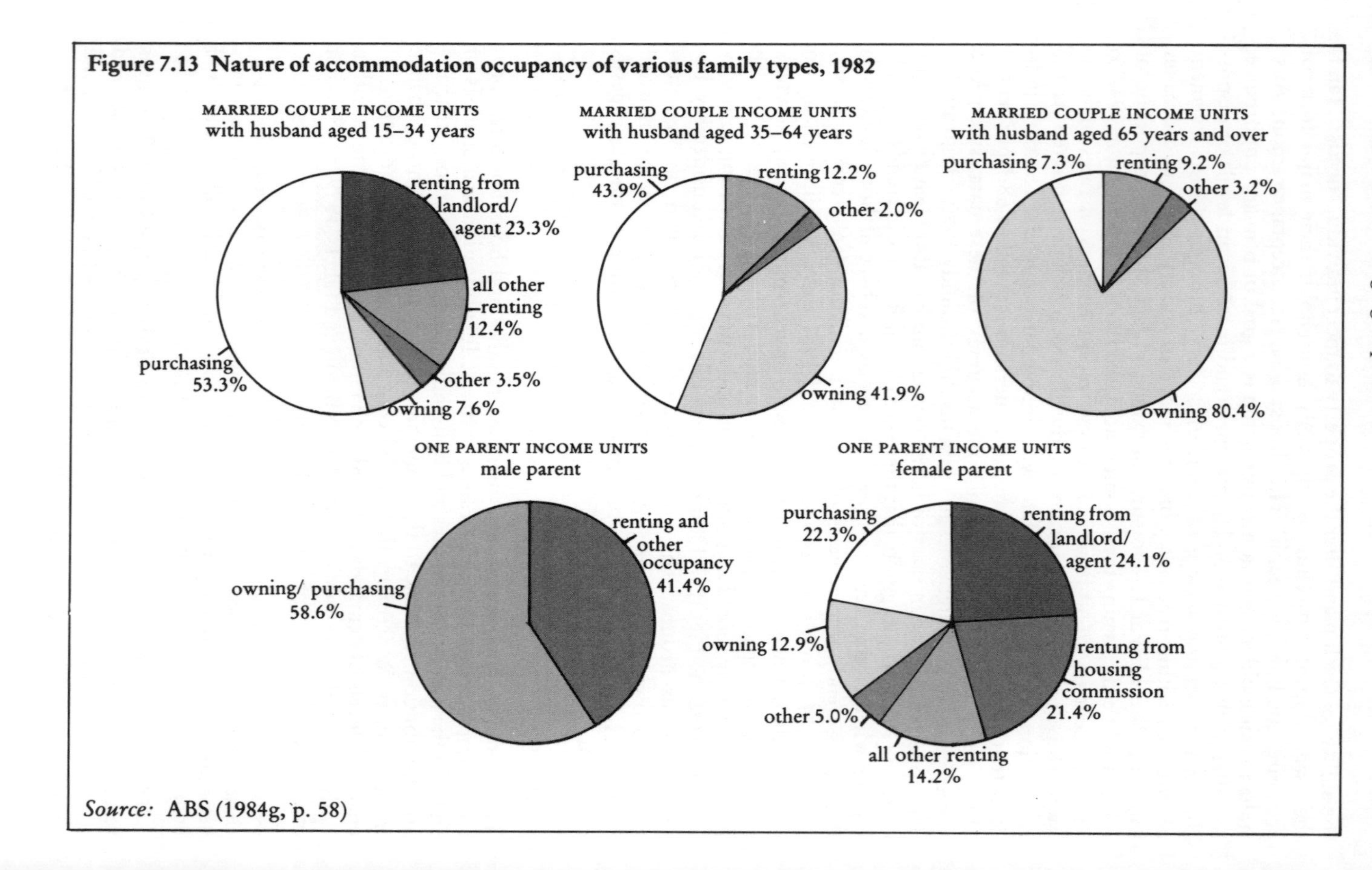

Source: ABS (1984g, p. 58)

indeed been major—to such an extent, in fact, that they have outpaced changes in the concepts and procedures used to collect family statistics at the census. It is apparent, for example, that our data are not adequate for analysis of alternative living arrangements among Australians who are not related by blood or marriage to each other. The use of the concept of 'primary households' employed by the US Bureau of Census since 1947 is worth investigating in this context (Stapleton-Concord 1982) as is the introduction of a 'partner or room mate' response category for household relationships. The latter was used at the 1980 United States census and provided easy recognition of unmarried adults sharing living quarters with non-relatives (Glick and Norton 1980, p. 21).

Much of the theory and methods employed in social science research in Australia is predicated implicitly or explicitly upon traditional life cycle ideas. As Stapleton (1980, p. 1103) has pointed out with respect to urban geography:

> Although the traditional family household (one male wage earner, plus spouse not earning and children) has now become a statistical abnormality, much of the research in urban geography continues to assume the less and less acceptable notion of an individual's progression through traditional life cycle stages.

Clearly the life cycle stage models advanced by Rossi (1955) and Simmons (1968) have limited applicability to the contemporary Australian family. To take one example, the family environment in which a majority of children grow up has been transformed with reductions in family size, acceleration of rates of family dissolution, and work outside the home being the norm for married women. What are the implications of these changes for child development and child welfare? It is clear that analysis of census data such as that undertaken here can tell only part of the story of change in Australian families and households. By charting the extent and characteristics of change, however, they do provide a necessary backdrop and starting point for detailed studies aimed at seeking a deeper understanding of those changes and a full appreciation of their social and economic implications. Demographers are sometimes accused by social science colleagues of sterile 'number crunching' of census data, yet the statistics presented in this chapter are far from being cold abstract figures—they tell several profoundly human stories. They are indicative of some very distinctive shifts in the most fundamental of our society's institutions. The extent of these drastic changes in the socio-demographic indicators briefly examined here demands the attention of policy maker and researcher alike.

8 Australia's Ethnic Mosaic

The 1970s saw the emergence in Australia as well as the United States and Canada of a 'new ethnicity', which has 'involved a rejection of the "melting pot" theory and a reassertion of ethnic identity by many groups' (Gelfand 1981, p. 91). Advocates of the 'new ethnicity' see it as a long-overdue societal and political recognition of the distinctiveness and value of the contribution to Australian society made by groups with different backgrounds to those of the majority's Anglo-Celtic heritage. The creation of a Department of Immigration and Ethnic Affairs, the establishment of an Australian Institute of Multicultural Affairs, the development of goverment-funded ethnic radio and television and major changes in education policies are only a few areas in which the new ethnicity has been reflected. It has also led to a widespread change in the attitude toward inclusion of an ethnic origin question in censuses. Earlier it was considered that such a question would encourage divisiveness in the society, exacerbate existing prejudices and play into the hands of factions favouring discrimination against particular groups. Indeed, such an atittude against inclusion of an ethnicity question in the national census is still dominant. For example, in Indonesia the inclusion of such a question is seen as being inimical to national unity. In the United States and the United Kingdom (e.g., Office of Population Censuses and Surveys 1982) the 1970s saw a build-up in the pressure to include an official question on ethnicity in national censuses, and much of that pressure emanated from ethnic minority groups themselves. In Australia similar pressure has led to the inclusion of an ethnicity question in the 1986 census.

All of the above raises the question of development of criteria to identity and define ethnic groups. Clearly ethnicity is primarily associated with groups of individuals and families feeling themselves as belonging to a distinctly separate group of people. Argument has continued as to whether language, birthplace, culture, custom, history, physical characteristics, etc. can be used in censuses and surveys to identify ethnic groups. For the 1981 census, as with earlier post-war censuses, we must rely chiefly upon birthplace and racial origin data to identify the characteristics and distribution of distinctive ethnic groups in Australian society. In this chapter we will consider separately the Aboriginal population, which can be identified from racial origin data, and those distinctive groups who can be identified by their overseas birthplace. The latter refers only to the first-generation migrants among particular ethnic groups, whereas with the passage of time and a downturn in immigration of many groups the second and third generations of their Australian-born offspring are assuming greater numerical significance. The census includes questions which can assist in identifying some of these groups. These include those relating to nationality, religion and especially to birthplace of parents. These have been used to estimate the size of various ethnic groups in Australia. In this chapter non-Aboriginal ethnic groups are taken to include persons born in a particular country and the Australian-born children of persons born in that country.

In Chapter 4 the major patterns of recent immigration to and settlement of immigrants in Australia were considered. We will extend this analysis here by examining the growth and some socio-economic characteristics of the major ethnic groups and some of the implications of these patterns for policy makers and planners. In particular we will be focusing on the extent of social and economic mobility within the various groups and upon some of the policy-related aspects of the changing age structure of the major ethnic groups.

GROWTH OF NON-ABORIGINAL ETHNIC GROUPS

In an earlier chapter the major contribution of post-war immigration to the growth in size and diversity of Australia's population has been outlined. However, consideration of birthplace data alone severely underestimates this contribution, since a significant proportion of the Australian-born population at the 1981 census are the children of immigrants who arrived in Australia during the post-war era. With the cumulative impact of the large waves of immigration of the first two and a half post-war decades and the subsequent decline in immigration numbers during the 1970s these Australian-born children are assuming greater relative and absolute numerical significance in the Australian population. However, they have been subject to surprisingly little research attention in comparison with the overseas-born population. A number of important research and policy issues immediately spring to mind. For example, to what extent have members of this 'second generation' been upwardly mobile with respect to education and occupation in comparison with their parents? To what extent has this generation retained the values, language and culture of its overseas-born parents? The implications of such questions for the established Australian immigration programme and the policy of multi-culturalism are obvious. Less obvious are the implications for broader social and economic policy. For example, how far have the Australian-born children of Southern European-born parents retained the customary attitudes towards inter-generational relations?—do they show a greater propensity to take aged parents into their households than Australian-born contemporaries? (Hugo 1984e).

The literature concerned with the second generation born to Australia's post-war immigrants is very limited, and this is despite the fact that a question on birthplace of parents has been included in successive Australian

Table 8.1 Ethnic origin of first and second generations in Australian population, 1978[1]

Origin	Generation I (birthplace) No.	%	Generation II (parents' birthplace) No.	%	I & II (ethnic origin) No.	%
England	874 523	31.2	666 815	33.6	1 646 289	34.4
Italy	285 836	10.2	243 283	12.2	534 705	11.1
Scotland	152 096	5.4	164 356	8.3	338 474	7.1
Greece	153 232	5.5	124 210	6.2	314 074	6.6
Slovenia, Serbia, Croatia & Macedonia	147 662	5.3	72 716	3.7	222 901	4.6
Germany	110 607	3.9	83 642	4.2	181 919	3.8
Netherlands	92 565	3.3	82 581	4.2	181 812	3.8
Ireland	67 349	2.4	99 873	5.0	178 144	3.7
New Zealand	105 365	3.7	58 137	2.9	165 202	3.4
Malta	56 837	2.0	50 779	2.6	107 546	2.2
Poland	57 439	2.0	36 174	1.8	103 626	2.2
Lebanon-Syria	50 645	1.8	29 658	1.5	72 015	1.5
Hungary	27 574	1.0	14 474	0.7	50 755	1.1
Wales	26 065	0.9	20 972	1.1	51 216	1.1
Egypt	30 738	1.1	14 299	0.7	45 037	0.9
USA	28 907	1.0	13 397	0.7	43 506	0.9
Latin America	38 131	1.4	5 932	0.3	43 897	0.9
Total South-east Asia[2]	63 913	2.3	15 467	0.8	35 756	0.8
China, Hong Kong, Singapore	43 672	1.5	17 540	0.9	34 000	0.7
India	38 501	1.3	16 164	0.8	20 011	0.4
Estonia, Latvia, Lithuania	26 435	0.9	13 586	0.7	42 924	0.9
Cyprus	24 490	0.9	11 096	0.6	35 586	0.7
Denmark, Norway, Sweden, Finland	25 282	0.9	18 173	0.9	43 499	0.9
Austria	23 692	0.8	13 468	0.7	37 184	0.8
Turkey	20 458	0.7	4 581	0.2	23 493	0.5
South Africa	18 280	0.6	7 568	0.4	19 336	0.4
Russia	14 836	0.5	8 380	0.4	30 919	0.6
Sri Lanka	16 190	0.6	3 925	0.2	20 015	0.4
Spain	14 806	0.5	7 692	0.4	23 505	0.5
Czech/Slovak	15 319	0.5	6 219	0.3	21 605	0.5
Ukraine	12 135	0.5	5 587	0.3	19 226	0.4
Canada	13 819	0.5	7 204	0.4	21 229	0.4
Generation total	2 806 646	100.0	1 985 914	100.0	4 792 560	100.0
Australians (third or later generation)					9 328 023	
Aborigines					142 495	
Total					14 263 078	

censuses since 1971. There are, however, some exceptions to this generalization. In particular, the foremost scholar of Australian post-war immigration, Charles Price, has placed great emphasis on the generation structure of immigrant groups. Especially in his work on Southern European settlement in Australia, Price (e.g., 1955, 1963) stressed the significance of the structure of generations in those communities.

With the development of a policy of multi-culturalism in Australia and growth of the 'new ethnicity' there has been a growing interest in the 'second generation' and in the estimation of the numerical size of the various ethnic groups which make up the Australian population. Price himself (1979, and in ESCAP 1982) has utilized not only census data but also other sources such as State registries of births by birthplace of father and mother to arrive at estimates of the 'ethnic origin' of the Australian population. A summary of the results of Price's judicious analysis is presented in Table 8.1. It will come as a surprise to many to see that fully a third of Australians are an immigrant or the child of an immigrant. The dominance of England as an origin of first- and second-generation immigrants is immediately apparent, accounting for fully one-third of them. Moreover, if one adds in the other Anglo-Celtic groups (from Scotland, Ireland, New Zealand and Wales) the proportion comfortably exceeds 50 per cent. The impact of post-war Southern European immigration is striking, with over one million Australians being first- or second-generation Italian or Greek or from what is now Yugoslavia. Southern Europeans account for a quarter of all the first- and second-generation immigrant population. The next largest group comprises people from the continental Western European countries (among whom the Dutch and German predominate), accounting for around 10 per cent, while those European countries further east provide nearly 5 per cent more. The more recently arrived groups from the Middle East and South-east Asia are very small, not only in the Australian population as a whole but also in the first- and second-generation immigrant population summarized in Table 8.1. This is of course partly a function of their recent arrival, which has given them only very limited opportunity to build up a second generation. Nevertheless, it is salutory in the context of any debate about Asian immigration to take into account the data in the table.

Price's estimate of the 'second generation' population in 1978 places it at around two-thirds the size of the first generation. The size of the 'second generation' population at a single point in time is of course largely a reflection of the size and distribution of immigration during earlier periods. As a result of post-war immigration the proportion of the Australian population born overseas doubled from 9.8 per cent at the 1947 census to 18.4 per cent in 1966, the highest level it had reached since the turn of the century. During the 1970s, however, the proportion born overseas remained fairly stable due to the slowdown in immigration and the inevitable increase in the

Notes to table on opposite page:
[1] major groups only—those comprising 0.5 per cent or more
[2] includes Burma, Thailand, Indo-China, Malaysia, Indonesia, Philippines, East Timor

Table 8.2 Parents' birthplace for Australians of immigrant extraction, 1971–81

	Both parents born in Australia		Father only born in Australia		Mother only born in Australia		Total overseas-born parent		Not stated	
	No.	%	No.	%	No.	%	No.	%	No.	%
1971	7724200	60.6	473100	3.7	886700	7.0	2118108	16.6	333974*	2.6
1976	8094800	60.0	535000	4.0	946400	7.0	2362247	17.4	372529	2.7
1981	8404795	57.7	687180	4.7	982854	6.7	2737537	18.8	251529	1.7

* Estimate, based on 1976 experience
Note: percentages are of total resident population, not just the Australian-born; they do not add up to 100 per cent because the overseas-born population is not included
Sources: J. Rowland (in ESCAP 1982, pp. 108–10) and ABS (1983c, 11)

Australian-born as the large numbers of arrivals in the 1950s and 1960s had children. Thus at the 1981 census 20.6 per cent of Australia's population was born overseas, but if one adds the second generation population of Australian-born with at least one parent born overseas, over 41 per cent of Australia's population in 1981 was associated with immigration. As of the 1981 census there were 2 989 068 Australian-born persons who had at least one parent born in a foreign country.

Table 8.2 presents estimates of the total second generation using the same definition as J. Rowland (in ESCAP 1982, p. 117), i.e., all Australian-born persons with at least one parent born outside Australia. This definition presents little difficulty when dealing with the total second-generation population, but this is not the case if we are attempting to identify the second generation of a particular immigrant group. In the case of individuals both of whose parents were born overseas, but in different countries, there will be double counting. Where this arises as a problem here we take the father's birthplace as an indication of the ethnic origin of second-generation individuals. Accurate estimation of the size of the second generation is also made difficult by the high level of non-response to this question in the census, especially in 1971 and 1976. In fact special efforts were made in 1981 to reduce this level of non-response and the success of this is reflected in Table 8.2. The proportion of Australians reporting that both parents were born in Australia fell by three full percentage points between 1971 and 1981 and it comes as something of a surprise that only 57.7 per cent of Australians in 1981 had Australian-born mothers and fathers. On the other hand, there has been considerable growth in the numbers and proportion with one or both parents born overseas. Table 8.3 clearly shows that the growth of the latter population during the 1970s was more than three times faster than that of the population with two Australian-born parents.

The second generation as defined here is only slightly less numerous than the total overseas-born population, numbering around 2.75 million and comprising around one-fifth of the total Australian community. More than half the members of the second generation have one parent who is Australian-born. Among the latter there is a predominance of Australian-born mothers—a reflection of the masculinity of many immigration streams.

Table 8.3 Australian-born population: percentage inter-censal growth in birthplace of parents categories, 1971–81

Period	Both parents born in Australia	Father only born in Australia	Mother only born in Australia	Total with overseas-born parent	Not stated
1971–76	4.8	13.1	6.7	11.5	11.5
1976–81	3.8	28.4	3.9	15.9	−32.5
1971–81	8.8	45.3	10.8	29.2	−24.7

Sources: J. Rowland (in ESCAP 1982, pp. 108–10) and ABS (1983c, p. 11)

Table 8.4 Australian-born population: country of birth of overseas-born parents, 1981

Birthplace of parents	Males	Females	Total	Percentage
UK & Ireland (Rep.)	645 961	689 248	1 335 209	44.67
Germany	53 194	53 854	107 048	3.58
Netherlands	55 754	53 789	109 543	3.67
Poland	21 232	20 694	41 926	1.40
Other Northern Europe	62 539	64 293	126 832	4.24
Greece	63 491	60 875	124 366	4.16
Italy	140 771	135 748	276 519	9.25
Malta	30 928	29 028	59 956	2.01
Yugoslavia	44 901	42 884	87 785	2.94
Other Southern Europe	9 837	9 575	19 412	0.65
Middle East	33 189	32 184	65 373	2.19
Vietnam, Laos, Kampuchea	1 567	1 432	2 999	0.10
Other Asia	42 770	42 151	84 921	2.84
New Zealand	48 415	50 172	98 587	3.30
Other and not stated	223 114	225 478	448 592	15.01
Total	1 477 663	1 511 405	2 989 068	100

Source: ABS (1981 census, one per cent sample tape of individuals)

However, it is instructive to note that over the 1971–81 period the proportion of 'mixed birthplace' parent pairs involving overseas-born mothers increased. The ratio of Australian fathers to Australian mothers in such mixed-parent pairs increased from 0.53 to 0.70 over that period.

Turning to the country of origin of overseas-born parents of the Australian-born at the 1981 census, Table 8.4 shows the numbers in the second generation for each of the numerically large groups. As stated earlier, where parents were born in different overseas countries the child is allocated to the father's birthplace. As the United Kingdom and the Republic of Ireland together have been by far the largest contributor of migrants with over one million people or approximately 37 per cent of all migrants over the 1947 to 1981 period, it is therefore to be expected that nearly half (44.7 per cent) of the second-generation Australians are of British ancestry. A more detailed breakdown of the mixed-birthplace parent pairs shows that the majority

(70.6 per cent) of the British second-generation group had only one parent born in Britain and one born in Australia, while 3.2 per cent had only their father born in Britain and their mother in another country besides Australia. Only 26.2 per cent of second-generation Australians of British origin had both parents born in Britain.

Perhaps one of the more important groups to look at with respect to the second generation is the Italians. Immigrants from Italy are the second largest group, representing approximately 9 per cent of the foreign-born population to settle in Australia. Table 8.4 shows that the second-generation Australians of Italian descent were also second in size only to the British, with 276 519 people or 9.25 per cent of the second-generation population. In sharp contrast to the Australian-born of British descent, nearly 69 per cent of the Australian-born of Italian descent had *both* parents born in Italy. These children, therefore, are predominantly growing up in a family where their Southern European traditions are strong and they therefore are likely to retain much of the heritage of their parents. Only 24.9 per cent had one parent born in Italy and one in Australia. The other major countries of origin of second-generation Australians are Greece (4.16 per cent), the Netherlands (3.66 per cent), Germany (3.58 per cent) and New Zealand (3.3 per cent). Among Greeks the pattern of only a very limited degree of first-generation outmarriage observed for Australian-born people of Italian descent was even more marked, with over 81 per cent of Australian-born having both parents born in Greece. In contrast to the Greeks and Italians, where ethnic social, community and family ties are strong, the majority of second-generation Australians of German, Dutch and New Zealand origin had one parent born in Australia.

Although the major influx of immigrants from Asia did not commence until the 1970s, second-generation Australians of Asian descent comprise nearly 85 000 individuals or 2.84 per cent of the second generation. Perhaps surprisingly, over 56 per cent of Asian immigrants married an Australian. Only 32 per cent of second-generation Asians had both parents born in Asia. As immigration from Indo-China has occurred only since the mid- to late 1970s there were only 3002 second-generation Australians of Vietnamese, Laotian or Kampuchean background, and for over 82 per cent of these both parents were born in Indo-China.

Most members of the second generation are very young and most are still living with their parents. Hence, it is not surprising that there is very close conformity in the spatial distribution of the two generations of the major birthplace groups. This is confirmed in Table 8.5 which shows very low Index of Dissimilarity (I_D) values[1] for the two generations of each of the major birthplace groups, indicating that the second generations tend to be distributed in a very similar way to their corresponding first generations in

[1] The Index of Dissimilarity (I_D), as was explained in Chapter 4, can be interpreted as the percentage of a particular sub-population which would have to change their place of residence if the distribution of that group between sub-areas of the region under study is to be made exactly the same as that of another sub-group.

Table 8.5 Melbourne, Sydney and Adelaide statistical divisions: indices of dissimilarity for first and second generations of major birthplace groups, 1981

Birthplace of parents	Metropolitan area		
	Melbourne	Sydney	Adelaide
UK & Ireland (Rep.)	9.14	9.54	15.39
Germany	5.88	8.01	4.40
Greece	6.08	8.35	5.86
Italy	7.92	10.26	6.78
Malta	7.62	8.52	24.95
Netherlands	4.24	7.70	6.40
Yugoslavia	9.32	13.33	11.24

Source: ABS (1981 census, local government area summary file)

Sydney, Melbourne and Adelaide. Hence, the spatial distribution of the various non-Aboriginal ethnic groups corresponds very closely with that of the corresponding birthplace groups considered in Chapter 4. This pattern, however, could change significantly during the next couple of inter-censal periods as the second generation ages into the stage of the life cycle of leaving the parental home, setting up independent households and beginning a family. Whether it does change is important, because the extent to which second generation children are living near or with their parents when their parents are old and infirm will bear on welfare programmes and policies designed for the so-called ethnic aged (Hugo 1984e).

THE AGE STRUCTURE OF FIRST- AND SECOND-GENERATION IMMIGRANT GROUPS

The specific phasing of immigration into Australia and the selection procedures which placed overwhelmingly heavy emphasis on young, economically and demographically active persons means that the bulk of Australia's overseas-born persons arrived here as adults in their twenties, thirties or forties in the 1950s and 1960s. Hence there are relatively few young overseas-born persons and, as Table 8.6 shows, most major birthplace groups have a median age significantly higher than the Australian-born population. Only groups which have recorded significant immigration gains in the last few years, like the New Zealanders and Lebanese, have median ages approaching those of the Australian-born. However, it will also be noted in the table that there is considerable variation between the birthplace groups in the proportion that are aged over 65 years. Those born in Italy, the Netherlands and especially the United Kingdom and Poland have especially high proportions aged above 65 years. Among the other groups, however, this proportion is lower than for the Australian-born, although their median age is greater than for the Australian-born. It is clear from Figure 8.1 that the overseas-born population is significantly older than the Australian-born. It will be noticed, however, that the greatest difference in the two age

Table 8.6 Median age and percentage aged 65+ for major birthplace groups, 1981

Birthplace	Median age (years)	Percentage aged 65+
Australia	26.3	9.2
New Zealand	28.3	7.2
Lebanon	29.8	3.0
Malta	38.1	6.3
Yugoslavia	38.8	5.5
Germany	40.7	7.8
UK & Ireland (Rep.)	41.2	16.9
Greece	41.7	6.7
Netherlands	42.4	9.9
Italy	45.8	11.2
Poland	57.5	21.5

Sources: ABS (1981 census); Department of Immigration and Ethnic Affairs (n.d.)

Figure 8.1 Age-sex composition of the Australian-born and overseas-born population, 1981

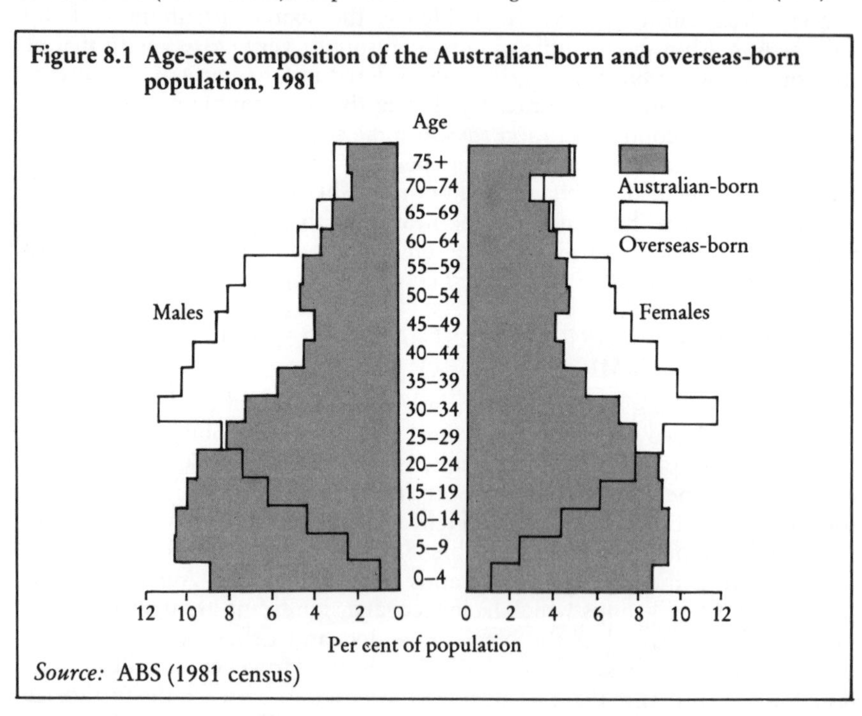

Source: ABS (1981 census)

distributions is in the 30–59 age groups and not in the oldest ages. The diagram shows that the top of the bulge in the overseas-born ages is around the 55–59 age group. During the 1980s this bulge will move up the pyramid into the 60+ age groups and in the 1990s into the seventies and so on. Hence, Australia is on the threshold of a period during which the number of overseas-born persons aged 60 and over will increase very significantly.

The rapidity of the growth of the overseas-born aged population in Australia is evident in Table 8.7, which shows the pattern of this growth over the last decade and the probable trends in the early 1980s. It can be seen from the table that the number of overseas-born aged grew more than twice as fast as the Australian-born aged during the 1970s and it seemed likely to grow three times as fast as the Australian-born population aged 60 years and over between 1981 and 1986. The contrast is even more striking if we include only immigrants from non-British countries of origin. Here the growth in the late 1970s has been more than four times as fast as that of the Australian-born and this difference is even greater in the 1980s. In sheer numbers the older persons born in the United Kingdom and the Republic of Ireland dominate the overseas-born aged, accounting for more than half in 1981. However, this dominance will be reduced in the early 1980s since the growth rate of the British Isles-born aged is considerably lower than that of other major groups. The growth of the Italian-, Greek- and Yugoslavia-born 60+ population is such that their numbers will have more than doubled between 1971 and 1986. The 'other European' category in Table 8.7 experienced peak growth in the early 1970s, and their numbers doubled during the 1970s. This is largely due to the ageing of migrants from Eastern Europe and the Baltic states, most of whom came to Australia in the immediate post-war years as young adult displaced persons. As Mykyta (1982, p. 1) has pointed out, 'they can be thought of as a single cohort. Their migration was largely concluded in the early 1950s and their numbers did not alter significantly thereafter'.

A set of longer-term projections of the ethnic aged have been prepared by the Australian Institute of Multicultural Affairs (1983a) and these have been summarized in Table 8.8. These indicate that by the end of the century one in three older Australians will have been born overseas, and nearly one in four will be an overseas-born person of non-British background. It will be noted that the older Australian-born population is projected to grow at a rate slower than all other major birthplace groups except some small Eastern European groups. The New Zealand- and United Kingdom-born populations aged 55 or more will grow considerably faster than the Australian-born. Their problems and needs of course are likely to be similar to those of the Australian-born, except for the fact that as immigrants they may not have as many relatives living nearby to call upon for support when needed. For the aged coming from non-English-speaking countries, however, the situation is different in that it may be complicated by problems associated with adjustment to a different cultural situation and difficulties in being able to communicate in English. Hence, the rapid growth of the aged among the overseas-born from non-English-speaking countries is of special significance. Among these Table 8.8 shows that the Italian-born are the largest group and their numbers in the 60+ age group will double during the 1980s. The Greek-, Yugoslavia- and German-born are also significant in numerical terms and their numbers will also double during the decade. The fastest rates of growth of the ethnic aged are projected for the Indo-Chinese-born groups; however, it is clear from Table 8.8 that this is a function of the very

Table 8.7 Total Australian population aged 60+, by country of birth, 1971, 1976, 1981 and (projected) 1986

Country of birth	Census population			Projected 1986 population		Percentage growth		
	1971	1976	1981	Without migration	With migration	1971–76	1976–81	1981–86*
UK & Ireland	231 737	246 442	258 375	240 574	276 796	+ 4.8	+ 4.8	+ 7.1
Greece	9 825	11 896	13 876	17 427	20 723	+21.1	+16.6	+49.3
Italy	28 206	36 168	44 775	55 662	59 671	+28.2	+23.8	+33.3
Yugoslavia	6 684	9 158	12 790	16 016	19 656	+37.0	+39.7	+53.7
Other Europe	46 879	80 233	104 290	120 695	126 126	+71.2	+30.0	+20.9
Asia & Middle East	12 497	20 911	29 694	23 833	33 890	+67.3	+42.0	+14.1
Other countries	31 140	18 924	36 656	37 013	44 249	−39.2	+93.7	+20.7
Total overseas	366 968	423 732	500 456	511 220	581 111	+25.8	+18.1	+16.1
Australian-born	1 199 871	1 377 375	1 496 919	1 598 080	1 571 680	+14.8	+ 8.7	+ 5.0
Non-British overseas	135 231	177 290	242 150	270 646	304 315	+31.1	+36.6	+25.7
Total	1 566 839	1 801 107	1 997 375	2 109 300	2 152 791	+15.0	+12.7	+ 6.1

* Calculated using projected 1986 population *with* migration

Source: ABS (1971, 1976 and 1981 censuses); Pollard and Pollard (in Howe 1981, p. 23)

Table 8.8 Projected growth of the overseas-born population aged 60+ by birthplace group, 1981–2001

Country of birth	Number 1981	1991	2001	Percentage growth 1981–91	1991–2001	1981–2001
UK. & Ireland (Rep.)	267 200	312 600	361 800	17.0	15.7	35.4
Italy	46 100	88 700	122 183	92.4	37.7	165.0
Poland	22 000	34 900	30 500	58.6	−12.6	38.6
New Zealand	17 700	24 600	33 800	39.0	37.4	91.0
Netherlands	16 700	28 200	35 700	68.9	26.6	113.8
Germany	14 300	31 200	43 800	118.2	40.4	206.3
Greece	14 300	33 700	65 800	135.7	95.3	360.1
Yugoslavia	13 200	32 400	59 700	145.5	84.3	352.3
USSR/Ukraine	12 400	15 400	13 000	24.2	−15.6	4.8
Baltic States	10 300	12 700	10 700	23.3	−15.7	3.9
Other Europe	29 500	58 600	85 800	98.6	46.4	190.8
Indo-China	900	7 500	19 400	733.3	158.7	2 055.6
Middle East	10 700	26 300	44 000	145.8	67.3	311.2
Other Asia	19 500	42 500	74 000	117.9	74.1	279.5
Other	12 200	25 800	49 600	111.5	92.2	306.6
Total overseas-born	516 200	795 500	1 086 100	54.1	36.5	110.4
Total non-British	249 000	482 900	724 300	93.9	50.0	190.9
Total Australian-born	1 544 720	1 856 100	1 960 500	20.2	5.6	26.9
Total	2 060 920	2 651 600	3 046 600	28.7	14.9	47.8

Source: Australian Institute for Multicultural Affairs (1983b, pp. 226–7)

small numbers of older people of that background in 1981, so that even with the high rate of growth their numbers will still be small by the end of the century.

For many of the non-British-born groups, then, there will be a more than doubling of their older populations by the end of the century. In terms of numbers and need for special attention, it is likely that the growth of the aged among the Greek-, Italian- and Yugoslavia-born populations is of most significance. If we focus attention on the changing age structures of these groups, the strong ageing trend among them is immediately apparent. Taking firstly the Italian-born population, Figure 8.2 shows that it is concentrated almost totally in the adult age groups, reflecting the lack of immigration from Italy over the last decade or so. A comparison of the Australian- and Italian-born age distributions in 1981 highlights this. The third diagram, which overlays the age distributions of the Italian-born in 1976 and 1981, shows clearly the 'upward movement' of the Italian-born age

Figure 8.2 Age-sex composition of Italian-, Greek-, Yugoslavia- and Australian-born persons, 1976 and 1981

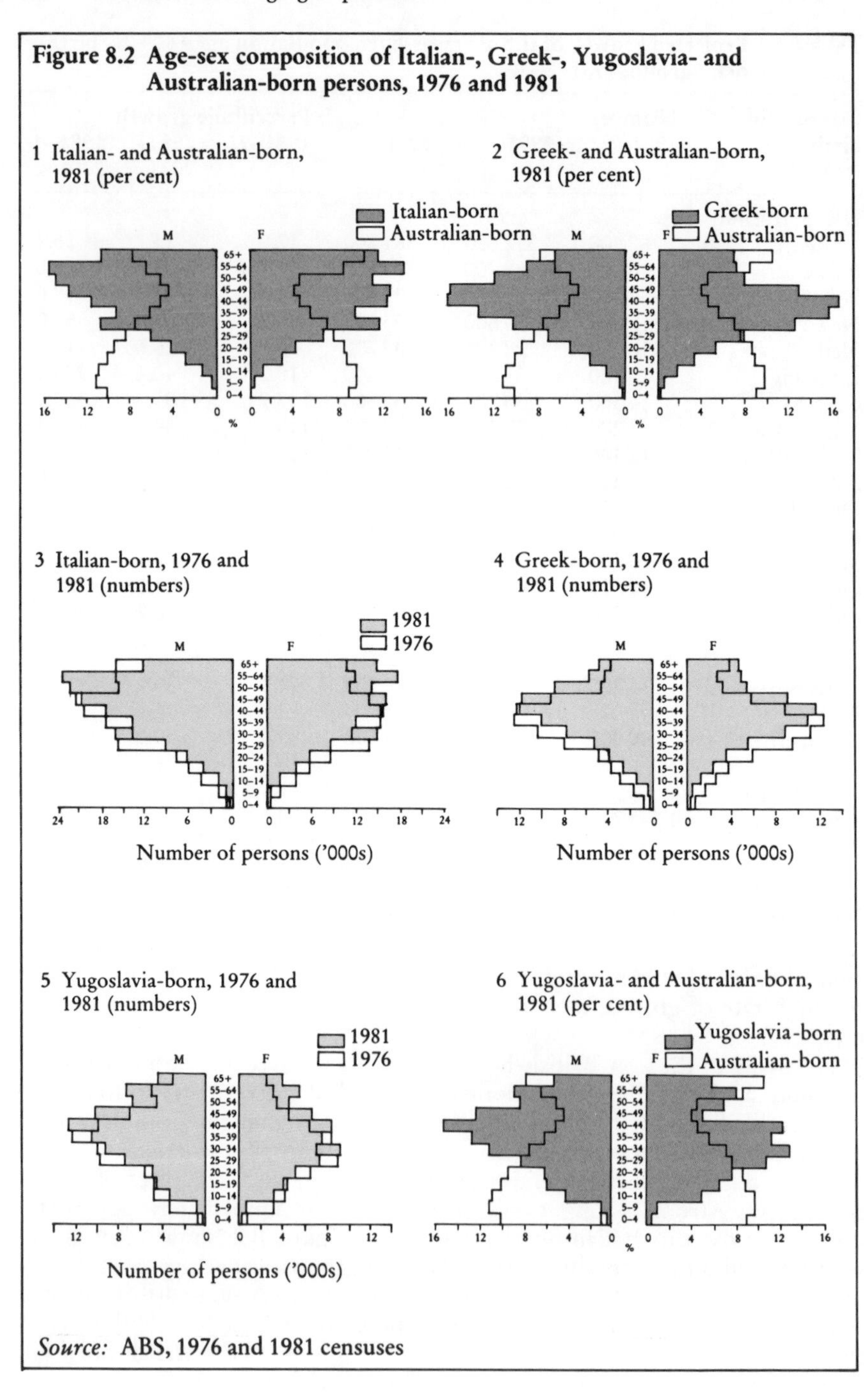

Source: ABS, 1976 and 1981 censuses

Table 8.9 Projected growth of non-British overseas-born aged population, 1981–2001

Age group (years)	Number 1981	2001 Low[1] migration	2001 High[2] migration	Percentage change 1981–2001 Low migration	High migration
40–59	603 794	803 405	1 088 300	33.1	80.2
60–64	79 701	173 613	204 863	117.8	157.0
65–69	64 251	143 942	170 466	124.0	165.3
70–74	45 411	120 568	143 623	165.5	216.3
75+	44 235	160 448	189 456	262.7	328.3

[1] Net migration gain 37 000 per annum.
[2] Net migration gain 107 000 per annum.
Source: Australian Institute for Multicultural Affairs (1983b, p. 230)

structure as it aged the five years between the censuses. Equivalent diagrams for the Greek-born population show a similar ageing pattern, although it is apparent that the Italian population is somewhat older than the Greek-born population and the main movement of Greeks into the older age categories is still to come—in the 1980s and early 1990s. The strong concentration of the Greek-born population in the 35–50 age groups in 1981 clearly presages an impending surge in the numbers of Greek-born persons among the older population; the proportion of the Australian-born in the 65+ age group was higher than that for the Greek-born. The pattern for the population born in Yugoslavia is a little different again. While they are considerably older than the Australian-born, there are larger proportions in the younger adult and teenage groups than is the case among the Greek- and Italian-born. Nevertheless, a significant shift in the age distribution toward the older ages between the 1976 and 1981 censuses is apparent in Figure 8.2. As with the Greek-born, however, the proportion in the 65+ age group was still a little lower than for the Australian-born at the 1981 census, although it can be readily seen that the 1980s and early 1990s will see a very rapid growth of the Yugoslavia-born in this age category.

The projected growth of the total overseas-born, non-British-origin older population is shown in Table 8.9. Even under the low migration assumption, there will be a doubling of the overseas-born aged population. Moreover, it is apparent that the fastest growth is in the oldest ages. These of course are the ages at which older persons are likely to have a greater need for specialized housing, health and other facilities and services.

It should be noted in passing that although the data presented in Table 8.9 are projections rather than predictions, we can be more confident in them than the bulk of projections since they are dealing with a population that is already in place and not subject to high levels of mobility. Unless there are unforeseen and extremely unusual circumstances, Tables 8.7, 8.8, and 8.9 provide us with an accurate indication of the dimensions of the impending growth of an aged overseas-born population.

Figure 8.3 Age structure of Australian-born persons with at least one overseas-born parent, 1981

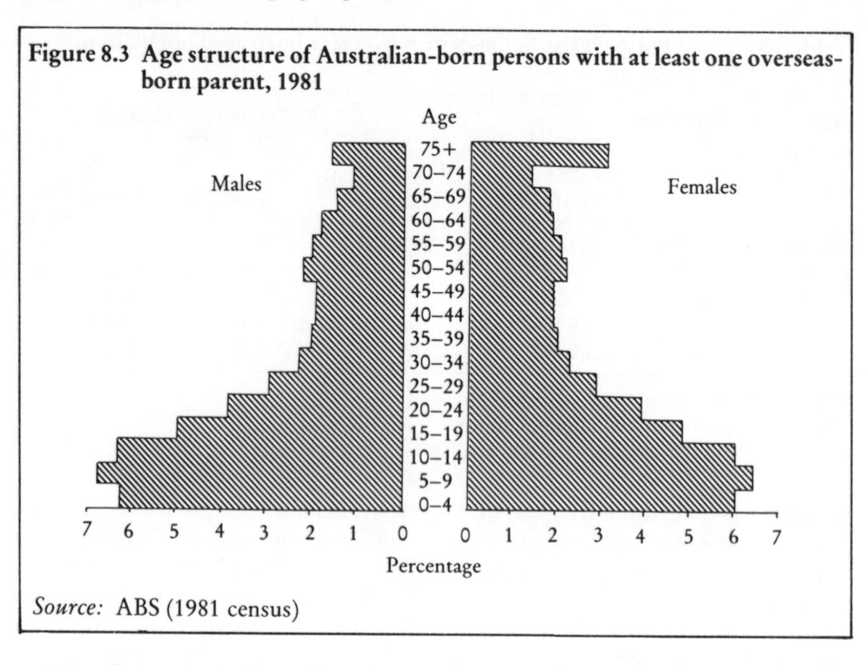

Source: ABS (1981 census)

Since the major influx of immigrants occurred in the 1950s and 1960s and was highly selective of young adults in the family formation age groups, the present 'second generation' of Australian-born persons with one or both parents born overseas is a very youthful population. At the 1981 census, 47.6 per cent of the second generation were aged less than 20 years compared to 33.7 per cent of the total population. Figure 8.3 shows that from the early thirties ages there are relatively uniform numbers in each older age group, with approximately 2 per cent of males and females in each age group. At ages 75 and over at the 1981 census there were 46 967 males, making up 1.6 per cent of the second-generation population, and 93 672 females, making up 3.1 per cent of that population. As would be expected, there is a balance between males and females in the second generation.

There is considerable variation between the ethnic groups with respect to the age structure of their second generation, reflecting largely an 'echo' effect of the phasing of the major periods of immigration of the respective groups. Nearly all of the 2.5 million settlers who arrived before 1939 were from the British Isles, with many being assisted by government-sponsored programmes to come to Australia. Thus the flow of British immigrants has been less subject to the short-term 'wave' effects that have influenced other groups, and hence the age structure of the second generation of British origin (Figure 8.4) is less dominated by particular age categories.

Figure 8.4 and Table 8.10 indicate that the second-generation populations of the other major birthplace groups, with the exception of those of Polish origin, are very young, with most groups having at least 65 per cent of its population aged under 20 years. This is largely a reflection of the changes in

Figure 8.4 Age structure of Australian-born persons with at least one parent born in an overseas country, by birthplace of parent(s), 1981

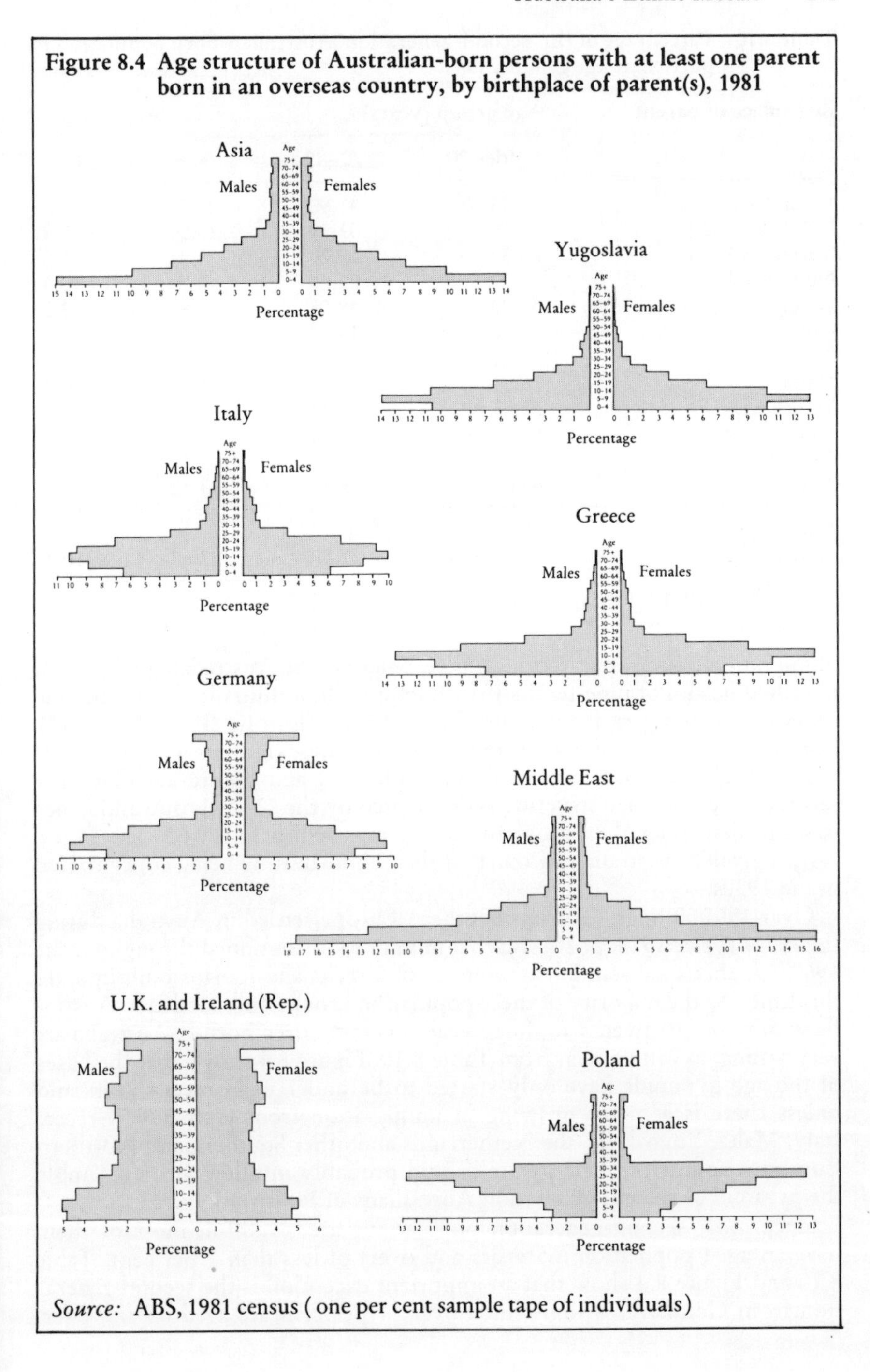

Source: ABS, 1981 census (one per cent sample tape of individuals)

Table 8.10 Percentage of the 'second-generation' Australian-born population in particular age groups, 1981

Birthplace of parents	Age group (years)			
	Under 20	20–49	50+	65+
Australia	36.03	41.90	22.06	8.79
UK & Ireland (Rep.)	35.09	31.39	18.00	15.47
Germany	66.37	17.29	5.27	11.08
Netherlands	75.62	23.27	0.79	0.34
Poland	38.09	58.08	1.83	2.03
Greece	79.40	18.08	2.13	0.40
Italy	68.82	28.13	2.14	0.87
Malta	76.54	21.92	1.40	0.14
Yugoslavia	81.55	17.28	0.88	0.30
Middle East	80.97	15.20	2.22	1.59
Asia	73.59	19.56	3.48	3.36
New Zealand	44.63	28.77	13.82	12.81
Total second generation	47.75	29.59	22.67	10.54

Source: ABS (1981 census matrix tapes)

immigration policy after World War II, whereby the Australian government modified its aim of nine-tenths British immigration. Initially this resulted in an influx of refugees from Central and Eastern Europe (Price 1975, A3), beginning in the late 1940s. Prominent among these refugees were people of Polish origin and it is noticeable in Table 8.10 and Figure 8.4 that their second-generation age structure is dominated by the 20–49 group and hence is somewhat older than those for the groups which followed. The Poles' early arrival in Australia saw much of their child-bearing being concentrated in the 1950s.

Over 196 000 migrants from Southern Europe settled in Australia during the 1950s (Price 1979, p. 10) and that immigration continued throughout the 1960s, so that a substantial community of Greeks and Italians built up over this time. As the majority of these population groups only settled in Australia within the last twenty to thirty years, their children born in Australia are very young, as can be seen from Table 8.10. Figure 8.4 shows that the bases of the age pyramids have only started to be undercut in recent years and unless there is a major upswing in immigration from Germany, Greece, Italy, Malta, Yugoslavia, the Netherlands and other Southern and Northern European countries, their pyramids will probably in a few years resemble the pyramid of second-generation Australians of Polish origin.

Since most second-generation populations are youthful, most of them have an aged population (65 years and over) of less than 1 per cent. Table 8.10 and Figure 8.4 show that an important exception is the second generation from Germany, within which over 11 per cent are aged 65 and over.

This is a result of large-scale German immigration to Australia being of much longer standing than the other continental European groups.

Restrictions on the entry of Asian permanent settlers were eased in the late 1960s and, after a slow beginning, by 1976 (or the mid-1970s) Asians constituted the largest group of new settlers except for the British. By the late 1970s over a third of immigrants were from Asia, with the largest groups being from Indo-China and East Timor. Thus, second-generation Australians of Asian origin were generally very young at the 1981 census. For the second-generation Asian population, 48.5 per cent are under 10 years of age and for the second generation of Middle Eastern origin the percentage was as high as 58.5.

THE ETHNIC AGED

It is apparent from the previous section that not only is Australia's older population the fastest-growing of any age group, but within that group, the non-British European-born community is growing even more rapidly. It must be stressed, however, that significant ethnic heterogeneity among our aged population is something quite new in Australian society. Just as the early post-war period saw a transformation of the degree of ethnic heterogeneity of our working-age and dependent child populations, the 1980s and 1990s will see a change of similar dimensions among our aged population. On the other hand, institutions and service personnel concerned with the aged have gained their experience in working with an aged population among whom the overwhelming majority were of Anglo-Celtic heritage and had spoken English as their first language for their entire lives. Such persons will remain a majority among our aged for the foreseeable future. However, there will be, as has been demonstrated here, significant minorities of aged persons coming from quite different backgrounds. As Schappi (1983, p. 21) has pointed out, the physical deterioration and psychological stress that accompany ageing inevitably befall all of us, irrespective of where we were born. However, it is in coping with the loss of physical mobility, the slowing down of bodily functions, the psychological changes, adapting to the loss of a spouse etc., that some significant differences begin to appear in the ability of some groups to call upon formal and informal support networks and services. What are some of the particular difficulties and issues which this trend will present to planners and service promoters?

First, and perhaps most obvious, is the question of language problems preventing migrants from non-English-speaking countries of origin being aware of, and/or able to use, existing services for the aged. The existing studies suggest that, except for the receipt of the pension, it would appear that there is significant under-utilization of services by the ethnic aged (Australian Institute for Multicultural Affairs 1983b, p. 25). Several studies have indicated that many among the ethnic aged, especially women, have a poor command of the English language, even though they may have been in Australia for many years.

Figure 8.5 Proportion of older persons in major birthplace groups who are not able to speak English well or not able to speak English at all, 1981

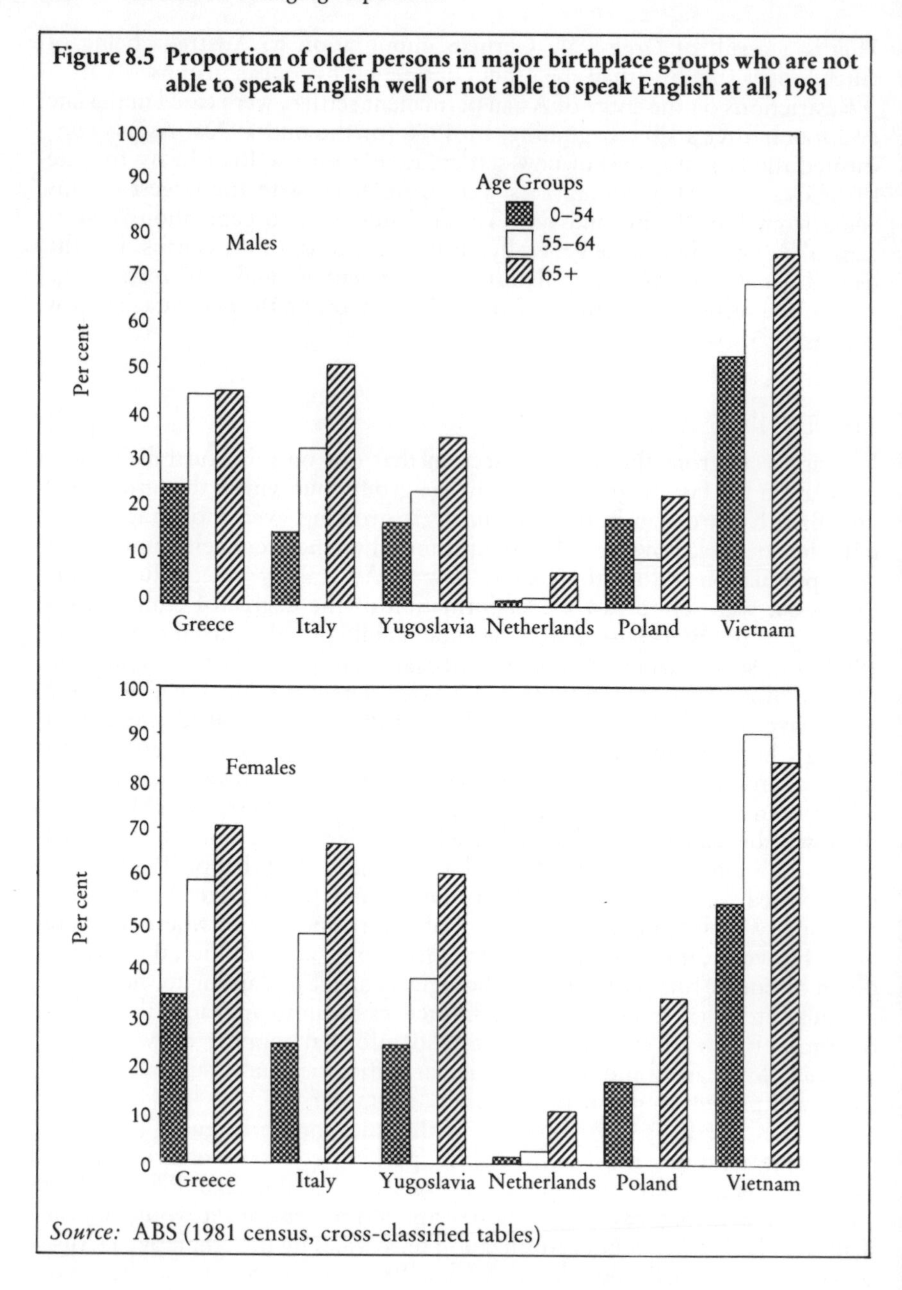

Source: ABS (1981 census, cross-classified tables)

The 1981 census collected information on the ability of the population to communicate in English. Figure 8.5 gives the percentage of older persons in the major groups of non-English-speaking origin that reported not being able to speak English well or not being able to speak English at all. A greater proportion of older people is unable to communicate effectively in English than is the case for younger people. These differences are in most cases quite large, the only exception being the Vietnamese-born population, among whom inability to speak English is fairly common in all ages and for whom the older section of the population is very small in number. Another universal feature is that within birthplace groups a much larger proportion of older women cannot speak English than is the case for older men. Among the 65+ age group this difference is very large, and among women of this age born in Greece, Italy and Yugoslavia, more than half cannot communicate effectively in English. The problem is thus especially pronounced among the groups of Southern European origin. Even among migrants who have been in Australia for decades, there are many who have little command of English, especially among women. Many of these people have had restricted interaction outside their homes or with other groups during their stay in Australia. Mykyta (1982, p. 8) has designated language and communication as 'perhaps the most central problem area' among aged migrants, and says that migrants who have a restricted command of English for everyday needs often have 'insufficient for the conduct of business transactions or health or welfare consultations'. He adds that there is a tendency among the aged for 'bilingual individuals to revert to their first language'.

The problems created for the aged person lacking the ability to communicate effectively in English are manifold. Most obviously they experience great difficulty in using existing services taken for granted by many of the aged. Even if such services provide an interpreter, the aged immigrant lacking English may never even hear of, or find out about, the relevant health or welfare agency. The language problem may also exacerbate stresses between generations with younger Greeks, Italians or others who have grown up in Australia perhaps preferring to use English in most day-to-day contexts. Others have argued that the language barrier becomes acute should an aged immigrant find it necessary to enter an institution where they are not able to communicate with those around them (Mykyta 1982; Clyne 1977).

It has been suggested by some (Schappi 1983, p. 21) that the communication difficulties referred to above are to some extent compensated for by the fact that among groups like Southern European migrants extended family loyalties are strong, so that the aged can expect to draw upon greater support and care from within the family than many of their Australian-born counterparts. However, some writers have found that such expectations may not be realized in the Australian context (e.g. Moraitis, in Howe 1981, p. 257), although the extent of breakdown in tradition is not known. While some suggest that it is substantial, Storer (1981, p. 10) reports a study in Melbourne where 80 per cent of immigrant families interviewed wanted grandparents to join them and many complained of loneliness due to migration severing extended family links. On the other hand, he also reports several studies which have documented significant incidence of inter-generational conflict arising from migration. Such problems include parent/child conflict over values, morality, arrangement of marriages, as well as different priorities between generations being given to the maintenance of traditions and customs. Clearly most of the second generation have gone to school and grown up in Australia and been subject to many non-traditional influences, while there are also other contextual factors which may reduce the amount of support provided for the aged within the family (Moraitis in Howe 1981, p. 257; Mykyta 1982, p. 10).

Nevertheless, analysis of 1981 census data has indicated that the distribution of family living arrangements among elderly immigrants differs from that among the Australian-born. While 24 per cent of native-born Australians aged 60 years and over lived alone, this applied to only 17 per cent of older persons born in non-English-speaking countries (Australian Institute for Multicultural Affairs 1983b, p. 6). For females 75 years and over the comparative proportions were 39 per cent and 24 per cent. However, the pattern is not uniform across all groups. For example, among men born in Eastern Europe there are high incidences of living alone which is consistent with feedback from social workers that this group suffers especially from social isolation and loneliness. For females the patterns are somewhat different, with substantially lower proportions of the overseas-born living alone.

It is also clear that there is a greater tendency for the family to support the older generation outside institutions among the major ethnic groups than is the case among Australians of Anglo-Saxon background. Ware (1981, p. 96), for example, in her study of the Italian community analysed 1976 census data for Sydney which 'confirms that the great majority of the Italian born aged live in private homes rather than institutions'. Among the Australian population aged 60 and over, 3.1 per cent were patients in nursing homes while only 1.4 per cent of the ethnic aged were in nursing homes. For females 75 and over, 11.8 per cent of Australian-born were patients in nursing homes while just 6.6 per cent of females aged 75 and over born in non-English-speaking countries were in nursing homes (Australian Institute for Multicultural Affairs 1983b, p. 25). Conversely, the 1981 census data show that there is a greater tendency for the family to support the older generation by co-residence among the major ethnic groups than is the case among Australians of Anglo-Saxon background (Hugo 1984e). Table 8.11 shows the proportion of older persons in major birthplace groups who were ancestors of the heads of the households in which they live. It provides evidence that Southern European and, to a lesser extent, non-English Northern European families show a greater propensity to take in their older relatives than is the case among the Australian-born. Among the oldest age groups the contrast is startling: 21.4 per cent of South Europeans aged 70–74 years live with their children, while this is the case with nearly a third of those aged 75 years or over. Among the Australian-born, on the other hand, only 4 per cent of those aged 70–74 years live with their children, as do 7.5 per cent of those aged 75 years and over. Clearly then, there are some major contrasts between the Australian-born and several of the major birthplace groups with

Table 8.11 Percentage of older persons in major birthplace groups living in a household where they are an ancestor of the household head, 1981

Age group (years)	Birthplace			
	Australia	U.K./Ireland (Rep.)	Northern Europe	Southern Europe
60–64	1.9	2.1	3.5	3.8
65–69	2.6	4.1	3.9	6.3
70–74	4.0	4.7	6.6	21.4
75+	7.5	11.5	12.5	32.2
Total	3.9	5.9	5.8	14.4

Source: ABS (1981 census, one per cent sample tape of households)

respect to living situations of their aged population. Of course, as Ware (1981, p. 97) has pointed out, data on living arrangements such as those quoted above 'cannot make any allowance for the presence of a daughter who lives next door or in the next suburb but pops in every day'. Nevertheless, it does point to the fact that, at least among Southern European immigrant groups, aged parents, especially if widowed, are much more likely to move in with their children and grandchildren than their Australian-born counterparts. On the other hand, living in non-private dwellings is much more common among the Australian-born aged. The above patterns should by no means be interpreted as indicating that extended family living arrangements are universal among aged immigrants of non-English-speaking origin. Schappi (1983, p. 22) concludes that 'extended family living arrangements are not as widespread within migrant communities as was generally assumed ... many migrant families adopt the nuclear family living arrangements where the second generation establishes their own households'. The proliferation of movements to establish birthplace-group specific aged homes within Australian cities suggests that nothing has happened subsequently to alter this conclusion.

In discussion of the well-being and support of the aged, marital status is a vitally important consideration. Couples are less likely to suffer loneliness and lack of physical and emotional support than widowed and other single persons. Table 8.12 shows the proportions of four age groups of persons aged over 55 years who were married at the time of the 1981 census according to their birthplaces. Some interesting patterns are evident here besides the well-known tendencies such as the fact that a greater proportion of aged males enjoy the support, companionship and comfort of a spouse than is the case for women. Almost universally there are greater proportions of immigrant males and females married than is the case for older native-born Australians. This pattern is a function, as Ware (1981, p. 101) points out, of the fact that however 'much they may be disadvantaged in other areas, immigrants enjoy a clear advantage in terms of mortality levels'. Despite the fact that with increased length of residence in Australia immigrant mortality is

Table 8.12 Percentage of population in various age-sex categories within major birthplace groups married at the time of the 1981 census

Birthplace	Percentage married at time of 1981 census			
	M	F	M	F
	aged 55–59		aged 60–64	
Australia	80.8	73.0	80.1	64.9
Germany	82.4	73.7	83.9	66.9
Greece	92.8	78.3	91.6	66.9
Italy	90.9	84.5	91.3	76.1
Netherlands	86.9	80.8	88.5	75.0
Poland	77.0	73.5	77.7	67.3
Yugoslavia	82.4	73.2	82.8	61.8
Vietnam	83.9	59.6	79.1	43.5
UK & Ireland (Rep.)	83.7	78.2	83.6	69.6
New Zealand	78.8	71.0	81.8	64.2
	aged 65–74		aged 75+	
Australia	76.5	48.7	59.8	18.7
Germany	78.9	51.2	60.9	17.3
Greece	85.5	45.0	63.3	18.8
Italy	86.5	57.5	65.6	24.2
Netherlands	85.3	62.1	74.3	28.3
Poland	73.4	52.9	64.0	21.0
Yugoslavia	76.1	44.7	60.4	19.8
Vietnam	73.4	33.8	50.0	8.6
UK & Ireland (Rep.)	79.6	50.9	62.7	21.2
New Zealand	80.2	48.4	62.5	22.1

Source: ABS (1981 census, cross-classified tables)

converging on that of the Australian-born (McMichael et al. 1980; Dunt 1982), the difference is still large enough to mean that a greater proportion of immigrants have the support of a spouse than is the case for the Australian-born. The differences are partly a result of the selective nature of the migration to Australia which would have favoured healthy, strong individuals. Despite this mortality difference it has been suggested (e.g., in Mykyta 1982, p. 11) that immigrants are disproportionately disadvantaged with respect to physical and mental health. This is a function of the fact that many are in the lowest socio-economic status groups and difficulties are experienced in gaining access to medical services. Some have also suggested that males in some migrant groups have been disproportionately represented in manual occupations with higher risk of injury or death than others, and that this could result in the incidence of some kinds of disability in old age being especially high in those groups (Hugo 1983f).

Lack of financial security is a major problem confronting the ethnic aged, as highlighted by the majority of organizations contacted in a Victorian study (Hearst 1981, p. 21). The 1981 census provides us with some data on differences between birthplace groups in their annual income. Table 8.13

Table 8.13 Income distribution of persons aged 65+ by birthplace group, 1981

Birthplace	No. of persons	Income None	$1–$4000	$4001–$10 000	$10 001–$15 000	$15 001–$26 000	$26 001 or more
Australia	633 012	4.0	46.5	37.3	7.0	3.9	1.3
Germany	8 290	5.0	63.0	21.2	5.4	4.0	1.5
Greece	9214	12.2	70.5	12.5	2.8	1.6	0.5
Italy	29 546	6.7	77.1	12.7	2.1	1.0	0.4
Netherlands	9 156	3.6	73.5	17.8	3.1	1.5	0.4
Poland	12 396	4.4	66.9	17.7	6.2	1.1	1.4
Yugoslavia	7 920	10.5	75.7	11.0	1.8	0.7	0.3
Vietnam	299	14.7	74.6	9.7	1.0	–	–
UK & Ireland (Rep.)	184 895	2.6	71.0	21.4	3.0	1.5	0.4
New Zealand	11 759	3.6	58.7	25.9	6.3	4.1	1.4

Source: ABS (1981 census, cross-classified tables)

shows that generally a higher proportion of immigrant aged reported receiving no income at all than was the case for the Australian-born, and for all immigrant groups the proportions in the two lowest income categories combined is substantially greater than is the case for the Australian-born. Whereas half of the Australian-born aged had incomes of less than $4000 per annum, this was true of more than 70 per cent of the aged from Yugoslavia, Greece, Italy and Vietnam, more than 70 per cent of those from the Netherlands, Poland and the United Kingdom and more than 60 per cent of those from Germany and New Zealand. These income data suggest that the incidence of poverty among the aged is greater among the ethnic aged than for the Australian-born.

It has been demonstrated in Chapter 6 that, like many minority groups, the aged in Australia tend to live in particular types of areas. The ethnic aged show an even more marked pattern of concentration. This spatial clustering of particular ethnic groups in particular communities is of more than esoteric interest in that it can be indicative of the presence of and access to kinship and friendship networks between people (including the aged) who share the same cultural and linguistic background. Moreover, knowledge of this spatial pattern is of basic significance in planning and carrying out the provision of services to the ethnic aged. Indeed, the very strong clustering of this group can be used to facilitate the cost-effective provision of specialized services to them. Elsewhere (Hugo 1983c, 1984e) it has been shown that the distribution of the overseas-born aged follows generally the patterns described for their respective entire birthplace groups in Chapter 4. They are over-represented in the major metropolitan areas, although those living in non-metropolitan areas tend to be more concentrated. Moreover, the small numbers of ethnic aged living in non-metropolitan areas may mean that they are more isolated from both formal and informal support networks than their urban counterparts. Within the metropolitan areas of Australia, older overseas-born persons tend to be distributed in very much the same way as their entire birthplace groups (see Chapter 4). This means that groups like the Greek- and Italian-born aged populations are highly concentrated in a few areas. The inner suburbs, which tend to be stereotyped as being the major areas of non-English-speaking background people, have high *relative* shares of the ethnic aged. However, overwhelmingly greater *numbers* of ethnic aged are distributed in the middle suburbs that were predominantly settled in the two decades following World War II. The major increase in demand for services for this group will therefore be concentrated in those areas. Moreover, it is in 'middle suburbs' of two types that the concentration occurs—the areas which formerly had or still do have significant market gardening activity (in the Adelaide case, the River Torrens Valley) and the lower socio-economic, heavily industralized suburbs (in Adelaide, the north-west sector of the metropolitan area). The degree of spatial concentration varies between birthplace groups, with those of Southern European origin being most concentrated while Eastern and Northern European groups tend to be more dispersed.

In this section we have only touched upon a few of the special difficulties which confront the overseas-born aged. Many other issues have been raised and dealt with in greater detail by other writers (Hearst 1981; Mykyta 1982; Schappi 1983; Moraitis, in Howe 1981; Australian Institute for Multicultural Affairs 1983a and b). The AIMA (1983b) suggests that the low utilization rates of existing age care services by the ethnic aged are explainable in terms of the services themselves and in terms of the needs and preferences of the ethnic aged. However, a significant element is that most of the ethnic aged are 'young-old' and some services such as nursing homes are not needed as yet by the vast majority. However, other services such as domiciliary and day services which seem to be of particular relevance to the ethnic aged are also under-utilized. The essentially demographic analysis undertaken here has indicated the scale and nature of some of the problems confronting planners in these areas, but much policy-oriented research remains to be done.

SOCIAL AND ECONOMIC MOBILITY OF IMMIGRANT GROUPS

There is considerable debate concerning the social and economic well-being of particular groups of immigrants arriving in Australia during the post-war period. The classical view is that of each new wave of immigrants initially filling the lower pay and status echelons of the occupational spectrum and, by dint of working hard and long hours and by virtue of their ingenuity and entrepreneurial skill, gradually working their way up the social and economic ladder. An alternative view is that the immigrants are forced into particular low-paid, manual labour niches in the economy from which it was virtually impossible to escape so that they are locked into a situation of poverty and deprivation, and they therefore form a disproportionately large section of the exploited proletariat. Obviously the experience of immigrants varies enormously between individuals and groups and it is difficult to generalize about that experience. Much of the debate about the upward mobility (or lack of it) among immigrants is informed only by analysis of aggregate census data on the occupation/industry/income experience of various groups according to birthplace or length of residence in Australia. Such analysis takes no account of the experience of immigrants who have returned to their country of origin, among whom lack of upward mobility must be widespread. Moreover, little consideration has been given to intergenerational changes. Our focus in this section is to be upon the social and economic situation of the 'second generation' of immigrant groups, and especially on how this differs from the situation of the first generation of overseas arrivals. Our analysis will be restricted to data from the 1981 census and to a limited range of socio-economic indicators, mainly those concerned with work-related variables.

Educational qualifications

One of the most significant socio-economic differentials is formal educational achievement. Despite major changes in the post-war period which have greatly reduced inequality in access to education, especially tertiary education, there are still inequalities. Table 8.14 compares the level of formal educational achievement as recorded at the 1981 census for the adult (15+ years of age) first and second generations of the major birthplace groups. The significant differentials apparent would be even more marked if the population

Table 8.14 Educational qualifications in population aged 15 years and above according to birthplace (first generation) or birthplace of parents (second generation), 1981.

Birthplace or birthplace of parents	Educational qualification (percentage distribution) Diploma or better		Trade certificate/other		No qualifications		Still at school	
	Generation 1st	2nd	1st	2nd	1st	2nd	1st	2nd
Australia	7.9	7.8	16.0	16.2	64.8	65.7	3.9	3.4
UK & Ireland (Rep.)	7.7	8.2	20.3	17.3	63.1	63.7	1.7	2.9
Germany	9.1	5.8	27.8	12.0	52.2	64.7	1.1	9.0
Netherlands	6.3	7.7	28.0	14.2	57.9	57.3	0.8	15.3
Poland	6.5	13.3	15.4	16.5	68.6	58.4	0.7	7.6
Greece	1.4	7.2	8.9	10.2	81.9	49.1	1.9	24.3
Italy	2.2	5.3	12.3	14.7	76.9	58.7	1.1	15.4
Malta	1.5	2.3	9.7	17.1	81.1	63.5	0.4	10.4
Yugoslavia	1.6	5.7	15.9	12.8	72.3	59.3	3.0	14.3
Middle East	2.8	8.7	9.3	12.7	78.7	61.2	3.3	10.2
Asia	18.7	14.0	13.3	12.5	55.8	57.1	5.4	11.1
New Zealand	9.4	14.4	19.2	18.1	62.6	58.9	2.1	3.4

Source: ABS (1981 census, one per cent sample tape of individuals)

'still at school' at the time of the census were excluded from consideration. Indeed in this respect it is interesting to note the very high proportions of some second-generation groups (e.g., Greeks) still at school. These groups maintain their children at school well beyond the compulsory leaving age. Clearly, while the stereotype of Southern European immigrants having less formal education than the Australian-born has validity, it most definitely does not apply to the second generation. A similar pattern prevails for the Middle Eastern groups. The high educational selectivity of Asian immigration is clearly evident in Table 8.14, with nearly a fifth of the Asian-born having a tertiary qualification. There can be no doubt that there has been a high degree of upward mobility among several of the Southern European groups, in that the proportion of the second generation going on to higher education is not only much greater than for their equivalent first-generation populations but also is higher than the Australian average. These patterns are particularly apparent if the proportions with 'no qualifications' are examined. For all Southern European groups there is a striking contrast with much lower proportions of the second generation reporting no qualifications.

Occupational status

One of the most useful indicators of the extent of socio-economic differences between generations is the occupation in which they are employed. Ware (1981, p. 60), for example, found strong evidence of considerable upward occupational mobility within the Italian community. Table 8.15 presents data on the occupations at the 1981 census of first-generation and second-generation populations of the major birthplace groups in Australia. Some striking patterns are evident. The UK/Ireland (Rep.) origin group is the largest, showing many similarities with the Australian-born population and little difference between generations. The main difference is the smaller proportion of the second generation in the 'tradesmen, process and production' workers category and more in the farming/clerical/sales categories. This does not give evidence of overall upward occupational mobility but reflects the fact that many British immigrants of the 1950s and 1960s were selected on the basis of their manual skills, whereas subsequent structural change in the economy has meant that jobs in these areas have not been so readily available to their Australian-born children who have come onto the job market in the last decade or so. The pattern among New Zealanders is somewhat similar.

Some of the largest differences are in the Southern European groups, supporting the observations of Ware (1981) on the population of Italian-origin. The pattern for the population of Greek origin is even more striking, with 11.6 per cent of the second generation having professional, technical or executive occupations compared to 1.5 per cent of Greek-born persons. For the population of Italian origin, the comparable proportions are 10 and 3.4 per cent respectively, and for the Yugoslav-origin group 14.8 and 4.9 per cent. It will be noted in Table 8.15 that there are inter-generational differences of similar magnitude in clerical occupations. On the other hand, the proportions employed as tradesmen, process and production workers and

Table 8.15 Occupational status according to birthplace of parents, 1981

Birthplace of parents	Occupational status (percentage distribution) Professional, technical, executive		Clerical		Sales		Farmers, fishermen, hunters		Tradesmen, process & production		Service, sport, recreation		Unemployed	
	Generation 1st	2nd	1st	2nd	1st	2nd	1st	2nd	1st	2nd	1st	2nd	1st	2nd
Australia	18.4	18.4	17.8	17.8	8.3	8.3	7.9	7.9	23.6	23.6	7.7	7.7	5.6	5.6
UK & Ireland (Rep.)	20.2	20.8	16.9	18.5	7.7	8.6	1.7	6.3	28.5	22.1	9.5	7.9	6.8	4.7
Germany	18.1	14.5	15.2	11.8	6.5	8.8	2.3	4.6	31.8	28.2	10.7	6.9	5.9	13.7
Netherlands	20.3	16.1	14.5	17.1	7.1	9.5	4.7	3.4	33.8	27.4	8.0	8.2	4.8	10.4
Poland	15.5	22.9	9.1	22.8	6.8	8.2	1.4	0.9	35.5	19.0	11.5	6.9	7.4	8.6
Greece	5.7	17.4	4.8	21.3	13.8	11.6	2.4	1.2	47.1	20.9	11.5	6.6	6.4	8.9
Italy	7.6	12.6	7.1	20.1	6.0	11.6	5.4	6.1	51.3	25.5	9.0	6.2	3.8	7.7
Malta	5.7	6.6	7.9	13.8	3.8	7.2	4.3	3.6	51.6	40.7	11.4	6.0	4.9	10.2
Yugoslavia	4.9	14.8	5.0	19.9	3.6	7.4	1.6	2.3	58.6	25.0	8.9	7.4	8.2	14.2
Middle East	6.4	17.5	6.8	19.8	8.5	15.9	1.0	5.6	47.8	15.1	6.8	6.3	12.7	9.5
Asia	25.5	22.6	17.0	17.1	4.5	10.1	2.1	2.0	22.2	23.1	10.4	12.1	10.3	6.5
New Zealand	19.7	21.6	15.9	18.0	8.4	9.6	2.8	4.9	26.4	18.6	10.7	8.7	7.1	6.1

Source: ABS (1981 census, one per cent sample tape of individuals)

service workers among the second-generation Southern European groups are around half those of the first generation. There is clear evidence here of movement from manual, blue-collar occupations toward higher-status white-collar employment. As Ware (1981, p. 60) has pointed out, 'In general these figures would suggest that the hopes and aspirations of those who came to Australia to find a better life for their children are in many cases fulfilled'. However, it will also be noted in Table 8.15 that the proportions of second-generation Southern Europeans in high-status professional and technical occupations are generally still below those of Australians of more than two generations standing. Thus, it would appear that although the second generations of Southern Europeans are in general considerably better off than their parents, they still have not quite achieved complete equality with longer-established Australians. It will be noted that there are especially high proportions of second-generation populations of Italian and Greek origin in clerical white-collar occupations but comparatively low proportions in the technical/professional occupations, suggesting that the shift has been made toward the lower-status end of the white-collar type of occupation.

The Middle East-origin community shows some interesting inter-generational differences in their occupational distribution. To a large degree its members parallel the experience of the Southern European groups, with the differences between generations being perhaps even more marked in the shift from the manual labour occupations to professional, technical and clerical forms of employment. On the other hand, persons of Asian origin show the least difference of any of the groups, due to the strong educational selectivity of Asian immigration to Australia.

The remaining continental European groups show a somewhat different pattern from the Southern European groups. The German-origin groups had lower levels of employment than longer-standing Australians in higher-status occupations but generally showed very little evidence of upward occupational mobility. On the other hand, the second-generation populations of Dutch and Polish origin notably had much higher proportions than their respective first generations in professional and technical occupations but also higher proportions than for the Australian-born with Australian-born parents. These groups also showed an inter-generational shift away from manual occupations to white-collar work, especially in the clerical area.

It is interesting to examine the extent of unemployment in the various groups shown in Table 8.15. It will be noticed that in most cases the level of unemployment in 1981 was higher among the overseas-born groups and their Australian-born second generation than for Australians of longer standing. Among the most recently arrived 'waves' of immigrants, the proportions unemployed were twice as high as those for the Australian-born. Hence, among the Middle East- and Asian-born, unemployment levels exceeded 10 per cent. Most of the second generation had levels of unemployment not only in excess of the other Australian-born population but also of their corresponding first-generation populations, who came at a time of economic expansion and full employment.

In short, there is evidence of upward occupational mobility across generations among the people of recent overseas origin. It is however not evenly distributed across groups, and it is more marked among groups whose first generation tended to go into the lower-status, manual occupations upon their arrival in Australia than among other groups or the Australian-born population of longer standing.

Income status

Table 8.16 shows the income distribution of individuals in the first and second generations. Although the differences are somewhat masked by the larger proportions of the second generation who are in the younger age categories and not earning income than is the case for the first generation, some interesting differences are in evidence. Another point that should be mentioned is the fact that the younger age structure of the second generation will generally mean that a much greater proportion of them will be in the early (and lower-paid) stages of their career life cycle than is the case for the first generation which has an older age structure. Both of these factors will of course tend to bias the second generation toward the lower end of the income distribution scale. However, despite this it will be noted in the table that in most groups the proportions of the second generation in the highest income bracket are greater than the proportions of their corresponding first-generation group. Thus again there is evidence of significant intergenerational upward mobility among the major post-war immigrant groups.

THE ABORIGINAL POPULATION

The most distinctive ethnic group in the Australian population is the Aborigines, who were counted at the 1981 census to number 159 897, or 1 per cent of the national population. It is indicative of the decimation and deprivation experienced by this group that despite rapid growth during the post-war period their numbers are now only half what they were prior to European settlement in Australia. Despite some significant improvements during the last decade the Aboriginal population demographically represents a 'Third World' sub-population within a dominant First World population. This was shown with respect to mortality and fertility in Chapters 2 and 3, but is true of almost every demographic parameter. Indicative of this is the poor quality of most demographic data relating to the Aboriginal population. Even at the 1981 census there was a massive discrepancy between the enumerated Aboriginal population and the more realistic estimates made by Gray and Smith (1983), using other sources, which are presented in Table 8.17. Earlier detailed analysis (NPI 1975; Smith 1980) explained these discrepancies in terms of different definitions of Aboriginal and changing patterns of self-identification, but Gray and Smith (1983, p. 8) maintain that

> we now have reached a stage where there is much less uncertainty about the size and definition of the population, and, where adequacy of enumeration rather than changing identification seems to be the main factor behind intercensal anomalies.

Table 8.16 Annual income of individuals according to birthplace of parents, 1981

Birthplace of parents	Income status (percentage distribution) None		$1–$8000		$8001–$12 000		$12 001–$18 000		$18 001 and over		Not stated	
	Generation 1st	2nd	1st	2nd	1st	2nd	1st	2nd	1st	2nd	1st	2nd
Australia	12.8	12.5	41.4	40.9	17.9	18.4	15.4	15.8	7.9	8.2	4.6	4.3
UK & Ireland (Rep.)	11.4	10.1	40.7	40.3	17.8	14.6	17.8	13.3	8.7	18.3	3.7	3.5
Germany	12.9	14.4	35.5	54.9	18.0	11.6	20.0	10.2	9.8	5.2	3.8	4.2
Netherlands	15.0	18.6	32.7	40.7	18.3	17.5	20.2	14.9	9.2	2.5	4.7	5.9
Poland	9.5	16.5	48.8	31.4	19.8	18.7	12.9	19.1	5.3	9.2	3.7	5.1
Greece	14.0	33.6	32.6	28.1	25.9	15.3	8.9	10.6	2.2	4.1	5.0	8.3
Italy	13.4	22.8	37.7	38.7	25.3	18.4	14.0	7.8	3.0	4.1	6.5	8.3
Malta	18.6	17.1	30.7	36.0	25.3	20.3	17.2	14.5	2.4	3.2	5.8	9.0
Yugoslavia	15.7	22.9	34.5	31.8	26.6	20.0	13.8	11.4	3.5	1.8	6.0	12.1
Middle East	22.6	18.4	35.1	37.8	24.6	20.9	8.9	9.7	3.0	7.2	6.1	6.1
Asia	19.9	18.7	30.6	38.8	19.4	17.2	17.2	14.2	8.8	6.4	4.1	4.7
New Zealand	14.1	11.4	32.8	44.4	19.0	14.5	17.9	16.3	10.9	10.1	5.3	3.4

Source: ABS (1981 census, one per cent sample tape of individuals)

Table 8.17 Changes in Aboriginal population, 1788–1981

Year	Estimated population	Year	Estimated population
1788	314 500	1933	67 314
1861	179 402	1947	70 465
1871	155 285	1954	75 567
1881	131 366	1961	106 124
1891	111 150	1966	121 697
1901	94 598	1971	139 457
1911	80 613	1976	156 556
1921	69 851	1981	171 151

Sources: NPI (1975, vol. 2, p. 478); Gray and Smith (1983, p. 8)

Figure 8.6 Age structure of Aboriginal and non-Aboriginal populations, 1981

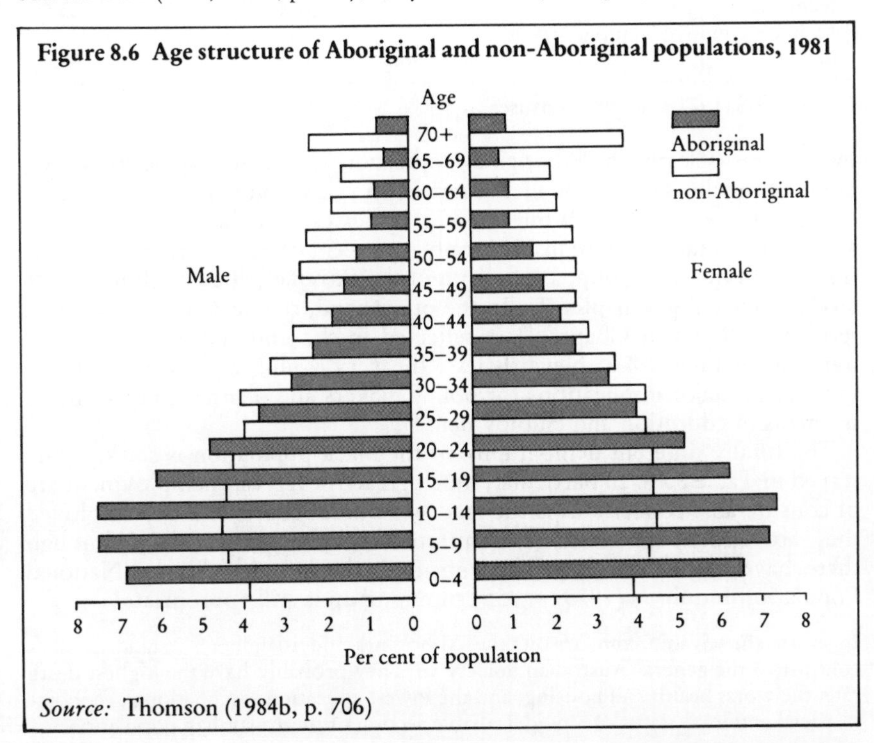

Source: Thomson (1984b, p. 706)

Nevertheless, it is apparent from Table 8.17 that after a century and a half of decline, the Aboriginal population began to increase slowly in the 1930s and more quickly during the 1950s and the 1960s. In the latter decade there was an increase of nearly a third in the Aboriginal population. Since then, chiefly due to the decline in fertility and maintenance of high overall mortality levels outlined in earlier chapters, the inter-censal growth declined to 12.3 per cent for 1971–76 and 9.3 per cent in 1976–81.

One of the major differences between the Aboriginal and non-Aboriginal population is depicted in Figure 8.6, which shows the age structure of the

Table 8.18 Comparison of various demographic characteristics of the Aboriginal and total population, 1971 and 1981

Characteristics	Aboriginal 1971	Aboriginal 1981	Total population 1971	Total population 1981
Expectation of life at birth (male)	52	49	68	71
Expectation of life at birth (female)	52	56	75	78
Infant mortality rate	120	24.5	11	10.7
Total fertility rate	5.97	3.32	2.95	1.94
Percentage in urban areas	44	60	85.6	85.8
Percentage aged less than 15	40	41	28	25
Percentage unemployed (males)	9.2	27.4	1.2	5.5
Percentage employed in professional/ technical	1.7	7.0	6.8	13.6
Percentage employed, employees or helpers	96.7	97.8	87.4	85.6

Source: ABS (1971 and 1981 censuses)

two groups. Clearly the Aboriginal population is a demographically young population with 41 per cent aged less than 15 years (compared to 25 per cent of the total population). While around 14 per cent of the total population was aged 60 years or more in 1981, only 4 per cent of the Aboriginal population was in this age group, a reflection of the extremely high adult mortality levels discussed in Chapter 2. On the other hand, the decline in Aboriginal fertility outlined in Chapter 3 is reflected in the undercutting of the age pyramid in Figure 8.6. Nevertheless, the very young age structure has a number of major implications for policy makers and planners, especially in the areas of education and employment.

The totally different demography of the black population is starkly portrayed in Table 8.18. In particular, much greater levels of unemployment are of considerable concern, as is the fact that where Aboriginals are employed they are disproportionately concentrated in lower-status jobs. Although there have been some improvements over the last decade, the National Population Inquiry's (1975, p. 455) summing up is still appropriate.

> In every conceivable comparison, the Aborigines and islanders ... stand in stark contrast to the general Australian Society.... They probably have the highest death rate, the worst health and housing, and the lowest education, occupational, economic, social and legal status of any identifiable section of the Australian population.

The Aboriginal population is much more evenly dispersed nationally than the total population which is heavily concentrated in the major cities and eastern coastal zone. Few aspects of Aboriginal demography have undergone as rapid a change, however, as their distribution; many moved into urban areas in the 1970s (Table 8.18).

Table 8.19 shows that the estimated distribution of the Aboriginal population between the States and Territories differs markedly from that of the total population. Queensland has the largest Aboriginal population and with

Table 8.19 Distribution of Aboriginal and total populations among States and Territories, 1981

State or Territory	Aboriginal population (est.)	Percentage of Aboriginal population	Percentage of total population
Qld	46 819	27	16
NSW	39 879	23	35
WA	31 347	18	9
NT	29 086	17	1
SA	9 830	6	9
Vic.	10 439	6	26
Tas.	2 936	2	3
ACT	815	1	2
Total	171 151	100	100

Source: Gray and Smith (1983)

Western Australia and the Northern Territory contains nearly two-thirds of the Aboriginal population but only a quarter of the total national population.

While the distribution of the Aboriginal population between States has changed little over the last two decades, there has been a transformation within the States. This change is readily apparent in Figure 8.7 which shows the changing proportions of the Aboriginal population living in urban and rural areas. Traditionally, since initial European settlement, the Aboriginals have been a predominantly rural minority in an overwhelmingly urban total population. As recently as 1961, 77.6 per cent of the Aboriginal population lived in rural areas or were migratory. Subsequently, however, there has been a continuing pattern of increasing concentration such that at the 1981 census only just over 40 per cent of Aboriginals were enumerated in rural areas. But the 1981 census results also indicated that the total Aboriginal population in major urban centres (with 100 000 or more) was 31 546 compared to 42 187 in 1976. While some commentators (e.g., Felton 1983, p. 32) suggest that the 1981 major urban figures are more like the actual situation than the 1976 figures, there is a strong body of opinion that the downturn in the graph for major urban areas in Figure 8.7 is largely due to undercounting: indeed, the Commonwealth Department of Aboriginal Affairs (1981) estimated that 75 per cent of Australia's Aboriginals lived in either cities (with populations of at least 20 000) or towns (including town reserves and fringe camps) in 1981. Nevertheless, it is clear that between two-thirds and a half of Australia's urban Aboriginals live in non-metropolitan centres with more than 1000, and less than 100 000 inhabitants, again presenting a major contrast with the total population (see Chapter 5).

The urbanization trends evident in Figure 8.7 represent a social change of very considerable dimensions, since it means that the bulk of Australia's adult urban Aboriginals are inmigrants. Burnley and Routh (1984, p. 1)

Figure 8.7 Distribution of Aboriginal and Islander population between urban and rural areas, 1961–81

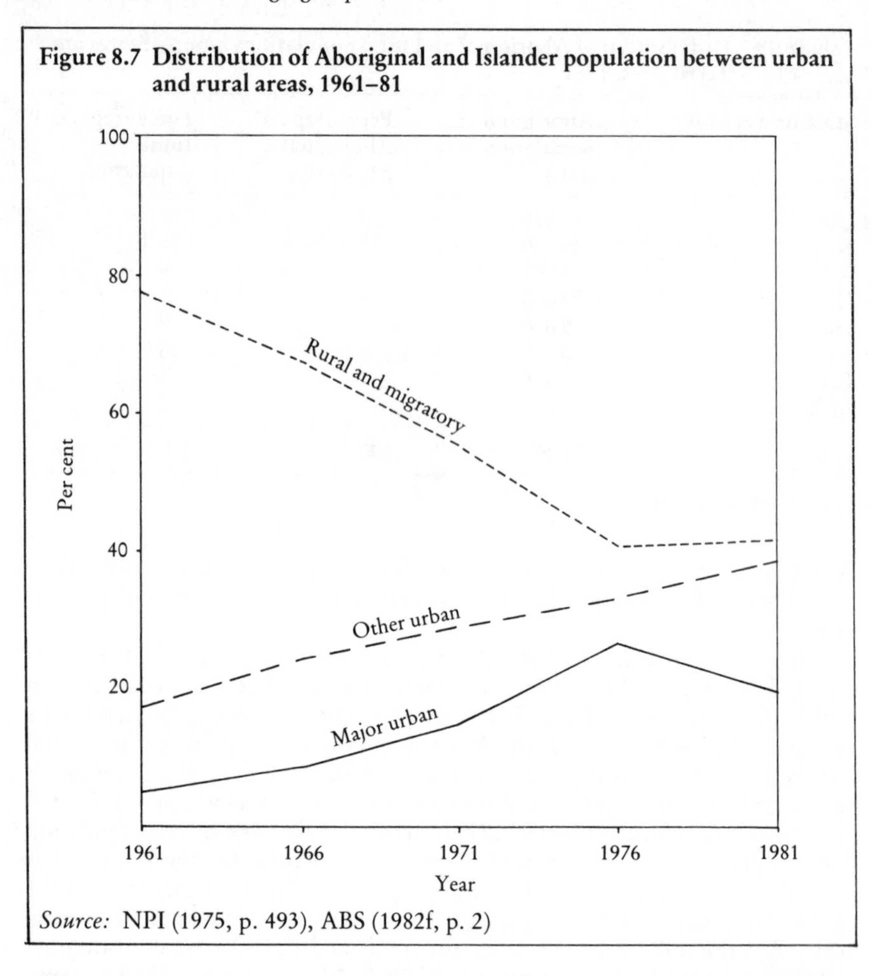

Source: NPI (1975, p. 493), ABS (1982f, p. 2)

found, for example, that 86 per cent of their sample of 150 Aboriginals in inner Sydney (1982–83) were inmigrants, while Gale's (1981) study of Aboriginals in Adelaide found that 71 per cent of households had been at a different address five years previously. Census data (Young 1982) indicate that Aboriginals have a significantly higher level of residential mobility than the non-Aboriginal population. Moreover, as Gale (1972, 1981) points out, once in the cities, inmigrant Aboriginals have been forced to undergo greater social change than most non-Aboriginal newcomers from other parts of Australia, because their social and cultural distance from urban society tends to be greater. The studies of urban Aboriginals show strong patterns of chain migration, with kinship and friendship bonds between early inmigrants and their places of origin being important. This also has led to spatial concentration in particular parts of the major cities, mainly in non-gentrified inner suburbs and areas of lower socio-economic status in the middle and outer suburbs (e.g., Gale and Wundersitz 1982)—especially those areas with significant amounts of public housing. However, some dispersal has occurred, in some cases due to a deliberate policy by State housing authorities of allocating Aboriginals housing in a wide spread of areas rather than concentrating them in particular suburbs (e.g., Gale 1981). Although much of the motivation for migration to major urban areas has been found to be rural poverty and unemployment, the same studies tend to indicate that high levels of unemployment, deprivation and welfare dependence also occur in the city (Burnley and Routh 1984).

In Chapter 2 the inferior and unacceptable health status of the Aboriginal population and its implications for policy were discussed. It is clear that those health inequalities can be seen as only part of a larger pattern of socio-economic inequality and deprivation. Policy makers and planners must confront this issue and as Thomson (1984a, p. 946) points out, 'Broad wide ranging programs must be aimed at alleviating Aboriginal poverty and powerlessness, at redressing the persisting effect of dispossession and of eliminating discrimination. The key to Aboriginal self determination is power'.

CONCLUSION

The Australian Council on Population and Ethnic Affairs (1982b, p. 8) wrote during the early 1980s that 'Since the early days of white settlement, the Australian population has always been a varied mix—not only in its ethnic origins but also in many other aspects such as religion, occupational class and regional alliances'. However, the 1947 census statistics reflect a relatively homogeneous, overwhelmingly Anglo-Celtic society—less than 2 per cent of the total population was born in a non-English-speaking country and there were only 70 468 Aboriginals. This chapter has demonstrated that one of the most dramatic changes in Australian society during the post-war period has been a substantial increase in ethnic heterogeneity. In 1981 the number of Australians born in a non-English-speaking country together with their Australian-born children exceeded two million persons, and more than 1 per cent of the population is Aboriginal. The new heterogeneity of Australian society has been brought about not only by shifts in immigration policy over the post-war years but also by immigrants themselves changing in manifold ways with the passage of time in their new country as they respond to different social, economic and different circumstances.

This transformation is of enormous significance in many areas of policy formulation and planning. Throughout the post-war years there has been a growing series of specific programmes of assistance to immigrants. Also, belatedly, new services were provided for Aboriginals to assist them to participate more fully in Australian society. These programmes have grown steadily over the last three decades. However, there are still a few areas of planning in which a greater understanding of, and sensitivity toward, the diversity of the cultural background of the population is necessary for meeting perceived needs and equitable provision of opportunities and services to that population. In this chapter we have provided a good case in point by focusing particularly on the ethnic aged, whose numbers will increase significantly during the 1980s, as will the proportion that they make up of their own population and of the total Australian aged community. Many of the needs of the ethnic aged are similar to those faced by the bulk of Australia's rapidly growing aged population. However, there are clearly some significant differences and these must be understood so that policies can be developed to cope with them. The special nature of many of the difficulties being confronted by the ethnic aged is gaining increasing public recognition, as letters and articles in the daily press testify (Richards 1982, 1983).

There are, however, wider and more general policy issues which are a source of continuing public debate. Official policies have undergone a major shift during the post-war period as the Government's statement to the 1984 International Population Conference (Department of Immigration and Ethnic Affairs 1984a, p. 22) demonstrates:

> Policies of assimilation and the integration of the individual into a basically mono-cultural society have given way to one of encouraging cultural diversity in which whole communities are integrated into a multi-cultural society. This policy emphasises the multi-cultural nature of society and recognizes and accepts the desire of ethnic groups to retain and foster their own cultures and languages while maintaining the cohesiveness of Australian society.

Hence, the policies of the 1950s and 1960s which emphasized the adjustment of minorities to established institutions gave way in the 1970s to one in which institutions were to be modified to accommodate the minority. While this policy of multi-culturalism has been taken up enthusiastically and intensely advocated in many areas (e.g., Australian Council on Population and Ethnic Affairs, 1982b), it also has been regarded with suspicion by others who see it as divisive and inequitable (e.g., see Knopfelmacher 1982; Chipman 1980). It remains to be seen whether the 'salad bowl' approach proves more effective than the 'melting pot' in achieving greater social justice for minority ethnic groups and Australians generally.

9 Australians at Work

Which Australians seek work outside the home, what types of work they are employed in and where that employment is located, have undergone major changes in recent years. These changes are of course a function of a wide range of technological, economic and social forces, some of which are internal to Australia while others are of more international applicability. It is beyond the scope of this chapter to deal comprehensively with these forces; I will focus upon how changes in the composition of the population have impinged upon the workforce and also how shifts in the workforce have influenced population change, especially since the early 1970s, when the Australian economy began to undergo considerable change. In particular, I will use results from the 1981 census to review major trends in labour force participation and the occupational and industrial composition of the workforce and from that analysis derive a number of policy-related implications.

CHANGING PATTERNS OF LABOUR FORCE SIZE AND PARTICIPATION

The Australian labour force (i.e., persons aged 15 years and over working or seeking work) has been growing more rapidly than the total population, as Table 9.1 shows. This has been due in part to the passage of the baby boom cohorts into the working age groups but also, as will be shown later, to a major increase in the levels of participation of women in work outside the home. However, there has been a convergence in the growth rates of the

Table 9.1 Growth of the Australian labour force, 1966–83

Period	Total labour force ('000s) at		Percentage increase	
	beginning	end	Workforce	Total population
1966–71	4902.5	5608.4	14.4	12.7
1971–76	5608.4	6190.5	10.4	7.4
1976–81	6190.5	6752.7	9.1	6.3
1981–83	6752.7	6980.1	3.4	2.3

Sources: Commonwealth Department of Employment and Industrial Relations (in ESCAP 1982, p. 328); ABS (1984i, p. 136)

Figure 9.1 Labour force participation rates, 1966–83

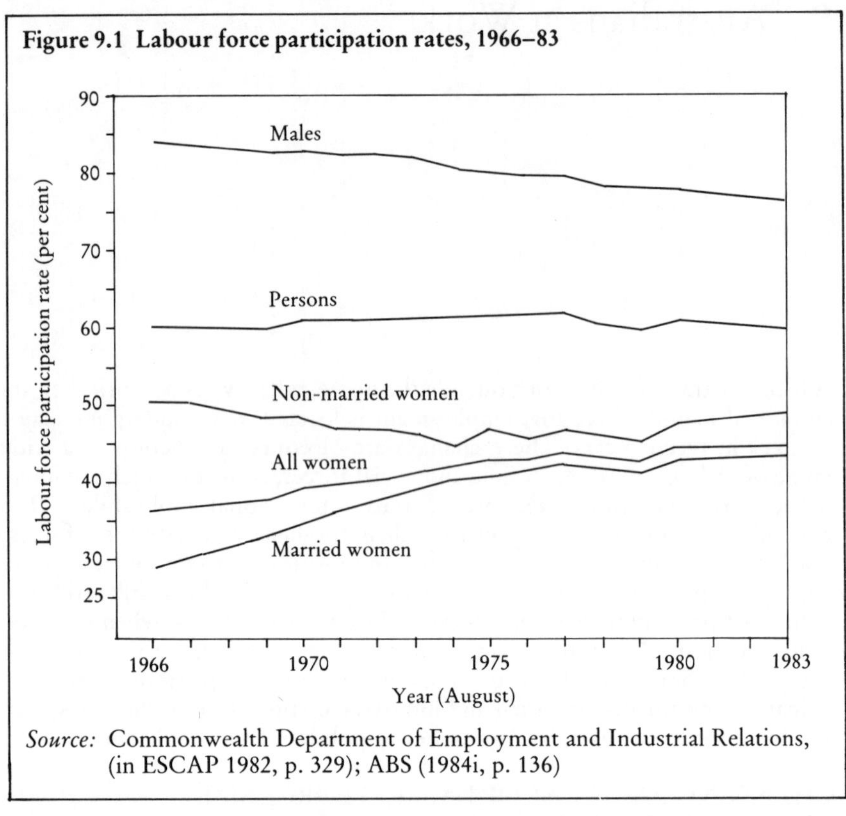

Source: Commonwealth Department of Employment and Industrial Relations, (in ESCAP 1982, p. 329); ABS (1984i, p. 136)

population and workforce in recent years, as the last of the baby boom cohorts enter the workforce ages.

Changes in overall participation rates of the population in the labour force (i.e. proportion of persons aged 15 years and over working or seeking work) are shown in Figure 9.1. This shows that the major changes in participation over the period since 1966 have been among married women. The proportion of adult males in the workforce has declined somewhat, largely because of reduced participation at older ages and perhaps increased participation in higher education among young men. Among unmarried women there has been little change over the last two decades in the rate of workforce participation. However, whereas in 1966 only 29 per cent of married women were in the labour force, this had increased to 42.6 per cent in 1983. This has seen the overall participation rate for women increase from 36.3 per cent to 44.8 per cent in 1983. It perhaps should be noted in this context that in the United States the 1980 census was the first in which more than 50 per cent of adult women reported working outside of the home, while in Sweden the female workforce participation rate was 74 per cent. Hence there appears to be scope for further increases in the female participation rate in Australia.

There have been some significant recent shifts in labour force participation rates in particular ages. Table 9.2, for example, shows that between the 1976

Table 9.2 Labour force participation rates, 1976 and 1981

Age	Males (percentage)			Females (percentage)		
	1976	1981	Change	1976	1981	Change
15–19	54.0	59.4	+5.4	48.5	53.5	+5.0
20–24	84.3	85.9	+1.6	61.8	68.0	+6.2
25–29	91.0	89.7	−1.3	48.2	54.0	+5.8
30–34	92.1	92.4	+0.3	48.7	51.4	+2.7
35–39	92.6	93.9	+1.3	55.7	57.3	+1.6
40–44	92.4	92.7	+0.3	56.9	59.8	+2.9
45–49	91.1	90.9	−0.2	53.4	55.7	+2.3
50–54	87.9	87.8	−0.1	44.3	45.2	+0.9
55–59	83.5	79.8	−3.7	33.7	32.2	−1.5
60–64	66.2	52.2	−14.0	17.5	15.0	−2.5
65+	16.2	12.0	−4.2	4.9	4.8	−0.1
Total	55.1	56.0	+0.9	31.1	33.7	+2.6

Source: ABS (censuses of 1976 and 1981)

and 1981 censuses there was somewhat increased participation at the younger ages but decreased participation among older workers, especially males in the 60–64 age group. This of course reflects the major move toward early retirement from the workforce, especially among men, and has major implications for planners (as discussed in Chapter 6).

It was mentioned in Chapter 3 that the major decline in fertility which Australia has experienced since the early 1960s has been partly a function of some significant changes in the position and role of women within Australian society. A major element in this has been the increasing participation of women, especially married women in working outside the home. This change is strikingly apparent in Figures 9.2 and 9.3, which are taken from Hull (1982, p. 8) who summarizes the situation thus:

> women, whether married or not, have moved into the labour force in a major way since the thirties such that today over half of all women are in the labour force at any given time, and over ninety per cent participate at some time during their lives.

It can be seen from Figure 9.2 that the major increase in participation of women in the workforce, especially in the main child-bearing ages of the twenties and thirties, occurred in each inter-censal period between 1961 and 1976. It will be noted in the diagram that the most recent inter-censal period (1976–81) saw the smallest increments in participation among women aged between 25 and 50 of the post-war period, while there was a reduction in participation of older women in the workforce. Thus, the late 1970s have seen a considerable departure from the trends of the earlier part of the post-war period, although it is unclear to what extent this is a function of female participation in the workforce having reached some kind of ceiling and how much it is due to the downturn in the economy and increased levels of unemployment.

The pattern for married women for the 1976–81 period is similar to that for all women, with only small increases in the level of participation of

Figure 9.2 Female labour force participation rates, by age, at censuses between 1911 and 1981

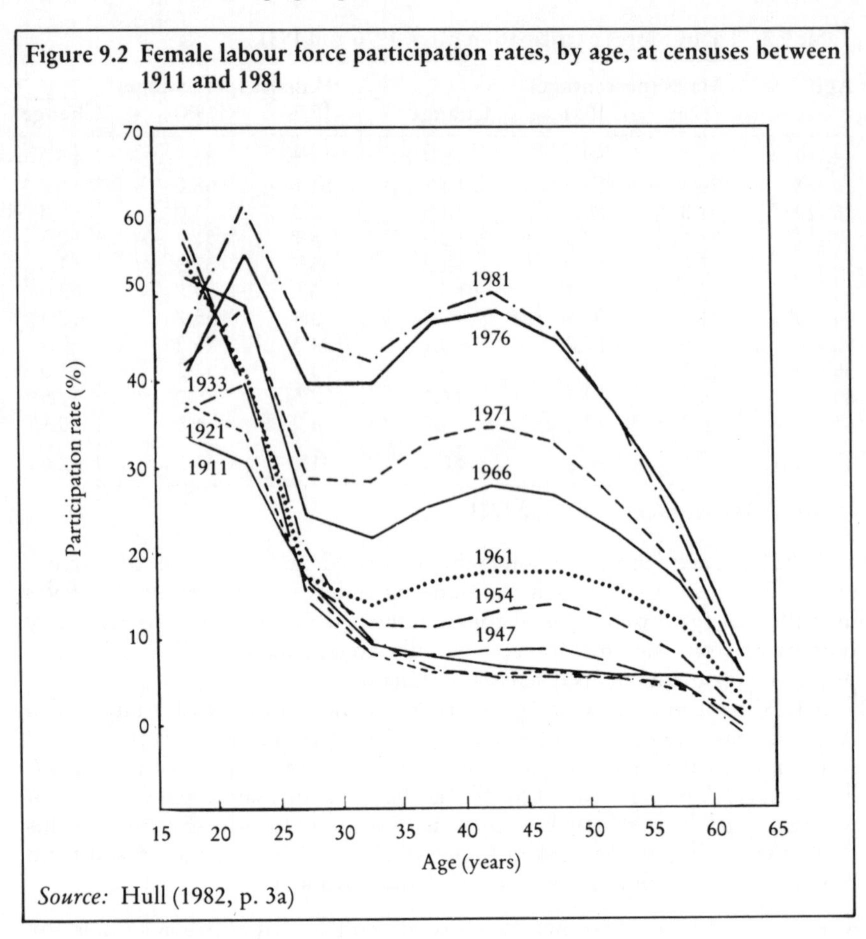

Source: Hull (1982, p. 3a)

women in the child-bearing age groups. Nevertheless, the fact remains that more than 50 per cent of married women in their early twenties, thirties and forties were working outside the home. The bimodal pattern in both Figures 9.2 and 9.3 reflects the pattern of many women leaving the workforce temporarily in their late twenties and early thirties to have children, to return once they have completed their child-bearing. This contrasts with the shape of the distribution in earlier years, especially for married women, when women tended to leave the workforce entirely after beginning child-bearing. In Chapter 3 it was shown that there is a clear pattern of women in all age categories who are wage and salary earners having substantially lower fertility than those not in the workforce.

The age structures of the workforce in 1976 and 1981 are shown in Figure 9.4. It can be clearly seen that the major increments to the workforce have been in the younger working age groups, reflecting the passage of the last

Figure 9.3 Married female labour force participation rates, by age, at censuses between 1933 and 1981

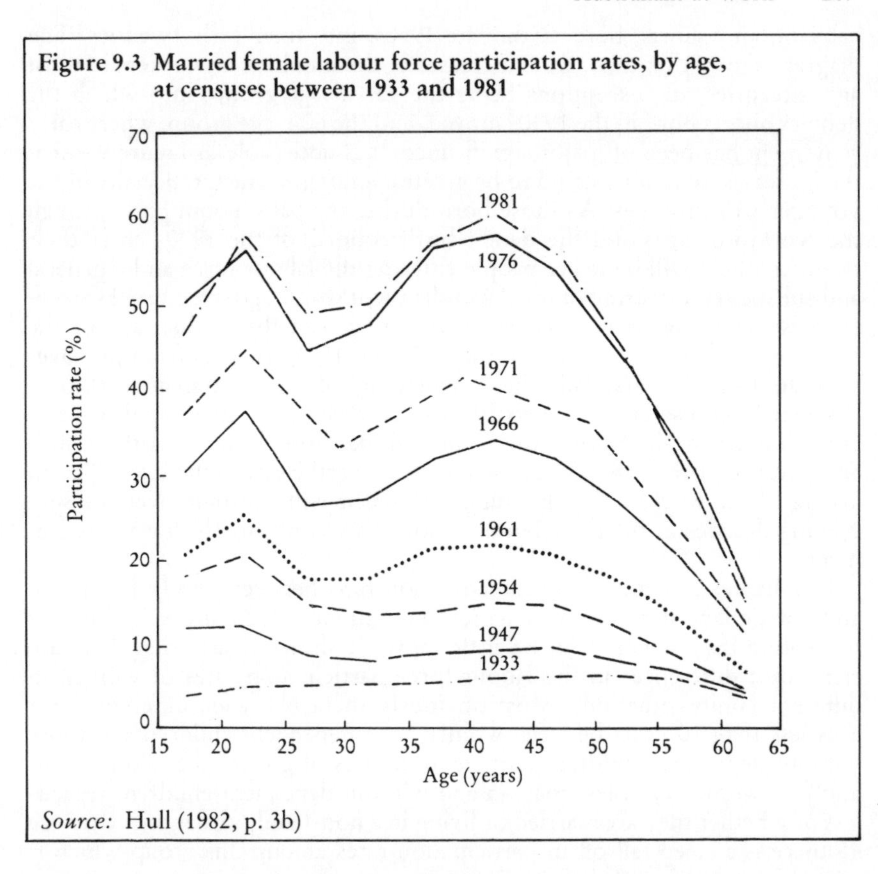

Source: Hull (1982, p. 3b)

Figure 9.4 Age structure of labour force, 1976 and 1981

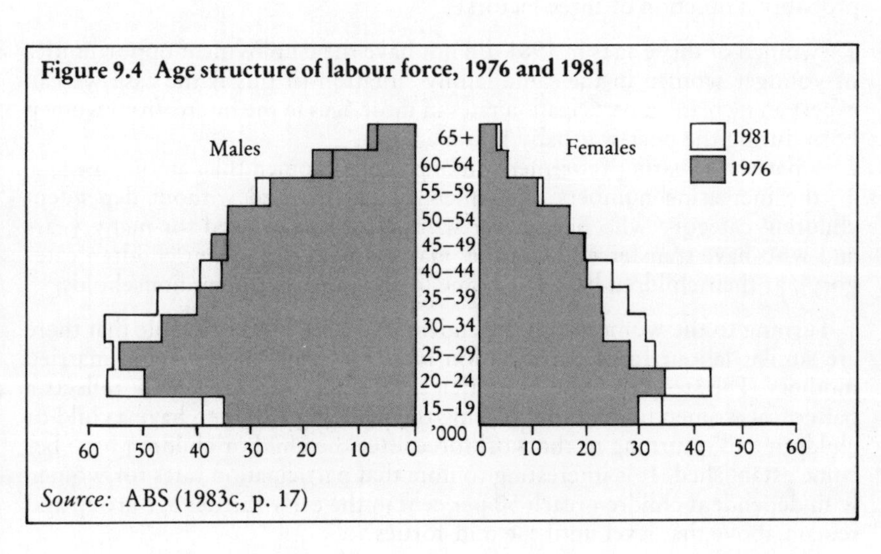

Source: ABS (1983c, p. 17)

baby boom cohorts, born in the late 1950s, into their early twenties. The diagram shows that there were increases in the numbers of workers in most age categories, the exceptions being the 45–49 age group, into which the deficit cohorts born in the 1930s moved, and the 60+ age group, where early retirement has been of major significance. It is noticeable in Figure 9.4 that the increases in numbers tend to be greatest among women, especially in the younger working ages. As those born during the baby boom pass through the workforce ages and the deficit birth cohorts of the 1970s enter their twenties, there will be fewer people entering the labour force and a general and substantial maturing of the Australian workforce age structure. However, this 'maturing' is not occurring as yet, in fact the median age of the workforce was reduced between the 1976 and 1981 censuses from just over 35 years to 34.1 years. This slight 'younging' of the Australian workforce happened because large cohorts born in comparatively high fertility years are still entering the labour force (and will be through much of the 1980s) and because of the loss of older workers. Nevertheless, in the late 1980s an ageing of the workforce will commence and it will continue over the succeeding decades as the baby boom cohorts move inexorably toward retirement.

In Chapter 3 some of the inter-relationships between family formation and female labour force participation were discussed. Figure 9.5 allows us to explore these relationships a little more. It shows clearly that there are significant differences in the labour force participation rates of women in different family situations. Most obviously there is a wide differential for ages less than 50 years between women with dependent children and those without dependent children. Participation rates of greater than 70 per cent apply to women aged less than 45 and without dependent children, regardless of whether they are married or living in a non-family situation. After age 45 there is a steep fall-off in participation rates among this group which is probably a function of three factors:

1 women of those ages in 1981 did not have the employment opportunities of younger women in the same family situation (if this is the case we can expect an increase in participation rates in those ages in the future, from women born during the post-war baby boom age);
2 a pattern of earlier retirement among career women than among men;
3 the increasing numbers of women in the 'married without dependent children' category who have never worked or not worked for many years and who have transferred from the 'married with dependent children category', as their children have left home to set up independent households.

Turning to the women with dependent children, it is noticeable that there are similar labour force participation rates for single mothers and married mothers. The steep increase in participation rates with age clearly reflects a pattern of women temporarily leaving the paid workforce to have a child or children and returning to the workforce after the child or children have become established. It is interesting to note that participation rates for women with dependent children reach 50 per cent in the early thirties age group and remain above that level until the mid-forties.

Figure 9.5 Labour force participation rates of females, by family status and age, July 1979

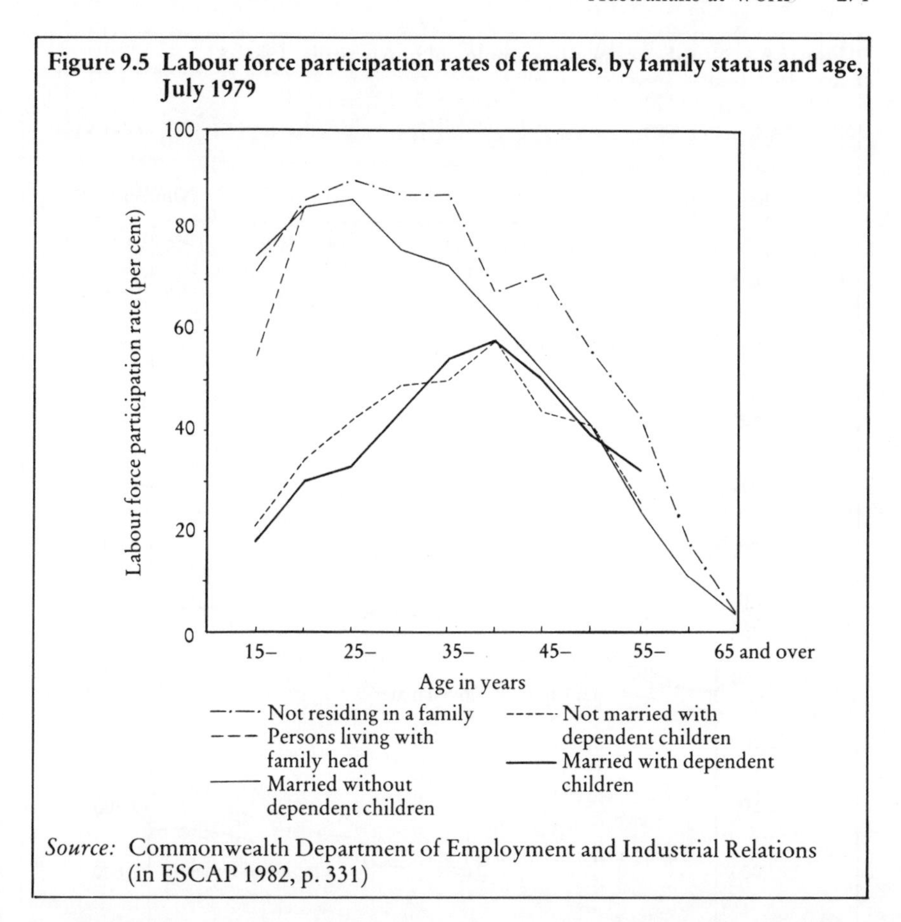

Source: Commonwealth Department of Employment and Industrial Relations (in ESCAP 1982, p. 331)

The growth in the various components of Australia's workforce over the 1966–83 period is shown in Figure 9.6. It shows the greater contribution of females than males to the growth of the labour force, with the steepest increase being of women in part-time employment. While more than a third of employed women were employed part-time in 1983, the equivalent proportion for men was only around 6 per cent. The overall growth of part-time employment over the 1966–83 period was more than 100 per cent compared to only 18.3 per cent in full-time employment. The ABS (1984e, p. 8) attributes this increase in part-time employment to 'increased labour force participation of married females, the expansion of service type industries with greater opportunities for part-time employment and the trend toward more time for leisure'. Perhaps the most striking pattern evident in Figure 9.6, however, is the pattern of an actual *decrease* in the number of males in full-time employment (and hence in total males employed) in the early years of the 1980s. This was accompanied by an increase in the number of part-time employed males and in the number of males who are unemployed—

Figure 9.6 Number of persons employed in Australia, 1966–83

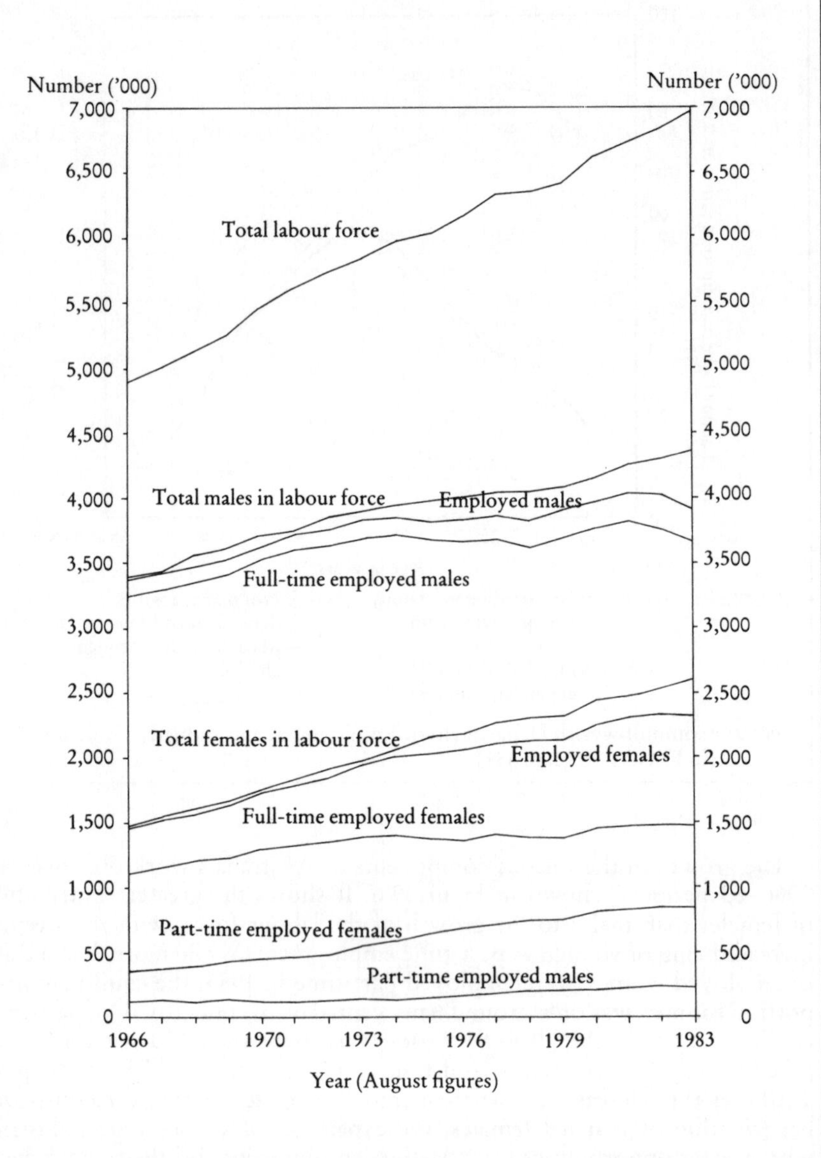

Source: ABS (1984e, p. 9; 1984i; p. 136); Commonwealth Department of Employment and Industrial Relations (in ESCAP 1982, p. 328)

hence the increase in the total number of males in the workforce. It is to a consideration of the unemployed that I will now turn.

UNEMPLOYMENT

Of all the social and economic changes in Australia during the 1970s, none was so dramatic as the shift from a quarter of a century of virtual full employment into an era of significant and increasing unemployment. Gregory (1984) has shown how the changing pattern of unemployment in Australia has been very similar to the experience of other Organisation for Economic Co-operation and Development (OECD) countries. In fact, during the 1960s, as Figure 9.7 shows, the unemployment rate was below 2 per cent; about two-thirds the average rate for the OECD countries. However, as Gregory points out (p. 3), 'Since 1975 there has been a remarkable change in Australia and in the rest of the world. Unemployment has increased in most countries to levels that were apparently normal before World War II'. Such an upward movement is apparent in Figure 9.7 after 1974. Thereafter, there has been a close correspondence with the OECD experience, described by Gregory thus (p. 4): 'a sudden upwards jump in 1974–75, then a pause and now beginning in 1980 an upward movement'. The rise in the early 1980s continued until 1984 when there was an improvement.

Examining changes in the actual numbers of unemployed persons is particularly appropriate here, because it indicates the scale of the problems to be tackled by policy makers and planners. Moreover, it demonstrates the dramatic change from the 1950s, 1960s and early 1970s, when the number of unemployed people was below 100 000—indeed, at that time it was often stated that a government which allowed unemployment to rise above 100 000 would almost certainly fall. Figure 9.8 shows that by 1983 unemployment had exceeded 600 000.

Unemployment falls disproportionately upon particular groups and it is important for planners to identify such groups. First, it is apparent from

Figure 9.7 Unemployment rates in Australia, 1966–84

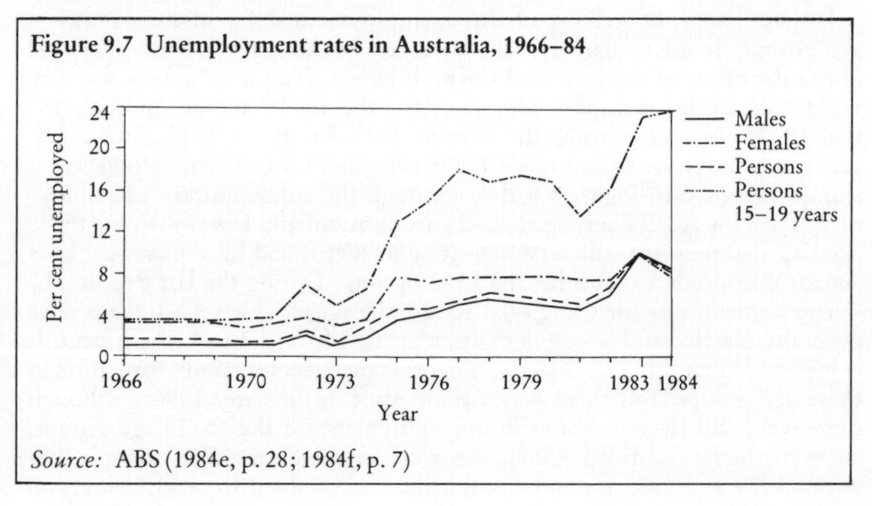

Source: ABS (1984e, p. 28; 1984f, p. 7)

Figure 9.8 Number unemployed, 1966–84

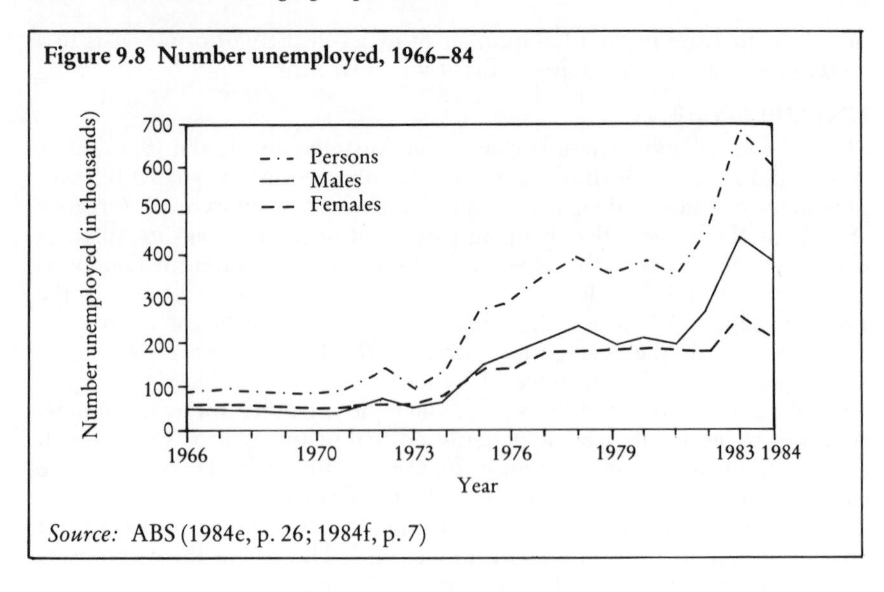

Source: ABS (1984e, p. 26; 1984f, p. 7)

Figure 9.7 that unemployment rates are higher for women than men but that the rates have been converging over time. Moreover, the gap between the number of unemployed men and women in Figure 9.8 is much smaller than that between numbers of employed men and employed women (Figure 9.6). In addition it is probable that many women (especially married women) who would like to work do not get counted as being unemployed (Merrilees 1984). A consistent pattern of female unemployment in ABS labour force surveys has been 'the high proportion looking for part time work' (Commonwealth Department of Employment and Industrial Relations, in ESCAP 1982, p. 347).

Perhaps the most striking of the unemployment differentials is between age groups. In particular, it is the younger working age groups that have borne the brunt of the increased unemployment. Figure 9.7 shows the very rapid increase in unemployment rates for the 15–19 age group since the mid-1970s. In fact, during the decade 1973–83 the unemployment rate increased nearly fivefold from 4.7 per cent to 22.6 per cent. However, it should be noted in Figure 9.9 that although the contemporary unemployment rates for Australians aged 20–24 are substantially lower than for those aged 15–19, they are still very high (one in seven) and have increased by a similar magnitude to rates for the 15–19 group. During the last decade, the unemployment rate for those aged 20–24, the age at which Australians have generally married and begun families, increased from 2.3 to 14.7 per cent. It is inevitable that this will have had a depressing effect on family formation in these age groups. But there was a slight shift in the early 1980s: although there were still large increases in unemployment for the 15–24 age groups, some of the largest relative increases were in older ages. For example, between 1979 and 1983 the unemployment rate doubled for each age group

Figure 9.9 Unemployment rates by age, 1966–83

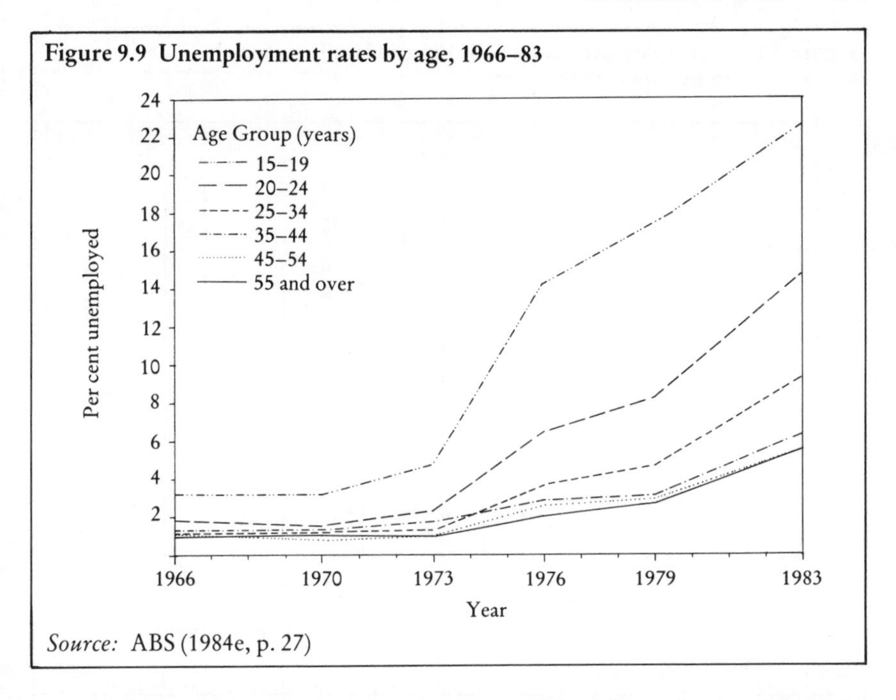

Source: ABS (1984e, p. 27)

over age 25 and by 1983 some 9.2 per cent of the labour force aged 25–34 was unemployed.

The full implications of the high unemployment rates on the young generations can only be guessed at. Experience of periods of unemployment and precarious tenure of jobs must influence a person's confidence about the future and commitments such as marriage, having children, buying a house, etc. These cohorts almost certainly will differ in many social and demographic respects from the earlier post-war baby boom cohorts who gained initial employment during periods of relatively low unemployment and who generally experienced long periods of two-income family living.

There are some significant differences in levels of unemployment according to family status. Figure 9.10 shows that the highest rates of unemployment in 1982 were among 'Female (not married) family heads'—among whom single mothers predominate. As was shown in Chapter 7, single-parent families tend to be the most vulnerable to poverty. Unemployment rates were also very high among people living alone or living with other people to whom they are not related by blood or marriage. Unemployment is much lower among people living in the stereotypical Australian family situation of husband and wife, or husband and wife and dependent children. The lowest rates, about 3 per cent, were recorded for husbands without dependent children. For married women the rates were significantly higher than for husbands, especially among those with dependent children.

There are a number of other significant unemployment differentials, some of which have been referred to in earlier chapters. For example, in Chapter 4

Figure 9.10 Unemployment rates according to family status of individuals, 1982

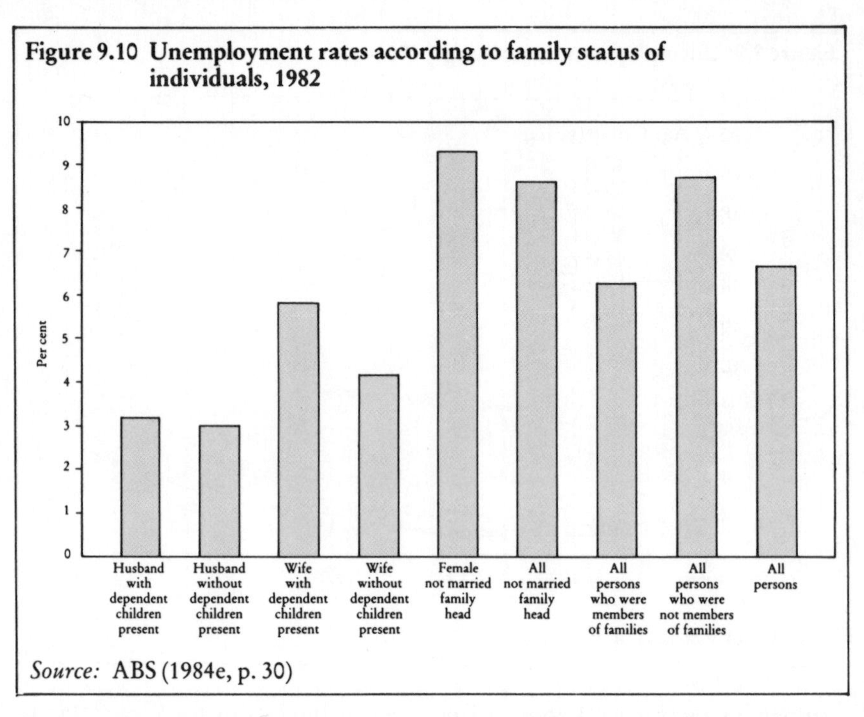

Source: ABS (1984e, p. 30)

it was shown that recently arrived immigrants had high levels of unemployment. Another group which is highly vulnerable to unemployment is Aboriginals, for whom unemployment is part of an all-pervading pattern of deprivation. Table 8.18 showed that between the 1971 and 1981 censuses the rates of unemployment among Aboriginal males increased from 9.2 per cent to 27.4 per cent. As Castle and Mangan (1984, p. 82) point out, 'Unemployment among Aboriginals is greater than unemployment in any other group of the Australian population, and is arguably the most obdurate social and economic problem in Australia'.

One aspect of the rapid increase in unemployment of recent years which is of particular significance to planners and policy makers is the spatial concentration of high levels of unemployment in particular areas. Maxwell and Peter (1982), for example, have analysed unemployment data for the 1971, 1976 and 1981 censuses at state, metropolitan/non-metropolitan and statistical division levels. Their findings were as follows:

1 There was little difference between the States in their unemployment experience during the 1970s, and the States react similarly to changes in economic conditions at a national level. As Table 9.3 shows, only South Australia was significantly different, with an average level of unemployment in the 1970s of one percentage point above most of the other States. But the interstate variations were significantly greater in the very high unemployment years of the early 1980s. South Australia and Tasmania had particularly high rates of unemployment.

Table 9.3 Percentage unemployed in States, Territories (metropolitan and non-metropolitan regions), 1971–84

	Percentage of total labour force				
	Average 1971–81	Census estimates 1971	1976	1981	Labour force survey Nov. 1984
Metropolitan					
Sydney	3.7	1.3	4.8	4.8	7.5
Melbourne	4.1	1.6	3.6	5.4	5.8
Brisbane	4.5	1.9	5.3	5.4	9.3
Adelaide	5.7	2.7	4.5	8.3	9.7
Perth	4.9	1.8	4.6	6.5	8.9
Hobart	4.5	2.1	3.4	8.3	9.2
Non-metropolitan					
NSW	4.8	2.1	6.1	6.3	10.6
Vic.	4.1	1.6	5.2	6.0	8.1
Qld	4.4	2.2	5.4	5.8	9.1
SA	4.1	2.3	3.4	6.0	8.8
WA	3.1	1.6	3.0	5.3	7.3
Tas.	4.2	1.6	5.5	7.0	9.9
States and Territories					
NSW	4.1	1.6	5.2	5.6	8.6
Vic.	4.1	1.6	4.2	5.6	6.5
Qld	4.4	1.8	5.3	6.0	9.2
SA	5.2	1.7	4.2	7.7	9.5
WA	4.3	2.0	4.0	6.3	8.5
Tas.	4.4	2.0	3.9	8.3	9.6
ACT	n.a.	1.4	2.6	5.1	4.0
NT	n.a.	1.8	3.2	4.9	5.7
Australia		1.7	4.7	5.9	8.1

Sources: Maxwell and Peter (1982); ABS (1984f)

2 In examining metropolitan/non-metropolitan areas separately, Table 9.3 shows that there are wider variations between metropolitan areas than States in average unemployment levels. Sydney and Melbourne experienced the lowest rates and Adelaide the highest. Again the widest variations were in 1981 with rates in Adelaide and Hobart being almost twice those in Sydney. In New South Wales non-metropolitan unemployment rates were higher than in Sydney, but in South Australia and Western Australia and Tasmania they were lower than in the State capitals.

3 At the statistical division level Maxwell and Peter found the following types of regions had significantly worse unemployment than their State capitals and stood out as potential problem areas: (a) Non-metropolitan manufacturing areas such as Barwon (Geelong), Illawarra (Wollongong) and Whyalla—areas with economic bases which rely very heavily on manufacturing, and where the downturn in manufacturing accompanying structural change in the Australian economy has been felt more heavily because of the

lack of alternative economic activity; (b) Coastal regions such as the New South Wales north coast, and the Queensland far north and the central highlands which paradoxically have experienced rapid population growth. These are attractive resort-type areas and Maxwell and Peter (1982, p. 4) suggest that there is 'a tendency for industrial development to lag behind this population movement generated in large part by a search for a better climate'. Some have suggested that such areas may in fact attract some unemployed persons who in failing to get work in the largest cities decide to at least have a pleasant environmental setting to live in.

In general, agricultural regions fared quite well with respect to unemployment in the 1970s, as did areas with economies dominated by mining activity.

It has also been demonstrated that unemployment is strongly concentrated within particular parts of Australia's major cities (Beed, Singell and Wyatt 1983; Forster 1983a and b; Burnley 1980; Vipond 1980a and b, 1981). The following common features have been identified by Forster (1983b, p. 131):

1 Male unemployment rates are generally highest in the inner older suburbs and fall off with distance from the city centre, especially in those sectors of the metropolitan area which tend to be of middle to high socio-economic status.
2 Female unemployment rates, on the other hand, are relatively low in the inner suburbs but are particularly high in outer working-class suburbs, especially in Sydney and Adelaide.

A range of arguments have been put forward to explain these patterns and Forster (pp. 131–2) has categorized them broadly into two groups. The first set of arguments suggests that the patterns of concentration are simply the spatial expression of other unemployment differentials—that persons at high risk of unemployment such as Aboriginals, young adults, recently arrived immigrants, lower socio-economic groups, single parents etc., tend to live in particular parts of the city. Alternatively, some argue that while aspects of the spatial organization of the city did not *cause* high unemployment they could have a significant compounding effect upon the problem in some areas, through poor accessibility to job opportunities and so on. Of course the respective schools of thought have opposite implications regarding the effectiveness of programmes aimed at reducing employment in these areas. However, at the very least one would argue that a sound knowledge of the spatial dimension of unemployment in Australian cities is of fundamental importance in the development and targeting of programmes aimed at reducing unemployment and ameliorating its effects.

STRUCTURAL CHANGE AND CHANGING PARTICIPATION IN EMPLOYMENT SECTORS

Structural change in the economy is a continuous process which has major ramifications not only for the level of employment but also for its distribution between sectors of the economy and the location of that employment. Structural change can result from a complex range of processes involving shifts in the pattern of world trade, technological innovation, changes in the nature and availability of resources, changes in the policies of governments and multinational organizations and changes in community expectations and tastes. The processes of structural change and technological innovation which create employment in some sectors of the economy and destroy jobs in other sectors will thus impinge unequally upon different groups in society and upon different regions and local economies.

The broad patterns of structural changes which have occurred in the Australian economy are reflected in Figure 9.11. This shows the changing shares of various industry sectors in the Australian economy since the early nineteenth century. Several significant shifts are evident, among which the following are particularly striking:

1 The long-term decline in the relative share of agriculture in gross domestic product (GDP) from over 50 per cent in the early 1800s (and until a quarter of a century ago) to the 1980 level of 6.4 per cent.
2 The fluctuating significance of mining reaching a peak share of 14.6 per cent in 1860, declining to 1.8 per cent in 1960 but increasing to 6 per cent in 1980 under the influence of the 1970s mining boom.
3 Of particular note are the patterns in manufacturing, which were of very minor significance in the early years of white settlement but gradually increased to 12.8 per cent of GDP at the turn of the century. The increase continued, especially in the post-war period, and in 1960 28.9 per cent of GDP was generated by manufacturing. However, in more recent years the most striking and important structural change has been the considerable reduction in the significance of manufacturing in the Australian economy. In 1980 manufacturing accounted for only 21.2 per cent of GDP and it is projected to decline further to 15 per cent by the end of the century.
4 One of the most stable sectors, at least in terms of its proportion of GDP, has been construction, although there was a decline from 7.7 to 6.6 per cent between 1960 and 1980.
5 The most striking change evident in Figure 9.11 for the 1960–80 period is the increased share of the services sector of the economy. Finance, insurance and business services increased its share of GDP from 7 to 10.5 per cent, while recreation, personal, entertainment and community services increased from 8.4 to 14.5 per cent.

It is noticeable in Figure 9.11 that of all the twenty-year periods shown some of the most marked sectoral shifts were recorded during the 1960–80 period. Structural changes in the economy have indeed been occurring apace in Australia since the early 1960s, although little attention was paid to them during periods of steady economic growth and low unemployment. In the later 1970s however, growing unemployment has stimulated much greater interest in structural change and its consequences. There is a growing literature which addresses these vitally important issues (e.g., Bureau of Industry Economics 1979; Linge and McKay 1981). All that will be attempted here

Figure 9.11 The changing importance of industries in the Australian economy, 1800–2000

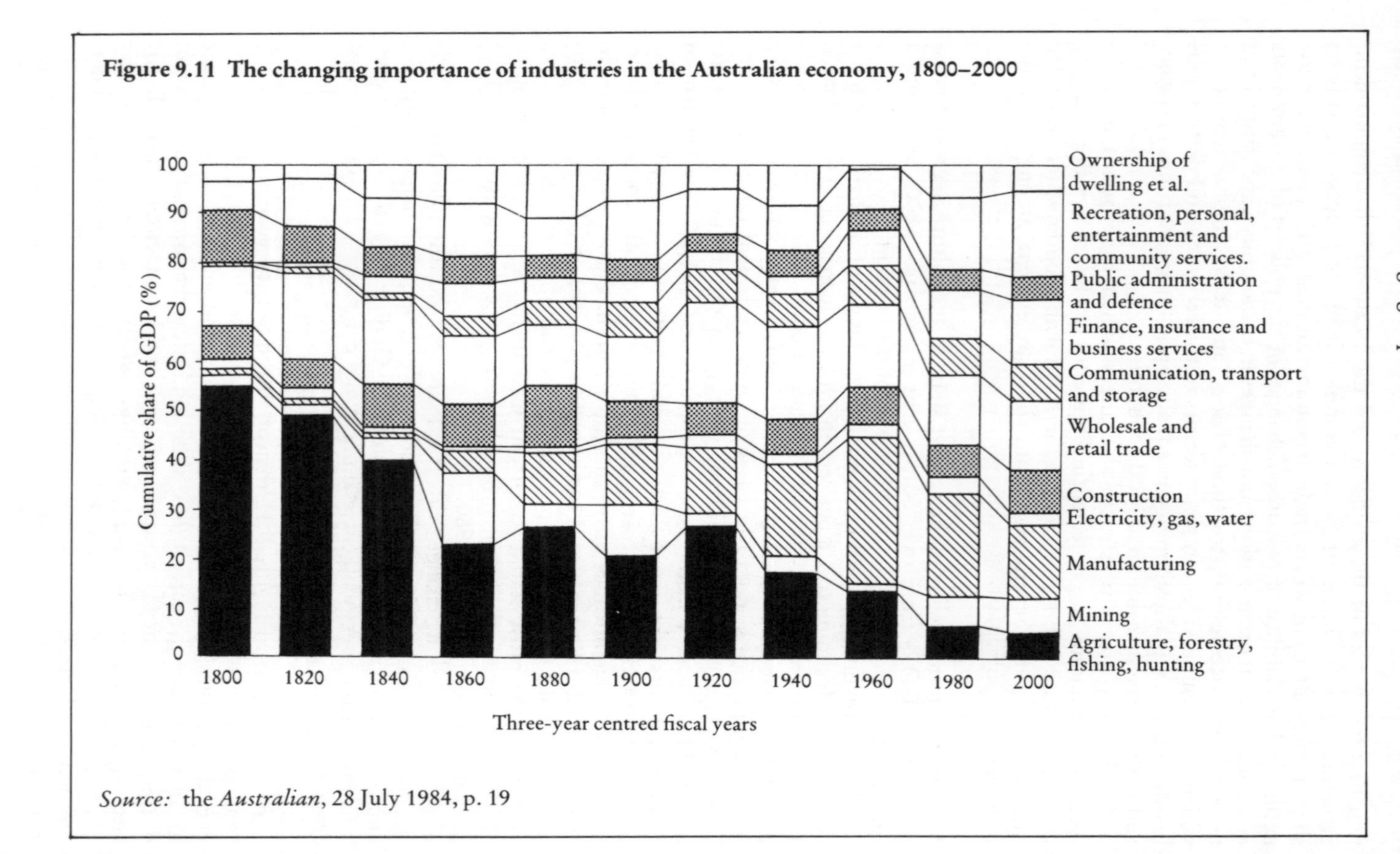

Source: the *Australian*, 28 July 1984, p. 19

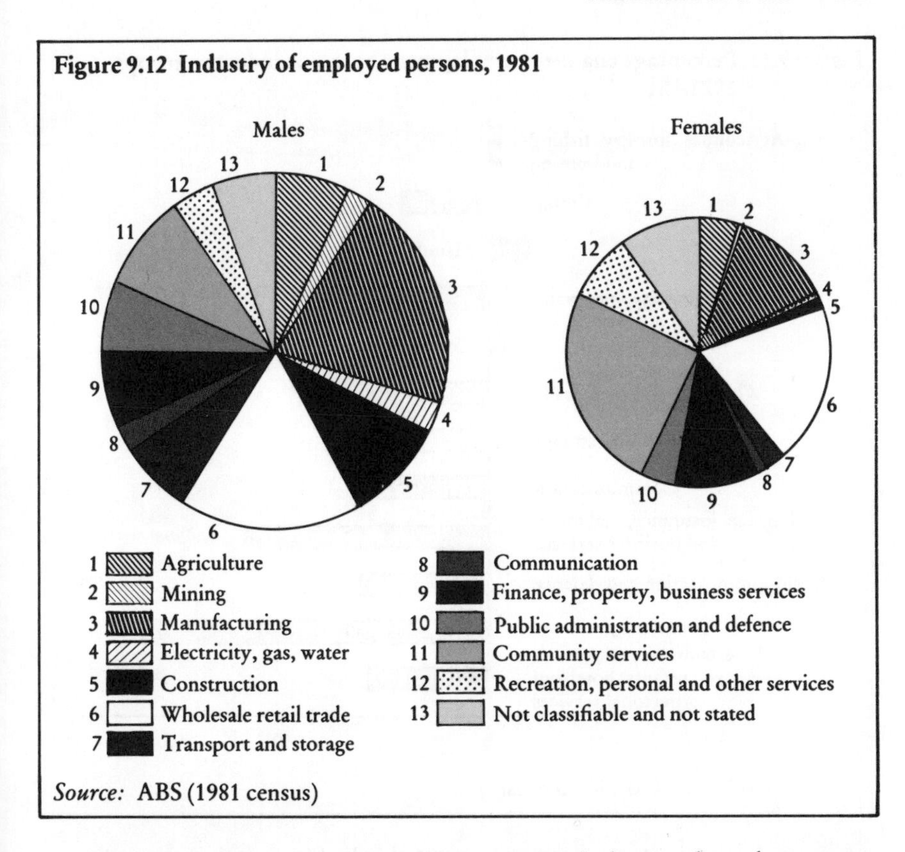

Figure 9.12 Industry of employed persons, 1981

Source: ABS (1981 census)

is to spell out what the effects of the structural changes have been upon employment in the various sectors of the economy.

Figure 9.12 shows the distribution of Australian employment between various sectors at the 1981 census. Slightly less than 18 per cent of the workforce was employed in manufacturing, 6 per cent in agriculture and 1.4 per cent in mining. In each of these areas there is an under-representation of women, with only 17 per cent of the female workforce being employed in the three sectors, compared to 30 per cent of employed males. Clearly, however, employment is dominated by tertiary-sector activities, especially among women. The only categories besides 'not stated' where employed women outnumber men are in community services and recreation, personal and other services, which account for a third of women and only 12.6 per cent of men in the labour force.

During the 1970s structural change had a noticeable impact on the level of employment in the various industry sectors. Figure 9.13 shows the extent and direction of these changes. There were three sectors in which an absolute decline in the number of employed was experienced—agriculture, manufacturing and construction. The shift away from manufacturing in Australia can be appreciated from the fact that in 1971 it accounted for 24.2

Figure 9.13 Percentage change in employment by major industry groups, 1971–81

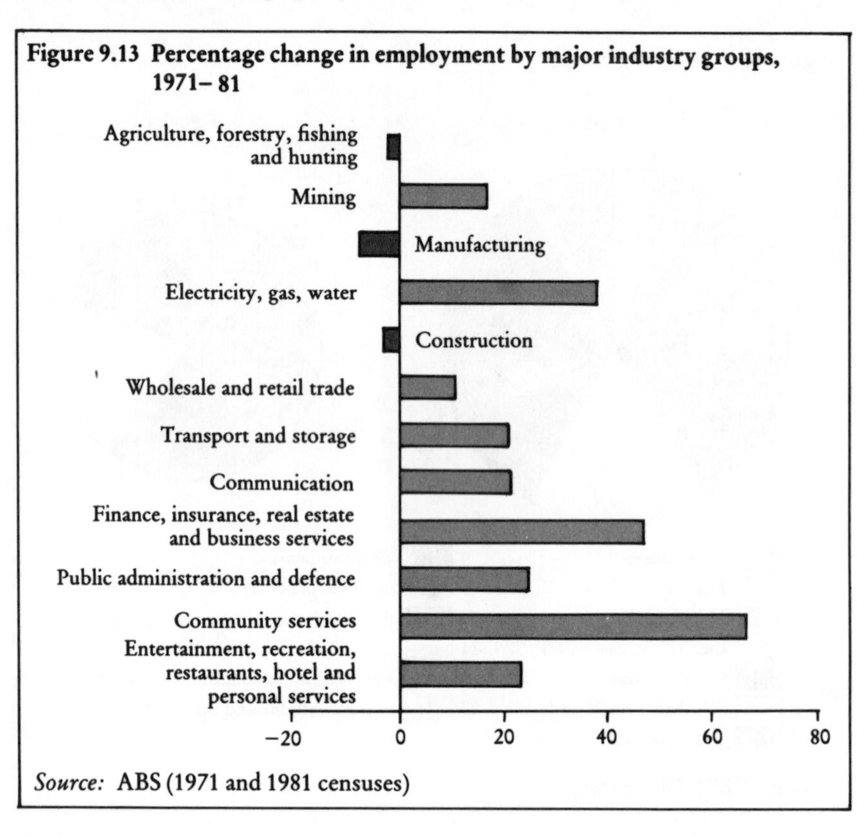

Source: ABS (1971 and 1981 censuses)

per cent of employed persons but by 1981 this had been reduced to 18.9 per cent (if 'not stated' is excluded). There was a net reduction in manufacturing of 100 950 jobs between 1971 and 1981. The decline in construction employment between 1971 and 1981 is not so readily explainable in terms of long-term structural change but more in terms of cyclical movement. The housing industry is especially susceptible to periods of boom and slump under the influence of recession, inflation, changes in interest rates and government policies, etc., and it happened that the 1971 and 1981 censuses tended to coincide with periods of boom and bust respectively in the housing industry. It is interesting to note that in the United States, employment in manufacturing and construction continued to grow through the decade 1972–82, albeit by only 2.1 and 9.7 per cent respectively (US Bureau of Census 1983d, p. 29).

This pattern of cyclical economic trends superimposed on longer-term structural shifts also applies to the agricultural sector. Figure 9.13 shows that there was only a small decline in the number employed in agriculture between the 1971 and 1981 censuses, despite the long-term decline in agriculture's share of GDP evident in Figure 9.11. In the United States there was a similar small absolute decline during the 1970s in the number of persons employed in agriculture. However, a comparison of 1971 and 1981 masks

Figure 9.14 Occupation of employed persons, 1981

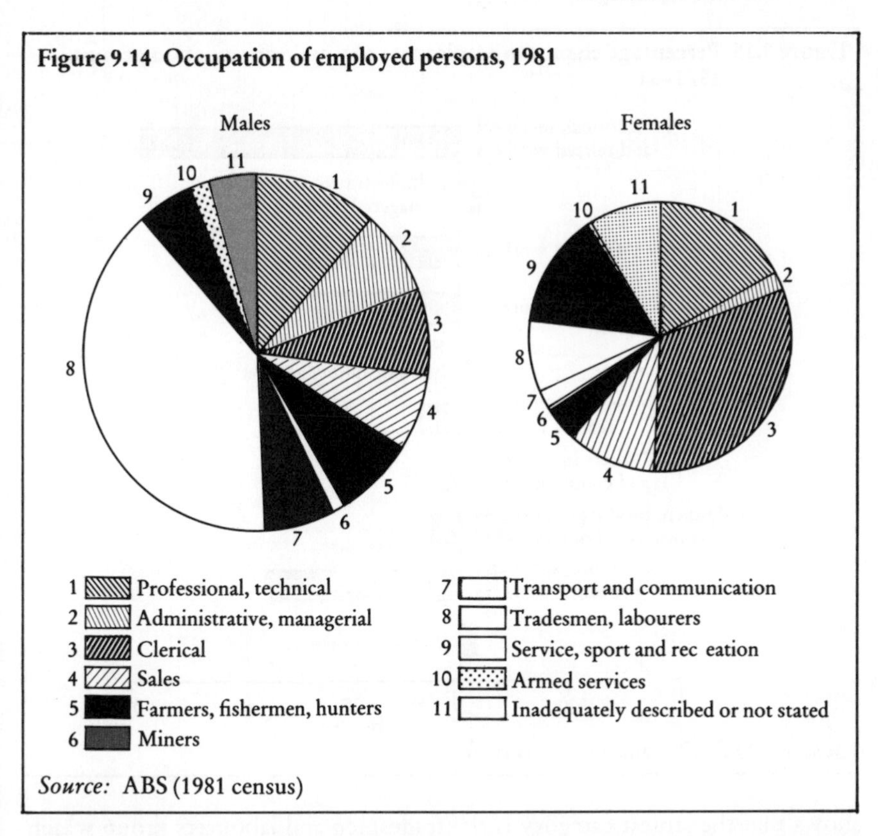

Source: ABS (1981 census)

some significant fluctuations during the intervening period. The 1968–72 period was one of severe rural crisis in Australia 'associated with severe drought and unpropitious world markets for wheat and wool' (Smailes and Hugo 1982, p. 172). This produced a significant attrition of the rural workforce so that the 1971 census was conducted at a low point in agricultural employment. Between 1972 and the late 1970s however, despite vicissitudes, the fortunes of the primary production sector on the whole were favourable. Indeed the rural recovery saw an increase of 4.7 per cent (18 170 persons) in the agricultural workforce between 1971 and 1976. However, between 1976 and 1981 the longer-term trend of attrition of the numbers employed in agriculture resumed and there was a loss of 25 189 agricultural jobs—a 6.2 per cent decline over the five-year period.

Among the industrial sectors in which there was a growth of employment between 1971 and 1981, only the mining category was not of a tertiary nature. Despite the 'mining boom' of the late 1970s and early 1980s, the growth in mining employment was only 17 per cent, reflecting the capital- rather than labour-intensiveness of most mining operations. Clearly, however, the major growth in employment has been in community services and finance, insurance, real estate and business services.

Turning to the occupational composition of the population, Figure 9.14

Figure 9.15 Percentage change in employment by major occupation groups, 1971–81

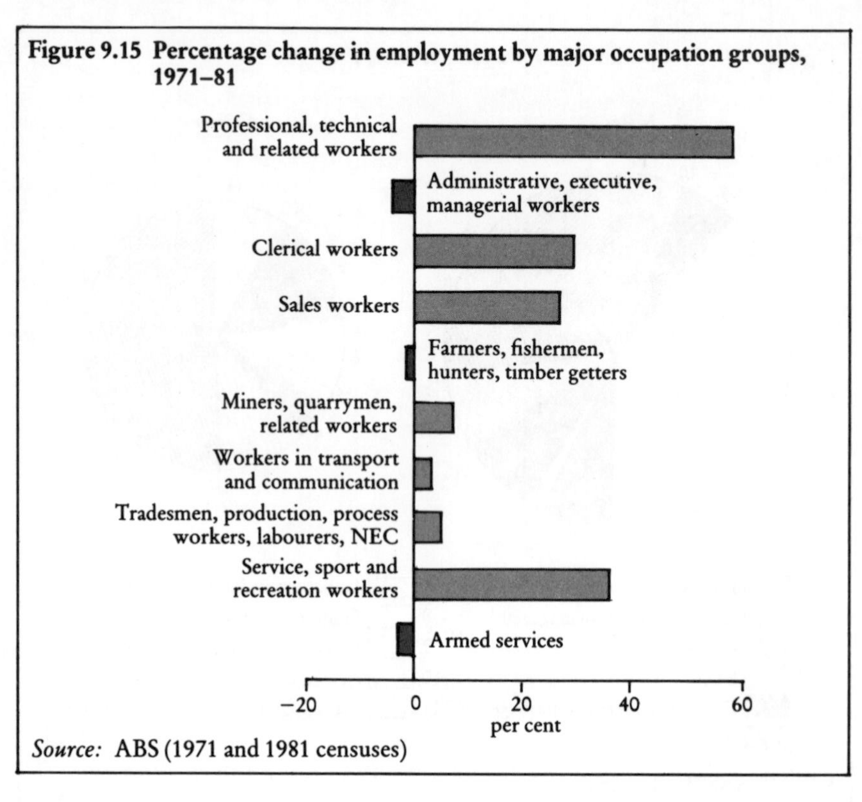

Source: ABS (1971 and 1981 censuses)

shows that the largest category is the tradesmen and labourers group which has 39.5 per cent of employed males and 9.1 per cent of females. The farmers and miners categories account for only 7 per cent of all workers and are dominated by males. The second largest individual category is of clerical workers, which has 8.3 per cent of males and 31.9 per cent of females. Other categories in which females outnumber males are sales workers and service, sport and recreation workers.

The impact of structural change in Australia's economy during the 1970s also has resulted in a shift in the distribution of occupations. Figure 9.15 shows that although employment in seven of the ten major occupational groups increased between 1971 and 1981, growth varied between those groups. The increases are dominated by growth in white-collar and service workers, which together accounted for 91 per cent of the total growth in employment. In particular, the number of professional, technical and related workers increased by almost 60 per cent between 1971 and 1981. It is interesting to note that in the United States this group was also the fastest-growing occupational category during the 1970s (US Bureau of Census 1983d, p. 26). In this category the most rapid growth was among engineers, architects, surveyors, health and law professionals, chemists, physicists, geologists and entertainers. Unlike the United States, however, Australia had a decline in the number of employed persons in the administrative, executive and managerial worker category during the 1970s. This decline was concentrated among employers and self-employed managers who were reduced by 14 per cent between 1976 and 1981, and reflects a decline in small enterprises and the increasing scale of operations of businesses during the 1970s.

The second largest increase was in the 'service, sport and recreation workers' category (36 per cent), as also occurred in the United States during the 1970s (US Bureau of Census 1983d, p. 26). The structural shifts in the economy are seen in the fact that although the 'tradesmen, labourers' category experienced a small increase, their share of the total workforce declined from 32.1 to 28.1 per cent between 1971 and 1981 and there was an absolute decline in the number of women employed in this blue-collar sector. The small decline in farm workers shown in Figure 9.15 is a little misleading since (as was explained earlier) there was in fact a much more substantial decline (6.6 per cent) in the later 1970s following a recovery in the early 1970s from a severe rural recession which prevailed at the time of the 1971 census.

THE CHANGING SPATIAL DISTRIBUTION OF EMPLOYMENT

The shifts in employment patterns considered above have spatial ramifications. The structural changes which have occurred in the Australian economy have resulted in some regional shifts in the location of economic activity, some of which have been explored in Chapter 5 in the discussion of causes of inter-regional migration. In particular it was shown (Table 5.6) that the increase in employment in the 1970s was disproportionately concentrated in New South Wales, Queensland, Western Australia and the Northern Territory. South Australia had virtually no increase in employment between 1976 and 1981. It was also shown that in the main sectors of employment decline—manufacturing and construction—the brunt of the loss was recorded by Victoria and South Australia (Table 5.7). Table 9.4 shows that of the net loss of 57 068 jobs in manufacturing and construction in Australia between 1976 and 1981, Victoria and South Australia accounted for fully 89 per cent.

The other sector in which there was substantial job loss between the 1976 and 1981 censuses was agriculture. The process of substitution of labour inputs by capital investments in mechanization etc., has been a long-standing one in Australian agriculture and, except during periods of extension of the agricultural frontier (e.g., the post-war soldier settlement schemes), there has been a continuous history of net displacement of labour during this century. In the early 1980s this was exacerbated by extended drought in several parts of south-eastern Australia. Table 9.4 shows that the heaviest losses of agricultural jobs were in New South Wales (6 per cent), Victoria (9 per cent), Queensland (5 per cent) and especially South Australia (11 per cent). Small net gains were recorded only in Tasmania and the Australian Capital Territory. The other primary production sector—mining—provides less than a quarter of the number of jobs in agriculture but there was a 22 per cent

Table 9.4 Some changes in employment patterns, 1976–81

	NSW	Vic.	Qld	SA	WA	Tas.	NT	ACT	Australia
1 Number unemployed in 1976	111 673	64 146	40 332	19 555	20 314	7 378	1 454	2 529	266 841
2 Number unemployed in 1981	132 899	99 616	60 370	45 556	36 876	14 116	2 862	5 404	397 699
3 % workforce unemployed in 1976	5.2	3.9	4.6	3.4	4.0	4.3	3.3	2.7	4.4
4 % workforce unemployed in 1981	5.6	5.6	6.0	7.7	6.2	7.7	4.9	5.1	5.9
5 Increase in employed	202 133	96 409	115 270	578	61 192	6 456	12 809	9 631	504 466
6 Increase in unemployed	21 226	35 470	20 038	26 001	16 562	6 738	1 408	2 875	103 858
7 Change in no. wage/salary earners	167 997	86 258	96 552	−1 031	47 369	5 500	11 787	8 026	422 454
8 No. in agriculture 1981	110 203	90 197	77 258	42 112	43 692	12 995	2 221	710	379 388
9 Change in no. in agriculture 1976–81	−6 605	−8 535	−4 090	−5 341	−796	279	−237	134	−25 191
10 No. in mining 1981	31 048	5 304	19 378	4 151	22 048	4 311	2 569	185	88 994
11 Change in no. in mining 1976–81	5 819	19	3 435	686	5 317	99	939	−8	16 306
12 No. in manufacturing/construction 1981	551 433	466 743	196 118	133 961	110 975	37 087	7 730	8 784	1 512 831
13 Change in no. in manufacturing/ construction 1976–81	829	−26 917	−581	−23 811	2 287	−3 175	−219	−3 823	−57 068
14 No. in utilities/transport 1981	215 864	149 509	94 043	45 111	50 322	16 198	4 706	5 099	580 843
15 Change in no. utilities/transport 1976–81	24 549	17 888	24 149	106	7 512	1 614	1 337	935	77 995
16 No. in trade, finance, services 1981	1 149 269	829 754	495 213	288 311	288 662	88 508	31 160	82 382	3 246 318
17 Change in no. in trade, finance, services 1976–81	98 947	90 514	84 288	20 570	106 212	7 736	10 058	13 265	394 879

Source: ABS (1976 and 1981 censuses)

increase in mining employment during the inter-censal period—most of it in New South Wales, Western Australia and Queensland.

The main areas of employment growth were in tertiary activities of wholesale and retail trade, finance, public administration, community services, entertainment and recreation in which there was a total net increase of 394 879 jobs between the censuses. It is interesting to note in Table 9.4 that more than a quarter of those jobs were in Western Australia, a quarter in New South Wales, with Victoria and Queensland having more than a fifth each. In the growth sectors of utilities, transport and communication, New South Wales and Queensland accounted for nearly two-thirds of the growth in jobs, reflecting the increasing concentration of economic growth and large development projects in these States.

If we turn to an examination of employment change between major urban, other urban and rural sectors, a deconcentration of employment opportunities occurred between 1976 and 1981 in Australia. This was discussed earlier in Chapter 5 at the national level, but Table 9.5 shows that this pattern was fairly consistent across the States. Only two of the States which had cities in the 'other urban' category recorded more rapid growth in total employment in another category, and in both of these (South Australia and Queensland) the rural sector had the most rapid growth. Only in the ACT was the most substantial growth in jobs in the major urban sector and as a virtual city-state it is not directly comparable to the other States and Territory. In fact there was an absolute decline in the total number employed in Adelaide and Hobart between the censuses. The most sustained growth of metropolitan job opportunities was, as would be expected, in the States with the most rapidly expanding economies—Queensland and Western Australia. In the major urban areas of New South Wales and Victoria, however, growth in the number of jobs was quite modest, especially in the latter.

In the 'other urban' category, very rapid growth of jobs was common. South Australia is the main exception, due particularly to the decline of Whyalla, where the economic base was heavily reliant upon steel manufacture and ship-building and very vulnerable to the effects of structural change. Despite these losses an overall modest gain was recorded. In the Northern Territory the recovery of Darwin from Cyclone Tracy as well as the generally rapid rate of economic development and greater exploitation of natural resources produced a 41 per cent increase in the number of 'other urban' jobs. Similarly in other rapidly developing States, provincial centres expanded apace—Western Australia (21 per cent), Queensland and New South Wales (17 per cent). The growth rates in Victoria and Tasmania were smaller but still were greater than those in any other sector, especially major urban areas.

The bounded rural localities and rural areas have traditionally (at least in the post-war period) been areas of substantial job loss. An array of processes produced this, including the progressive substitution of capital and scientific input for labour inputs in primary production and the greater centralization of manufacturing and tertiary activity made possible by improved transportation and made necessary by the need to achieve economies of scale

Table 9.5 Changing employment patterns in rural and urban areas of States and Territories, 1976–81

State or Territory	Total persons employed	Major urban	Other urban	Bounded rural locality	Rural
NSW	1981	1 537 159	433 147	35 953	224 541
	% change 1976–81	7.26	17.46*	8.67	16.72
Vic.	1981	1 206 869	259 143	28 909	181 093
	% change 1976–81	4.61	13.17*	−1.37	7.77
Qld	1981	453 983	293 776	30 973	173 058
	% change 1976–81	10.76	16.55	10.30	18.18*
SA	1981	371 611	84 082	15 876	76 021
	% change 1976–81	−0.89	2.38	−3.20	4.07*
WA	1981	350 247	110 795	20 144	71 674
	% change 1976–81	12.17	20.96*	1.15	5.48
Tas.	1981	54 325	72 978	11 663	30 998
	% change 1976–81	−2.75	9.06*	0.17	6.79
NT	1981	–	44 350	4 120	6 906
	% change 1976–81	–	40.87*	−5.35	0.83
ACT	1981	100 394	–	110	1 016
	% change 1976–81	11.09*	–	−2.66	−27.17
Australia	1981	4 074 588	1 298 271	147 748	765 307
	% change 1976–81	6.38	15.72*	3.38	11.70

*Highest inter-censal growth rate for that State or Territory
Note: Major urban = urban centres with a population of 100 000 and over
Other urban = urban centres with a population of 1000 to 99 999 persons
Bounded rural locality = population clusters of 200 to 999 persons
Rural = remainder of the State
Source: ABS (1976 and 1981 censuses)

(Hugo in Burnley 1974, p. 93). In the late 1970s, however, which have seen unprecedented overall levels of unemployment in Australia, there has been a significant growth of jobs in the rural sector. Victoria, South Australia and the Northern Territory lost jobs in their bounded rural locality category, although there was strong growth in Queensland and New South Wales in such centres. In many purely rural areas, however, job growth was more substantial and widespread. Again, Queensland and New South Wales are especially prominent. In the rural sector of both States there was a substantial decline in agricultural jobs (from 160 147 in 1976 to 145 442 in 1981) but significant growth in other sectors of the economy, especially in all types of tertiary activity (from 87 397 jobs to 123 961). These point to some very important structural changes in the rural population, and it should be noted that the percentage of rural workers employed in agriculture declined from 49 to 38 per cent in New South Wales and from 45 to 35 per cent in Queensland. In South Australia the growth in rural jobs was more modest at 4 per cent, but it was substantially higher than in other settlement categories in that State.

There is insufficient space here to consider job growth and decline at a local level, although in Chapter 5 it was shown that job growth is strongly correlated with population growth and both are strongly concentrated in particular areas. This growth was especially concentrated in the settlement zone designated IB1, the coastal areas in Queensland, New South Wales and Western Australia which are at or slightly beyond the outer limits of the commuting zone of the capital cities of those States. As was pointed out in Chapter 5, we must be careful in using census employment data for locational analysis, since it allocates workers to their place of usual residence not their place of work. Hence, an important question remains as to the proportion of these workers whose job is located outside a major urban or other urban area and to the incidence and rate of long-distance commuting among workers living in rural areas. Knowledge of commuting patterns in Zone IB1 would be useful to planners, but at present the ABS only tabulates such data for people living in and near metropolitan centres.

INCOME AND INCOME DISTRIBUTION

A question on income has been included in the Australian census only since 1976. Table 9.6 summarizes some of the median levels of income at the 1976 and 1981 censuses for individuals, families and households. The large difference between male and female median incomes is immediately apparent, and reflects not only inequalities of access to higher-paid jobs but also the fact that a majority of women who work outside the home do so part-time. Census data suggest that female incomes have not increased as fast as those of males over the 1976–81 period. Nevertheless, it is indicative of the social changes which have occurred in Australia during the 1970s that nearly eight

Table 9.6 Median income in Australia, 1976 and 1981[1]

Group	Median annual income (A$) 1976	1981	Change 1976–81 (%)
Individuals, males	7 005	10 906	+55.7
Individuals, females	3 363	4 952	+47.2
Families[2]	8 274	12 365	+49.4
Households[3]	10 116	15 227	+50.5
Consumer price index[4]	70.01	110.2	+57.4

[1] Calculation excludes all 'not stated' responses and people reporting no income.
[2] Family income is the combined income of head and spouse if present.
[3] Household income combines the income of all persons in the household 15 years of age and over.
[4] weighted average for six State capital cities
Source: calculated from ABS (1976 and 1981 censuses; 1984i, p. 119)

out of ten Australian women aged 15 years or over received an income in 1981. In passing, it is interesting to note that this was also the figure calculated from the 1981 census data in Canada (Pryor and Norris 1983, p. 28). Clearly it is due to an increase in female participation in the labour force and changes in availability of government-provided pensions (especially age and supporting mother pensions). The significance of multiple income earning within families is reflected in the higher median income levels for families and households than individuals, as shown in Table 9.6.

It is difficult to establish trends over time in income using census data. The US Bureau of Census (1983d, p. 30) has shown that during the 1970s there was an overall decline in the purchasing power of families, since there was a 3 per cent gap between the increase in family income and that of consumer prices between 1971 and 1981. Australia would also appear to conform to this pattern: Table 9.6 shows that the increases in incomes were not as great as the increase in prices during the late 1970s, especially for women and families. The pattern is also evident in the findings of the 1981–82 ABS income and housing survey (ABS 1983d): the mean income of all income recipients had increased 29.6 per cent over the previous survey in 1978–79, while the weighted average consumer price index had risen by 33 per cent.

The US Bureau of Census (1983d, p. 30) shows that an important underlying factor affecting changes in median family income has been the unprecedented increase in the number of families maintained by women. It is clear that in Australia there are important variations between family types in their incomes. This is apparent in Figure 9.16, which shows the distribution of gross weekly income for different family types in 1982. Married-couple income units, which comprise a husband, wife and dependent children (if any), not only have very high median incomes compared to other types of families but the distribution over the various income categories is relatively even. A major factor in these high incomes is the increasing participation of married women in the workforce mentioned earlier. Indeed, at the time of the 1982 survey in 48.2 per cent of married-couple income units the wife was in the labour force. Moreover, since this includes wives older than 60 years (and hence past retirement age) it underestimates the participation of young married women in the workforce. Some 51.1 per cent of married women with dependent children worked outside the home (ABS 1984g, p. 42). Only 27.9 per cent of married women with a dependent child under 1 year of age worked, but 62.6 per cent of those with a dependent child aged 10 years or more worked.

Turning to the income of single-parent families (of which 90 per cent are headed by women), not only is the median income less than half that of married couples but the distribution is strongly skewed to lower incomes. Only 42.8 per cent of women heading these households with dependent children were in the workforce, and only 23.2 per cent were employed full-time. Note that the equivalent figures for married-couple women with dependent children were considerably higher—51.1 per cent and 35.5 per cent respectively. Moreover, the proportion of single mothers who were unem-

Figure 9.16 Income unit types by level of gross weekly income, 1982

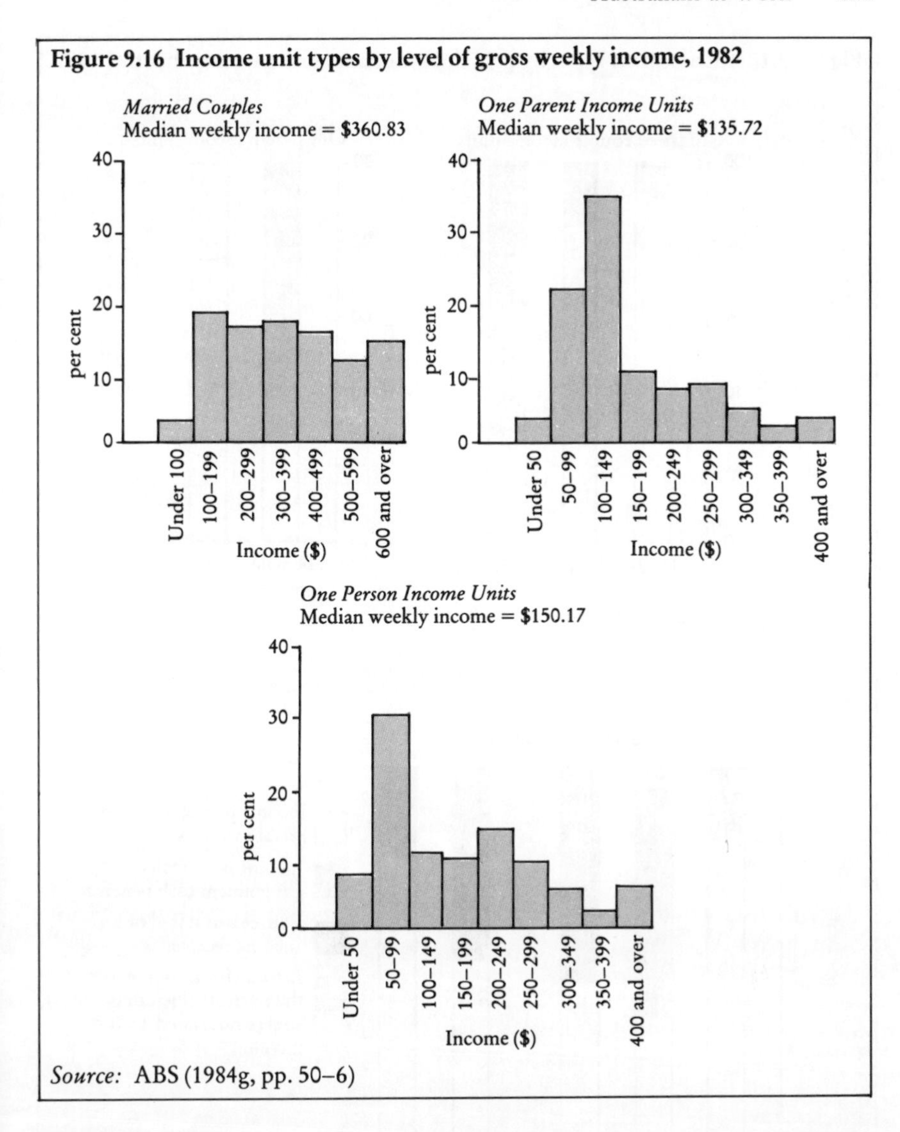

Source: ABS (1984g, pp. 50–6)

ployed (10.1 per cent) was more than twice that of wives with dependent children (4.7 per cent).

The third category in Figure 9.16 is one-person income units, comprising persons aged 15 years and over but excluding students. It includes, as well as individuals living alone, groups like non-dependent offspring, non-family individuals not living alone, single parents without dependent children, etc. While there is a concentration of persons in this category in the low-income group there is a wider spread of incomes and higher median income than for

Figure 9.17 Income unit types by principal source of gross weekly income, 1982

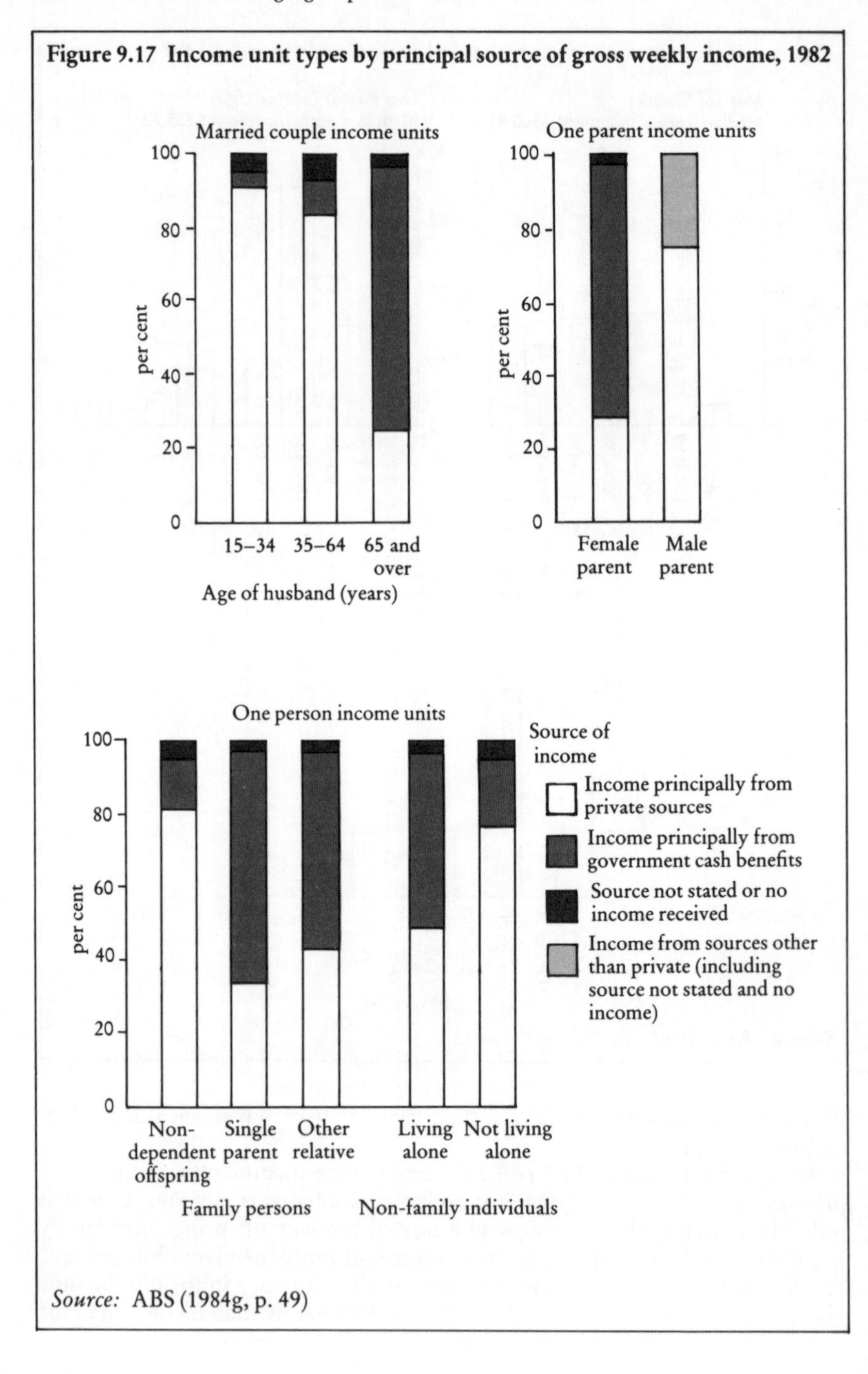

Source: ABS (1984g, p. 49)

Figure 9.18 Proportion of income earners in income groups, males and females, 1981

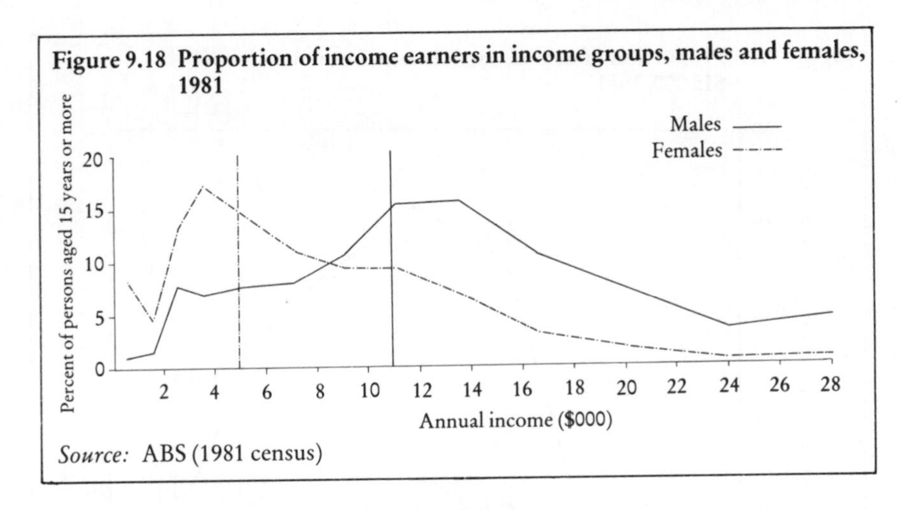

Source: ABS (1981 census)

single parents. People in the low-income group tend to be outside the workforce and many are recipients of social welfare benefits from the government. As can be seen from Figure 9.17 there are some categories of one-person income units in which government cash benefits are the primary source of income. Most of these are single parents and older persons who receive the age pension and who are living with relatives, primarily their adult children

The major source of income of younger married couple families is clearly earned income from wages, salaries and other private sources. On the other hand, pensions are the major source of income of older married couples. The heavy reliance of single parents (mostly mothers) upon cash benefits from the government is also readily apparent from Figure 9.17.

There is insufficient space here to examine exhaustively the differences in income between various groups in Australian society; however, it is useful to briefly examine some income differences between sex and age groups. Figure 9.18 shows the distribution of annual income for males and females at the 1981 census. This indicates that whereas income for males approaches normal distribution about the average annual income of around $11 000, the distribution for women is heavily skewed toward the lower income levels. Some indication of age differentials is to be seen in Figure 9.19, which shows the proportion of income earners with annual incomes in excess of $15 000 per annum in different age groups. It is interesting to note that the peak is not in the older workforce ages for either males or females. It would thus appear that seniority in years is not as strongly associated with income as would perhaps have been expected. This contrasts with age-earnings profiles which show peaks at around 45–50 years and suggests that at older ages there is much greater inequality in earnings, with high earnings being concentrated in a smaller proportion of individuals than is the case for earners in their late thirties and early forties. High proportions of men in their late thirties and early forties are in the highest earning categories. This has

Figure 9.19 Proportion of income earners with annual incomes over $15 000, 1981

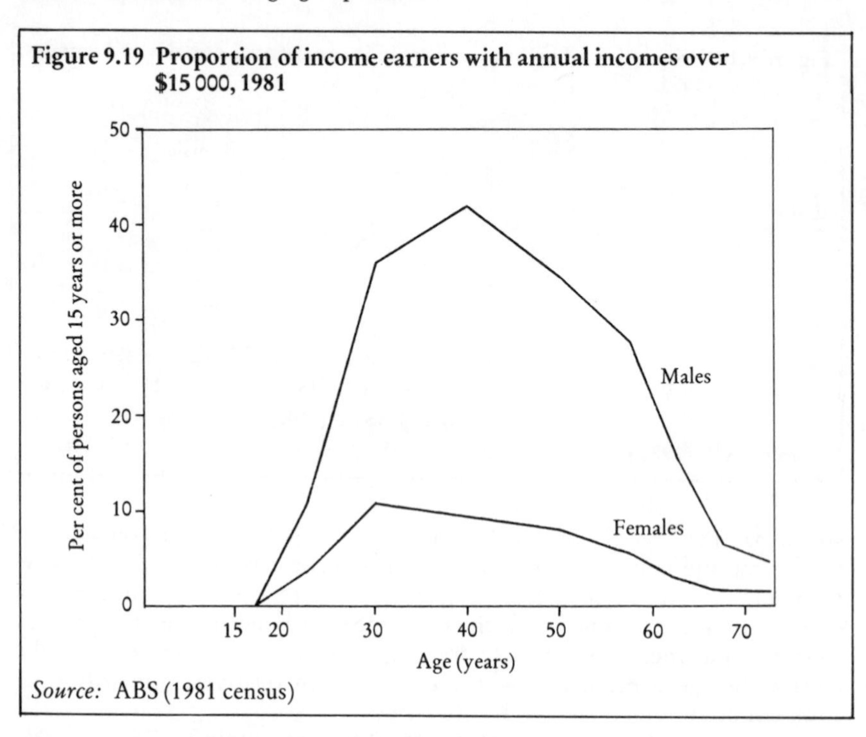

Source: ABS (1981 census)

obvious implications for marketing, since there is a clear concentration of individuals and families with significant disposable income in this age category, especially when it is considered that more than half of these men have wives working outside the home (many on a part-time basis). The profile for women earning in excess of $15 000 per annum is much lower, and the peak is at a younger age.

One important aspect which should also be considered here is the distribution of income, which gives some indication of the degree of inequality within Australian society. Table 9.7 shows the Gini Coefficients for individual income recipients for 1973–74, 1978–79 and 1981–82. (The Gini Coefficient is one of the most widely used measures of income inequality. It can be interpreted as the proportion of individuals who would have to change the income class in which they fall for perfect equality to be achieved.) It would appear from Table 9.7 that there has been little change in the level of inequality among Australian income earners, with a marginal decline between 1973–74 and 1978–79 and an increase between 1978–79 and 1981–82 bringing it back to 1973–74 levels. The increase in inequality can be seen in the fact that in 1981–82 the top 10 per cent of income recipients received 29 per cent of all income whereas the bottom 20 per cent received only 1.9 per cent, compared with 27.8 and 2.7 per cent in 1978–79.

Given that the family is the major unit of consumption in Australia, it is important to examine the pattern of inequality in the incomes of families.

Table 9.7 Gini Coefficients for income distribution of individuals and families, selected years

Year	Males	Females	Total individuals	Families
1968–69	n.a.	n.a.	n.a.	0.33
1973–74	0.35	0.53	0.47	0.31
1978–79	0.35	0.48	0.44	0.39
1981–82	0.36	0.50	0.47	0.45

Source: ABS (1975, p. 8; 1980b, p. 158; 1983d, p. 6; 1984h, p. 6)

Table 9.7 shows that the Gini Coefficients for families tend to be lower than for individuals. This is due to the large number of women working part-time and contributing with their husbands to a family income. This would appear to apply particularly to families where husbands are on relatively low incomes. It would also appear that there was an increase in income inequality between families during the 1970s.

SOME POLICY IMPLICATIONS

There have clearly been a number of significant changes in the pattern of labour force participation and structure during the last decade. One of the most important implications of this change for government is the rapid increase in the numbers and proportion of adult Australians who are reliant upon government cash benefits as their principal source of income. As Table 9.8 shows, between 1973–74 and 1981–82 there was not only a substantial reduction in the proportion of men and women who were wage and salary earners but also an absolute decline in numbers. The table shows that part of this was made up by an increase in the numbers having their own business, trade or profession over that period. However, it is apparent that the major increase has been in the number of recipients of government cash benefits. Over the 1981–82 year 633 900 males (13 per cent of income recipients) and 1 647 000 females (34 per cent of income recipients) received more than 90 per cent of their total income from government cash benefits. This of course represents a significant strain on Commonwealth government expenditure. In Chapter 6 the implications of the growth of the number of old age pensions were explored. Table 9.9, however, shows that the exponential growth in government expenditure on unemployment has been even more rapid than that on the aged. Some 6 per cent of Commonwealth expenditure is now on unemployment benefits.

In such circumstances, the future growth of the Australian workforce is a matter of major concern. A decade ago the National Population Inquiry (1975) made a set of detailed projections of the Australian labour force and nothing has happened in the interim to invalidate the broad patterns projected by the NPI. The reduction in Australian fertility of the 1970s has ensured that in the absence of massive immigration gains the increments to the Australian labour force during the 1990s will be less than in the previous

Table 9.8 Principal source of income of all income recipients, 1973–74 and 1981–82

Principal source of income	Males No. ('000s)	%	Females No. ('000s)	%	Total No. ('000s)	%
Wages and salary						
1973–74	3353.1	75.1	1968.4	46.1	5321.5	60.9
1981–82	2778.2	57.0	1575.7	33	4353.8	45.1
Own business, trade or profession						
1973–74	556.5	12.5	263.6	6.2	820.1	9.3
1981–82	776.2	15.9	436.1	9.1	1212.3	12.5
Government cash benefit						
1973–74	415.7	9.3	1748.2	41.0	2163.9	24.8
1981–82	886.8	18.2	2178.6	45.5	3065.5	31.7

Source: ABS (1980b, p. 159; 1983d, p. 7).

Table 9.9 Commonwealth government expenditure on unemployment benefits, between 1974–75 and 1983–84

Year	Expenditure ($m)	Percentage of total expenditure
1974–75	477.0	2.67
1979–80	1104.7	3.32
1983–84	3369.4	5.94

Source: ABS (1984i, p. 521; 1979b, p. 512); Department of Social Security (1984a, p. 28)

two decades. In the United States some demographers have suggested that there will be labour shortages before the end of this century. For example Butz et al. (1982, p. 11) suggest that one consequence of the post–1960 'baby bust' will be

> The declining numbers, first of young adults, then of the entire adult population, [which] will cause tighter labour markets. At the end of the 1980s, and especially in succeeding decades, employers will be forced to raise wages in order to compete for the dwindling numbers of workers. We anticipate that young women will respond by working longer hours and in greater numbers than they do now. We also expect that many older workers contemplating retirement will seek to keep their jobs, perhaps part time, for additional years. The average retirement age will then increase, reversing the 35 year decline.

Such a statement, however, takes no account of the labour-displacing impact of technological change or the international division of labour which is resulting in labour-intensive industry moving to low-wage countries in South-east Asia. In Australia the major labour force problem over the next decade is likely to be our high levels of unemployment, and government efforts need to be directed to increasing labour demand.

Table 9.10 Projections of increase in the Australian labour force and its relation to total projected population

Years	Average annual increase No immigration	Net immigration 50 000 p.a.
1976–81	102 400	130 400
1981–86	79 600	111 000
1986–91	59 200	93 800
1991–96	50 200	86 400
1996–2001	48 000	88 200
	Labour force as a percentage of total projected population	
1976	45.7	45.7
1981	47.7	47.7
1986	48.7	48.8
1991	49.0	49.2
1996	49.1	49.4
2001	49.4	49.8

Note: projections assume increasing participation rates.
Source: NPI (1975, p. 342)

While the undercutting of the age pyramid in Australia is not nearly so marked as in the United States, there can be no doubt that the pressure placed on the Australian labour market by young people entering the work-force ages will be reduced in the 1990s. The NPI labour force projections are summarized in Table 9.10 (the annual migration gain of 50 000 is probably most realistic). The actual annual average increment to the labour force between 1976 and 1981 was 127 109 and hence very close to the projected figure shown in Table 9.10. The migration levels of the early 1980s exceeded the assumed 50 000, so that the actual average increment to the labour force over the 1981–84 period of 126 700 was somewhat larger than the projected figure. Nevertheless, there is no reason to suggest that projected declines in increments for the late 1980s and early 1990s shown in Table 9.10 will not occur.

Unemployment must be a priority area of concern among Australian policy makers, and while the major influences on it will be economic factors (beyond the scope of this study), there is no doubt that the demographic pressure exerted on the labour market by young people seeking their first job will be reduced over the next decade as the 'baby bust' cohorts move into the working ages. There still appears to be scope for increased participation of women in the workforce, and an improvement in the economy and in employment opportunities may see a resumption of the trend of increasing participation by women evident before the late 1970s. Another element which has to be considered by planners is the labour force participation of older workers. The recent reduction in the participation rate has both voluntary and involuntary components (Stretton and Williams 1984) so that an upturn in the economy may also see an increase in the participation of older workers. This raises a number of policy-related issues, such as the concept of phased retirement for older workers so that they are retained in the labour force over a longer period, but working part-time in the latter years.

The age structure of the Australian labour force has been shown here to be a young one, which raises a number of issues other than unemployment to manpower planners. One such consideration is upward mobility among the labour force. It was established earlier that the greatest concentration of high-income earners is in their late thirties and early forties indicating a similar concentration of people in middle and senior positions. This represents something of a blockage to younger workers in the middle and later 'baby boom' cohorts. Clearly the opportunities for upward mobility of workers in these groups are going to be extremely limited over the next two decades. If this generation is to maintain interest and enthusiasm in their work they are going to have to satisfy their aspirations via lateral rather than upward mobility. This too represents a challenge to planners to develop and provide such options.

The findings of this chapter underline the difficult labour market situation faced by women, especially single older women and single mothers. They continually recur as one of the most underprivileged groups in Australian society. Many of these women cannot fit in to existing traditional job structures; however, their position could be improved through thoughtful planning. Such planning would include the encouragement of more flexible work patterns through job-sharing and more flexible time requirements, as well as greater provision of child care.

CONCLUSION

A thorough economic analysis of Australia's changing labour force is beyond the scope of this study. However, the growth, structure and distribution of the workforce is influenced by demographic as well as economic factors. The last decade has seen continued rapid growth of the labour force due to the continued passage of the baby boom cohorts into the working ages and increased female participation. However, unlike the previous decade there has been a massive increase in unemployment, a substantial shift away from manufacturing and agriculture to tertiary industries and a slight but noteworthy trend toward deconcentration of employment opportunities away from the major metropolitan centres. The extent to which these and other trends are continued over the next decade of course cannot be predicted with confidence but there is no indication of any imminent dramatic turnaround in them.

10 Conclusion

Writing immediately after the end of World War II, Glover (1946) summarized the likely outlook for patterns of population change in Australia up to the end of the twentieth century as follows: 'The indications at the present time are that Australia will attain its maximum population of approximately nine million persons at the end of the twentieth century'.

In fact, the nation's population had reached nine million by late 1954 and even the 'low' series of assumptions in the most recent ABS projections (ABS 1984i, p. 90) indicate that Australia is likely to have double that number by the year 2000. Clearly demographers do not have any special window to the future which is denied other social scientists. In the context of one and a half decades of very low fertility and virtual zero net migration gains in which Glover was writing, he could hardly be expected to have anticipated the post-war baby and immigration booms which caused such unprecedented population growth in the two decades following World War II. The accurate prediction of such 'parametric shocks' which involve a dramatic and sudden swing in demographic processes and which bear little or no relationship to trends in the immediately preceding period is a matter as much of luck as informed judgement. Such dramatic shifts aside, however, many population trends can be anticipated with a degree of certainty and demographic analysis can yield insights which are helpful to planners and policy makers. The preceding chapters have attempted to illuminate patterns of impending change in Australia's population through the close analysis of contemporary trends, especially those revealed by the results of the 1981 census.

THE FUTURE OUTLOOK

There are some shifts in Australia's demography which can be readily anticipated. This especially applies to changes in particular sub-groups in the population. There is, for example, little that is hypothetical in our projections of the growth of the aged population—most of the aged pensioners of the late 1980s and 1990s are here. That growth is inevitable and can be projected with a substantial degree of certainty so that there is time to design adequate pension and other support systems. Similarly the passage of the 'baby bust' cohorts into the ages of entering tertiary education, household formation and entry to the workforce has important implications for planning in universities and colleges of advanced education, the housing industry and in the manpower area. Of course other factors also will shape participation rates in higher education, household headship rates and labour force participation (especially among women and older workers). Nevertheless, although there are a range of important intervening variables, demographic trends remain a fundamental and underlying determinant of the extent of demand and need for employment, housing, goods and services.

Australia seems set on a path toward zero population growth, at least so far as the natural increase component of population change is concerned. There is no evidence to suggest that intrinsic fertility will rise above replacement level in the foreseeable future. It is difficult to see any substantial change in such contemporary trends as increasing age at marriage, low levels of marital fertility, increasing popularity of a completed family size of two children, an increasing proportion of women remaining childless, high rates of divorce and high levels of female participation in the workforce. The early 1980s have seen relative stability in fertility levels in Australia and most commentators suggest that this pattern will be maintained, at least until the late 1980s. As was demonstrated in Chapter 3, the 'echo effect' of the post-war baby boom (the baby 'boomerang') is producing, and will continue to produce, an increasing number of births each year in the 1980s, but intrinsic fertility has remained at low levels.

In the recent past mortality levels in Australia were considered to be so stable that the National Population Inquiry (1975, p. 256) stated that 'There is little evidence which suggests that a major improvement in mortality rates is imminent. If population changes were only a function of mortality future population could be projected with great certainty'. However, as has been demonstrated in Chapter 2, there have subsequently been significant improvements in mortality, especially in older age groups. While there is some conjecture about the future course of mortality, the general consensus is that life expectancy will continue to increase during the rest of the 1980s. This will make little difference to the projected number of persons under retirement age, but it does make a significant difference to the number of persons of pensionable age. This represents a major change from the past, when contemporary mortality fluctuations were not a significant determining factor in changes in the growth of the elderly population or the proportion that they made up of the total population.

The least predictable element in national population growth remains immigration. There are so many imponderables, both internal to Australia (levels of unemployment, changes in government, shifts in public opinion, etc.) and external (the political situation in South-east Asia, extent of refugee movement, extent of pressure from international bodies, etc.). As was pointed out in Chapter 4, there are strong pressures for both a decrease and an increase in immigration. However, in the high levels of unemployment prevailing in the mid-1980s it is difficult to see the high immigration levels of the early 1980s being sustained. Attempts to anticipate the composition of the intake are as problematical as those to predict the numbers involved. A number of possible scenarios were discussed in Chapter 4, but it would appear that a programme which is predominantly 'humanitarian' in orientation is likely to continue for the near future at least, so that the intake will be dominated by family reunion and refugee category settlers rather than as part of some manpower planning policy or programme.

Shifts in age structure can be discussed with greater precision, since all but the youngest Australians of the later 1980s and early 1990s have already been born. The rapid growth of the older population for the remainder of the 1980s presents a challenge to policy makers and planners. The problem will be ameliorated in the 1990s and 2000s with the passage of the 1930s and early 1940s babies into the pensionable ages. However, as is shown in Chapter 6, this constitutes the 'calm before the storm' with the baby boomers beginning to age into their late sixties in the second decade of the next century. The Australian age structure is dominated by the baby boom cohorts, who will move through young and middle adulthood up to the end of the century. The passage of the deficit baby bust cohorts following them will see reductions in the numbers entering the labour force, higher education and initial separate household formation as the century progresses. On the other hand, the baby boom echo cohorts will produce increasing enrolments in kindergartens and primary schools, although current indications are that the strength of the echo is greatly attenuated in comparison to the resounding boom of the two decades following World War II.

Chapter 7 has shown that dramatic changes have occurred in the ways Australians group themselves into living units. Despite the baby bust cohorts reaching the stage of 'leaving the nest' in the 1990s, it is likely that the rate of household formation will continue to outpace overall population growth as it has throughout the post-war period, due to a number of other trends encouraging smaller household size. It seems likely, for example, that high divorce levels will continue, leading to splitting of households. Moreover, the current thrust of aged care policy, encouraging older people to remain in independent accommodation as long as possible (e.g., Parliament of the Commonwealth of Australia, 1982) will lead to longer survival of separate households among older people. Despite occasional media statements that 'the family is dead', the stereotypical two-parent family will remain the context in which most Australian children are raised. Nevertheless, even the most conservative of projections would anticipate a greater diversity in living arrangements in Australia over the next two decades. Single-person households and single-parent families will almost certainly grow more rapidly than husband-wife households, and there will be an increase in non-family households in which persons who are not related by blood or marriage cohabit. This has important implications for housing policy. The type of structure, tenure, location and cost of housing has to be increasingly tailored to the needs of singles, single-parent families, the elderly and couples. So far in Australia these challenges have been taken up in a comprehensive way by only a few public housing authorities and the private sector has restricted its limited activity to the upper income end of these non-traditional markets.

As the baby boomers passed into the adult working ages in the late 1960s and 1970s, the Australian labour force grew very rapidly, especially since this was accompanied by high intakes of immigrants in the economically active age groups and a sharp reversal of the pattern of most married women not working outside of the home. The demographic pressure on employment in the 1990s will be reduced as the 'baby bust' group reaches adulthood. However, a considerable volume of labour absorption is required to take up the current backlog of more than half a million unemployed and the large amount of 'hidden' unemployment, especially among women. There would certainly appear to still be considerable potential and desire for increased female participation in the workforce. The two-income family has become the established norm, and the trend is very unlikely to be reversed. However, structural change is likely to produce continued reductions in the manufacturing and agricultural workforce, while the tertiary and quaternary sectors will become even more dominant. The extent to which the current tendency toward early retirement is or is not sustained will also strongly affect the future size of the workforce.

Few population issues are more controversial in Australia than the ethnic composition of the population. One of the major changes in post-war Australia has been the increase in ethnic heterogeneity. Although Aboriginal fertility has fallen dramatically, the black population will continue to grow somewhat faster than the population as a whole, especially if the scandalously high levels of Aboriginal mortality can be reduced. Nevertheless, the proportional representation of Aboriginals in the total population is unlikely to undergo significant change. Smith's (1980, p. 281) projections, which assume declining fertility and mortality, suggest that the Aboriginal population would number around 300 000 in 2001. The projection of the non-Aboriginal ethnic population is much more difficult, since it is heavily dependent on future immigration policy and procedures. The Department of Immigration and Ethnic Affairs has produced a series of projections of the birthplace composition of the Australian population in the year 2001 under a number of immigration scenarios. Table 10.1 presents the distribution of birthplace groups at the end of the century if the 1982–83 intake composition is maintained throughout the period. It must be remembered that these projections include only first-generation immigrants and exclude their Australian-born children. There are substantial differences between the projections although the predominance of the Australian-born is consistent, as is that of the United Kingdom- and Ireland-born. The widest differences tend to be for the Asian-born component with their population being projected to double by the year 2001 under the low immigration assumption and treble under the 100 000 per annum net gain scenario. Price (1984, p. 16) has made estimates of the size of the ethnic Asian population (as distinct from the Asian-born population) and projected them forward to the year 2001, assuming a continuation of current trends. His calculations put the contemporary ethnic Asian population at 2.5 per cent of the Australian population (a total of around 435 000, including 186 000 Turkish and Arabic persons, 77 500 South Asians, 77 500 Chinese and 94 000 South-east Asians). Price's projection of current trends would see Australia's Asian population at the

Table 10.1 Projected population by major birthplace group, according to selected migration scenarios, 2001

Major birthplace group	Actual 1983	Projected 2001				
		Average annual net migration gain				
		Zero	50 000	100 000	150 000	200 000
		Number (millions)				
Australia	12.1	14.2	14.6	14.9	15.2	15.6
UK & Ireland (Rep.)	1.2	1.0	1.3	1.5	1.7	1.9
Other Europe	1.2	1.0	1.2	1.4	1.6	1.8
Middle East	0.1	0.1	0.1	0.2	0.2	0.2
Asia	0.3	0.3	0.6	0.9	1.3	1.6
Other	0.4	0.4	0.5	0.6	0.7	0.8
Total	15.3	17.0	18.3	19.5	20.7	21.9
		Percentage				
Australia	79.0	82.9	79.7	76.5	73.8	71.4
UK & Ireland (Rep.)	7.8	6.1	6.9	7.5	8.0	8.5
Other Europe	7.6	6.0	6.7	7.3	7.8	8.3
Middle East	0.8	0.7	0.8	0.8	0.9	1.0
Asia	2.1	1.9	3.5	4.9	6.1	7.2
Other	2.6	2.4	2.6	3.0	3.4	3.7

Source: Goddard et al. (1984, p. 58)

end of the century comprising around 7 per cent of the total. However, any projection of immigration intake or composition is at best extremely conjectural. As Goddard et al. (1984, p. 57) point out,

> Whilst determination of size of each birthplace group in the intake is largely beyond the current non-discriminatory immigration policy, intake composition by birthplace can be influenced by eligibility category size. For example, a relatively large Refugee category would currently result in a relatively large Asian intake.

Forecasting changes in the distribution of the population is as difficult as anticipating future levels of growth. As Reynolds et al. (1980, p. 11) have put it in the American context, 'As for how many Americans will decide to live in Schenectady vs. Houston 10 years hence, you might do better playing the tables in Las Vegas'. It would seem that overall levels of residential mobility may fall somewhat with the passage of the large baby boom age cohorts into the less mobile middle adult years. The current trend toward a northward shift in the distribution of population between the States is likely to be continued, at least in the short term. The ABS projections of the population for States and Territories assume a continuation of this pattern, and Table 10.2 shows the shifts in the balance of population between the States which this implies. If existing patterns of interstate differentials in growth were maintained to the end of this century, the proportion of the national population in the south-eastern quadrant of Australia would decline from 74.8 to 70.2

Table 10.2 Percentage distribution of the population among the States and Territories, 1981 and (projected) 1991, 2001 and 2021

	Actual 1981	Projections					
		Series A (low)			Series B (high)		
		1991	2001	2021	1991	2001	2021
NSW	35.1	34.4	33.8	32.8	34.6	34.1	33.5
Vic.	26.5	25.4	24.6	23.1	25.4	24.6	23.4
Qld	15.7	17.3	18.8	21.5	17.2	18.6	20.7
SA	8.8	8.2	7.6	6.3	8.1	7.5	6.3
WA	8.7	9.3	9.7	10.8	9.4	10.0	10.9
Tas.	2.9	2.7	2.6	2.3	2.7	2.5	2.2
NT	0.8	1.0	1.3	1.7	1.0	1.2	1.6
ACT	1.5	1.5	1.6	1.6	1.5	1.5	1.5
Australia	100.0	100.0	100.0	100.0	100.0	100.0	100.0

Source: ABS (1983e, p. 9)

per cent by 2001 and 66.1 per cent by 2021. The table shows that the biggest shifts would be away from Victoria and South Australia and toward Queensland and the Northern Territory.

Internal migration patterns between metropolitan and non-metropolitan areas have changed significantly in the last decade and it is difficult to state with any confidence whether these tendencies will continue. On the one hand, the 'turnaround' in Australia has not reached the dimensions that it has in the United States, suggesting that there is still considerable scope here for deconcentration. Moreover, most of the structural and behavioural changes identified in Chapter 5 as being associated with population deconcentration appear to be still in evidence in Australia. On the other hand, little is yet known about the possible retarding impact of escalating costs of fossil fuels on population deconcentration. Also in some parts of the world there is evidence of a resumption of the concentration trends which prevailed prior to the 1970s. For example, several Nordic cities such as Copenhagen, Stockholm and Helsinki have returned to a pattern of net migration gains in the early 1980s after experiencing net losses in the late 1970s (Municipality of Oslo, 1983, Table 14.3), while in the United States there exist some preliminary indications of such a pattern (Richter 1983; Forstall and Engels 1984).

PROJECTIONS OF AUSTRALIA'S POPULATION

At several points in earlier chapters, reference has been made to the series of projections produced by the ABS. Those used here employ the 1981 estimated resident population as a base (ABS 1982c, 1983e). We must at the outset make a clear distinction between what is meant by the terms population *projections* and population *forecasts.* A *projection* indicates how a population will change on the basis of certain assumptions regarding the determinants of change. A *forecast*, on the other hand, is a single projection

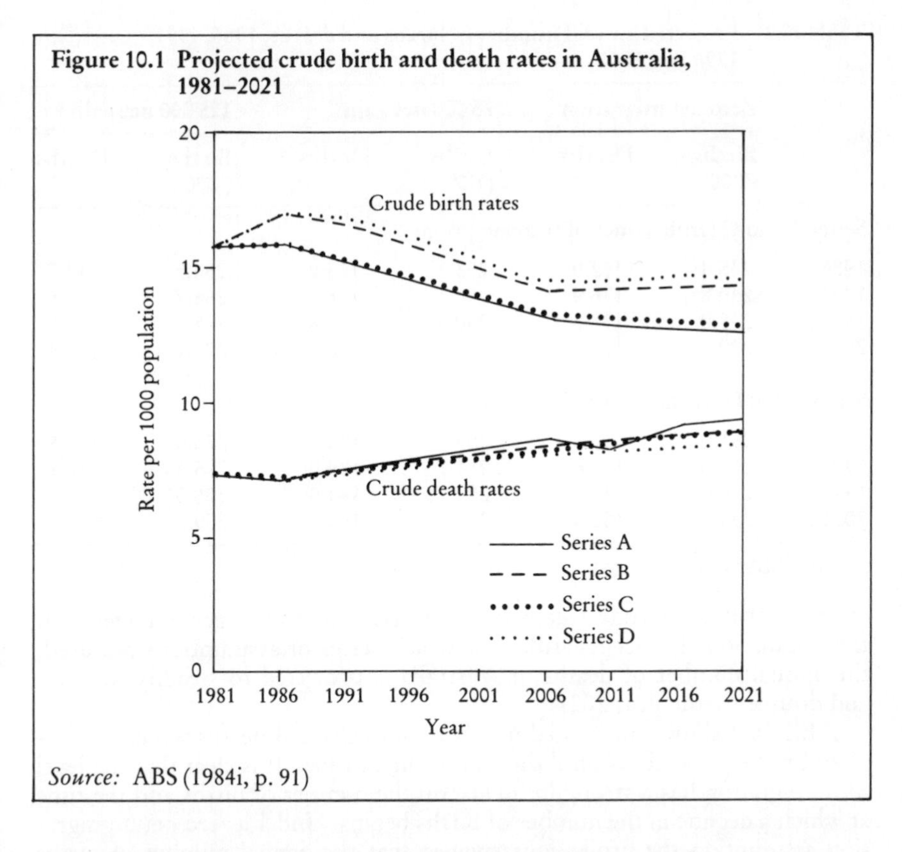

Figure 10.1 Projected crude birth and death rates in Australia, 1981–2021

Source: ABS (1984i, p. 91)

which is described by the demographer who made it or a subsequent user of it, as indicating the *most likely* population at a given date. Hence, all forecasts are projections but not all projections are forecasts.

Before examining the results of the ABS projections it is necessary to briefly recapitulate the assumptions upon which they are based. The ABS has identified four different scenarios in its projection series and these are based on various combinations of assumptions regarding future fertility, mortality and immigration levels. Like most official projections, they tend to be conservative and based solidly on a continuation of recent trends rather than upon hypothetical speculation. Figure 10.1 shows the birth and death rates assumed by the various projection series.

First, regarding fertility the Series A and C projections assume a decline to a Total Fertility Rate of 1.9 in 1987 (10 per cent below replacement level) and stability thereafter. The Series B and D assumptions suggest a recovery to replacement level in 1987 and stability thereafter. Hence, neither set of fertility assumptions envisages Australian fertility rising above replacement level. Only one set of mortality assumptions is used in the projections, and these assume a fairly rapid improvement to 1987 and thereafter a slower improvement in life expectancy. Figure 10.1, however, shows that despite this

Table 10.3 Projected annual number of births and deaths, 1986, 1991, 1996 and 2001

	Zero net migration		75 000 net gain		125 000 net gain	
	Births ('000)	Deaths	Births ('000)	Deaths	Births ('000)	Deaths
Series A and C fertility/mortality assumptions						
1986	245.4	112.9	253.3	113.9	258.5	114.7
1991	240.8	126.4	256.5	128.7	266.7	130.5
1996	238.0	138.8	260.6	142.8	275.2	145.8
2001	229.8	150.2	259.1	156.1	278.1	160.4
Series B and D fertility/mortality assumptions						
1986	261.0	113.0	269.5	114.0	275.0	114.8
1991	267.5	126.6	284.9	129.0	296.3	130.8
1996	264.6	139.1	289.7	143.0	306.0	146.1
2001	255.9	150.5	288.5	156.4	309.7	160.7

Source: ABS (1982c)

improvement the Crude Death Rate will rise due to the general ageing of the population. In fact regardless of which series of assumptions are used, the annual number of deaths in Australia is projected to steadily increase and double by the year 2021.

Table 10.3 shows the annual numbers of births and deaths which are implied by the projections until the end of the century. It is clear that the level of immigration has a strong influence on the number of births and the time at which a decline in the number of births begins. Under a zero net immigration assumption the projections suggest that the annual number of births will decline from the mid-1980s under the low fertility assumption and the early 1990s should the higher fertility assumption hold. With a net immigration gain of 75 000 persons the peak occurs in the mid-1990s and with a gain of 125 000 there is a steady increase in the number of births up to the turn of the century.

The smoothness of the birth and death curves in Figure 10.1 when compared to the actual curves shown in earlier chapters reflects the artificiality of the constant fertility and mortality assumptions. However, they are indicative of the future results of what now seem reasonable assumptions, except perhaps that of a return to replacement fertility by 1987. The convergence of the birth and death rate profiles in Figure 10.1 indicates of course a general decline in natural increase rates over the projection period. This is reflected in a fall-off in the projected rate of growth of the population over the period depicted in Figure 10.2.

The importance of net migration gains to the overall population growth rate is readily apparent in Figure 10.2. The two sets of net migration gain assumptions are of 75 000 (Series A and B) and 125 000 persons (Series C and D) respectively. In the mid-1980s the former appears the most realistic,

Figure 10.2 Projected annual rates of net migration gain and of population growth, 1981–2021

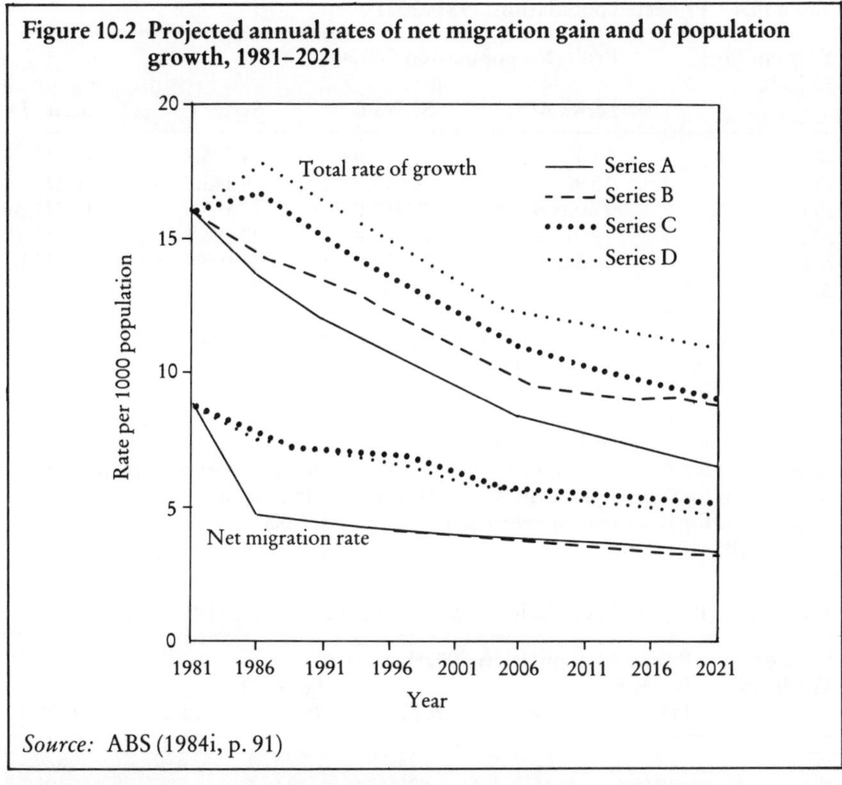

Source: ABS (1984i, p. 91)

although immigration levels are notoriously volatile and difficult to project. In Chapter 4 the growth implications of a wider variety of immigration level assumptions are considered and these give Australia total populations at the end of the century ranging from 17.13 million (zero net migration) to 21.82 million (annual net migration gain of 200 000 persons). It is noticeable in Figure 10.2 that with the progressive decline in natural increase the relative importance of net migration in overall population growth increases.

The future national population totals implied by the four ABS assumption scenarios are presented in Table 10.4. These have a narrower range of net immigration assumptions. Each of the series envisages a continuation of growth through to the year 2021, with population totals at the end of the century ranging between 18.9 million (Series A) and 20.56 million (Series D). Present trends would suggest that the lowest of those totals is the most likely. As was indicated earlier in this chapter, the ABS has also projected how this population would be distributed between the States should contemporary differences in population growth trends be maintained. The population totals obtained are shown in Table 10.5. Perhaps the most striking pattern in the table is that for South Australia, which shows a period of absolute decline in population between the years 2001 and 2021, under the lower fertility and immigration assumptions. It is important to bear in mind, however,

Table 10.4 Projected population, 1981–2021

Year ending 30 June	Projected population ('000s) Series A[2]	Series B	Series C	Series D
1981[1]	14 926.8	14 926.8	14 926.8	14 926.8
1986	15 981.1	16 006.9	16 243.8	16 270.1
1991	17 008.6	17 169.0	17 555.8	17 721.3
2001	18 916.7	19 365.4	20 084.1	20 555.1
2011	20 557.1	21 332.9	22 408.5	23 235.0
2021	22 062.1	23 337.1	24 653.4	26 026.1

[1] Base population = estimated resident population at 1981 census
[2] Projection assumptions are as follows:
Series A: TFR declines to 1.9 in 1987 and is constant thereafter
Mortality declines
Net migration 75 000 p.a.
Series B: as for A, except TFR recovers to 2.11 in 1987 and is constant thereafter
Series C: as for A, except net overseas migration = 125 000 p.a.
Series D: as for B, except net overseas migration = 125 000 p.a.
Source: ABS (1984i, p. 90)

Table 10.5 Projected population of States and Territories, 1981–2021

State or Territory	Projected population ('000s) Series A 1981	2001	2021	Series D 1981	2001	2021
NSW	5237.1	6399.5	7240.9	5237.1	7007.7	8708.7
Vic.	3948.6	4653.1	5086.7	3948.6	5066.0	6080.5
Qld	2345.3	3559.5	4745.1	2345.3	3813.2	5377.8
SA	1319.3	1429.3	1399.7	1319.3	1534.0	1642.4
WA	1299.1	1859.0	2375.7	1299.1	2054.5	2844.5
Tas.	427.3	484.3	499.0	427.3	511.2	564.3
NT	122.8	237.0	371.1	122.8	254.7	417.6
ACT	227.3	294.9	343.7	227.3	314.0	390.3
Australia	14 926.8	18 916.7	22 062.1	14 926.8	20 555.1	26 026.1

Source: ABS (1983e, pp. 10–11)

that very little credence can be placed in any projections over a forty-year period. It is highly improbable that the components of population change will remain stable over such a long period. Clearly any projection will only be as accurate as its assumptions and as time passes the probability that the assumptions will become less valid increases. The average annual rates of population growth for the States and Territories which are implied by the high and low projections are presented in Table 10.6 and show very wide differentials between the States, especially in the high series. As was indicated earlier, if these interstate differentials are maintained over an extended time, such as that of the projection period, a significant northward shift in Australia's population distribution will occur. However, it would seem

Table 10.6 Average annual rates of population growth, actual and projected, 1971–2021

State or Territory	Actual growth rate (%) 1971–81	Projected growth rates (%) Series A 1981–91	1991–2001	2001–21	Series D 1981–91	1991–2001	2001–21
NSW	1.03	1.13	0.89	0.62	1.58	1.36	1.09
Vic.	0.92	0.91	0.73	0.45	1.33	1.18	0.92
Qld	2.39	2.32	1.90	1.45	2.68	2.24	1.73
SA	0.95	0.55	0.25	−0.10	0.88	0.63	0.34
WA	2.11	1.99	1.63	1.23	2.53	2.11	1.64
Tas.	0.71	0.79	0.47	0.15	1.03	0.77	0.50
NT	3.66	3.69	2.99	2.27	4.12	3.32	2.50
ACT	4.16	1.45	1.17	0.77	1.76	1.49	1.09
Australia	1.34	1.31	1.07	0.77	1.73	1.49	1.19

Source: ABS (1983e, p. 7)

Figure 10.3 Median ages for projected population, 1981–2021

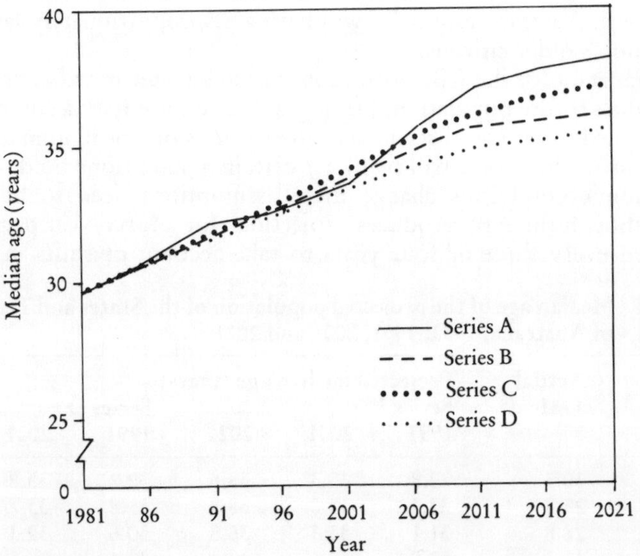

Source: ABS (1984i, p. 91)

highly unlikely that contemporary differentials would be maintained over such a long period.

At several points in this study, the pattern and implications of ageing of the Australian population have been stressed and it is important to examine the extent of ageing implied by the ABS projections. Figure 10.3 shows that under each of the four series of projections there will be a steady increase in the median age of the Australian population through to the end of the century. It will be seen that the major differences between the various series become apparent in the first two decades of the next century, where there is a difference of more than two years in the median age of the low-fertility, low-immigration and the higher-fertility, high-immigration scenarios. This projected ageing of the population has been discussed in some detail in Chapter 6 and it should be stressed again that the projections of the aged population, at least to the end of the century, are much less hypothetical than those for the very young. The aged population of the next two decades is in the main already resident in Australia, and indeed resident in the area where they will be requiring specialized services. The general ageing of the population, however, not only affects the growth of the pensionable population; there will be a general increase, for example, in the average age of the workforce as the baby boom moves up the age pyramid and this has significant implications for manpower planning.

The differentials in projected growth between the various States and Territories obviously have implications for ageing and these are spelt out in Table 10.7. Again we should be cautious about taking the figures for 2021 too seriously. It is unlikely that present trends will be maintained over such an extended period. Nevertheless, it is clear that if present patterns are maintained, South Australia especially will have a disproportionately large share of the nation's older citizens.

It is important for the ABS projections *not* to be interpreted as predictions of Australia's future population. Demographers do not have a complete prescience denied other social scientists. Their role is one of illuminating what populations of the future will be like *if* certain assumptions hold. As social and economic conditions change these assumptions need to be revised. Hence although the ABS produces projections for a forty-year period, they are revised every three or four years to take account of shifts in fertility,

Table 10.7 Median age of the projected population of the States and Territories of Australia, 1981, 1991, 2001 and 2021

State or Territory	Actual 1981	Projected median age (years) Series A			Series D		
		1991	2001	2021	1991	2001	2021
NSW	30.3	32.8	35.3	38.6	32.2	33.8	35.6
Vic.	29.8	32.3	35.0	38.8	31.8	33.7	35.7
Qld	28.8	31.1	33.3	36.8	30.6	32.3	34.7
SA	30.3	33.8	37.6	43.6	33.4	36.5	39.9
WA	28.5	31.2	33.6	37.0	30.7	32.5	34.7
Tas.	28.8	32.2	35.8	41.1	31.8	34.8	38.3
NT	24.5	25.9	27.8	31.3	25.6	27.1	30.0
ACT	26.8	30.1	32.6	37.6	29.8	31.9	35.2
Australia	29.6	32.2	34.7	38.2	31.6	33.4	35.5

Source: ABS (1983e, p. 7)

mortality and migration. All decision-making requires judgement about future conditions and demographic projections can assist this judgement. As Morrison (1971, p. 58) points out, 'Decision making involves hedging bets against identifiable consequences. Demographic information can support this effort by illuminating the contingent as well as charting the probable'.

SOME OBSERVATIONS ON POLICY ISSUES

As was pointed out in Chapter 1, there is a complex two-way inter-relationship between demographic processes on the one hand and the role of planners and policy makers on the other. Many nations have initiated policies and plans which seek to alter the level or nature of population growth, composition or spatial distribution and Australia is no exception. But equally, as Borrie (1982, p. 1) has pointed out, policy measures are 'required to cope with economic, social and cultural problems that arise from demographic factors such as a baby boom, change in marriage patterns, sudden fluctuations in the level of births, the ethnic composition of immigrants or such structural changes as ageing'. Thus policy can be both cause and effect of changes in demographic processes.

At the 1984 International Conference on Population held in Mexico City, the head of the official Australian delegation, also then the Minister for Immigration and Ethnic Affairs, stated that 'Policies in Australia are not designed to directly affect demographic processes. Our policies are pursued to meet basic needs of the population'. While it is true to say that Australia has no official stated policies which explicitly seek to intervene in demographic processes within the nation, it is clear that such interventions have been and are being made, albeit in an *ad hoc* and often indirect way. It is not intended to reiterate here the policies and programmes which have sought to shape the size, growth rate, ethnic composition and spatial distribution of the population. However, it is apparent that there is division of opinion within the Australian community in this area, especially regarding the scale and composition of immigration. Moreover, these divisions are very complex and cut across many conventional political and socio-economic groups. Perhaps partly as a result of this, the level of debate has not been high, despite the vital importance of these issues to the future of all Australians. It must first be acknowledged that we do have policies in place which are influencing and will in the future influence our population; the public should be fully informed concerning them and there must be the fullest posssible opportunity for public discussion of them. As Betts (in Birrell et al. 1984,. p. 73) put it:

> open debate is necessary if policy is to serve not the ends of special interest groups but ends that we as members of a democratic polity, have decided to accept on the grounds of morality, equity and a sustainable future.

Most of the debate and attention on population policy in Australia will undoubtedly continue to focus upon immigration. As has been documented earlier, the pro- and anti-immigration lobbies are both strong, and there is no current indication that either view will prevail for the remainder of the century. The view of Australia's senior demographer, Professor W. D. Borrie, is that an analogy of Australia's immigration programme first presented sixty years ago (Wickens 1925) will continue to be relevant. It is suggested that Australia will, like a boa constrictor, 'go on taking its meals of immigrants in great gulps with quiescent periods in between to aid the processes of digestion' (Borrie in ESCAP 1982, p. 558). With respect to fertility policy, it is unlikely that Australia will, or indeed should, adopt pro-natalist measures to counter low fertility, although some needed policies addressing goals of social equity may have implications for fertility. For example, provision of child-care and creche facilities and reduction of male/female inequalities in various areas of society, especially in the workforce, could influence fertility patterns.

A major objective of this study has been to establish and demonstrate the vital importance of decision-making in policy and planning formulation being informed by, aware of and responsive to contemporary and impending changes in demographic processes. If, for example, we examine the major areas of expenditure of Commonwealth funds listed in Table 10.8, almost all sectors are strongly influenced by demographic change. Indeed, several of the changes in relative significance of various sectors between the early 1960s and 1980s evident in the table are associated with demographic (as well as economic and social) shifts. The relative significance of the education and repatriation budgets has been strongly influenced by the passage of the baby boom cohorts through the education system in the intervening period. What are some of the resource shifts which are implied in contemporary and likely future demographic changes? Here we will touch briefly only on three of the larger expenditure areas in Table 10.8—education, health and social services. The importance of the changing demographic context for these

Table 10.8 Commonwealth government expenditures, classified by purpose, 1961–62 and 1981–82

Purpose	1961–62 $m	per cent	1981–82 $m	per cent
General public services	105	4.3	2 878.7	6.7
Defence	400	16.4	4 135.4	9.6
Education	35	1.4	3 347.9	7.8
Health	174	7.1	4 071.6	9.4
Social security & welfare	587	24.1	10 120.4	23.4
Repatriation	205	8.4	1 387.9	3.2
Housing and community amenities	2	0.1	442.3	1.0
Recreation and culture	3	0.1	463.1	1.1
Economic services	144	5.9	1 969.7	4.6
Transport & communication	27	1.1	2 497.9	5.8
Immigration	22	0.9	–	–
Other	730	30.0	11 879.8	27.5
Total	2434	100	43 194.7	100

Source: ABS (1967, p. 762; 1984i, p. 521)

policy areas as well as others has been examined in more detail in earlier chapters.

In no area of social planning has the swing from 'baby boom' to 'baby bust' been more severely felt than is the case in education. The 1950s and 1960s saw a progressive overcrowding of kindergartens, primary schools, secondary schools and then universities as what the National Population Inquiry referred to as the 'educational shock waves' of the baby boom hit these institutions; and these systems were under enormous pressure just to keep pace. Planning consisted predominantly of gearing up to meet the burgeoning demand for teachers, buildings, etc. However, just as this 'gearing up' has been achieved, the 'baby bust' cohorts have begun to work their way through the age structure, first of all causing reductions in growth and then an absolute reduction in numbers of new entrants to primary schools and eventually to higher educational systems. As a result, new sets of problems have confronted educational planners. Moreover, this pattern of periodic swings from situations of shortage to surplus is going to continue as the baby boom and bust 'echo' through future generations. The advantage which planners have is that there is time available to plan for these swings, although this planning, especially its manpower aspects, is going to have to be flexible and innovatory. There has been a tendency for educational bureaucrats and planners who 'cut their teeth' in the heady days of massive expansion to view this future scenario of moderate overall growth with despondency or even alarm. However, the National Population Inquiry (1978) correctly sees the forthcoming period as one of great opportunity in this area. There are, for example, opportunities to strive for greater equity in the availability of educational opportunities and perhaps also to partially compensate for some of the inequities which have applied in the past. High school completion rates and higher education participation rates in Australia are still low by North American and OECD standards, and there is considerable scope for improvement in those areas. Moreover, there are many Australian adults who passed through the young adult years when educational opportunities were restricted and were unable to develop their potential and interests fully, but who could be given the chance to 'catch up' through adult education, mature age entry schemes to tertiary institutions, etc., especially during periods of low intake of 'normal' age entrants. For example, in the United States Butz et al. (1982, p. 31) have suggested in this context that

> In the next decade, the baby boom cohorts, the largest group of citizens in the nation's history, will pass through the age bracket 35–45. It is at this stage in life that many housewives enter or re-enter the labour force, and many other workers seek to reroute their energies.

Moreover, accelerated structural and technological change means that there will be increasing numbers of candidates for mid-life career redirection.

One of the major adaptations to the boom/bust demographic cycle must be in the area of teacher training. It is clear that imaginative manpower and management strategies will be required if the teaching profession is to retain a throughput of young, talented and motivated recruits and not to stultify. This can be achieved in a low-growth situation through a number of avenues. An obvious need is for selective inservice upgrading and retraining to be encouraged and supported. Also, as is argued in more detail elsewhere (Hugo 1980b, p. 62), the dominance of the school teaching workforce by women in their twenties and thirties opens up a number of possibilities. For example, the authorities might decide to make it very easy for women or men to teach full-time for a period of six or seven years and then, following a short period of leave to have a family, to return on a half-time basis to teach out the rest or a major part of their career. This would mean not simply making such an alternative a possibility but making the bureaucratic adjustments which will positively encourage teachers to opt for such a strategy if it is what they would prefer. This would open up a greater range of career options, especially to women teachers, who are so often faced with a dichotomous decision of either teaching or working in the home. It would also allow for there to be a moderate continuous intake of new teachers so that education planners are not faced with the future prospect of a large proportion of their teaching force retiring within a decade or so. A strategy of a steady intake of teacher trainees would appear to be much more cost-effective than boom-to-bust swings of oversupply and undersupply of trained teachers. The present age structure of teachers, coupled with the recent severe cutbacks (which affect most severely newly trained people) could lead to severe problems in the future; but this could be obviated by more flexible staffing policies and careful manpower planning. In this context it is interesting to note that the Commonwealth Public Service is moving toward having permanent part-time workers.

Some of the most pressing problems in educational planning relate to the changing spatial distribution of demand. The numbers of potential primary and secondary school students can fluctuate much more widely on a local scale than on a city-wide or nation-wide scale. There is a real need for research intended to predict these local fluctuations in demand for educational services, so that appropriate planning measures can be implemented. Clearly, sections of cities pass through a 'life cycle' in which the demand for educational services will vary in both type and volume. There is at present a lack of knowledge concerning the nature of this 'life cycle of a suburb' and its implications, with the work of Rowland (1983) being the major exception. In any event, it would at present seem premature for educational authorities to divest themselves of property and buildings in the inner and middle suburbs of declining population. It may well be that the increasing costs of personal transport in Australia may encourage more people to settle in these inner suburban areas, closer to places of work in the centre of the city. At the very least there is a need for thorough investigation of current intra-urban migration trends and the impact that rising transport costs are having upon them. Obviously, too, many of the problems raised by these issues are architectural. There is a need, for example, for school buildings to be designed so as to combine features which satisfy all the educational needs of students and features which allow them to be readily shifted to a growth suburb as their original location reaches a mature stage in the suburb life cycle. Alternatively, such buildings should be designed so that their function can be readily changed from educational to other uses.

In the area of health care, two major demographic changes documented here are of particular significance. They are the increased longevity of older Australians and the consistent ageing of the population. A corollary of the former trend is increased rates of morbidity among older people, so that not only are the numbers of older people increasing faster than the population as a whole but the incidence of illness among them is increasing. Hence, the pressure on health services in the upper ages is double-edged. The implications for health policy, planning and decisions of these trends are enormous. Obviously, as has been discussed in Chapters 2 and 6, older people make greater demands on the health system than younger people. Moreover, their illnesses generally are chronic rather than the acute illnesses which predominate among the young and require different types of treatment. A major restructuring of the health delivery system is needed, away from the current emphasis on high-cost, high-technology medicine focused upon the treatment and curing of acute disease. Moreover, attention should be paid to the 'compression of morbidity' model of health policy. This model suggests that there are a range of preventive health strategies (most of them requiring changes in lifestyle) which can 'delay significantly the onset of morbidity either due to chronic diseases or to the ageing process itself' (Fries 1984, p. 354). This model suggests that much of the morbidity among older people can be postponed and compressed into the very final period of the life span. It implies a health strategy which attacks chronic disease among the elderly at its social, behavioural and educational roots—which in part lie in the lifestyle adopted by the population in the adult years prior to the final stage of the life cycle.

Earlier it was shown that continuance into the future of the current pattern of health expenditure on the aged would require massive increases in public expenditure, even when it is not allowed that the incidence of morbidity will increase among the aged. The current model of heavy institutionalization of care of the dependent aged population is coming under increased attack, and new strategies which strongly support the family and local community adopting as much responsibility for the well-being of their older dependants as they currently do for their young dependants should be explored and developed. It has been shown here that glib arguments for a simple transfer of government resources which had previously been spent on the dependent young (mainly in the area of education) to pay for care of older people have limited utility. As Butz et al. (1982, p. 32) succinctly put it, it is not 'easy to close down an occasional school in order to open an occasional nursing home'. Moreover, current public spending on each aged dependent Australian is three times that on each young dependent Australian.

The implications of current and impending demographic shifts for the social security system are considerable and have been touched on in almost all of the chapters in this study. Most obviously, expenditure on social security for the aged is poised to grow exponentially. In Japan and the United

States, where the demographic pressures of ageing have come sooner than in Australia, the financial soundness of the social security system for the aged has been eroded and is at crisis point. While their systems are very different from that in Australia, we do share an important common feature: in all three countries social security is financed on a pay-as-you-go basis. Responsibility for support of the aged therefore falls on the younger age cohorts. The balance between the younger and older age groups thus becomes a crucial consideration and makes the entire social security system highly vulnerable to demographic shifts. While the likely degree of aged dependency in the latter years of this century and especially after 2011 has been greatly exaggerated in some quarters, even a small shift in this balance will greatly increase the tax burden upon the working generation at the input end of the pipeline. It is a politically difficult issue to address, but it will have to be addressed, and the later it is left the more drastic will have to be the legislative measures taken to cope with it.

Other demographic pressures on the social security system which have been focused upon in earlier chapters include the plight of single-parent families which are overwhelmingly headed by women. On almost any criteria of well-being, this family type has a greater incidence of hardship than any other. It is apparent that the demands made in this area upon the welfare budget will continue to increase. However, there are other measures which clearly should be taken in addition to the provision of the welfare safety net. Encouragement and assistance of single mothers to enter the paid workforce via privileged access to child-care and creche facilities, for example, is one obvious area which needs to be explored. The demographic pressures on unemployment will be reduced in the near future, but the backlog of presently unemployed people and the displacement of labour caused by structural change and fluctuations in the economy will undoubtedly maintain substantial pressure in this area of social security.

CONCLUSION

In this final chapter we have only briefly glanced at a few of the implications of the changing Australian demographic context for policy making and planning in some public-sector areas. In each chapter both the changes and their implications are spelled out in greater detail. The purpose here was to simply illustrate the significance of demographic analysis to this decision-making. As Butz et al. (1982, p. v) point out, understanding of the evolving demographic environment, 'and the direction of demographic trends, is requisite to shaping the future rather than simply reacting to it'.

This study has attempted to analyse recent trends in the growth, structure and distribution of the Australian population and indicate the probable outlook for the future. Clearly many other elements beside demographic factors have to be considered in assessing likely future patterns of population growth and structure. However, it has been shown that even under present conditions significant changes are taking place in the Australian population. The slow-down of growth and its impact on the structure of the population, as well as household formation and the forces making for a changing spatial distribution of the population, are all of significance in assessing future demand for services. As we move toward zero growth it is certain that the pressures to increase provision of a wide range of services will be less than they were during the period of rapid growth during the three decades following World War II. It seems, however, that total population growth will continue at least for another four decades, albeit at a slower rate than has been the case prior to the mid-1970s. Major readjustments in age structure and population distribution will continue to affect the demand for services.

The directions that Australia takes in the remainder of this century are dependent upon a myriad of interacting political, social and economic forces, the accurate anticipation of which is extremely difficult, if not impossible. As Borrie (1979, p. 63) has pointed out, 'the future, when it becomes the present, seldom coincides with our former expectations—values will have changed, new and almost unforeseen technologies will have been introduced, social patterns will have deviated from defined paths'. Yet looking forward and attempting to anticipate the future and to prepare for it with insight and flexibility is essential for the welfare of society and is an important responsibility of social scientists. We do not have a magical set of infallible techniques which allows us to see what will happen in the future, but we are too often surprised by demographic changes which are readily identifiable and predictable.

The demographic trends evident in the results of the 1981 Australian census and analysed here present a number of challenges and opportunities to planners and policy makers. Yet we have no guarantees that these challenges and opportunities will be met, since so much decision-making in government and business is based on reacting only to contemporary circumstances. Such decision-making too often fails to achieve goals of a fair and just, as well as efficient, allocation of scarce resources. There can be no doubt that better understanding of demographic change and the short- and long-term problems which it engenders can greatly improve the quality of decision-making in both the public and private sectors.

List of Tables

List of Figures

Appendix

Topics covered in 1981 Australian census of population and housing*

Demographic topics
Name
Age
Sex
Marital status
Duration of marriage
Issue (all issue)
Relationship (family structure)

Internal migration
Place of usual residence
Residence 1 year ago
Residence 5 years ago

Ethnicity and related topics
Birthplace
Resident/visitor status
Year of arrival
Citizenship (nationality)
Language (proficiency in English)
Religion
Aborigines/Torres Strait Islanders

Education
Attendance at an educational institution
Highest qualification obtained
Age left school

Income
Income (amount-ranges)

Labour force
Occupational status
Employment status
Occupation
Industry
Hours worked

Mode of travel
Mode of travel to work
Journey to work

Housing
Type of dwelling
Number of rooms
Nature of occupancy
Reason dwelling unoccupied
Mortgages—monthly payments
Rent—amount paid per week
Rent—type of landlord
Rent—furnished or unfurnished
Motor vehicles garaged
Material of outer walls

*For a comprehensive coverage of items covered in the previous census (1976) see Choi (in ESCAP 1982, pp. 559–74).

Bibliography

Armstrong, B. and de Klerk, N. 1981. 'A Comparison of Premature Mortality Due to Cigarette Smoking and Road Crashes in Australia'. *Community Health Studies* **5**, 3, 243–9.

Australian Bureau of Statistics 1967. *Official Year Book of the Commonwealth of Australia*. Commonwealth Bureau of Census and Statistics, Canberra.

———1975. *Income Distribution, 1968–69*, consolidated and revised edition, ABS, Canberra, reference no. 17. 17.

———1978. *Housing Survey, 1978 Sydney, Newcastle, and Wollongong*, part 3, 'Anticipated Residential Movement and Satisfaction with current Housing Conditions,' ABS (NSW office), catalogue no. 8713.1.

———1979a. *Birth Expectations of Married Women, Australia, November 1976*, ABS, Canberra, catalogue no. 3215.0.

———1979b. *Year Book Australia, 1979*, No. 63, ABS, Canberra, catalogue no. 78.8293.6.

———1980a. *Birth Expectations of Married Women, Australia, June 1979*, ABS, Canberra, catalogue no. 3215.0.

———1980b. *Social Indicators, Australia, no. 3, 1980*, ABS, Canberra, catalogue no. 4101.0.

———1980c. *The Housing Intentions of South Australians*, ABS (SA office), Government Printer, Adelaide, catalogue no. 8705.4.

———1981a. *Survey of Handicapped Persons, Australia, February–May 1981 (Preliminary)*, ABS, Canberra, catalogue no. 4342.0.

———1982a. *Deaths Australia 1981*, ABS, Canberra, catalogue no. 3302.0.

———1982b. *Estimated Resident Population by Sex and Age: States and Territories of Australia, June 1971 to June 1981*, ABS, Canberra, catalogue no. 3201.0.

———1982c. *Projections of the Population of Australia 1981 to 2021*. ABS, Canberra, catalogue no. 3204.0.

———1982d. *Australia's aged population 1982*, ABS, Canberra, catalogue no. 4109.0.

———1982e. *Australian Families, 1982 (Preliminary)*. ABS, Canberra, catalogue no. 4407.0.

———1982f. *Census of Population and Housing, Counts of Aboriginals and*

Torres Strait Islanders, Australia, States and Territories, 30 June 1971, 1976, 1981, ABS, Canberra, catalogue no. 2164.0.

———1982g. *Deaths Australia 1980*, ABS, Canberra, catalogue no. 3302.0.

———1982h. *Births Australia 1981*, ABS, Canberra, catalogue no. 3301.0.

———1983a. *Deaths Australia 1982*, ABS, Canberra, catalogue no. 3302.0.

———1983b. *Births Australia 1982*, ABS, Canberra, Catalogue no. 3301.0.

———1983c. *Summary Characteristics of Persons and Dwellings, Australian Census of Population and Housing. 30 June 1981*, ABS, Canberra, catalogue no. 2443.0.

———1983d. *Income and Housing Survey. Income of Individuals, Australia, 1981–82 (Preliminary)*, ABS, Canberra, catalogue no. 6501.0.

———1983e. *Projections of the Population of the States and Territories of Australia 1981–2001*, ABS, Canberra, catalogue no. 3214.0.

———1983f. *ABS Information Paper 1981 Census of Population and Housing: Dwelling Household and Family*, ABS, Canberra, catalogue no. 2150.0.

———1984a. *Estimated Resident Population by Sex and Age: States and Territories of Australia, June 1983*, ABS, Canberra, catalogue no. 3201.0.

———1984b. Australian Health Survey 1977–78, magnetic tape, ABS, Canberra.

———1984c. *Australian Demographic Statistics, September quarter 1983*, ABS, Canberra, catalogue no. 3101.0.

———1984d. *Births, Australia 1983*, ABS, Canberra, catalogue no. 3301.0.

———1984e. *Employment, Underemployment and unemployment 1966–1983, Australia*, ABS, Canberra, catalogue no. 6246.0.

———1984f. *The Labour Force, Australia, November 1984, Preliminary*, ABS, Canberra, catalogue No. 6202.0.

———1984g. *Australian Families 1982*, ABS, Canberra, catalogue no. 4408.0.

———1984h. *Income of Income Units, Australia 1981–82*, ABS, Canberra, catalogue no. 6523.

———1984i. *Year Book Australia 1984*, ABS, Canberra, catalogue no. 131.0.

———1984j. *Internal Migration, Australia Twelve Months Ended 30 June 1983*, ABS, Canberra, catalogue no. 3408.0.

———1984k. *The Labour Force Australia May 1984*, ABS, Canberra, catalogue no. 6203.0.

———1984l. *Income and Housing Survey, Income of Individuals*, ABS, Canberra, catalogue no. 6502.0.

———1985a. *Births Australia 1984*, ABS, Canberra, catalogue no. 3301.0.

———*Yearbooks, Australia*, Canberra.

Australian Council on Population and Ethnic Affairs 1982a. 'Recent Trends in Immigration', *Population Report 6*, Australian Government Publishing Service, Canberra.

———1982b. *Multi-culturalism for All Australians: Our Developing Nationhood*. AGPS, Canberra.

Australian Institute for Multicultural Affairs, 1983a. *The Ethnic Aged: An*

Annotated Bibliography and Selected Statistics. AIMA. Melbourne.
———1983b. The Ethnic Aged Project, briefing papers for members, second biennial meeting of members, Melbourne, October.
Australian Parliament 1979. House of Representatives Standing Committee on Aboriginal Affairs. *Aboriginal Health*. AGPS, Canberra, 1979.
Bane, M.J. and Weiss, R.S. 1980. 'Alone together: the world of single parent families', *American Demographics* **2**, 5, 11–15.
Beed, C., Singell, L. and Wyatt, R. 1983. 'The Dynamics of Intra-City Unemployment Patterns', *Australian Bulletin of Labour* **10**, 1, 36–46.
Beegle, J.A. 1966. 'Social Structure and the Changing Fertility of the Farm Population', *Rural Sociology* **31**, 415–27.
Bell, M., 1978. Non-Metropolitan Population Growth in South Australia, unpublished B.A. (Hons) thesis, Flinders University of South Australia.
Benjamin B. and Overton E., 1981. 'Prospects for Mortality Decline in England and Wales', *Population Trends* **23**, 22–28.
Birrell, R. 1975. 'Population and Planning: The Consequences of Ignoring Demographic Realities', *Royal Australian Planning Institute Journal*, July–October, 87–94.
———1978. 'The 1978 Immigration Decisions and their impact on the Australian Labour Force', *The Australian Quarterly*, **50**, 4, 30–43.
———and Hay, C. (eds) 1978. *Immigration Issue in Australia: a sociological symposium*, Department of Sociology, School of Social Science, La Trobe University, Melbourne.
———and Birrell, T. 1981. *An Issue of People: Population and Australian Society*. Longman Cheshire, Melbourne.
———Hill, D. and Nevill, J. (eds) 1984. *Populate and Perish? The Stresses of Population Growth in Australia*, Fontana, Sydney/Australian Conservation Foundation, Melbourne.
Bongaarts, J. 1983. 'The formal demography of families and households: An Overview', *International Union for the Scientific Study of Population Newsletter* **17**, 27–42.
Bonnell, S.M. and Dixon, P.B. 1982. 'The Impact of Structural Change on Employment of Migrants in Australia during the Seventies', Chapter 4 in D. Douglas (ed.) *The Economics of Australian Immigration* Proceedings of the conference on the economics of immigration, 8–9 February, Sydney University extension programme.
Borrie, W. D. 1979. Population and Society, pp. 63–75 in S.T. Waddell (ed.) *Prospect 2000*, ANZAAS, Perth.
———1982. 'Reflections on Population Policy Options', paper presented to the first Australian Population Association conference, 31 October–2 November, Canberra.
———and Mansfield, M. (eds) 1982. *Implications of Australian Population Trends*, proceedings of a conference held by the Academy of Social Sciences in Australia, 21–22 September 1981, Canberra.
Borthwick, T. 1891. A contribution to the Demography of South Australia, unpublished M.D. thesis, University of Edinburgh.
Boundy, J. 1980. Housing and Housing Development, draft chapter pre-

pared for ESCAP (1982), mimeo.
Bouvier, L.F. 1980. 'America's Baby Boom Generation: The Fateful Bulge', *Population Bulletin* **35**, 1, 1–35.
Bracher, M.D. 1981. *Are Australian Families Getting Smaller? A Study of Patterns and Determinants of Fertility in Melbourne*, Australian Family Formation Project monograph no. 8, Department of Demography, Australian National University, Canberra.
Brown, D.L. 1981. 'A quarter century of trends and changes in the demographic structure of American families', pp. 9–25 in R.T. Coward (ed.) *The Family in Rural Society*, Westview Press, Boulder, Colorado.
Bureau of Industry Economics 1979. *Australian Industrial Development—Some Aspects of Structural Change*, Australian Government Publishing Service, Canberra.
Burnley, I.H. (ed.) 1974. *Urbanization in Australia: The Postwar Experience*, Cambridge University Press, Cambridge.
———1975. 'Ethnic Factors in Social Segregation and Residential Stratification in Australian Large Cities', *Australian and New Zealand Journal of Sociology* **11**, 12–20.
———1976a. *Social Environment*, McGraw-Hill, Sydney.
———1976b. 'Greek Settlement in Sydney 1947–1971', *Australian Geographer* **13**, 3, 200–14.
———1977. 'Mortality Variations in an Australian Metropolis: The Case of Sydney', in N.D. McGlashan (ed.) *Environmental Studies Occasional Paper 4*, University of Tasmania, Hobart.
———1980. *The Australian Urban System*, Longman Cheshire, Melbourne.
———1982. *Population, Society and Environment in Australia*, Shillington House, Melbourne.
———and Routh, N. 1984. *Aboriginal Migration to Sydney*, School of Geography, University of New South Wales, Sydney.
Butz, W.P., McCarthy, K.F., Morrison, P.A. and Valana, M. 1982. *Demographic Challenges in America's Future*, Rand Corporation, Santa Monica.
Caldwell, J.C. 1982a. *Theory of Fertility Decline*, Academic Press, London.
———1982b. Prospects for fertility in western countries, paper prepared for Australian Population Association Conference, Australian National University, Canberra, November.
———1984. 'Fertility Trends and Prospects in Australia and other Industrialised Countries', *Australian and New Zealand Journal of Sociology* **20**, 1, 3–21.
———and Cameron, M. 1972. Demography in the Universities of Australia and New Guinea, paper presented at the second Asian population conference, Tokyo.
Cary, L. 1980. 'The return of the prodigals', *Time*, 13 October, p. 90.
Castle, R. and Mangan, J. 1984. *Unemployment in the Eighties*, Longman Cheshire, Melbourne.
Champion, A.G., 1981. 'Population Trends in Rural Britain', *Population Trends* **26**, 20–3.
Chipman, L. 1980. 'The Menace of Multi-Culturalism', *Quadrant*, September–October, 3–6.

Clark, R.L. and Spengler, J.J. 1980. *The Economics of Individual and Population Aging*, Cambridge University Press, New York.
Clifford, W. and Marjoram, J. 1979. *Suicide in South Australia*. Australian Institute of Criminology, Canberra.
Clyne, M.G. 1977. 'Bilingualism in the elderly', *Talanga* **4**:45–56.
Commission of Inquiry into Poverty, 1975. *Poverty in Australia: First Main Report* (2 volumes), Australian Government Publishing Service, Canberra.
Commonwealth Department of Aboriginal Affairs, 1981. Statistical Section newsletter number 12, Canberra.
Commonwealth Department of Education, 1980. *Population Growth and Educational Development*, Australian Government Publishing Service, Canberra.
Cook, B. 1980. Migration patterns of the elderly, paper presented to the fifth annual meeting of the Regional Science Association, Australian and New Zealand Section, Tanunda, South Australia.
Crimmins, E.M. 1981. 'The Changing Pattern of Mortality Decline 1940–1977 and its Implications for the Future', *Population and Development Review* 7, 2, 229–54.
Dasvarma, G.L. 1977. 'Causes of Death Among Males of Various Occupations', in N.D. McGlashan (ed.) *Environmental Studies Occasional Paper 4*, University of Tasmania, Hobart.
———1980. Differential Mortality in Australia (with special reference to the period 1970–1972), Ph.D. thesis, Department of Demography, Australian National University, Canberra.
Davidson, B.R. 1965. *The Northern Myth*, Melbourne University Press, Melbourne.
Day, L. 1971. 'Differential fertility in Australia', *International Population Conference* **3**, 2043–52 (published by the International Union for the Scientific Study of Population, Liège).
———1979. 'Those Unsatisfactory Statistics on Divorce', *Australian Quarterly* **51**, 26–31.
Department of Housing and Community Development (DHCD). 1976. *Aged Persons Housing Survey*, vols I and II, Australian Government Publishing Service, Canberra.
Department of Immigration and Ethnic Affairs (DIEA) 1983. *Australia: Population Forecasts for 1983–86 with projections for selected years to 2021*, Australian Government Publishing Service, Canberra.
———1984a. *Australia*, statement prepared for the international conference on population, Mexico City, August 1984, Australian Government Publishing Service, Canberra.
———1984b. Immigration Policy Categories and Population Projections, paper presented to the seventh Commonwealth/State population workshop, 18–19 October.
———1984c. *Australian Immigration*, Consolidated Statistics no. 13, 1982, Australian Government Publishing Service, Canberra.
———(n.d.). 1981 census: Birthplace × Age × Sex, *Australia Statistical Note* no. 17.
Department of Social Security, 1983 and 1984. *Pocket Compendium of In-*

come Security Statistics, December issue, Statistics section, Research and Statistics Branch Development Division, Canberra.

Di Iulio, O.B. 1976. Household Formation 1911–2001, *National Population Inquiry Working Paper No. 24*, Australian Government Publishing Service, Canberra.

Di Iulio, O.B. and Choi, C.Y. 1982. Early 1981 Census Results: The Growth, Distribution and Composition of the Population, paper presented to first Australian Population Association conference, Canberra.

Dixon, D.A. and Crompton, C. 1983. Social Welfare financing: implications of an ageing population, paper presented at Australian population issues seminar, Australian National University, Canberra, 18 August.

Dobson, A.J., Gibberd, R.W., Wheeler, D.J. and Leeder, S.R. 1981. 'Age-Specific Trends in Mortality from Ischaemic Heart Disease and Cerebrovascular Disease in Australia', *American Journal of Epidemiology* **1**, 4, 404–12.

Douglas, D. (ed.) 1982. *The Economics of Australian Immigration, Proceedings of a Conference*, 8–9 February, Sydney University extension programme.

Downie, M.C. 1980. The Nature of the Future Demand for Services by the Elderly Population of Noarlunga, unpublished B.A. (Hons) thesis, Flinders University of South Australia, Adelaide.

Doyle, B. 1982. The 1981 Census: early results and evaluation, paper presented to the first Australian Population Association conference, Canberra.

Dunt, D.R. 1982. 'Recent Mortality Trends in the Adult Australian Population and its Principal Ethnic Groups', *Community Health Studies* **VI**, 3, 217–22.

Dyer, K. 1979. 'Infant Mortality In Our Cities', *Scientific Australian* August, 14–16.

Easterlin, R.A. 1980. *Birth and Fortune: the impact of numbers of personal welfare*, Basic Books, New York.

ESCAP (Economic and Social Commission for Asia and the Pacific) 1982. *Population of Australia* (country monograph series no. 9), 2 vols, United Nations, New York.

Espenshade, T. 1984. *Investing in Children: New Estimates of Parental Expenditures*, The Urban Institute Press, Washington.

Faulkner, C.J. 1980. Intra-urban migration and the life cycle in Metropolitan Adelaide, unpublished B.A. (Hons) thesis, Flinders University of South Australia, Adelaide.

Felton, P. 1983. 'Confusing Information on the Census Aboriginal Population—1981', *Australian Population Association Newsletter* **8**, 27–34.

Fisher, N.W.F. 1969. Some aspects of interstate migration in Australia, paper presented to 41st Congress of the Australian and New Zealand Association for the Advancement of Science, Adelaide.

Forstall, P.L. and Engels, R.A. 1984. Growth in Nonmetropolitan Areas Slows, mimeo, US Bureau of the Census, Washington.

Forster, C. 1983a. 'Spatial Organisation and Local Employment Rates in

Metropolitan Adelaide: Significant issue or spatial fetish?', *Australian Geographical Studies* **21**, 1, 33–48.

———1983b. 'Australian Profile: Unemployment in the Cities', *Geographical Education* **4**, 131–40.

Frejka, T. 1980. 'Fertility Trends and Policies: Czechoslovakia in the 1970s', *Population and Development Review* **6**, 1, 65–93.

Fries, J.F. 1984. 'The Compression of Morbidity: Miscellaneous Comments About a Theme'. *The Gerontologist* **24**, 4, 354–9.

Gale, G.F. 1972. *Urban Aborigines*, Australian National University Press, Canberra.

———1981. 'Adjustment of migrants in cities: Aborigines in Adelaide, Australia', in G.W. Jones and H.V. Richter (eds) *Population Mobility and Development*, Australian National University Development Studies Centre, Canberra.

Gale, G.F. and Wundersitz, J. 1982. *Adelaide Aborigines: A case study of urban life 1966–1981*, Australian National University Press, Canberra.

Gelfand, D.E. 1981. 'Ethnicity and ageing', in C. Eisdorfer (ed.) *Annual Review of Gerontology and Geriatrics* **2**, Springer, New York.

Gibson, D.M. and Rowland, D.T. 1982. *Community Versus Institutional Care: The Case of the Australian Aged*, working paper no. 20, Ageing and the Family Project, Australian National University, Canberra.

Gifford, R.M., Kalma, J.D., Aston, A.R. and Millington, R.J. 1975. 'Biophysical Constraints in Australian Food Production: Implications for Population Policy', *Search* **6**, 6, 212–23.

Glick, P.C. and Norton, A.J. 1980. 'New Lifestyles Change Family Statistics', *American Demographics* **2**, 5, 21–3.

Glover, A.T. 1946. 'The Patterns of Population Change in Australia', *Royal Australian Historical Society Journal and Proceedings* **XXXII**, 295–340.

Goddard, R.G. 1983. Rural Renaissance—but where?, paper presented at 53rd Congress of the Australian and New Zealand Association for the Advancement of Science, Perth.

———, Sparkes, L.H. and Haydon, J.A. 1984. 'Demographic Consequences of Immigration', chapter 3 from *The Economics of Immigration*, Committee for the Economic Development of Australia and Department of Immigration and Ethnic Affairs, Canberra.

Gogulapati, R., de Ravin, J.W. and Trickett, P.J. 1984. *Projections of Australian Mortality Rates 1981–2020*, occasional paper no. 1983/2, Australian Bureau of Statistics, Canberra.

Gordon, A.R. 1977. Home Ownership in Australia—1966, 1971 and Beyond, paper presented to conference of economists, Hobart.

Gray, A. 1982. An historical perspective on recent changes in Aboriginal fertility, paper presented to Australian Population Association conference, Canberra, November.

———1984. 'Changes in Aboriginal Family Formation and Fertility', in *Australian Family Research Conference Proceedings* vol. 1, Institute of Family Studies, Melbourne.

———and Smith. L.R. 1983. 'The Size of the Aboriginal Population',

Australian Aboriginal Studies **1**, 2–9.

Graycar, A. 1981. 'Ageing in Australia: a pointer to political dilemmas', *The Australian Quarterly* **53**, 2, 280–300.

———and Kinnear, D. 1981. 'The Aged and the State', Social Welfare Research Centre Reports and Proceedings, working paper no. 5, (revised edition, September), University of New South Wales, Sydney.

Gregory, R.G. 1984. 'The demise of full employment', in R. Castle and J. Mangan (eds) *Unemployment in the Eighties*, Longman Cheshire, Melbourne.

Harrison, B.R. 1981. *Living Alone in Canada: Demographic and Economic Perspectives* Statistics Canada, Ottawa.

Harrison, D.S. 1983. The Impact of Recent Immigration On The South Australian Labour Market, working paper no. 52, National Institute of Labour Studies, Flinders University of South Australia, Adelaide.

Hearst, S. 1981. *Ethnic Communities and Their Aged*, Clearing House on Migration Issues, Melbourne.

Hecht, J. 1982. 'From a third to a second child: Recent changes in French Population Policy', *Federal Institute for Population Research* (Germany) **7**, 71.

Heeren, H.J. 1982. 'Pronatalist Population Policies in Some Western European Countries', *Population Research and Policy Review* **1**, 137–52.

Hetzel, B. 1982. 'The Diseases of Affluence', in R. Birrell, D. Hill and J. Stanley (eds) *Quarry Australia*, Oxford University Press, Melbourne.

Hicks, N. 1978. *The Sin and Scandal: Australia's Population Debate 1891–1911*, Australian National University Press, Canberra.

Hogan, W. 1984. Issues in Immigration and Migrant Settlement Problems, revised version of paper presented to the forty-first ordinary general meeting of the Institute of Public Affairs, Sydney, 3 July.

Howe, A.L. (ed.) 1981. *Towards an Older Australia*, University of Queensland Press, Brisbane.

Hugo, G.J. 1975. 'Postwar Settlement of Southern Europeans in Australian Rural Areas: The Case of Renmark, South Australia', *Australian Geographical Studies* **13**, 2, 169–81.

———1979a. 'Some Demographic Factors Influencing Recent and Future Demand for Housing in Australia', *Australian Quarterly* **51**, 4, 4–25.

———1979b. 'Population Projections and Planning', in T.K. Bell et al. *The Future of Local Government in South Australia*, (monograph series, no. 4) Centre for Applied Social and Survey Research, Flinders University of South Australia, Adelaide.

———1980a. 'Some demographic aspects of changing patterns of housing demand and home ownership in Australia', in *Home Ownership in Australia: A Perspective for Future Policies*, Housing Industry Association, Canberra.

———1980b. Some Demographic Factors Influencing Recent and Future Demand for Educational Services in Australia, paper presented at 50th congress of the Australian and New Zealand Association for the Advancement of Science, Adelaide.

———1983a. 'South Australia's Changing Population', *South Australian*

Geographical Papers no. 1, Royal Geographical Society of Australasia (SA Branch), Adelaide.
———1983b. *The Changing Australian Family: Structure and Characteristics of Households and Families in Australia at the 1981 Census*, 1981 census project paper 9, National Institute of Labour Studies, Flinders University of South Australia, Adelaide.
———1983c. *Changing distribution and age structure of birthplace groups in Australia 1976–1981*, 1981 census project paper 5, National Institute of Labour Studies, Flinders University of South Australia.
———1983d. *Population Change in Urban and Rural Areas 1976–1981* 1981 census project paper 7, National Institute of Labour Studies, Flinders University of South Australia.
———1983e. *Interstate Migration in Australia, 1976–1981*, 1981 census project paper 1, National Institute of Labour Studies, Flinders University of South Australia.
———1983f. Immigrants in the workforce: a demographic perspective, paper prepared for public forum on the 'ethnic disabled as a result of occupational injury and diseases' organized by the Council for the Ethnic Disabled of South Australia, Adelaide.
———1983g. *The Ageing of Ethnic Populations in South Australia*, South Australian Ethnic Affairs Commission, Adelaide.
———1984a. 'Projecting Australia's aged population: problems and implications', *Journal of the Australian Population Association* **1**, 41–55.
———1984b. *Patterns and Components of Regional Population Change 1976–1981*. 1981 census project paper 3, National Institute of Labour Studies, Flinders University of South Australia.
———1984c. 'Internal Migration in Australia—some First Glimpses From the 1981 Census', in *Migration in Australia*, proceedings of symposium held in Brisbane, 1–2 December 1983, by the Royal Geographical Society of Australasia (Qld Inc) and Australian Population Association (Qld Regional Group).
———1984d. 'Changes in the demographic structure of Australian families: An analysis of census data', in *Australian Family Research Conference Proceedings*, vol. 1, Institute of Family Studies, Melbourne.
———1984e. 'The ageing of ethnic populations in Australia with special reference to South Australia', *Occasional Paper in Gerontology*, no. 6, National Research Institute for Gerontology and Geriatric Medicine, Melbourne.
———, Rudd, D.M., Downie, M., Macharper A. and Shillabeer, A. 1981. *A Demographic Profile of the Present and Likely Future Population of the South Coast-Fleurieu Peninsula Regions of South Australia with Particular Emphasis on the Aged Population*, Discipline of Geography, Flinders University of South Australia.
———and Menzies, B.J. 1980. 'Greek Immigrants in the South Australian Upper Murray', in I.H. Burnley, R.J. Pryor and D.T. Rowland (eds) *Mobility and Community Change in Australia*, University of Queensland Press, Brisbane.
———, Downie, M. and Rudd. D.M. 1981. Changing patterns of concentra-

tion and migration of the older population in Australian cities: a case study in Adelaide, paper presented to 51st ANZAAS Congress, Brisbane.

———, Rudd, D.M. and Downie, M. 1984. 'Adelaide's aged population: changing spatial patterns and their policy implications', *Urban Policy and Research* **2**, 2, 17–25.

———and Smailes, P.J. 1985. 'Urban-rural migration in Australia: a process view of the turnaround', *Journal of Rural Studies* **1**, 1, 11–30.

———and Wood, D. R. 1983. *Recent Fertility Trends and Differentials in Australia*, 1981 census project paper 4, National Institute of Labour Studies, Flinders University of South Australia.

———and Wood. D.R. 1984. *Ageing of the Australian Population: Changing Distribution and Characteristics of the Aged Population*, 1981 census project paper 8, National Institute of Labour Studies, Flinders University of South Australia.

Hull, T.H. 1982. Conflict on the homefront: work, housework and the future of fertility, paper presented to seminar on conflict and consensus, Research School of Social Sciences, Australian National University.

Indicative Planning Council for the Housing Industry 1984. *Long-Term Projections Report 1984*, Canberra.

Irwin, R. 1977. *Guide for Local Area Population Projections*, technical paper no. 39, US Bureau of Census, Washington.

Jarvie, W.K. 1981. 'Internal Migration and Structural Change in Australia 1966–71. Some Preliminary Observations', in *Papers of the Australian and New Zealand Section of Regional Science Association*, sixth meeting, 25–55.

———1982. Changes in age specific patterns of inter-regional migration in Australia, 1966–71 to 1971–76 and their relationships to the changing pattern of job opportunities, paper presented to the Australian Population Association conference, Canberra.

———1984. Internal migration in Australia 1966–71 to 1971–76, Ph.D. thesis, School of Social Sciences, Flinders University of South Australia.

———and Browett, J.G. 1980. 'Recent changes in migration patterns in Australia', *Australian Geographical Studies* **18**, 135–45.

Jones, G.W. 1982. 'Population Trends and Policies in Vietnam', *Population and Development Review* **8**, 4, 783–810.

Jordan, A. 1979. Changing Family Patterns and Social Security Protection: The Australian Scene, research paper no. 3, Research and Statistics Branch Development Division, Department of Social Security.

Kain, B. 1977. *Retiring to the Seaside*, Routledge and Kegan Paul, London.

Kendig, H. 1981. *Buying and Renting: Household Moves in Adelaide*, Australian Institute of Urban Studies, Canberra,

———1982. *The Cumulation of Inequity: Housing in Old Age*, working paper no. 28, Ageing and the Family Project, Research School of Social Sciences, Australian National University.

Keyfitz, N. 1972. 'On future population', *Journal of the American Statistical Association* **67** (338), 347–63.

Khoo, S. 1984. 'Family formation and ethnicity', in *Australian Family*

Research Conference Proceedings, vol. 1, Institute of Family Studies, Melbourne.

Knopfelmacher, F. 1982. 'The Case against Multi-culturalism', in R. Manne (ed.) *The New Conservatism in Australia*, Oxford University Press, Melbourne.

Krout, J.A. 1982. Seasonal migration of the elderly, paper presented to annual meeting of the Population Association of America, San Diego.

Kuroda, T. 1977. *The role of migration and population distribution in Japan's demographic transition*, papers of the East-West Population Institute, no. 4, Honolulu.

Lavis, D.R. 1975. *Oral Contraception in Melbourne: An Investigation of the Growth in Use of Oral Contraceptives and their Effect Upon Fertility in Australia 1961–71*, Australian Family Formation Project, monograph no. 3, Department of Demography, Australian National University, Canberra.

Levy, R.I. and Moskowitz, J. 1982. 'Cardiovascular Research: Decades of Progress, a Decade of Promise', *Science* **217**, 121–9.

Lindblad, J. 1976. 'Where the Dropouts Are', *Bulletin* 27 March, 32–9.

Linge, G.J. and McKay, J. (eds) 1981. *Structural Change in Australia*, publication HG/15, Department of Human Geography Australian National University, Canberra.

Lipset, S.M. (ed.) 1980. *The Third Country: America as a Post Industrial Society*, University of Chicago.

Logan, M.I., Whitelaw, J.S. and McKay, J. 1981. *Urbanization: The Australian Experience*, Shillington House, Melbourne.

Long, J.F. 1981. *Population Deconcentration in the United States*, US Bureau of Census, Washington.

Long, L. and DeAre, D. 1982. 'Repopulating the Countryside. A 1980 Census Trend', *Science* **217**, 1111–16.

Long, L.H. and Hansen, K.A. 1979, *Reasons for Interstate Migration* current population reports, no. 81, US Bureau of Census, Washington.

Lopez, A.D. and Ruzicka, L.T. 1977. 'The Differential Mortality of the Sexes in Australia', in N.D. McGlashan (ed.) *Environmental Studies Occasional Paper 4*, University of Tasmania, Hobart.

Lovering, K. 1984. *Cost of Children in Australia*, working paper no. 8, Institute of Family Studies, Melbourne.

Lumsdaine, S. 1983. Power and Prejudice. The impact of new life styles on the Nannup Shire, paper presented at 53rd ANZAAS congress, Perth.

MacKellar, M.J.R. 1980. Population, immigration and the domestic market, address to the Australian Chamber of Shipping, 27 June 1979; reprinted in *Issues in immigration*, Australian Government Publishing Service, Canberra.

Madigan, F.C. 1957. 'Are Sex Mortality Differentials Biologically Caused?', *Milbank Memorial Fund Quarterly* **35**, 202–23.

Maher, C.A. 1984. *Residential Mobility Within Australian Cities, An analysis of 1976 Census Data*, census monograph series, catalogue no. 3410.0, ABS, Canberra.

Maher, C. and Goodman, A. 1984. *The Nature of Interstate Movement: A*

Demographic Analysis, working paper no. 2, 1981 Internal Migration Study, Department of Geography, Monash University, Melbourne.

Manton, K.G. 1982. 'Changing Concepts of Morbidity and Mortality in the Elderly Population', *Milbank Memorial Fund Quarterly* **60**, 2.

Maxwell, P. and Peter, M. 1982. Regional Variations in Unemployment and Participation Rates: An Intercensal Review 1971–1981, paper presented to Regional Science Association Conference (Australia and New Zealand section), Canberra.

McCaskill, M. 1982. 'The Tasman connection: aspects of Australian-New Zealand relations', *Australian Geographical Studies* **20**, 3–23.

McDonald, P.F. 1974. *Marriage in Australia: Age at First Marriage and Proportions Marrying in Australia, 1860–1971*, mongraph no. 2, Australian Family Formation Project, Department of Demography, the Australian National University.

———1984. 'The baby boom generation as reproducers: Fertility in Australia in the late 1970s and the 1980s', in *Australian Family Research Conference Proceedings*, vol. 1, Institute of Family Studies, Melbourne.

McKay, J. 1984. *Migration of the Labour Force: Interstate Patterns*, working paper no. 3, 1981 Internal Migration Study, Department of Geography, Monash University, Melbourne.

McKay, J. and Maher, C. 1984. *A Review of Migration Studies*, working paper no. 1, 1981 Internal Migration Study, Department of Geography, Monash University, Melbourne.

McMichael, A.J. 1982. *A Social and Epidemiological study of the Health of Southern European Migrants in Australia*, Commonwealth Scientific and Industrial Research Organisation (Division of Human Nutrition), Adelaide.

———, and Hartshorne, J.M. 1980. 'Cardiovascular Disease and Cancer Mortality in Australia, by Occupation, in Relation to Drinking, Smoking and Eating', *Community Health Studies* **4**, 76.

———, and Hartshorne, J.M. 1982. 'Mortality Risk in Australian Men by Occupational Groups 1968–1978', *Medical Journal of Australia* **1**, 253–6.

———, McCall, M.G., Hartshorne, J.M. and Woodings, T.L. 1980. 'Patterns of gastro-intestinal cancer in European Migrants to Australia', *International Journal of Cancer* **25**, 431–7.

McQuin, P., 1978. *Rural Retreating: A Review and an Australian Case Study*, Department of Geography, University of New England, Armidale.

Menzies, B.J. and Bell, M.J. 1980. Peri urban Development in the Adelaide Hills, paper presented to 50th ANZAAS congress, Adelaide.

———1981. *Peri-Urban Development: A Case Study of the Adelaide Hills*, research monograph no. 2 Extension Research and Evaluation Unit, Department of Agriculture, South Australia.

Merrilees, W.J. 1984. 'Hidden unemployment among married women', in R. Castle and J. Mangan (eds). *Unemployment in the Eighties*, Longman Cheshire, Melbourne.

Miller, P.W. 1982. The Economic Position of Migrants: Facts and Fallacies—a Preliminary View', *Australian Bulletin of Labour* **8**, 4, 229–48.

———1983. The impact of Immigration on the South Australian Labour Market, An Analysis of the 1976 Census, paper prepared as part of the National Institute of Labour Studies' research project: The Impact of Recent Immigration on the South Australian Labour Market. National Institute of Labour Studies, Flinders University of South Australia, Adelaide.

Moraitis, S. 1981. 'The migrant aged', in A. Howe (ed.) *Towards an Older Australia*, University of Queensland Press, Brisbane.

Morrison, P.A. 1971. *Demographic Information for Cities: A Manual for Estimating and Projecting Local Population Characteristics*, Rand Corporation, Santa Monica.

———1977a. 'Emerging public concern over U.S. population movements in an era of slowing growth', Rand paper series, no. P5873, Rand Corporation, Santa Monica.

———1977b. 'Demographic Trends that will Shape Future Housing Demand', *Policy Sciences* **18**, 203–15.

———1978. Overview of Demographic Trends Shaping the Nation's Future, testimony before the Joint Economic Committee, US Congress.

———1979, 'The Shifting Regional Balance', *American Demographics* **1**, 5, 9–15.

Municipality of Oslo 1983. *Statistical Yearbook of Oslo*, 84th issue.

Murphy, P. 1979a. Migration of the Elderly and Non-Metropolitan Change, unpublished paper presented to Regional Science Association, (Australia and New Zealand Section) fourth annual meeting, Albury-Wodonga.

Murphy, P.A. 1979b. 'Migration of the elderly: a review'; *Town Planning Review* **50**, 84–93.

Myers, G.C. 1982. 'The ageing of populations', in *International Perspectives on Aging Population and Policy Challenges*, United Nations Fund for Population Activities, New York.

Mykyta, L.J. 1983. Aged Migrants in Australian Society, paper presented at the second regional conference, International Association of Gerontology (Asia/Oceania Region), Singapore.

NPI (National Population Inquiry) 1975. *Population and Australia: A Demographic Analysis and Projection*, two volumes, Australian Government Publishing Service, Canberra.

———1978. *Population and Australia: Recent Demographic Trends and their Implications*, Australian Government Publishing Service, Canberra.

Newman, P., Annandale, D. and Duxbury, L. 1984. 'The rise or decline of the Australian inner city? An analysis of recent trends in population, housing, age structure and occupation', *Urban Policy and Research* **2**, 1, 7–16.

New Zealand Government Statistician, 1981. 'Part A—a cross sectional analysis of New Zealand fertility 1962–1979', *Demographic Bulletin* **4**, 1, 5–19.

Norton, A.J. and Glick, P.C. 1979. 'What's Happening to Households?', *American Demographics* **2**, 1, 19–22.

O'Connell, M. and Rogers, C.C. 1982. 'Differential fertility in the United States: 1976–1980', *Family Planning Perspective* **14**, 5, 281–6.

Office of Population Censuses and Surveys, 1982. 'Sources of Statistics on Ethnic Minorities', *OPCS Monitor* 82/1.

Ogden, P.E. and Huss, M.M. 1982. 'Demography and pronatalism in France in the nineteenth and twentieth centuries', *Journal of Historical Geography* **8**, 3, 283–98.

Omran, A.R. 1971. 'The Epidemiologic Transition: a Theory of The Epidemiology of Population Change', *Milbank Memorial Fund Quarterly* **49**, 4, 509–38.

Parliament of the Commonwealth of Australia 1982. *In a Home or At Home: accommodation and home care for the aged*, report from the House of Representatives standing committee on expenditure. Australian Government Publishing Service, Canberra.

Paterson, I.G., Kirkham, D.O. and Gilmore, K.C. 1978. *The Changing Rural Environment—A Study of Rural Retreats New Life Styles and Land Use in Southern Tasmania*, Environmental Studies occasional paper no. 6, University of Tasmania, Hobart.

Pollard, A.H. and Pollard, G.N. 1981. 'The demography of ageing in Australia', in A.L. Howe (ed.), *Towards an Older Australia*, University of Queensland Press, Brisbane.

Population Reference Bureau, 1982. 'U.S. Population: Where We Are: Where We're Going', *Population Bulletin* **37**, 2.

———1983. 1983 World Population Data Sheet, Washington.

———1984. 1984 World Population Data Sheet, Washington.

Powles, J. 1982. 'Health and the Escalation of Industrialism', in R. Birrell, D. Hill, and J. Stanley (eds) *Quarry Australia*, Oxford University Press, Melbourne.

Powles, J. and Birrell, R. 1977. *Mortality in Victoria 1969–1973*, Environmental Research Associates, Monash University, Melbourne.

Pressat, R. 1970. *Population*, Penguin, Harmondsworth.

Price, C.A. 1955. *The Italian population of Griffith*. Australian National University, Canberra.

———1963. *Southern Europeans in Australia*, Oxford University Press, Melbourne.

——— 1975. *Australian Immigration, a review of the demographic effects of post-war immigration on the Australian population*, research report no. 2, National Population Inquiry, Australian Government Publishing Service, Canberra.

———(ed.) 1979. *Australian Immigration: A Bibliography and Digest*, no. 4, Department of Demography, Australian National University, Canberra.

———(ed.) 1981. *Australian Immigration: A bibliography and digest*, no. 5. Australian National University, Canberra.

———1984. 'International Migration to and from Australia', *Journal of the Australian Population Association* **1**, 9–17.

——— and Martin, J.I. (eds) 1975. *Australian Immigration: A Bibliography and Digest*, no. 3, Department of Demography, Australian National University, Canberra.

Prinsley, D.M., Kidd, B., Howe, A.L. and Cameron, K. 1979. *The Experience of Retirement Migration to Phillip Island and its impact on the community*, occasional paper in Gerontology, National Research Institute for Gerontology and Geriatric Medicine, University of Melbourne.

Pryor, E. and Norris, D. 1983. 'Canada in the Eighties', *American Demographics* **5**, 12, 25–29 and 44.

Pryor, R.J. 1977. 'Preferences versus Policies? The politics of population distribution in Australia', *Australian and New Zealand Journal of Sociology* **13**, 1, 23–8.

———1978. Population Redistribution Policies in Developed Countries and the Case of Australia, paper presented at International Geographical Union commission on Population Geography Symposium, Oulu, Finland.

Retherford, R.D. 1972. 'Tobacco Smoking and the Sex Mortality Differential', *Demography* **9**, 203–16.

Reynolds, R.T., Robey, B. and Russell, C. 1980. 'Demographics of the 1980's', *American Demographics* **2**, 1, 11–14.

Richards, I. 1982. 'A Struggle As They Grow Old', *Advertiser*, 30 March, 6.

———1983. 'Ethnic Aged Problems Ignored', *Advertiser*, 14 April, 5.

Richter, K. 1983. 'Nonmetropolitan Growth in the Late 1970s: The End of the Turnaround?', *Center for Demography and Ecology, University of Wisconsin-Madison, Working Papers*, 83–20.

Roder, D. 1980. *Mortality Rates in South Australia from 1953 to 1978*, South Australian Health Commission, Adelaide.

Rossi, P. 1955. *Why Families Move*, The Free Press, Glencoe, Illinois.

Rowland, D.T. 1979. *Internal migration in Australia*, ABS, Canberra.

———1982a. 'The vulnerability of the aged in Sydney', *Australian and New Zealand Journal of Sociology* **18**, 229–47.

———1982b. 'Living arrangements and the later family life cycle in Australia', *Australian Journal on Ageing* **1**, 2, 3–6.

———1982c. 'A research response to ageing in Australia', *Australian Foreign Affairs Record* **53**, 12.

———1983. *Population and Educational Planning: The Demographic Context of Changing School Enrolments in Australian Cities*. Education Research and Development Committee Report no. 36, Australian Government Publishing Service, Canberra.

Rowland, J., Allan, A. and Hocking, A. 1980. Birth expectations of married women: preliminary findings of a survey, paper presented to 50th ANZAAS congress, Adelaide.

Russell, C. 1981. 'Inside the Shrinking Household', *American Demographics* **3**, 9, 28–33.

Ruzicka, L.T. 1974. 'Nuptiality and fertility of birth cohorts', *Demography* **11**, 3, 397–406.

———1977. 'Premarital pregnancies in Australia', *Journal of Marriage and the Family* **39**, 387–95.

———1979. 'Age at marriage and timing of the first birth', *Population Studies* **30**, 527–38.

———, and Caldwell, J.C. 1977. *The End of the Demographic Transition in Australia*, Australian Family Formation Project, monograph no. 5, Department of Demography, Australian National University.
———, and Choi, C. 1981. 'Recent decline in Australian fertility', *Year Book Australia*, no. 65, Australian Bureau of Statistics, Canberra.
Salas, R.M. 1982. 'Ageing: a universal phenomenon', *Populi* **9**, 4, 3–7.
Samuelson, R.J. 1979. 'Baby Boom Impact Has Twisted Economy', *Washington Post*, 6 February.
Schappi, U. 1983. 'Options for migrant communities', *Australian Journal on Ageing* **2**, 1, 21–8.
Scott, P. 1957. 'The changing population of Tasmania', *Geographical Studies* **4**, 1, 13–29.
Siedlecky, S. 1983. 'Trends in teenage pregnancy in Australia, 1971–1981', *Australia and New Zealand Journal of Obstetrics and Gynaecology* **23**, 129–35.
Siegel, J.S. 1979. 'Prospective Trends in the Size and Structure of the Elderly Population, Impact of Mortality Trends, and Some Implications', *Current Population Reports*, series P. 23, no. 78, US Government Printing Office, Washington.
———and Taeuber, C.M. 1982. 'The 1980 Census and the elderly: new data available to planners and practitioners', *The Gerontologist* **22**, 2, 144–50.
———and Hoover, S.L. 1982. 'Demographic aspects of the health of the elderly to the year 2000 and beyond', *World Health Statistics Quarterly* **35**, 314, 133–202.
Simmons, J.W. 1968. 'Changing Residence in the City: A Review of Intra-Urban Mobility', *Geographical Review* **58**, 4, 622–51.
Smailes, P.J. and Hugo, G.J. 1982. 'Rural communities and small area forecasting: some examples from South Australia', *Australian Geographical Studies* **20**, 2, 159–82.
———1985. 'A process view of the Population turnaround: an Australian case study', *Journal of Rural Studies* **1**, 1, 31–43.
Smith, L.R. 1980. *The Aboriginal Population in Australia*, Australian National University Press, Canberra.
Social Welfare Policy Secretariat, 1984. *The Impact of Population Changes on Social Expenditure: Projections from 1980–81 to 2021*, Social Welfare Policy Secretariat, Canberra.
Soldo, B.J. 1980. 'America's Elderly in the 1980s', *Population Bulletin* **35**, 4, 1–48.
South Australian Health Commission, 1980. A Demographic Social and Health Status Profile of South Australian Children, SAHC, January, 1980. Prepared by Dr G.D. Vimpani and Ms. A. Blood.
———1982. Comparative Mortality Rates in South Australia and Other States and Territories, mimeo, Epidemiology Branch, South Australian Health Commission, Adelaide.
———1983. *Cancer in South Australia: Incidence, Mortality and Survival, 1977–1981*, and *Incidence and Mortality, 1981*, South Australian Central Cancer Registry, Adelaide.

Spengler, J.J. 1966. 'Values and Fertility analysis', *Demography* **3**, 109–30.

Stapleton, C.M. 1980. 'Reformation of the Family Life Cycle Concept: Implications for Residential Mobility', *Environment and Planning* **A12**, 1103–18.

Stapleton-Concord, C.M. 1982. 'Spatial Distribution of Primary Individuals', *Professional Geographer* **34**, 2, 167–77.

Stevenson, T.L., 1982. South Australia in transition: a geographical interpretation of the beginning of fertility decline, 1836–1901, Ph.D. thesis, Flinders University of South Australia, Adelaide.

Stewart, J. 1977. Non-metropolitan Growth Resurgence: Trends and Factors in Growth, unpublished paper, Department of Environment, Housing and Community Development, Canberra.

Stilwell, F.J.B. 1974. *Australian Urban and Regional Development*. Australia and New Zealand Book Company, Sydney.

Stimson, R.J. 1970. 'Patterns of European Immigrant Settlement in Melbourne', *Tijdschrift Voor Economische En Sociale Geografie* **61**, 114–26.

Stone, L.O. and Fletcher, S. 1980. *A Profile of Canada's Older Population*, Institute for Research on Public Policy. Montreal, Quebec.

Storer, D. 1981. *Migrant Families in Australia*, working paper no. 3, Institute of Family Studies, Melbourne.

Stretton, A. and Williams, L.S. 1984. *Participation at Older Ages: Policy Implications from BLMR Research*, conference paper no. 43, Bureau of Labour Market Research, Canberra.

Stricker, P. and Sheehan, P. 1981. *Hidden Unemployment: the Australian Experience*, Institute of Applied Economic and Social Research, University of Melbourne.

Sullivan, D.A. and Stevens, S.A. 1982. Snowbirds: Seasonal migrants to the Sunbelt, paper presented to the annual meeting of the Population Association of America, San Diego.

Taeuber, C. 1979. 'A Changing America', *American Demographics* **1**, 1, 9–15.

Thomson, N. 1982. Patterns of Aboriginal Mortality 1976 to 1981, paper presented to Australian Population Association conference, Canberra.

———1984a. Australian Aboriginal Health and Health-Care. *Social Science and Medicine* **18**, 11, 939–48.

———1984b. 'Aboriginal Health—Current Status', *Australian and New Zealand Journal of Medicine* **14**, 705–18.

Uhlenberg, P. 1977. 'Changing structure of the older population of the U.S.A during the twentieth century', *The Gerontologist* **17**, 3, 197–202.

United States Bureau of Census 1982a. 'Number of One Parent Families Rises Sharply: Census Report', *US Department of Commerce News*, 17 June.

———1982b. 'One Child in Five Lives in a Single Parent Family: Census Bureau Reports'. *US Department of Commerce News*, 19 August.

———1982c. *Marital Status and Living Arrangements March 1981*, series P. 20, no. 372, US Government Printing Office, Washington.

———1983a. *Households, Families, Marital Status and Living Arrange-*

ments: 1982, series P. 20, no. 376, US Government Printing Office, Washington.
———1983b, *World Population 1983, Recent Demographic Estimates for the Countries and Regions of the World* US Department of Commerce, Washington.
———1983c. *Geographical Mobility: March 1980 to March 1981*, series P. 20, no. 377, US Government Printing Office, Washington.
———1983d. *Population Profile of the United States: 1982*, current population reports, special studies series P. 23, no. 130, US Government Printing Office, Washington.
Van De Kaa. D.J. 1981. 'Population Prospects and Population Policy in the Netherlands', *The Netherlands Journal of Sociology* **17**, 73–91.
Verbrugge, L.M. 1984. Longer Life But Worsening Health? Trends in Health and Mortality of Middle-Aged and Older Persons, *Health and Society Millbank Memorial Fund Quarterly*, **62**, 3, 475–519.
Vimpani, G.V. and Blood, A. 1980. *A Demographic Social and Health Status Profile of South Australian Children*, South Australian Health Commission, Adelaide.
Vining, D.R. Jr. and Kontuly, T. 1978. Population dispersal for major metropolitan regions: an international comparison', *International Regional Science Review* **3**, 1, 49–73.
Vipond, J. 1980a. 'The impact of higher unemployment on areas within Sydney', *Journal of Industrial Relations* **23**, 326–41.
———1980b. 'Intra-urban unemployment differentials in Sydney, 1971', *Urban Studies* **17**, 131–8.
———1981. 'Changes in unemployment differentials in Sydney, 1947–76', *Australian Geographical Studies* **19**, 67–77.
Wait, S. 1979. Retirement Migration: A Case Study of Mildura. B.A. (Hons.) thesis, Monash University.
Ware, H. (ed.) 1973. *Fertility and Family Formation, Australasian Bibliography and Essays*, Australian Family Formation Project, Department of Demography, Australian National University, Canberra.
———1975. 'Immigrant fertility: behaviour and attitudes', *International Migration Review* **9**, 3, 361–78.
———1979. The Status of women in Australia, paper delivered to Conference on Population and Australia, Department of Immigration and Ethnic Affairs, Canberra.
———1981. *A Profile of the Italian Community in Australia*, Australian Institute of Multicultural Affairs, Melbourne.
Wickens, C.H. 1925. 'Australian Population—its nature and growth', *Economic Record*, 1, pp. 1–16.
Wilson, M.G.A. 1971a. Australian Urban Fertility: a preliminary consideration, paper presented at 43rd congress of the Australian and New Zealand Association for the Advancement of Science, Brisbane.
———1971b. The spatial dimension of human reproduction in Victoria. *Proceedings, 6th New Zealand Geography Conference, 258–64.*
———1972. 'A Note on Infant Deaths in Melbourne', *Australian Paediatri-*

cians Journal **8**, 61–71.
———1978a. 'The pattern of fertility in a medium-sized industrial city: Wollongong, N.S.W.', *Tijdschrift Voor Econ. en soc. Geografie* **69**, 4, 225–32.
———1978b. 'A spatial analysis of human fertility in Scotland: reappraisal and extension', *Scottish Geographical Magazine* **94**, 3, 130–43.
———1979. 'Infant Death in Metropolitan Australia 1970–1973', *Canadian Studies in Population* **8**, 127–42.
Wiseman, R.F. 1979. 'Regional patterns of elderly concentration and migration', in S.M. Golant (ed.) *Location and Environment of Elderly Population*, W.H. Winston and Sons, Washington.
Wood, D.R. 1982. The Spatial Distribution of Infant and Perinatal Mortality in South Australia and the Influence of Social, Economic and Demographic Factors, 1970–1981, unpublished B.A. (Hons) thesis, Flinders University of South Australia, Adelaide.
Wood, D.R. and Hugo, G.J. 1983. *Recent Mortality Trends in Australia*. 1981 census project paper 2, National Institute of Labour Studies, Flinders University of South Australia, Adelaide.
———1984. *Distribution and Age Structure of the Australian Born with Overseas Born Parents*, 1981 census project paper 6, National Institute of Labour Studies, Flinders University of South Australia, Adelaide.
Wright, J. 1982. Migration of School Leavers: a case study in the Southeast of South Australia, unpublished B.A. (Hons.) thesis, School of Social Sciences, Flinders University of South Australia, Adelaide.
Young, C.M. 1976. *Mortality Patterns and Trends in Australia*, Research Report of the National Population Inquiry no. 5, Australian Government Publishing Service, Canberra.
Young, C.M. and Ware, H. 1979. 'Contraceptive use in Australia', *Australian and New Zealand Journal of Obstetrics and Gynaecology* **19**, 1, 1–6.
Young, E.A. 1982. Characteristics of Contemporary Aboriginal Mobility, paper presented at first Australian Population Association conference, Canberra.
Yusuf, F. and Briggs, D. 1979. 'Legalized abortion in South Australia: the first 7 years experience', *Journal of Biosocial Science* **11**, 179–92.
Yusuf, F. and Eckstein, G. 1980. 'Fertility of migrant women in Australia', *Journal of Biosocial Science* **12**, 179–90.
Yusuf, F. and Rockett, I. 1981. 'Immigrant Fertility patterns and differentials in Australia, 1971–76', *Population Studies* **35**, 3, 413–24.
Zuiches, J.J. and Brown, D.L. 1978. 'The Changing Character of the Nonmetropolitan Population, 1950–75', in T.R. Ford (ed.) *Rural U.S.A: Persistence and Change*, Iowa State University Press, Ames.

Index

Note: citations of places/categories in Tables and Figures are not listed in the Index—they can often be found near the relevant text reference, or in other cases by consulting the list of Tables and Figures.